Meaning, Communication,
and Value

Meaning, Communication, and Value

By
PAUL KECSKEMETI

THE UNIVERSITY OF CHICAGO PRESS

CHICAGO · ILLINOIS

THE UNIVERSITY OF CHICAGO PRESS, CHICAGO 37
Cambridge University Press, London, N.W. 1, England

PREFACE

THE present book is the fruit of long meditations. Its first version was finished just when the second World War started. Since then, the author has resumed work on it repeatedly but has had to let it lie for long periods because of other obligations. This explains what may strike the reader as a certain unevenness in presentation. But the essential thing for the author was not to produce a finished system but rather to initiate discussion about a problem area in philosophy which he considers vital. This area is that of evaluation and, more generally, of interpretation of meanings. Here, the author feels, a new departure is needed.

In recent philosophical thinking, in fact, emphasis has been placed more and more exclusively upon the *impersonal* disciplines of formal, logical deduction and empirical fact-finding. A high degree of rigor and sophistication has been reached in these fields, and the author fully recognizes the importance of these gains. But he feels that there is a certain danger in restricting philosophical thought to an ever increasing refinement of the impersonal methods of formal deduction and empirical fact-finding. The danger is that, in this fashion, all those operations which, like interpretation and evaluation, inevitably include an element of *personal* judgment and decision will come to be treated as wholly arbitrary, subjective, and unworthy of serious philosophical thought. By accomplishing such an act of renunciation, philosophy would render a grave disservice to itself and to human culture in general.

The present book represents an attempt to show that problems of meaning, not reducible to formal logic and to empirical fact-finding, are nevertheless amenable to rational analysis and that such an analysis is indispensable to a well-rounded philosophy.

P. K.

FIRENZE
August 1952

v

TABLE OF CONTENTS

INTRODUCTION
THE CONCEPT OF MEANING
1. MEANING AND DISCOURSE

THE subject of this study is "meaning," that is, anything that is or may be "interpreted." We shall examine the various types of interpretable entities, as well as the acts of interpretation themselves. The instance of interpretation most frequently studied is that of communications by means of the symbols of a language. In this instance the "meaning" interpreted is that of a message; and it is clear that interpretation of the message presupposes interpretation of the meaning of the various symbols of which it is made up. We shall deal with the interpretation of symbols and messages in some detail; clearly, it is this part of the study of meanings and interpretation that has the greatest practical importance. For the practical purpose of a communicated message is that of helping to create a consensus about facts of the world and, in general, about the presuppositions on which men may take concerted action. Symbols (or rather messages consisting of symbols) can, however, contribute to creating such a consensus only if they have a fixed, reliably interpretable meaning; for instance, we cannot ask whether a sentence is "true" before we can specify what it *means*. But we must add, right at this point, that the over-all problem of the meaning and interpretation of communications by means of symbols does not concern merely this type of "meaning": meaning as a preliminary condition for the ascertainment of the "truth" of a declarative sentence. There are also messages affirming values, and these are also important to the task of providing a basis for concerted action. Hence we must also concern ourselves with the meaning of nondeclarative messages—those expressing value judgments and value attitudes. In this way the study of meanings or of messages embraces the entire domain of human discourse. To what extent do the symbols used in communication—factual as well as evaluative—make consensus possible in principle? Is the "meaning" of *all* messages communicated by symbols such as to permit in each case a reliable, objective determination of the "truth," "correctness," or "validity" of the message? Or is this true only of one class of messages, those couched in "scientific" language, whereas acceptance or rejection of all other messages is an arbitrary matter, subject to nonrational factors, such as instinct and suggestion? Or is there an intermediary alternative such that some messages, while not fully and reliably verifiable, are also not completely arbitrary and irrational? We shall seek to provide an answer to these questions.

But we cannot start investigating the meaning of various types of messages and its degrees of "reliability" before looking at the problem of meaning and interpretation from a broader point of view. In fact, symbol meaning is not a self-contained phenomenon that could be understood and analyzed without reference to the "real" world outside language. To be sure, it is possible to deal with the meaning of the symbols of a language solely in terms of the relations obtaining between symbols as such. For instance, one may try to specify the "meaning" of an individual symbol by "defining" it, where the operation of "defining" a symbol consists in supplying other symbols, or combinations of symbols, already understood, which are synonymous with the symbol to be defined. It may be added that the language in which certain things about the words of a language are stated (e.g., that these words are "synonymous" with, or "equivalent" to, certain other expressions of the same language) must be considered as belonging to another language than the words discussed. The language in which we refer to words of a certain language is a "metalanguage" in relation to this latter language. Such analyses, however, cannot tell us all we want to know about the "meaning" of words and its interpretation, for the way in which the use of words fits in with extra-linguistic behavior is precisely one of the most important aspects of the communication of meanings.[1] Hence, before taking up in detail the problem of the meaning and interpretation of symbols and messages, we must look at the "interpretation" of "meaningful" signs in immediate, nondiscursive experience.

2. MEANING-IN-BEHAVIOR

Such interpretation of meanings is not found only on the human level. A grazing animal which chooses its food may be said to be "interpreting" its visual and other impressions. This example of "interpretation" illustrates for us the most fundamental layer of "meaning": the meaning of a familiar situation. Back of this case of interpretation we find a vital tension and selective responses to features of the environment which lead to the reduction of the tension.

1. Cf. George H. Mead, *Mind, Self, and Society* (Chicago: University of Chicago Press, 1934), pp. 71 ff.

What we see in the case of the animal is meaning grasped "in behavior." There is no question here of a conscious act of interpretation, with reflection upon a "meaning" grasped as such. The "interpretation" is merely a feature of behavior. What the animal does "makes sense," in that it selects items from its environment on which it can feed. This selection has been learned; and theories of learning[2] have been developed to show how needs acutely felt lead, first, to a systematic (and, at the same time, random) exploration of the environment, and then to stabilized habits of selecting items of the environment and of performing responses, which are associated with the reduction of those needs. One should not try to break down such sequences into isolated "stimuli" and "responses." It is not a "stimulus" as such that evokes a "response," but a stimulus plus an acutely felt need or "press" (to use H. A. Murray's term) and, beyond these, the over-all nature of the situation. There are many conditions that must be fulfilled before an animal organism will perform an available habitual response to a stimulus associated with need-reduction. The need must be acutely felt, and, at the same time, there must be no disturbance present such that fear or panic will impede the response appropriate to reduce the need. In other words, habits will be operative only in a sufficiently familiar situation. It is the over-all situation that ultimately determines which of the responses available to the animal will materialize. We must not only ask what stimuli are present; the main question is: Which of these stimuli will give the situation its dominant color? And that depends on many things, such as the intensity of the needs felt, the previous learning process which the organism has gone through, and the familiarity of the entire prevailing environmental setup. A stimulus will call forth an appropriate, learned response only if the situation is organized around it, Gestalt-wise: the stimulus is the "figure," and everything else is "background." Habituation is necessary not only to develop responses appropriate to a class of stimuli but also to enable the organism to treat everything else as "mere" background. This is the main reason why a cut-and-dried stimulus-response schema cannot account for behavior. For what is mere "background"—and therefore is not a stimulus for any response—is just as important for the organization of behavior as are the stimuli themselves.

In what sense can we say that the appropriate, learned behavior of the animal embodies an element of "interpretation"? Certainly, not everything the animal does will be akin to what we call "interpreta-

2. A survey of learning theories is found in Ernest R. Hilgard, *Theories of Learning* (New York: D. Appleton–Century Co., 1948).

tion of a meaning." For instance, the final consummation—the eating of something selected as food—as well as its enjoyment, has nothing in common with interpretation. Mere looking around, searching and "scanning" the environment, is also something different from interpretation-in-behavior. But we may speak of interpretation-in-behavior when we see an animal turn toward an item in the environment which attracts it as a clue to the possibility of some enjoyment. The "interpretation-in-behavior" belongs to the preliminary phase before some consummated enjoyment; it consists in selecting and seizing certain things or performing certain acts, as a learned preparatory step toward reducing a felt need.

Thus we may distinguish, in a behavior cycle, various phases. There is, first, the preparatory phase or "scanning"; this embodies no "interpretation" of the environment and reveals no meaning in itself. As long as the environment is merely scanned, it is without structure or meaning; such a structure emerges only gradually as the scanning reveals familiar features on which learned, appropriate behavior may be pegged. Next we enter into the phase of "interpretation" proper: the situation emerges as structured around "meaningful" signs, that is, items whose presence does not in itself reduce a need but points toward a reliable way in which need-reduction may be effected. Finally, we have the consummation itself. This lies beyond the phase of "interpretation-in-behavior" and thus beyond meaning; but the meaning grasped "in behavior" is *relative* to some consummation and enjoyment.

Each of these phases of the cycle of behavior has a different "objective" counterpart. During the unstructured "scanning" phase the organism is confronted with an undifferentiated objective field. During the "interpretation" phase the objective counterpart[3] of the act performed is a (dominant) *sign*. During the consummation phase the counterpart of the act—the object enjoyed—may be called a "correlate."

Our study of "meaning" and "interpretation," then, will start from

3. All these "objective" counterparts of the acts composing the cycle may be fantasied rather than real. Hallucinations are cases in point. These need not consist in the "conjuring-up" of objects made familiar by learning, as the following example shows: A young starling was brought up in an environment in which there were no flies or other flying insects. One day the bird, which had never seen a fly, suddenly darted at an invisible object, caught it in mid-air, carried it back to its perch, and hacked away at it with its beak, as starlings usually do with captured flies (Gustav Bally, *Vom Ursprung und von den Grenzen der Freiheit* [Basel, 1945], p. 132). In this case the "correlate" of the enjoyment phase was hallucinated without previous learning, suggesting that the consummation phase may not be "learned" at all.

this middle phase of a behavior cycle running from unstructured "scanning" to consummated enjoyment. It is not suggested that *all* meaning is to be construed as such a "middle phase" of a behavior cycle; we shall see that there are types of meaning and interpretation which are not relative to the immediate satisfaction of a pressing biological need. Moreover, interpretation properly so called is not mere "interpretation-in-behavior" but the conscious assignment of a meaning to an item of an environment. Interpretation-in-behavior, however, exemplifies, on a primitive biological level, the essential formal structure of all interpretation.

3. THE MEANING RELATION

The interpretation-in-behavior, as we have seen, bears upon a *sign*. How can we, then, circumscribe the "meaning" of the sign? We shall say: *The meaning of a sign S is that when S is present in a situation, it determines one kind of response that is "good" in that situation—* "good" in terms of the possibility of attaining some satisfaction. Throughout this study we shall understand, by "meaning," this kind of rather complicated relation: the meaning of an object A consists in determining which response is "good" (or "bad") in the situation in which A is present. "Good" and "bad" are taken here in the most general sense possible; *any* standard by which the result of a response may be judged satisfactory may define meanings. In the example we have chosen—the behavior cycle of the grazing animal—the "standard" was biological need-reduction. Later we shall see examples of meaning based upon other standards. We shall also deal with meaningful objects other than signs (e.g., symbols). What must be borne in mind is only that "meaning" cannot be construed as the actual response which the meaningful object calls forth. Almost the entire existing literature of meaning is to some extent vitiated, in my opinion, by confusion of the "meaning" of signs and symbols with their actual (or intended) behavioral *effects*. I shall argue that a "meaning" is not the response actually called forth by a sign, but something more abstract, namely, the way in which a situation is structured for an organism by that sign. To say that the sign S has meaning is to say that *when S* is present, the response R is "good" in terms of some standard; to say that the organism O "interprets" S in terms of this meaning is to say that for O the situation will be structured around the possibility of the "good" result that may be attained by performing R. How O will actually respond depends on many factors; for instance, the "good" response may be inhibited by some other sign *S'*, whose interpretation will cancel the seeking of the goal toward which *R* is oriented. Even in this case, however, the meaning of *S* will somehow be part of the structure of the situation. The "meaning" of *S* provides something like a "map," indicating possible routes in the field of behavior—it organizes the field in this sense.

4. MEANING AND INTERPRETATION

One may ask, at this point, whether "meanings," as defined above, are observable entities and whether they have any place in the scientific analysis of behavior if they are not "observable." And, further, one may ask what "interpretations" are and whether they have a place in the scientific analysis of behavior, if they are to be understood to be something different from the mere recording and analysis of factual data.

My answers to these questions is as follows:

A "meaning" is not an observable entity but a pure construct. As such, it may help us in analyzing the situation and behavior of organisms. For a large part of the study of behavior the concept of "meaning" is not even needed; we can describe learning processes without ever explicitly referring to the "meaning" of signs. This is particularly true as long as the only "meaning" we are dealing with is meaning-in-behavior. We can observe such behavior and note the characteristic "curve" which the learning process follows, without explicitly referring to "meanings" and without using the concept of "interpretation." The concepts of "meaning" and "interpretation," however, are implicit in the organization of such studies. For instance, we have to classify actual observed responses as "good" or "bad" according to some biological standard, such as need-reduction; that we adopt such a classification implies the concept of "meaning," even if we need not use it explicitly. Behavior studies differ in this respect from all other studies in "natural" science. In no other field of natural science are we compelled to resort to such dichotomies of "good" and "bad" responses. I think this peculiarity of the study of behavior has great methodological importance; in this field the scientist cannot maintain the completely detached impartiality that is generally taken to be characteristic of the scientific attitude as such. The reason for this is that the life and behavior of organisms are themselves centered around "demands" upon an environment; and we cannot by-pass these "demands" and reduce them to "neutral" structural properties. Hence such constructs as "meaning" and "interpretation" are concealed in the organization of studies about behavior, even where they need not be used explicitly. At the level of interpretation-in-behavior, the observer need not refer to "meaning" or "interpretation," but the philosopher, whose job is not to make observations but to account for the organization of the observer's activities, must refer to them. On "higher" levels of behavior, where acts of interpretation are performed explicitly by the organisms observed—e.g., where the organisms observed use symbols—the observer himself, too, must refer to "meanings" as such. Behavior involving explicit interpretation (rather than mere interpretation-in-behavior) cannot be properly described and analyzed unless the observer himself "interprets" the signs that are also "interpreted" by the observed organism. In doing so, the observer must use, if not precisely the same standards, at least the same kinds of standards as those on which the explicit "interpretive" behavior of the observed organism is based. When performing intelligence tests, the tester must be able to solve the problems on the basis of which intelligence is rated. There is a real flow of communication between the tester and the subject of the test: a question is asked and answered in a language understood and used by both. This is radically different from the relationship that obtains between the scientific observer and the objects he observes in inanimate nature. To be sure, we may say metaphorically that the experimenter "puts a question" to nature, but the question is not a verbal one in this case, and the object does not answer the experimenter in the language which the latter uses in intercourse with his fellows.

To what extent the standards defining the meanings interpreted by the observer can diverge from those defining the meanings interpreted by the subject is a difficult question, basic to "interpretive" sociology; it will be discussed in some detail later. At this point, we wish merely to stress again the difference between the position of the scientist studying inanimate nature and the scientist studying behavior, particularly symbol behavior. The former records facts and constructs theories using the observable (measurable) data recorded; the latter deals not only with "facts" but also with meanings, and his theories are built not only upon factual description and measurement but also upon interpretation. It is true that the natural scientist also makes use of "constructs" as well as of manifest data; but his constructs differ from the special class of constructs that meanings are. The constructs of natural science are conceptual tools that provide a framework for keeping manifest data together in the unity of a theory. Meanings, on the other hand, are derived in a different way; they are derived by means of acts of "interpretation."

This takes us to the second question raised above. What kind of operation is this "interpretation"? Thus far, we have said only what it is *not*—it is *not* a descriptive operation, that is, one by which we ascertain and record observable data, and it is also not the elaboration of a theoretical construct like the ones used in analyzing events in inanimate nature. Is this "interpretation," then, something intangible and mystical, an intuitive act beyond analysis?

By no means. Acts of interpretation are essential components of human intercourse; they permeate every phase of "normal" life. The only "abnormal" thing about them—that which distinguishes them from such operations as the ascertainment of a factual datum—is that, in "interpreting" meaning, we perform an act which cannot be recorded without in some sense duplicating it. In studying symbol behavior, I cannot say whether a subject has or has not "understood" a symbol unless I first "understand" the symbol myself. That is, I must know the language to which the symbol belongs; I must know how to apply the rules of that language (which are the "standards" defining "good" or "bad" responses to the symbol as symbol). In other words, in this field the observer cannot limit himself to recording "brute" facts; he must go by standards of meaning in order to characterize his data. If we remember this, we shall be able to say what an "interpretation" is: it is not the response to a stimulus as it actually occurs, but it is the actual or possible response *judged* as to whether it is "good" or "bad" in terms of some standard. Or, to put the same thing in different words, an interpretation is an act in which a meaning is grasped, a "meaning" being a construct or matrix, indicating not which response will actually occur in the presence of a stimulus but which response is "good" or "bad," respectively, by some standard, *if* it occurs.

There are, no doubt, experimental situations in which the observer may assume that the responses which he observes will be "good" responses, at least with a very high probability. In such cases actual responses will enable him to fix meanings. Thus, under certain circumstances, an observer studying the language behavior of people whose speech he does not understand may reconstruct the rules of that foreign language from the actual language behavior. In general, if I do not know the rules of a language, I can ascertain them only from actual behavioral clues.[4] But, in order to do so, I must assume that the actual response I take as my clue is itself "correct" behavior in terms of those rules. I must have confidence in my guide and judge his conduct to be a valid standard. Dictionaries, for instance, may be considered as containing records of *actual* responses to symbols which have to be taken as standard, paradigmatic responses. No rule of language can be ascertained without some judgment concerning the "good" or "bad" quality of an actual response.

5. BRUTE FACT AND MEANING

In view of the foregoing, we must, I think, distinguish between two kinds of data: those which can and those which cannot be ascertained without recourse to "meaning," i.e., without making some judgment about the datum in the light of some standard. The first kind of datum may be characterized as "brute fact." To establish it, it is enough to ask what happened, without also asking whether that event was "good" or "bad" in terms of some standard. The second type consists of "meaning" phenomena, i.e., phenomena which cannot be identified merely by asking "what happened." To identify them, the observer must *judge* them.

Examples of "brute fact" are events which can be properly described, identified, and put into the framework of a theory merely by reference to their measurable characteristics. In a sense, of course, everything that is read can be "measured": what we would call a "meaningful" event, such as the use of a symbol in communication, is *also* a physical occurrence that can be described in terms of electronic and acoustic processes. The point is, however, that such descriptions will not characterize the event as a "meaningful" one; they will not relate it to the rules of a language. And yet it is only in so far as the event is taken as exemplifying the use of a language governed by rules that it becomes for us an instance of "communication" behavior. To treat of this event as an instance of "communication by symbol," we have to relate it, not to a body of theory correlating vibratory or electronic data, but to a body of rules that we ourselves apply in communicating with others.

At the risk of appearing pedantic, we shall once again try to characterize the difference we see between the ways in which the two classes of scientists go by "rules" in fixing their data. Of course, the

4. Cf. Rudolf Carnap, *Introduction to Semantics* (Cambridge: Harvard University Press, 1942), pp. 12 f.

scientist who performs merely acts of measurement and pure factual description also has to follow "rules"; there are rules to be observed in measuring things and other rules governing the formulation of findings and the conclusions that may be drawn from them. But all this merely amounts to saying that scientific activity itself is always a "meaningful" activity and not that it always deals with phenomena which are meaningful in themselves. There are meaningful activities, involving the use of symbols, which bear upon mere "brute fact," as distinct from other meaningful activities that we perform upon objects which themselves exhibit "meaning." Physical science belongs to the first group; in biology, meanings begin to inform the object of observation, at least implicitly; and within the sciences of behavior and in philosophical reflection the character of meaningfulness is essential to the objects observed or reflected about.

6. The Concept of Meaning and the Unity of Science

Now the question arises: Is this dichotomy within science an ultimate, genuine one, or is it mere appearance? The scientific as well as the philosophical temper is deeply attracted toward unity and shrinks from the idea of an irreducible dualism. This, at least, has been the dominant trend of Western thought throughout many of its vicissitudes. It is true that there is also a dualistic tradition in Western thought; it is deeply characterized by dichotomies of "body" and "soul," "matter" and "mind," and so on. But the two terms of such dichotomies are almost never considered to be on the same footing and to have equal dignity. It is either the one or the other term which is accepted as representing ultimate reality. On the metaphysical or ontological plane the two terms collapse into one. We have materialistic or idealistic ontologies; in developing its initial dualistic schemes, the Western mind finally manages either to dismiss matter as a mere "privation" of being or to reduce mind to the status of an "epiphenomenon" or "reflection" of matter. In the light of this characteristic trend of Western thought, we must expect that there will be considerable reluctance to accept our distinction between sciences of "brute fact" and sciences of "meaning" as final and irreducible.

The typical reaction, Western style, to such distinctions is likely to be: If there are two types of "science," both cannot be "science" in the proper sense. It is impossible for the two types of science to have equal rank and equal dignity. One of the types must be the prototype; and the other can have the dignity of science only in so far as it can ultimately become similar to the paradigm.

Now there is no doubt that physical science is generally accepted today as the paradigm of science. Those who accord physical science this paradigmatic status will be inclined to dismiss our concept of meaning as ultimately and metaphysically irrelevant. Their argument will run approximately as follows: To be sure, in using symbols in communication and in many other cases, we make choices governed by rules or value standards. And it may also be admitted that we cannot at present replace the vague predicates "good" and "bad," on which these choices are based, by precise, quantitative terms. At present, for instance, we must be content with saying that a certain response will reduce a tension in the state of an organism; we shall be able to observe, in a more or less intuitive way, that such an event takes place; but we cannot express in purely quantitative terms the difference between the "tense" and the "saturated" state. We can make many measurements of the various states of the organism and find many measurable symptoms or concomitants of the two states, but we cannot define the organic states themselves in a purely quantitative way. We possess no "neutral" observational model or structure from which we can deduce what will happen within an organism. This, however, is merely a temporary state of affairs. When biology *really* becomes a science, it will possess a model of just this kind. And then we shall be able to dispense with value predicates such as "good" or bad"; we shall be able to treat the entire subject matter, including all levels of "interpretive" behavior, by means of purely descriptive models. As in all science, we shall have to provide links—correlation indicators—between our models and the extra-scientific categories of ordinary human experience—but this matter no longer concerns science as such. And even now, although we do not yet have a "science" of life, we must try to overcome this state of affairs by doing everything in our power to discard the category of "meaning" as quickly as possible; the less we use it and the more we cling to purely descriptive, factual, quantitative concepts, the more "scientific" will our science be.

I cannot say whether this argument will ultimately turn out to be correct, in so far as the future evolution and the final state of the sciences of life and behavior are concerned. It may be that, in the end, we shall possess "neutral," descriptive models of all organic processes, so that we can dispense with the categories of meaning and interpretation in accounting for the behavior of organisms. This does not mean that the categories of meaning and interpretation will themselves lose *all* application. As long as man is man, he will communicate by means of symbols, and, in order to do so, he will have to learn rules and attend to meanings; as a subjective experience, meaning will be as important as ever. It is only in the scientific explanation of behavior that these categories will no longer have room, if the scientific critic of the concept of meaning turns out to be right. Then science will have its own fully developed language alongside that of everyday communication; when translated into this scientific language, all statements about rules and "value-oriented" behavior will become purely descriptive statements; meaning and value concepts will survive only in nonscientific, everyday language.

If this possible outcome materializes, the unity of science will be achieved—together with a sharper dichotomy between "scientific" and "nonscientific" discourse. This, however, will not disturb the adherent of the scientific outlook, for, he holds, the language of science will be universal and self-contained; it will be able to express whatever the nonscientific, everyday language can express; and it will be merely a matter of convenience if people still cling to nonscientific discourse in everyday life.

Now, as I said, it cannot be proved that this scientific utopia will not one day be fulfilled. I think, however, that there are some very good reasons for considering such an outcome extremely improbable. For what does the prophecy really imply? It implies, for instance, that future scientists of behavior, when observing a conversation among people whose language they do not understand, may nevertheless be able, under certain conditions, to determine what each of them will say. This means that our hypothetical scientist will be able to "catch up" with others having more information than he has himself. But this would be an extremely paradoxical achievement. For our remarkable scientist would be able to tell other people, simply by analyzing the communication process going on between them, what they themselves do *not* know; at the same time, he would also be able to listen to other people's conversation without learning from it what they *do* know.

What is "information"? We mean by it knowledge communicated by way of transmitting symbols, as distinct from knowledge acquired at first hand. Such "information" may, of course, be about brute facts—facts which do not call for interpretation. But information as such is something that must be understood, something that must be interpreted. We cannot grasp information as information without performing an act of interpretation, that is, without making a choice among possibilities that can be "good" or "bad." Only a being which can interpret meaning can receive and use information.

7. MEANING AND MECHANISM

Now we ask: Is the capacity to interpret meaning—to make a choice, in this sense, between "good" and "bad" possibilities—the exclusive possession of living organisms? Or can it be possessed and exercised by machines as well? "Cybernetics"[5] is the name of a new discipline which deals with this question. One of the topics studied by cybernetics is information transmitted not to living organisms but to calculating machines. Information of this sort does not consist only in the transmission of an impulse; to be operative, the impulse must fit the construction of the machine. It must be patterned as an appropriate "taping," that is, a behavior map specifying the "good" choices that have to be made on the basis of the "information." If the "taping" is appropriate, the machine, barring accidents, cannot miss giving the "correct" response.

The scientific utopia outlined above implies that, even if the scientist, observing behavior, cannot directly interpret as meaningful information certain impulses that he sees transmitted to other organisms, he can, nevertheless, reconstruct their "meaning" from firsthand observation of the impulse and of the receiving organism. Something superficially similar to this may be accomplished by the scientist who examines a calculating machine: if he is conversant with the principle according to which the machine is constructed, he will know what the machine will be expected to do with any tape that is fed into it. But this case is really not at all analogous with that postulated by the scientific utopia. For one thing, the scientist who "understands" the machine will also "understand" the "meaning" of the "information" contained on the tape. For another, the "information" given to the machine differs in principle from the "information" received and interpreted by human beings. The former, in fact, may be described as an "instruction" rather than as "information" proper. The machine is "instructed" to perform certain operations according to the tape fed into it; it is not merely "informed" of a certain state of the world. It cannot help performing the "good" response if it is properly constructed and if the tape which is given it makes sense in terms of its construction. Human "information" cannot be accounted for in this

5. Cf. Norbert Wiener, *Cybernetics* (New York: John Wiley & Sons, 1948), pp. 74 ff.

way. I believe that in the case of "information" received by human beings, we are in the presence of two relatively independent systems of behavior: the one concerns the interpretation; the other concerns the ultimate behavioral choices that depend also on "firsthand" knowledge of the world. Both systems have their own array of "meanings" (i.e., definitions of "good" choices), and they are relatively independent, in the sense that the interpretation of the information need not determine the ultimate behavioral choice. Human beings may disbelieve any information they receive; in fact, in human intercourse, information may be deliberately misleading as well as truthful, and this alternative is the crucial element of all human information as such. Here is a radical difference between calculating machines and human beings. The former are incapable of doubt; nor would there be any point in "lying" to them. Hence a model based upon "instructions" given to machines is radically insufficient to account for information interpreted by human beings. The latter will influence behavior only by being incorporated into the system of meanings based on "firsthand" knowledge—as when the sender of the information is "trusted" by the receiver.

Machines might be "taught" to check information before they act on it; in this way, some features of the double behavioral system of man could be built into the machine. But the similarity would still be very limited. For in this case, too, the machine would "unfailingly" act upon the instruction fed into it; it would not "reject" any information supplied to it but rather wait, as instructed, until an incomplete instruction is completed in a certain way. A machine constructed to disobey instructions is a contradiction in terms.

Now there exists also a different class of behavior-duplicating machines: the "walking toys." These have a primitive "motor" apparatus, enabling them to move ahead and to turn, and a primitive "sensory" apparatus, enabling them to receive light and touch impulses. The motor apparatus is so connected with the "receptors" of the machine that the former's movements are guided by the stimuli which the latter receive. These devices duplicate, in a way, sensory-motor circuits that exist in living organisms; and the remarkable thing is the high degree of "spontaneity" and learning ability they display. Sometimes they are considered as providing proof that most, if not all, features of "higher" behavior can be adequately reproduced by simple mechanisms. Thus, one experimenter writes:

It seems to me important to realize that of the many features of the mind and behaviour which are quoted against mechanistic philosophies, there are some at least which are easily mimicked by machines. Exploration, curiosity, free-will in the sense of unpredictability, the seeking of goals, self-regulation, the avoidance of danger, a scale of values and relative importance, self-recognition, the avoidance of dilemmas, foresight, memory, learning, forgetting, association of ideas, form, recognition, original creation and the elements of social organization are all within the capacity of purely mechanical devices, and the responsibility seems to me to rest now with the transcendentalists to define some further aspects of behavior or experience for the other side to attempt to reproduce.[6]

What is the purport of this argument? It seems to me to be this: Earlier mechanistic philosophies contended that the laws of mechanics would ultimately provide an explanation for every detail of the behavior of organisms. But, even though the laws of mechanics obviously were "valid" within the organisms and many processes occurring in animal behavior could be described with their help, all attempts to reduce *all* behavior to mechanical processes have failed. For the things that animals were doing (acting upon significant cues, "exploring" their environment, and so on) were radically different from all phenomena studied in mechanics. To derive such complicated patterns of behavior from laws involving only the variables of Newtonian mechanics was an altogether hopeless task. Now, however, the situation is different. Instead of trying to explain living behavior in terms of classical mechanics, we can now use, as an analogon of the organism, a new type of machine—that type which operates, not with wheels and levers, but with a "feed-back" device. Cybernetics has shown that those aspects of animal and human behavior which are least explicable in terms of classical mechanics can be quite well approximated by mechanisms having a "feed-back" feature, such as thermostats and calculating machines.[7] Behavior based upon feedback, which is exhibited by machines as well as by animals, is, in a sense, meaning-oriented behavior.

In view of this analogy between the animal and the machine, the

6. W. Grey Walter, "The Functions of Electrical Rhythms in the Brain," *Journal of Mental Sciences*, XCVI, No. 402 (January, 1950), 4.

7. "What cybernetics does is to show us at least one new kind of machine. One way of putting this is to say that they are not machines in the Newtonian sense. Nor, however, are they machines in the Maxwell or Einstein sense. A Newtonian machine, for example, is one for which we can calculate velocities and positions resulting from given velocities and positions. Now a cybernetic machine does not violate the principles of such a machine; it is simply that feed-back mechanisms go beyond them" (J. O. Wisdom, "The Hypothesis of Cybernetics," *British Journal for the Philosophy of Science*, II, No. 5 [May, 1951], 22).

question arises as to whether animal behavior is "nothing but" the functioning of a complicated set of feed-back mechanisms—mechanisms which can be duplicated in inanimate machines. Perhaps we shall be able, in not too long a time, to show in detail the working of the feed-back mechanisms controlling the activities of nerve cells. But this will still not settle the question of whether "meaningful" live behavior, including the interpretation of information, does or does not transcend anything that can occur in inanimate systems. To the skeleton as a system of levers, we shall add the brain and the nervous system as feed-back mechanisms. Since the brain and the nerves are physical objects, it is obvious that their mode of functioning can be described in terms of *some* physical law. If the laws of feed-back processes are suitable for this, it is all to the good. This still does not mean that nothing happens within a living organism that would not also happen in an inanimate mechanism having analogous feed-back features. The seemingly "intelligent" behavior of calculating machines mirroring the functions of the brain and of the nerves need not be the same thing as truly intelligent behavior *in vivo*. We can design automatons that will make "intelligent" choices, obeying a certain rationale, as the calculating machines do; but it is we who have prescribed these choices and imposed the pattern of "meaning" that governs the automatons' behavior. And we can also design automatons whose behavior will be partly governed by "meaning" and partly unpredictable even to the designer, such as the walking toys; but in this case, too, the "value" pattern is imposed by us, while the range of unpredictability is also provided by our design. It is no novelty that we can produce devices whose behavior will be purely random and unpredictable; dice and coins are excellent examples of this. The "walking toys" somehow combine properties of the dice with those of the calculating machine; the former properties, in a way, mirror "free will," and the latter, in a way, mirror "intelligence"; but there is no fusion between the element of free choice and the element of intelligence. Both, in fact, have been built into the machine by a freely choosing, intelligent being, who wanted to duplicate himself and succeeded merely in making something that combines randomness without intelligent choice and intelligent choice fully prethought and prearranged by the designer. To me, the assumption that we are made in the same way smacks of too much "transcendentalism."

But, apart from this, the "walking toys," remarkable as they are, provide no parallel for the human peculiarity we are examining at present: the "double system" incorporating both "firsthand" knowledge and knowledge through "information." The interesting thing is that, while the calculating machines act only upon "information" (or rather "instruction") and know nothing about the world at first hand, the toys have only firsthand knowledge of their environment and do not incorporate symbolic communication into their behavior. The toys reproduce the working of a crude sensory-motor circuit; they fail to reveal those aspects of behavior which are characterized precisely by the *inactivation* or *suspension* of sensory-motor circuits.

In order to provide a real mechanical counterpart of human behavior, one should construct a machine that responds to both "information" and "firsthand" stimuli and welds these two behavior cycles together. No machine constructed so far can do this, for none has as yet progressed to the stage of "information" beyond that of "instruction."

Thus we may conclude that mechanical models are incapable of duplicating some of the essential features of human information. It may be added that communications to animals also lack some of these essential features. Animals, too, are devoid of the two relatively independent systems of "meaning" which are fundamental to symbol behavior. To be sure, animals' behavior does depend, in part, on "communications" which they receive, either from human masters or from animals of the same species. But these communications are either "instructions" or "signals": they do not represent pure information about the state of the world, which has to be interpreted as such and then "evaluated" as to its truth. Rather, they point to presently available goals of behavior; and it may be said that, as regards acting upon instructions, animals are inferior to machines. After all, they have not been constructed with a view to making them obey instructions of any given degree of complexity, as machines have. Carrying out instructions must be foisted upon their fully developed "natural" behavior system in which other factors are necessarily dominant.

In spite of the duplication by feed-back mechanisms of many features of living behavior, it is entirely possible that life-phenomena transcend everything that can be constructed from nonliving materials.[8] If this were the case, we should be entitled to say that our distinction between the "meaningful" and the purely "factual" has an objective basis in the very nature of things. The distinction would then have to be recognized as an absolute, ontological, and insuper-

8. Cf. *ibid.*, pp. 22, 23.

able one. For that which is "emergent" in organic life beyond the phenomena of inanimate nature could be only the fusion between "being" and "meaning" that is characteristic of the organism. We mean the fact that "to be," for an organism, means to impose upon its environment a pattern of *demands* based upon what is "good" for the organism itself. Machines with a feed-back device also impose upon the environment a pattern of demands aiming at the preservation of equilibrium within the system; in this sense, they also may be said to be functioning in "meaningful" fashion. But the question is whether having such demands is an intrinsic feature of the very being, the existence of the mechanism, in the sense in which it is an intrinsic feature of the being of the organism. Are these demands real "needs" rooted in the very being of the inanimate feed-back systems? Or are they mere "quasi-needs," originating with the designer of the systems? The question is admittedly somewhat vague and "metaphysical," but it is by no means idle. I think it is possible to examine experimentally the question of whether the "needs" built into inanimate models simulating life-phenomena do or do not differ in their manifestations from the "needs" of living organisms. A better knowledge of this would bring us closer to answering the question as to whether organic life "transcends" all inanimate phenomena.

But what if the "antitranscendentalists" turn out to be right? What if one can construct from inanimate materials a model duplicating every feature of organic life, including the possession of genuine needs and demands rooted in the model's very existence? In that case, meaning, as an ontological category, might lose its status as something emergent beyond and irreducible to mere fact. For each "interpretation," one might then be able to produce a pure factual description that would be equivalent to it. We could, as it were, look behind that mysterious "unity of meaning and being" which is characteristic of organic life and is the fundamental layer of all meaningfulness that we can experience.

Such an ontological devaluation of the category of meaning would, however, still not signify that we as human beings could actually do without performing acts of interpretation—that we could actually disregard meaning. For, to say the least, the knowledge he can acquire at first hand could never be sufficient for man—he certainly needs knowledge by information. All information, however, must be interpreted explicitly, unlike mere "meaning-in-behavior," which requires no explicit interpretation. If the "antitranscendentalist" hypothesis is true, it follows merely that man would know how to derive the knowledge conveyed by a message carrying information without interpreting it as such. It does not follow that man would or could actually forego interpretation in favor of this other type of "factual" analysis. For "interpretation" would, in all probability, still be the far more efficient operation; by-passing information would be extremely complex and laborious and might be impossible to carry into effect in many cases in which it would be feasible "in principle." Hence, even if ontologically devalued, meaning would still be an indispensable category within the framework of human practice. This justifies, in any case, our endeavor to study "meaning" and "interpretation" as something different from "fact" and "observation."

8. Science and Meaning

Science as an activity consists in the collection, organization, and transmission of information; it is an activity carried out completely within a medium of meaning. Yet scientific work has the tendency to avoid meaning as a topic. Our skill in using language, which alone enables us to cultivate and to acquire scientific knowledge, is imparted not by science but by prescientific education. Science "presupposes" this skill, just as it presupposes certain basic interpretations that are needed to define the subject matter of certain sciences. Interpretation tends to play an implicit role within science, as something presupposed or taken for granted. In so far as the explicit content of scientific statements is concerned, it is likely to be entirely factual and non-interpretive. This is understandable. Science aims at maximum objectivity and reliability; and this goal seems to be jeopardized whenever one engages in explicit acts of interpretation. For one cannot interpret anything meaningful without referring to some demand or value, and how can one refer to values without the risk of saying things which are subjective and unreliable?

On the other hand, it is an illusion to believe that science can do entirely without ever considering "meaningful" aspects of phenomena. We grant that the task of science is never to "interpret" things but to ascertain facts or, rather, connections among facts. But it is impossible to ascertain all relevant connections among facts while completely ignoring problems of meaning and interpretation. There is no watertight separation between "fact" and "value." For instance, not all facts are "neutral" or "brute" facts; not all can be stated in purely "descriptive" terms. No purely "descriptive" model of the organism is now available, and it may be doubted whether it will ever be possible to construct such a model. In other words, many facts of organic nature apparently are "nonneutral": they can be grasped only by acknowledging that something, while existing, necessarily imposes a demand upon its environment. The science of life must take this into account.

Of course, biology does not attempt to "interpret" the meaning of organic life; it simply takes the fundamental meaningfulness for granted. But if we study animal and human behavior, we encounter many data which cannot be either isolated or used without being interpreted. No matter how squeamish a scientist may be about attributing "goals" and "demands" to the systems he studies, he cannot avoid it when he deals with live behavior. And this means that he must be "subjective" to a certain extent—not, to be sure, in the sense of indulging his tastes or predilections but in the sense of using concepts derived from nonneutral, emotionally charged experience. It would be wrong to say that a scientific theory of behavior "interprets" behavior: no theory can do that; the task of theory-construction is not to arrive at an interpretation but to make explanation and prediction possible. It is only that, in order to construct a theory of behavior, we need data, not merely "described," but "interpreted" in terms of meaning. As soon as science begins to interest itself in behavior, it must overcome its reluctance to rely on interpretation.

What we said about the "reluctance" of the scientific mind to resort to explicit interpretation applies, of course, only to nonformal, empirical sciences. The formal sciences—mathematics and logic—do nothing but explicate meanings; this is why they can be conceived as "normative" sciences. They deal only with meaning, and their propositions have no "factual" content.

We may, then, arrange the various sciences in a series, according to the extent to which their subject matters involve meaningful, interpretable materials. Physics uses descriptive variables exclusively; its whole content can be presented without either resorting to or presupposing acts of interpretation other than interpretation of the symbols used in scientific discourse as such. Biology is no longer devoid of interpretive content: its basic concept, that of the organism, presupposes "meaning," which, however, need not be interpreted explicitly but can be taken for granted. The sciences of behavior include among their data many which have to be interpreted explicitly. Finally, the formal sciences—mathematics and logic—have no descriptive, factual content but work exclusively with materials which are "given" only as interpretables, that is to say, materials consisting entirely of symbols.

9. THE METHODOLOGICAL AUTONOMY OF INTERPRETATION

I hold that, with the increase of the component of "meaning" in the subject matters of the various sciences, their methods must change. The method of mathematics differs widely from that of physical science; but that of biology, though closer to that of physics, is also by no means the same. Some of the basic concepts of biology cannot be reduced to those of physics. In the science of human behavior, we make a still greater methodological jump, since we have to resort to explicit "interpretation" of meaning. In my opinion, *"interpretation" is an autonomous method* that cannot be reduced to neutral fact-finding. The following analysis will serve, in part, to establish the methodological autonomy of interpretation.

Does such an attempt endanger the unity of science? On the contrary, I think that only the recognition of the autonomy of interpretation enables us to conceive of the unity of science in a reasonable way; for the usual attempt to save the unity of science by foisting the method of physics upon all other sciences suffers from a fatal flaw: it creates an unbridgeable gap between "empirical" and "formal" science, between "nonanalytical" physics and "analytical" mathematics. Now I suggest that the method of "interpretation" occupies, as it were, a middle position between the analytical and the nonanalytical. It is postulational and empirical at the same time. The existence of such a method shows that science is, after all, a unity—not in the sense that it uses the same method in every field, but in the sense that its various autonomous methods together make up a spectrum of intellectual activity that has its place within the entire behavior system of man.

This is not to say that, within each science, only one specific method, distinct from that of any other science, can be appropriate. Rather, there will be room for various methods within each science. In the sciences of behavior, for instance, observation, causal (statistical) analysis, and experiment coexist with methods of "interpretation" by which some of the most important types of data used in these sciences are secured.

But meaning and its interpretation have for us an interest reaching far beyond the methodological role they play in the various sciences. Our entire life flows, as it were, through a medium of meaning. Both as biological organisms and as members of a human culture, we constantly interpret meanings on various levels, and our specific capacity for "contextual" interpretation of symbols (see chap. i) is perhaps the most outstanding mark of our "human" nature.

My purpose in this study is to work out what is specific to meaning and its interpretation, as distinct from mere fact and its description. I have already mentioned the theoretical possibility that all interpretation might turn out to be reducible to some equivalent factual description. But this "ontological devaluation" of the category of meaning, which is problematic in itself, would not, if successfully consummated, diminish the overwhelming practical importance of interpretation as a component of our life; for, as choosing beings, we have to base our choices upon "meaning," upon a distinction between "good" and "bad." Choice in the human sense would be impossible if we could choose only among things differentiated exclusively in "descriptive" terms. And, as social beings, we could not communicate with one another if the only knowledge we cared to have were knowledge acquired at first hand.

I. MEANING AND SITUATION

CHAPTER I

THE CATEGORIES OF MEANING

1. Types of Meaning

IN THE Introduction we referred to various types of meaningful entities: "signs" and "symbols," "information" and "instruction." We shall now present a more systematic classification of such "interpretable," "meaningful" entities.

Let us recapitulate some of the conclusions we have already reached. We said that the "meaning" of any meaningful object does not consist in the response that it actually evokes but in a relation obtaining between that object, a situation, and an organism such that, *if* the object is present in the situation, a certain kind of response on the part of the organism will be "good" by some standard. All "meaning" in our sense of the term exhibits this general structure; but, as we shall see, an extraordinary variety of types of meaning and interpretation emerges as soon as we explore the general scheme a little more closely.

For instance, our definition suggests that all meaning is relative to "an organism," in terms of what may be "good" and "bad" for that organism. But this does not say that *all* meaning can be reduced to some immediate biological advantage or disadvantage; responses may also be guided by other standards. Further, it is not asserted that all meaning has to be "interpreted" by the organism itself whose potential responses are qualified as "good" or "bad" by the meaning relation. An outside observer *A* may very well survey the situation in which an organism *O* finds itself and "interpret" that situation and the meanings encompassed in it from the point of view of *O*. Finally, not everything that is interpreted (either by *A* or by *O*) has an equally close and direct bearing upon *O*'s prevailing situation and the course that *O* should take in order to make the best of that situation. It is apparent, then, that we must make some fundamental distinctions between types of meaning. We have to distinguish types of meaning, first, in terms of the standards on which they are based; second, in terms of the perspective from which they are interpreted; and, third, in terms

25

of the directness of the contribution they make to resolving impending situational problems. This last distinction is perhaps the most fundamental one, and it is the one we shall take up first.

a) COMMUNICATIVE MEANING

This directness, or closeness to the core of the situation, is, in fact, what makes the difference between "sign meaning" and "symbol meaning." *All* meaning defines a type of "good" response in the situation in which it is present; but not all "good" responses defined in this way have a direct bearing on what is to be done in order to secure a "good" denouement, a desirable or favorable sequel to the prevailing constellation of circumstances. Only "signs" have this kind of meaning; "symbols" by themselves have not. When a "sign" is present in a situation, then it points indeed to what should be done to take care of the situation adequately; the interpretation of the meaning of the sign consists in specifying a map of "good" or "bad" behavior routes, spelling out possible sequels to the situation itself. But when a symbolic message or "communication" is presented, the interpretation of the communication as such is neutral toward the question of what are the possible "good" or "bad" routes in the situation. The primary "meaning" of the communication concerns a different kind of "map" of responses; these possible responses are purely "linguistic" in the sense that their "goodness" or "badness" is defined by the rules of the language in which the communication is couched. It is only after this first or linguistic interpretation—the interpretation of the symbol meaning as such—is completed that we may consider the communication as "sign," that is, its contribution to the elucidation of the meaning of the situation itself. I am not saying that these two steps are always performed separately. More often than not, a communication is interpreted as to its symbol meaning automatically and instantaneously and is treated like every other sign—we take the second step without being conscious of having taken the first one. But, for the analysis of the meaning of the communication, the distinction is vital. We cannot get at the essence of the symbol meaning as such by relating it immediately to the situation. If we try to do this, our thinking about the meaning of symbols immediately bogs down in a host of irrelevancies; for instance, we shall say that the meaning of the word "house" is something different for each person who uses the word and also different in each situation in which the word is used. What I am asserting is that both the private "aura" surrounding each word and the unique application to which each actual use of the word points are irrelevant to the meaning of the word as such, that is, the meaning which is being communicated. *This* meaning is fixed by the rules of the English language, not too rigorously, of course, but rigorously enough to permit communication by means of the word. The rules are precise enough to enable all users of language to fit the symbol into their various private "associational auras" and into the "situational contexts" in which the communications are made. The rule which makes this fitting possible is the linguistic meaning and not the actual instances in which the fitting is performed. The main point I want to stress in this connection is that, although the "linguistic" meaning is *invariant* toward possible sets of "situational" meanings, the set of "linguistic" meanings is not self-contained, as it were. To "understand" a language does not mean merely familiarity with rules relating symbols to one another. It also means familiarity with ways in which the interpretation of symbols can be fitted into the nonlinguistic context of the "live" situation. The fundamental idea upon which the present analysis of meaning is based is that, though the "symbol" cycle and the "sign" cycle in behavior are relatively independent, neither is self-contained.

Responses within the "symbol" cycle as such are, so to speak, "incomplete" responses (unless they are "analytical," a case which will be discussed later) that must be supplemented by "fitting" them into the live context; this fitting alone endows them with full meaning. The reverse does not hold: the "live" context does no*t always* call for a "symbolic" supplement. But among human beings it most frequently does; few human situations are "symbol-free." In human behavior, responses are usually guided by symbolic communications, including some addressed by the self to the self, as in verbal thinking; and, even when no actual symbol communication takes place, there is at least a constant readiness to switch over to the "symbol cycle" and enrich the "live context" by "fitting" a symbolic communication into it. This constant moving back and forth between the two cycles is a fundamental human need. Isolation from human intercommunication by symbols creates anxiety, and, if it is severe and protracted, leads to grave trouble. Man's "symbol need" is so strong that he often uses symbols, as it were, for the pleasure of it, without the possibility of any immediate "fitting" into the live situational context. This does not mean that such "gratuitous" communications have no relation at all to the "live" situational context. If they do not point to a possible way of dealing with the present situation, they may provide "maps" to be stored away in memory for potential use in future situations. And, even if they have no conceivable "practical" application of this kind, they still may serve to relieve anxiety, simply by making the world more transparent. Furthermore, one of the functions of communication by symbol is the establishment of circuits of confidence among members of a group. As we shall see, confidence in the source of a communication is crucial to the fitting of the communication into the live context of the situation; and such confidence cannot be established without a great deal of "gratuitous" communication, which serves purely to create familiarity and a good emotional atmosphere.

But let us return to our analysis of symbol meaning. We said that it has to be interpreted, as it were, on two levels: the linguistic and the situational. On the first level the communication has to be understood as "text"; on the second, it has to be interpreted in the situational "context." The transition from one level to the other may be effected in various ways.

For instance (and this happens frequently), we may immediately take the message literally *as if* it were a "sign" of some existing state of things. It is important to realize, however, that the communication itself is never a "sign" of the existence of the state of things which it asserts. The "meaning" of a *declarative* communication, for instance, is merely that, *if* it is "true," such and such a state of things (which may be ascertained independently) actually exists. That "if" is always a question mark, and, in order to fit the communication into the situation, the question of *whether* the communication is true must be answered. This answer is not provided by the *text* of a declarative, nonanalytical communication. *Analytical* communications, indeed, are such that the interpretation of their meaning immediately reveals their truth or falsehood; but this is merely to say that they neither call for nor permit any "fitting" into the situational context. They are compatible with any situational context and hence devoid of information. Here, however, we are concerned only with communications that *do* convey information; and we say about them that they are not "signs" of the existence of the facts which they *assert*.

Communications, however, may—and even must—be considered as "signs" of some existing state of things also. Regardless of whether they are true or false, they may reveal the state of mind or the intention of the sender. One way of "fitting" the meaning of the "text" into the situational "context" consists precisely in this kind of interpretation of the communication as the *sign* of an intention or state of mind.

Finally, we have to reckon with the possibility that the meaning of the "text" cannot be "fitted" into the "context," because the "text" cannot be interpreted on the first level at all. Faced with such a deadlock, we may ask ourselves whether we have understood the message correctly; it may turn out that we ourselves are at fault, being unfamiliar with the rules of the language. Or the case may be that the sender of the communication has violated some linguistic rule. Such cases are methodologically interesting, for we can deal with them only by acts of *interpretation*. We have to ask ourselves not only what happened but also how the actual happenings are to be related to rules of behavior (here, linguistic behavior) which we ourselves are supposed to apply. Sometimes we resolve the difficulty by learning our rules better or by emending our partner's "text" to fit the rules and give a clear meaning (as when we correct printers' errors). Other cases are also conceivable. We may come to the conclusion that the message was indeed nonsensical; and in this case we may interpret it as a "sign" of some pathological state in the sender or of an intention to confuse. We may also conclude in certain cases that our symbol system itself is at fault—that we are trying to communicate by symbols which have no clearly defined meaning. In this case we may decide to revise the rules of our language to make possible a good "fitting" into the context. What we are concerned with in this last case is not the "fitting" of the textual meaning into a context but the *possibility* of "fitting" any and all communications to be made in a certain language. This, again, is a problem concerning "interpretation" and hence a value problem in its own right.

We can now try to indicate a little more precisely what happens when we interpret the "meaning" of any communication on the two separate "levels." Interpretation on the *first* level enables us to see how the message *could* be "fitted" into any situational context; on this level we get a meaning that is invariant with regard to all situational contexts. On the second level we perform the "fitting" itself. As we have already indicated, we may stop short of this "second-level" interpretation of symbolic communications; we may be content with determining how the communication *could* be fitted into any of a set or class of situations.

Interpretation on the first level will tell us what kind of communication we are dealing with—whether it is analytical or nonanalytical, declarative or nondeclarative, and so on. Let us look more closely at these various possibilities.

1. If the message turns out to be analytical, first-level interpretation completes the whole operation: the "fitting" cannot and need not be attempted. In all other cases first-level interpretation must be supplemented by a contextual "fitting." In the course of this "fitting" operation (or second-level interpretation), we may consider the message itself as a "sign" or *confront it* with situational "signs."

2. If the message is declarative, first-level interpretation tells us what the state of the world is in some respect, at some points, *if* the message is "true." We shall see later that pure "textual" interpretation of any declarative message does not specify, in reality, an individual, concrete state of things as "existing in reality" *if* the message is true. What it does specify is either that a *class* of possible states of things is *not empty if* the message is true or that one such class is "contained in" or "excluded from" another. *We cannot convey by a pure symbol "text" that a uniquely identifiable state of the world exists;* to make an assertion of this degree of concreteness, we must use not only a symbolic "text" but also some contextual indicators that fit the text into the situation. In other words, interpretation of any message as describing an actual state of the world presupposes the combination of a symbolic "text" with some nonsymbolic "fitting" devices. This "nontextual" component of sentences asserting actual states of things will be discussed later (see chap. vi).

3. If firsthand interpretation indicates that the message is declarative in form, the next problem is how to fit it into the situational context. It may be the case that the message is immediately applicable to the *present* situation: it asserts something that, if true, makes a difference here and now. But this need not be the case. The assertion may refer to concrete states of things remote in time and space. Then we can "fit" it into the *present* situation only by drawing "world lines" from it and stating that—provided that the message is true—we *would* find such and such a state of things if we moved from "here" along such and such co-ordinates for such and such a distance. (Such a statement, incidentally, involves the use of the "nontextual" devices mentioned in the preceding paragraph.) Or the message may be of a "general" form: it may assert that a *class* of state of things is not empty or includes another. Then we can attempt to "fit" it into the situation by trying to produce an *example* of the class relationship asserted. Finally, the message, though declarative in form, may be purely *imaginative*

in content: we cannot "fit" it into any actual situation but might *imagine* a situation into which it would fit.

4. First-level interpretation may indicate that the message is non-declarative. For instance, it may be a question or a command (or request). If so, the "fitting" will consist in scrutinizing our situational context to find out whether we can or should satisfy the sender and in discovering by what means he could be satisfied or resisted. In such cases the first-level interpretation will tell us what we are requested to do (supply a piece of information or perform an operation); second-level interpretation tells us *whether* and *how* we should do it. Such nondeclarative messages may, of course, also be distinguished as to whether they refer to the immediately given situation or to a remote one; whether they concern actual entities or class relationships; and whether they are meant realistically or as imaginative fiction.

5. Finally, messages may convey neither factual information nor a command or request but an *interpretation*. The interpretation of an interpretive statement (or value judgment) also proceeds on two levels. First-level interpretation will tell us what meaning relationship is asserted in terms of what standard (e.g., a reader may remark that what is said here is "nonsense"), second-level interpretation will consist in judging the matter interpreted in the message in terms of the standards which we ourselves accept as valid for us.

This classificatory survey of types of symbol meanings has given us a wide and varied array—pure declarative sentences of varied degrees of remoteness and concreteness; "realistic" and "imaginative" messages; nondeclarative sentences like questions, commands, requests, etc. (all these being subsumed under the general term "demand"); and "interpretive" messages, which are "declarative" in form but must be distinguished from purely *factual* sentences (the only ones we shall call "declarative"). We shall not prejudge at this point whether the "interpretive" statements are a subclass of "demands" or whether all are synonymous with a "demand." All we say is that they can be interpreted only with reference to some standard of "good" or "bad." The "objectivity" or "subjectivity" of all or some such standards will be discussed later.

Before we close our survey of the varieties of symbol meaning, one further matter should be mentioned. Messages consist of individual symbols, and the question arises how the "meaning" of a symbol as such is related to what we have discussed so far—the "meaning" of a message. On this I would point out the following: Individual symbols, such as words, are, of course, meaningful entities. *In themselves,* however, they have only what I have called "textual" meaning; they cannot be fitted into a *situational* "context" in and by themselves but only by way of a message (declarative sentence, demand, etc.) of which they form a part. A word as such does not "mean" anything situationally, although it can be "understood" or "not understood" when presented in isolation. (It is obvious, however, that a communication may consist of one single word and that in this case such a use of the single word will convey a "fittable" meaning.) We may try to clarify the difference between the meaning of a symbol as such and of a *symbolic communication* by saying: The meaning of a declarative sentence is that, *if* it is true, the state of the world is such and such; the meaning of a word is that, if it is put into such and such a sentence in a given situation, that sentence will be true (or false).

In our explication of symbol meanings, we have referred to other kinds of meanings—that is, sign meanings—and also to "facts" or "states of things." What we understand by the terms "sign" and "sign meaning" has already been made clear in our preceding discussions: the meaning of a "sign" is that, if it is present in a situation, such and such a response is good or bad by some standard. But, in defining the "meaning" of a declarative sentence, we referred to its "truth" and to a "state of things" or "fact": the meaning of the declarative sentence is that it is true if a certain state of things exists. As to the term "true," it clearly points to the specific standard in terms of which the meaning of the declarative sentence is defined; here the "meaning relation" is that, if the sentence is asserted, the "state of the world" being such and such, "acceptance" or "rejection" is the "good" response by the standard of "truth." Now we have here an intermediary term in our relation—the "state of the world." This intermediary term cannot be explicated in terms of sign meanings, for a factual state of affairs does not determine a "good" response in itself; the intermediary term refers, rather, to *classes* of meanings. We shall deal with this in our next section, where we take up sign meanings.

Before we start this discussion, however, we shall introduce a terminological distinction. The array of meanings we have surveyed in this section—meanings of words and of messages of various kinds—will henceforth be subsumed under the common heading "communicative meaning." The other great division of meanings, thus far called "sign meanings," will be called "situational meanings." As already pointed out, there is no watertight separation between these two main classes of meanings—a message is not fully interpreted until it is fitted into a context of situational meaning, and any situational meaning may be conveyed by symbolic communications. The distinction is made merely in order to stress the fact that communicative meanings have a first-level interpretation and a set of standards (rules of language) of their own, regardless of how they fit into an actual situation.

b) SITUATIONAL MEANING

By a "situation" we mean the totality of responses by which an organism or group of organisms can achieve something "good" or "bad" for itself in terms of some standard. Of course, nobody can achieve anything by a response unless that response is available to him; hence it would seem appropriate to define a situation as a sum of *available* responses. Such a definition, however, would lead to somewhat awkward consequences; for the *lack* of an adequate response may very well be crucial to an organism in a situation. In analyzing the situation of an organism, then, we must refer also to "required" responses which are not available (e.g., owing to lack of adaptation or training). But, on the other hand, it would be senseless to include in our analysis of a situation some purely imaginary responses that would solve a quandary or problem (e.g., "If I had wings, I would fly away"). Hence we shall include in our definition of the situation of an organism those responses which *are* available to it and those which *might* become available by learning or adaptation. Obviously, an organism can "interpret" its situation only in terms of the responses available to it; it is only the outside observer who can spell out the meaning of a situation in terms of responses that would achieve some good *if* they were available. From either point of view, the meaning of the situation can be spelled out in terms of the various "signs" that specify which response is "good or "bad," respectively.

If we now consider the situation not from the viewpoint of the outside observer but from that of the organism whose situation it is, we shall say that the situation may be either "familiar" or "baffling." The difference concerns the more or less ready availability of "good" responses. In an unfamiliar or baffling situation, "signs" which the organism can interpret are lacking; in such a situation it will experience a quandary, it will be perplexed. When this is the case, responses will be nonspecific—not related to any "sign." The organism will "scan" its environment in an effort to *find* some "signs," some clues pointing to a possible need-reduction.

This "scanning" behavior is characterized by randomness. No direction in movement is preferred to any other; no goal is sought directly. This nonpreference may also lead to immobility—a frequent, and often enough "adaptive," consequence of perplexity. In appropriate circumstances, random scanning behavior may lead to the discovery of sign meanings; certain directions and goals of movement will become "preferred" and stabilized, if they have been found to lead to need-reduction in a reliable way. This is the "law of effect," one of the fundamental laws of learning theory. What happens in these cases is a reduction of the "entropy" or randomness of behavior. The situation becomes more and more structured; more and more elements in it acquire "meaning."

Such behavioral randomness and its reduction are absolute necessities for animal organisms; for a fundamental feature of animal life is that the animal does not live in a "saturated" environment. The things which it needs to sustain life are scattered in its field of behavior and can be reached only by vigorous scanning or by a choice of "improbable" routes. (Plants can live, by and large, only in a "saturated" environment.) But these "improbable" routes are not necessarily mapped on the inherited behavior pattern of the animal. It must often discover them by probing and scanning; and the life-history of the organisms which cannot sustain themselves by random scanning consists in a series of cycles in which initial "random scanning" is reduced to a stable pattern. Where this is done often, quickly, and efficiently, we speak of "intelligence." Intelligence is the measure of the ease with which initial randomness is overcome and supplanted by an adaptive preferential order. Preferential routes may also be selected instinctively, on a basis of inheritance; in such cases we do not speak of "intelligence." In other cases the preferred routes may be learned from a parent or teacher: this mode of supplanting randomness by order may be called "information" or "example." (In our usage the term "information" is reserved for transmission of knowledge by symbols; we do not call familiarity with sign meanings, as such, "information.") Information is, of course, a powerful adjunct and tool of "intelligence."

Of course, animal species differ greatly as to the degree of their "intelligence" and as to the relative importance of "scanning" and "learning" in their lives. Fast-moving animals like fish, flying insects, and birds rely to a great extent on scanning and to a less extent on learning: their rate of movement is such that they can find their food by a largely *random* covering of their field of behavior. However, for nesting and reproduction, they need "preferential" places and routes. We often find rigid "preferences" for specific spawning and nesting places in fish and birds, based on inherited instincts. (In plants, food is obtained through "stationary" routes, and we find random scattering in their *reproduction* cycle.)

Man's life-situation, however, is such that he is absolutely dependent on both intelligence and information. He cannot achieve much by random scanning alone: his movements and reflexes are so slow that most of his life-situations would turn out disastrously for him if he could rely only on "scanning" before he hit upon the right response. Man must anticipate; but he cannot anticipate on the basis of an inherited map of preferential routes. He must map his situation himself; he must interpret sign meanings. But even that is not enough; the human individual could not subsist by his own intelligence. He is dependent on "information," the transmission of knowledge acquired by other human beings. The human brain and nervous system are not merely organs of "learning"; they are, to a great extent, organs of communication, receptors for information. Man needs two "higher" behavior systems—the "situational" one of learning and the "communicative" one of information; he could not subsist on the human level without possessing either and without knowing how to integrate the two. This integration of two "higher" (that is, noninstinctive) behavior systems is the specific characteristic of man; it determines the nature of specifically human "intelligence." It is this "contextual" use of symbols that makes the difference between human and other animal organisms.

We are, however, concerned here with the "situational" cycle proper, that of the "sign meanings" which define a set of good or bad responses in terms of some "situational" standard—that is, all standards except the "communicative" ones, the "rules of language." The question which is answered by the interpretation of a "sign" is what should be done in view of the presence of that sign, in order to give the situation a favorable turn. A "sign," as something "interpreted" as to its meaning, should not be defined as a "stimulus." The sign is not the stimulus as such (i.e., an impulse that could be recorded by every suitable receptor, such as a photographic film); it is an element of a "situation," characterized by the needs felt by an organism and by the array of available or desirable response patterns related to the reduction of those needs. The behavior, therefore, should not be considered as being controlled by "stimuli"; it is not even "controlled," properly speaking, by the "signs" and their meanings. For the meaning (as ascertained by a neutral, outside interpreter) does not call forth behavior appropriate to it. Behavior will follow "meaning" only to the extent that the appropriate response has been learned and is not inhibited by extraneous circumstances (including other "sign meanings" present and all kinds of other disturbances). We can only say that signs will "tend to" evoke a response appropriate to them, to the extent that their meaning has been learned and to the extent that they are "dominant" over competing meaningful and nonmeaningful components of the situation. It is not one sign in isolation that "determines" the response actually made, but a sign constellation in which certain signs are dominant; and in such a constellation the response actually forthcoming will be one that is both available and uninhibited by disturbances. Of course, by "sign" we do not mean an external object, event, or "stimulus" but a situational relationship whose terms include the needs of the organism. When we want to single out the "external" term of this relation, we speak of the "sign correlate."

A "dominant" sign correlate or event may also be called a "signal." Smoke may be a "signal," not for the event "fire," but for a situationally dominant response of doing something about the fire. Dark clouds may be a "signal" for looking for shelter. Signals may thus be provided by "nature," but they may also be produced artificially. Traffic lights, for instance, are artificial "signals." Such artificial signals have something in common with symbolic communications, in that they transmit from one organism (or mechanism) to other organisms a situational map of good responses which the latter could not discover by themselves. Such "communication by signal" is possible for animals too. But we should not confuse communication by signal with communication by symbol.[1] A signal, as such, calls for interpretation on the situational level: when it is present, it thereby spells out the meaning of the situation. Symbolic messages may, of course, serve as "signals"—what I am saying is that their "signal" meaning is their "second-level" or situational meaning.

Signals that have been designed so as to cause the receiving organism

1. We reject the view often expressed in writings about the theory of meaning that symbols are merely artificial signs, i.e., that they differ from other signs only as to their origin; cf. Charles Morris, *Signs, Language, and Behavior* (New York: Prentice-Hall, 1946), p. 25; L. S. Stebbing, *A Modern Introduction to Logic* (2d ed.; London, 1933), p. 11.

(or mechanism) to act in accordance with them may be termed "instructions." Mechanisms may be constructed in such a way that they will unfailingly act upon instruction; and organisms may be "conditioned" so as to obey signals automatically, in which case the signal will be an "instruction." Instructions differ from other signals, in that they do not allow for nonperformance due to disturbances or competing elements in the sign constellation. Hence they are rather exceptional in human or animal behavior; for the main characteristic of such behavior is precisely the great instability of responses to signs and sign events. Reflexes, of course, occur "unfailingly" in animal organisms; but they cannot be classified as "meaningful" responses, even though they may be "adaptive." "Adaptive" reflexes may be said to be "meaningful" only in the sense in which physiological processes can be called "meaningful," that is, in a metaphorical sense. At this point we shall consider as "meaningful" only responses in which a certain behavior route is chosen (or preferred) on the basis of an available behavioral map. There is no such choice involved in a reflex movement. Conditioned reflexes (or "instructions") also lack this element of choice, and for this reason they will not be called "meaningful" responses. Part of the response to symbols, however, is also automatic; symbols are, in part, "instructions." But the automatic response to a symbol stops short of its "contextual" interpretation.

The distinction we made between "sign" and "signal" refers to position in a sign constellation. We may call any member in a sign constellation a "sign," whether dominant or not; a "signal" is a dominant sign. It will be seen, however, that the human situation cannot be broken down into a mere constellation of signs or signals represented by clearly identifiable events playing the role of sign correlates. Much of the meaning of a human situation is "produced" or "projected" onto it by the interpreter.

On the animal level, specific adaptation to a type of sign events or "correlates" is the main basis on which situations are interpreted, and this kind of interpretation is what we called "interpretation-in-behavior." On the human level, this kind of "learned response" is present, too, but is far from being predominant. The chief characteristic of human intelligence is not that it enables its possessor to "come in out of the rain." Its basic trait is not adaptation but judgment, not implicit but explicit interpretation.

The difference is briefly this: A response based on adaptation can take place only when a type of sign constellation, the meaning of which has been learned, recurs. Responses based on judgment are not limited in this way. What is characteristic of them is that the dominant meaning in the situational context is treated as an x, an unknown, and determined by systematic questioning.

Let us consider an example. A traveler on vacation finds himself in a strange town. Not knowing what to do, he asks the hotel clerk to make some suggestions. The clerk mentions a beach about twenty miles away, a fair that is being held in a neighboring town, and a hike in a near-by forest. Our traveler is not tempted by all this; he asks whether there is a movie theater in town. The answer is Yes. "What are they showing?" "I don't know," the clerk says, "because the program is due to change today, and I haven't looked at the movie announcement yet; here is the paper." The traveler looks at the advertisement, finds he has seen the picture to be shown, and decides to go for a swim.

Let us analyze the little scene. Initially, no "signal" is presented; what the best response is remains to be determined. Our traveler does this by trying to ascertain the relevant facts. He collects factual information and learns about a beach, a fair, a forest, and a movie, all within reach. He then projects all these items of factual information upon his situation and confronts the resulting situational "map" with his needs. The factual information representing the best "route" on the map is the one about the beach. Had the movie theater been showing a different picture, that might have been preferred.

What happens when the "meaning" of the situation—that is, the best possible response—is determined on the basis of "facts"? Note that the information about the various facts as such is no "sign" determining a "good" response. The clerk will give the same information to any traveler, regardless of what the latter's tastes are; the announcement in the paper is made to all and sundry, whether they have seen the picture and like the star or not. We may say that the "facts" asserted in these items of information represent not the meaning of any situation but something common to, and invariant with regard to, many situations; we can define a "fact" in this sense as a *class* of sign meanings. Many people, having different wishes and standards of value, may make their response in the situation depend on "what the facts are"; but their decision, of course, is something different from, and superimposed upon, the ascertainment of the facts as such. In order to reach a decision, the subject must "judge" the facts—he must determine what the "fact," which is a common element of many situations, "means" to him in his prevailing situation. The fact is "fitted into" a situational context. This is possible if the subject possesses the faculty of making his response dependent not on the recurrence of a familiar type of sign but on the "class" to which his situation will be found to belong.

The "type of sign" calling for an adapted response also defines, in a primitive way, a "class" of situations. But, as long as an organism relies on adaptation, it can recognize a situation as belonging to a "class" only when some recurrent sign happens to be present, and such a recognition of the class membership of the situation immediately defines a "good" response. When, however, a decision is based on a survey of "facts," it is possible to recognize a class membership of the situation, and, as we have seen, even *many* class memberships, without prejudging what the "best" response will be. Factual knowledge may be collected as such, without acting upon it; when we do this, we deal with relationships between a situation and a class of situations or with relationships between classes of situations, without making any judgment as to what response such class relationships warrant. Such collection of factual knowledge involves no interpretation of meaning; it is in this sense that we speak of "brute" facts. Our present discussion, however, concerns not factual knowledge as such but the situational interpretation of such knowledge, the "judgments" based upon "fitting" the "fact" into the situational context.

This expression recalls a similar discussion we had in the preceding paragraph, when we spoke about the "first-level" and the "second-level" interpretation of symbolic communications. We said there that any symbolic communication has to be interpreted first as to its linguistic meaning and then "fitted into" a situational context. For instance, we determine the first-level meaning of a declarative sentence: this meaning is that the sentence is true if the state of the world is such and such. Then we may ask *whether* the sentence is true: this is not yet the "second-level" interpretation, since the truth or falsehood of the sentence does not yet determine how we should act; when we know that a sentence is true, we merely know to which *class* of situations our situation belongs. We can use this factual information by answering the question as to what behavioral route should be preferred, the facts being such and such.

In our scene the intermediary question of truth did not arise; the traveler had confidence in the assertions of the clerk and in the announcement in the newspaper. Believing both, he treated their messages as indicators of the existence of a state of things. His problem was reduced to confronting his prevailing situation with the situation-class pattern as represented by the facts about which he received information; this is the operation I call "judgment." A judgment is the interpretation of a situation, "the facts being such and such." Its schema is: "The facts being such and such, this is the good response by some standard." The "checking" (that is, verification or falsification) of a declarative sentence is obviously a judgment; it follows the schema: "The facts being such and such, the good response, by the standard of truth, is to accept (or reject) the sentence." In this case, judgment about a fact sentence S will be based on its agreement or disagreement with another fact sentence S'.

Our traveler implicitly believed what he was told; he was interested in "judging" the situation on the basis of fact statements which he believed, and not in "judging" the truth or falsehood of those statements. Nevertheless, the inference that our traveler implicitly believes everything he is told would be erroneous. He would not have asked the clerk or looked at the newspaper, had he not had confidence in them as sources of factual information; in a different situation, for instance, in a conference with business competitors, he might well be more wary about what others told him.

Facts, of course, may be ascertained at first hand, too; they need not necessarily be discovered by way of receiving truthful information. Actually, however, man discovers surprisingly few facts for himself; most of his firsthand knowledge of the state of the world is not factual knowledge but "knowledge by familiarity." We are "familiar" with the streets of our home town but know few "facts" about them at first hand. Familiarity is a category of adaptation, not of judgment; the presence of familiar objects endows the situation with a diffuse background "meaning," the gist of which is not that a certain response is required or desirable but that *no* being on the alert, exploration, or scanning for possible dangers or surprises is called for. In the presence of the familiar, we are relaxed and sometimes bored; we let the situation present its meaningful "signs," knowing we shall be able to cope with them, even if we make no effort to anticipate them. It is difficult to ascertain facts about the familiar; for, in order to establish facts at first hand, we have to break up the pattern of our situation in order to discover the class relationships that connect it with other situations. The flavor of familiarity, which clings to something unique, must evaporate during this operation. Some facts may be noted without words, e.g., one may have a "diagram" of a certain fact; but, mostly, the establishment of a fact will be accompanied by verbalization, either to others or to one's self. It may be added that most of the "facts" that we know at first hand, which are imbedded in a "familiar" background, involve the presence of symbols (e.g., names on shop signs in the familiar street).

In actual human behavior, then, the "signals" for appropriate behavior include, in addition to "typical" signs the meaning of which has been "learned" through adaptation, a different class of signs which have no "typical" meaning but acquire their dominant-sign or "signal" character on the basis of a judgment which relates them to a body of factual information. We shall call these signs, in contrasting them to "typical" signs, "contextual" signs, to indicate that ther meaning accrues to them through their being imbedded in a "context" of facts, on the one hand, and predispositions, preferences, and standards, on the other. Human behavior is characterized by the use of contextual signs. Animal behavior does not go beyond the level of typical signs.

The reader may have noted that the cycle in which contextual signals are established recalls in a way the cycle running from random scanning to the established "good" response in adaptive behavior. In the contextual cycle, too, we start from an unstructured situation in which no "signal" is present, and we institute questioning in order to work out a "map" of meanings. This questioning, however, is not wholly random behavior: it is based upon a pre-existent structuring of the situation. The traveler, for instance, chose for questioning a source in which he had confidence; and he framed his question in such a way as to elicit information relevant to a given array of possible preferences, those which vacationists may be supposed to have. Questioning may be relatively specific or relatively vague, depending on whether merely factual information about a definite region of the world is asked for or suggestions about possible satisfactory routes are to be elicited. In any case, however, the contextual cycle of questioning runs from meaning to meaning and not from complete lack of meaning to a structured situation. A question itself is a meaningful communication; it is based upon a meaningful patterning of the situation and helps improve that pattern further.

In all interpretation, whether interpretation-in-behavior or contextual interpretation, we may distinguish, as it were, two "poles": the unique situation "here and now," which is to be judged and in which a choice is to be made, and the recurrent meaningful characteristics, whether typical or contextual, which make it transparent and judge-able. It seems that animal organisms can intrepret the recurrent mean-ingful "types" of correlate only in their bearing upon the "unique" pole of the meaning relationship. Human beings can also identify and "interpret" the recurrent elements of situations as such, regardless of their bearing upon any actual situation. In other words, they can deal with types of possible meaning out of context. We say that these types represent "potential" meaning for any situation, as distinct from the "actual" meaning of the prevailing situation.

To sum up: Sign meanings may be classified into "dominant" and "nondominant" ones, on the one hand, and "typical" and "contextual" ones, on the other. The active organism interprets its situation in terms of dominant sign meanings; the nondominant ones can be perceived only by an organism which assumes the position of a detached ob-server toward another organism or toward itself. As to the difference between typical and contextual signs, the former may be interpreted "in behavior," whereas the latter can be interpreted only by an explicit judgment. It is characteristic of interpretation by judgment that it gets at a meaning by way of class relationships among situations. Class relationships in terms of which the dominant meaning of a situation may be contextually determined concern "facts" or "states of the world."

2. FACT AND MEANING

We have seen in the preceding section that facts or states of the world play a crucial role in the interpretation of contextual meaning. We have also seen that a "fact" in itself is not a sign but something invariant with regard to a number of signs. "Fact" is not a situational category: a "situation" can be analyzed only in terms of meanings; it is not a collection of facts that may be observed and described. An observer cataloguing all the facts he can observe around him does not characterize his "situation"; he merely specifies a number of situation classes to which his situation belongs. This operation has great situ-ational relevance, since contextual interpretation will hinge on it; but it does not represent interpretation of meanings in itself. I shall attempt to name a few categories that are used in ascertaining facts. As we shall see, these categories somehow correspond to the categories of meaning (signs, signals, sign correlates, symbols, symbolic communications) that we specified above; inevitably so, since the "fact" categories are categories of invariants or classes of sign meanings.

Let us follow our observer in his work. He may make a catalogue of the "objects" surrounding him. He may note "events" taking place in his environment. And he may distinguish "properties" of his objects and the way in which such "properties" appear to be coupled in a sequence of "events." In this way he may arrive at the establishment of regularities or "laws."

What is an "object"? Consider a commonplace object such as a drinking glass. In many situations—when we use the glass—it plays the role of a "sign correlate": in the meaningful situation in which our thirst drives us to use the glass, we can isolate the latter as an identifiable, relatively independent vehicle of part of the meaning of our situation. It is that which enables us to make a quantity of water available for drinking in the manner to which we are accustomed. But we can also consider the glass as such, when it does not enter into any situation as a sign correlate; then we look at it as a phsyical "object" having such and such enduring "properties." The observer is not interested in the various roles which the glass can play as a sign correlate; the properties he wants to ascertain are invariant toward all these roles. These properties may be geometrical shape and measurements, chemical composition, optical and electrophysical characteristics, and the like; if our observer is interested in economics, he may note the price at which the glass has been purchased or might be replaced; if he is a physician, he may be induced to ascertain the bacterial flora of the glass; and so on. In all these cases some operation is performed on the glass: it is made to respond to various manipulations, and these responses will enable the manipulator to characterize the glass by some "index." All these indices will be *meaningful* in terms of some manipulatory complex, such as a scientific theory: they will be geometrical or physical or economic, etc., indices. When such indices are established within the framework of a well-developed theory, it will be possible to deduce other indices which the theory will enable us to expect the glass to exhibit under specifically altered circumstances.

There is an apparent contradiction in the preceding analysis. We started out by saying that pure factual observation is not concerned with sign meanings; and in the end we found that it results in the ascertainment of "meaningful" indices. But there is nothing anomalous in this. Observation, as a human activity, is obviously meaningful; it is neither completely random nor a mere automatic functioning. The ascertainment of the properties of an object is a goal-directed activity which has its "standards" of meaning. Our point is, however, that the "meaning" of observation, as an operation, presupposes a neutral viewpoint toward every possible sign-correlate role of the object observed; in order to perform it well, we have to focus solely on the question of what the object is like, regardless of how we might use it to satisfy some need arising within our situation. This descriptive activity need in no way be absolutely disinterested, for we have seen how factual knowledge will help toward the contextual interpretation of the situation. But it is relatively disinterested, in that we make no contextual judgment involving the object as sign correlate while we are performing our descriptive operation. The only meanings that inform the operation are (a) the "meaning" of the indices, as possible values of the variables that make up a scientific theory, and (b) the communicative meaning of the statements we make about our observations.

We have already discussed communicative meaning in a preliminary way; but a few words have to be said about the "meaning" of observational indices as values fitting into a theory. The purport of this meaning is that we may treat the object as a "phenomenon" to be explained by such and such a physical or other theory. This *is* a situational meaning like any other; it involves a meaning relation to the effect that, the object being present, one or another type of "explanation" of its properties will be a "good" or a "bad" response. This "meaning relation," however, must be set apart from others, in that it refers to a situation in which we deliberately choose a neutral position toward all situations belonging to a certain class. What we do in this observational or theoretical situation will possibly help us or others when we have to determine what the best response will be in one particular situation; but, as long as we remain in the "theoretical" situation, we merely clear the ground for such possible choices. We are concerned not with the choice of a "route" but with the tracing of a "map." We are doing what the learning process does for the organism, not what the organism does when it responds on the basis of learning. Our own responses, in the observational situation, are "verbal" and "communicative": they have a remote rather than a close bearing upon any of a class of situations that may emerge.

It is not only scientific observers who may engage in observational activities. Anyone can identify and describe objects as such; he may classify them as to shape, color, size, and possible use or from any other point of view, without relating his findings to any elaborate theory. All such activities, whether of the "scientific" or of the "everyday" type, have something in common: they result in the ordering of objects within a classificatory and manipulatory scheme, and they represent an interruption of the cycle of situational choices. The observational situation is, in this sense, a situation *behind* the situations in which choices have to be made; we can enter into the observational role only when no vitally urgent choice has to be made. The collection of "facts" can start only when we can live, so to speak, on our reserves. Curiosity—the drive behind fact-finding—presupposes saturation. It is present in animals, too; but in their case it serves only to enrich their familiarity with the various elements—potential sign correlates—of their prevailing situations rather than to the exploration of situation-class relationships.

A "factual" category we mentioned above is that of "event." The distinction between "object" and "event" is not fundamental; we may look upon an "object" as a sequence of "events." From the subjective point of view of the observer, however, it may be practical to make the distinction, according as the thing he observes is something characterized by a great concentration and stability of combinations of observable properties or by a more or less rapid change in such a combination. Since, in the case of "objects," the combination is stable, it makes no difference *when* the observation is made; it must only be borne in mind that no stability of properties is absolute and that allowance must be made for more or less gradual changes in the descriptive properties of all objects. It also goes without saying that the descriptive "indices" of all objects depend on the kind of operation or manipulation by which they are elicited. Some of these things were perfectly familiar to Aristotle, who is full of warnings against confusion between "things" and "words" and against overlooking the possibility—nay, the certainty—that a thing or person will change its "accidental" and "relational" properties while remaining the same thing or person. It is a kind of irony that these insights, freshly "discovered" by charlatans, now go under the title of "non-Aristotelian" logic.

The main characteristic of an event is that it is "datable": it is a process taking place in space and time (and this is why an "object," described in terms of its full biography, may be considered as an "event"). In describing an event, we must also use "indices"; these "indices" ascribe properties not to enduring "objects" but to time-space points or intervals. Apart from this difference in focus, the observational attitude is the same, whether we describe objects or events; and if we put our description of an event into the framework of a theory, we can also anticipate future or past indices from presently observed ones.

This attention to "theory" is an essential characteristic of the observational attitude. The ascription of indices to objects or to time-space regions is not an end in itself even within the observational cycle of behavior; it is being undertaken with an eye to relating it to some deductive framework into which the indices fit. The observer is interested in describing events, not just for the sake of describing them, but in order to derive or apply some general knowledge about uniformities characterizing index combinations. I shall not deal here with the *derivation* of "laws" from "observations" of events, that is, with the problem of induction; I shall rather discuss briefly the *reverse* operation, the "explanation" of an observed event by means of a theory.

Let us suppose that we observe the indices $x_1, x_2, \ldots, x_n$. We can try to "explain" the occurrence characterized by this combination, provided that the "theories" we know include an equation satisfied by this set of values. A simple case of "explanation" is one in which the indices refer to the position of the same body at different times. If these indices fit into the equation of "free fall," we may offer the "explanation" that the body was dropped to the earth. If the indices refer to the observed positions of the sun at the same hour on different days, we may "explain" this series of observations in terms of a theory of the solar system. Not all cases of explanation are so simple as these; we often have to invoke different functions and different theories until all our data are accounted for.

It may happen that the indices we observe could be equally well accounted for by different explanations. For instance, if all we observe is some loud noise, the explanation may be that a heavy object has dropped to the earth, that a motorcar has blown a tire, or that a revolver has been fired, and so on. To find the "correct" explanation, we must look for other indices characterizing the event. If we look down the street, we may see a motorist changing a tire on his car; this new datum would support the explanation that the noise was, in fact, caused by a punctured tire. Further data (e.g., a report by the motorist that his mishap occurred before or after we heard the noise) may invalidate the explanation; then we have to look for data which will fit together as values satisfying some equation. Once an explanation is found by which all data we can discover are accounted for, we may treat the originally described event, together with its explanation, as an "event" requiring explanation in terms of a more general "theory." During this new cycle of explanation, we again perform the same kind of operation: we fit indices as values into some equation or "law" that we know. In so doing, we shall always be able to fill out lacunae in our observations, for our explanation will enable us to calculate or deduce indices attributable to space-time regions in the neighborhood of our observed indices. In this way an explanation will always imply a number of "predictions" of indices, and, in fact, we can use these "predictions" to check the correctness of our explanation. If some observation we make in the course of our investigations contradicts a prediction implied by our explanation, we have to abandon or amplify the latter. During the entire operation, we always treat observed indices as indicators of indices not observed.

Now this relationship between indices—namely, that an observed index "indicates" one not yet observed, as a value satisfying the same equation—is often taken to be the prototype of the "sign" relationship: the observed index is said to be a "sign" of the index deduced from it with the help of some theory, or for the event characterized by this latter index. For instance, it is customary to say that smoke is a "sign" of fire or "means" fire. This usage, of course, is inconsistent with our definition of the "sign" relationship: we cannot treat an event as the "sign" of another event, for *our* definition of "sign" and "meaning" involves not only events as such but also organisms, their standards or needs, and a hypothetical "good" response as defined by the "meaning" of the sign.

The distinction which our definition implies between the "causal" or "functional" relationship obtaining among events, on the one hand, and the "meaning" relationship, on the other, is not that the former is something purely "objective," whereas the latter is something essentially "subjective." The description of any event involves "subjective" terms, for the indices in terms of which the description is given depend on the nature of the recording instrument or sensory organ used; and, on the other hand, we can look at "meaningful" situations in an "objective" way, as when a neutral observer discusses the possible responses whereby an organism *could* achieve satisfaction. The distinction concerns, rather, the kind of thing we are talking about—in the one case, we discuss events that take place, no matter how they affect the needs and behavioral standards of organisms; in the other, we look at the events in terms of the contribution they might make to the determination of a "good" choice. Now, of course, there is no way of proving that the one or the other way of using the term "sign" or "meaning" is the only correct one; to say that the event "smoke" is a "sign" of the event "fire" corresponds very well to current usage, and *our* definition, which excludes this manner of speaking, is certainly the one that departs from usage. This is a weakness in our terminology; but we have accepted this disadvantage, in order to be able to keep apart two types of relationship that must be distinguished. What we maintain is that the connection we assert between "smoke" and "fire"—a causal connection on the basis of which we "explain" the occurrence of the former—is different from the connection between an interpretable sign and what it "means," i.e., the potential "good" response. For there is nothing in the relationship between "smoke" and "fire" suggesting that the one may gradually come to terms with the other and change its behavior during the process, whereas this is precisely the kind of thing we observe when we look at a sequence of meaningful responses in a live situation. We speak of "meaning" only in connection with phenomena which exhibit this kind of plasticity and perfectibility of behavior. All other connections among phenomena—uniformities in the combined occurrence of indices and so on—are free of "meaning"; they do not "mean" anything in themselves, nor does one part or component in such a configuration "mean" another.

This is not to say that fact-finding as an operation is devoid of "meaning." Our own exertions, undertaken to be able to "explain" and to "predict" phenomena, exhibit precisely the plasticity and perfectibility of meaning-oriented behavior. The causal connection between smoke and fire is one thing; our ability to grasp it and base explanations and predictions on it is another. The former does not involve the kind of relationship we called the "meaning" relation; the latter does. We may say in this sense that the observation of smoke becomes "meaningful" in so far as we can relate it to a theory in terms of which we can explain it. Thus, after all, we may make use of the expression "smoke means fire" as a shorthand expression for the clumsy and involved statement that the observation of smoke is "meaningful" to an observer in so far as he can explain it correctly by means of a theory causally relating it to fire. This kind of "meaning," however, concerns only the behavior (the possible "appropriate" response) of the observer as observer; no other possible "meaning" of the occurrence of smoke (and fire) is involved.

All this seems to suggest a rather clear-cut separation between the role of the "observer" and that of the "actor," who is interested not in describing and explaining events but in responding to them in a more "active" way in order to achieve an advantage that is not purely intellectual. Now we hear many warnings (particularly from pragmatists and instrumentalists, and most characteristically from John Dewey) about the inadvisability of setting up a partition wall between "theory" and "practice." All theoretical inquiry, Dewey insists, is merely a phase in a process pointing to some "more than purely intellectual" satisfaction; it does not stand in a vacuum all by itself but is a phase in a complete sequence of behavior governed both by "intellectual" and by other needs. "Knowing" and "acting" are inseparably linked together.

I may recall at this point that my position, as set forth in the preceding sections of this analysis, also stresses the principle that the cycle of "knowing," "fact-finding" behavior is not self-contained: it is intimately tied in with the cycle of "choosing" behavior. No life-history, whether of an individual or of a group, can be limited to a sequence of "recording" or fact-finding operations alone. What I would urge is merely that it is possible to distinguish, within each life-history, various "roles" and that the "role" of fact-finding is different from the "role" of choosing the best situational route in terms of the information thus made available. We may stress as much as we want that the former "role" makes sense only in so far as it prepares and contributes to the latter; it still remains true that it has a character and rationale of its own and that it can be played only during periods of lull between urgent "choice" situations. Further, it is not correct to say that it is possible to seek knowledge *only* in order to gather information relevant to the solution of some situational perplexity or quandary clearly present in consciousness. To what choice, if any, the knowledge acquired will be relevant may be left entirely open. Sometimes we embark upon research with a clear idea of what kind of application we can make of our findings; at other times, all we are interested in is the perfecting of the deductive patterns available for explaining and predicting phenomena. We *may* be convinced that, by doing so, we improve the chances of solving situational quandaries; that is, the more things we can predict in the most economical way, the more generally "useful" will our knowledge be. But we go ahead building and perfecting theories even if we have no idea of a concrete "payoff," and all we care about is to get the most powerful deductive-explanatory framework possible. We act *as if* the building of the "best" (most inclusive and economical) theory were an end in itself, and in a sense it is, for its possession reduces our anxiety and gives us a sense of power and freedom that has spiritual significance for us. What we gain may be "only" that our situation becomes more trans-parent without being more satisfactory in other ways. It may even be-come *less* satisfactory as a result of increased knowledge, as when scientists discover new techniques of mass destruction or ways of rendering superfluous the contributions of many individuals to the social output; such gain in knowledge may aggravate or generate social conflicts.

The cycle of "information" may be integrated with the cycle of "choice" in many ways. One possibility is that a person faced with a situational problem consults others to find the information relevant to his problem. Another is that specialists devote themselves to the gathering of information that they know will be useful to others, and then set themselves up as consultants. And, finally, the building of a comprehensive and well-structured body of information may itself be-come the paramount "situational problem" to be solved, regardless of how the information might become relevant to other situational prob-lems. Those who choose this latter "route" will, of course, also face *other* situational problems (they have to eat, for instance); but their behavior shows that great satisfaction may be derived from just partic-ipating in the creation of such a comprehensive, well-structured body of knowledge. Perhaps we should not say that knowledge in this case is treated like an "end in itself": it is sought "for the sake of" the rapture, the feeling of triumph and liberation, which one may derive from having pierced the riddle of the universe. But, after all, this *is* what we mean by something being an "end in itself."

Thus, we say that "knowing" both is and is not separated from "acting." *The more knowledge is immediately applicable, the more clearly we can distinguish the role of the "actor" from that of the "knower."* Then, indeed, we may see how knowledge, accumulated before a practical problem has arisen and acquired at leisure, will be exploited to solve the problem. The same separation will be apparent when one sets out to *generate himself* the kind of knowledge he needs to solve his problem. To do this, he must assume a new role. He must, above all, take leisure away from his pressing problem and *forget* his need; otherwise, he would gather wishful knowledge which would not help him. In these cases both the integration and the separation of the two cycles is clear-cut. It is only when we deal with *pure* theorists that we are at a loss; in so far as they are concerned, their "knowing" is also their "acting," both pointing to some mysterious source of satisfaction to which no "body of facts" but only the mastery of facts—whatever they be—is relevant. The reason why the theorist investigates into facts is not that it matters to him one way or the other what the facts are; the realm of facts is fascinating to him in itself, although, or rather because, the facts as such do *not* affect him. Of course, theorists may, and most often do, have goals and ideals other than their interest in pure theory. But in so far as they have, they play a dual role. In their role as theorists, they seek the "value" of illusionless clarity about the organization and structure of events surrounding man. This *is*, of course, a spiritual value to them: this is what Kant had in mind when he spoke about the absolute value of the contemplation of the starry heavens above us. In the spiritual joy of this contemplation, the content of what is found to be the truth counts for little; if there were other stars and their motions were different, the spiritual joy would be the same, provided only that everything could still be explained by a well-structured theory, reducing seeming disorder to clarity and uniformity. The achievement of this alone is significant.

But whether we seek "pure" or "applied" knowledge, we are interested in describing, explaining, and predicting "events" and "objects." The scientist moves within the categories of "fact" rather than "meaning," and this limitation to the categories of "fact" *is* the "meaning" of his situation. This makes it understandable that the scientist, studying behavior, seeks to articulate it in terms of "events," that is, observable "stimuli" and observable "responses." There is no doubt that each sequence within behavior can be *described* in such terms. In a sequence of "interpretation-in-behavior," for instance, we may isolate the "events" associated with the sign correlate, the so-called "stimuli," and the "events" making up the actual response. This is no problem; the problem is how we can "explain" the latter in terms of the former. To do this, we need a theory that would correlate together index values of "stimuli" and index values of response-events. I believe that this objective is unattainable. A theory of this kind cannot be constructed, no matter how many observations about stimulus-response sequences we may accumulate.

First of all, observation so far has revealed only that the observational indices of "stimuli" are utterly irrelevant to the nature and the observational indices of the "responses." In order to have the faintest guess about what the response will be, we have to know something, not about the stimuli as such, but about the previous history of the organism and the role which the *type* of stimulus in question has played in it. In other words, the theory we want to develop cannot contain indices of stimuli as independent variables. The theory must begin with structured situations into which the stimuli enter not as events of a certain descriptive character but as concomitants of the tense and satisfied phases of the life-history of an organism. We may then forget (within rather wide limits) the physical characteristics of the stimuli and focus on their role in the need-reduction process. Apart from tropisms and other unconditioned reflexes, the events we deal with and their "explanations" will be found to be organized in terms of tension-frustration-satisfaction sequences or anxiety-scanning-familiarity sequences. Of course, it is possible to associate descriptive indices with any of these phases: for instance, we may well ascertain measurable shifts in the exchange of energy between an organism and its environment which are characteristic of "hunger." We know that states of prolonged net loss of energy to the environment will result in a need for food and in food-seeking behavior. But we do not know *why* this should be so. We do not have a theory that would explain why an organism has the "demands" it has—why, for instance, it seeks to restore its energy balance. In other words, we do not have a theoretical schema of the organism from which we could deduce the fact that its behavior will be governed by such a principle. What this means from a methodological point of view is that in biology our questioning of "why's" must stop rather early, before the stage of fundamental schemata has been reached; in physics, we are more fortunate, although, of course, there, too, questioning must stop *somewhere*. Until we discover a fundamental schema of the organism, biological theory must be a low-level theory, that is, it must take much for granted before it can start explaining things.

This does not prove, however, that on this level of abstraction a purely descriptive theory of behavior cannot be developed. Learning theory, for instance, is aware of the fact that it is impossible simply to correlate descriptive indices of "stimuli" and descriptive indices of "responses." It is generally admitted that, if we want to explain the "events" that occur in animal behavior, we must study sequences of adaptive responses. This is done by controlled experiment: the organisms studied are placed in various situations of tension, need, frustration, etc.; then various stimuli are administered; and the sequence of responses is recorded in terms of various descriptive indices. These studies enable us to find index correlations characterizing the process of adaptation to what we called "typical" signs. A "learning curve" is such a function, correlating indices of events in the sequence of adaptive behavior. The correlations, however, are specific to one given kind of organism and even to individual organisms, and they vary according to the type of experiment performed. Types of correlation valid for *all* animal behavior are extremely general and poor in content. We know that adaptive responses to a type of stimulus will be "reinforced" if satisfaction reliably follows the presentation of the stimulus and that they will be "extinguished" if it does not; and we know that, if the observational indices of stimuli vary but a little, their reinforcing function will be unimpaired but that it will vanish if the variation exceeds some critical value. We may learn things of this general nature from controlled experiments on animals in various states of need and gratification or withdrawal of gratification.[2]

But does all this amount to a "theory" of animal behavior? A purely factual theory consists of a body of equations which take observational indices of events as the values of their variables, equations so comprehensive and powerful that a limited number of index data, gathered in *any* situation, will be sufficient to deduce unobserved index data characterizing any number of events preceding or following those observed. Ideally, then, a theory of behavior would enable us to describe unobserved responses in terms of "indices" with nothing to go on but a few crucial observational tests, a few "indices" of stimuli and responses. If we have to perform a large number of tests to make just a few vague predictions, indicating the general nature of the unobserved response rather than deducing its "indices" from functional relationships among the observed indices, we have no "theory."

This, however, is the state of our ability to predict behavior, in spite of our diligence in specifying all "indices" of the events we observe in the laboratory. Let us try to predict how an animal will respond to some novel stimulus in its natural habitat. We have nothing to go on, unless we gather a large number of observations on the habits

2. A rigorously quantitative, systematic treatment of this problem is found in Clark L. Hull, *Principles of Behavior* (New York: D. Appleton–Century Co., 1943).

and preferences of the animal in question; then, after many such observations, we may try to guess what its response *might* be, depending on its state of saturation, on the relatively frightening or innocuous nature of the new stimulus, and on the way in which it can be fitted into the already established behavioral "map" of the animal. Our guessing will not be helped by functions correlating index values of observed events; it will be helped by familiarity with the animal's map of "meanings." That is, careful and long observation of the animal's habitual goal behavior will help us somewhat in anticipating the kind of behavior it will show in choosing some *new* goal. An enormous amount of observation will yield just a little prediction, and the only way to cut down the amount of observation needed and increase the amount of prediction attainable is to forget about measurable indices and focus upon bundles of "meaning." We can approximate the laboratory situation and come up with "quantitative" predictions if, for instance, we have the good fortune so to contrive things that the new and unfamiliar stimulus will conceal the *only* piece of food the hungry animal can hope to find. Then, at last, we can consult our "learning curves" and predict—provided that we also know *how* hungry the animal is—how long it will take for the animal to get at the concealed food. In other words, we can extrapolate knowledge gathered in the laboratory situation to other situations duplicating the laboratory situation in every relevant respect. Otherwise, our index correlations will not be transferable to new situations—and yet such transferability is the goal for the sake of which the building of theories is undertaken.

The plain fact is that we can get behavior patterns which depend on "events" and on their indices only if we artificially restrict the situation to alternatives between "events." In the laboratory environment, indices of events make all the difference; in the natural environment of animals, situations are not structured by index differences. All significant behavior elements come in "bundles" and configurations, setting them off against everything else. Such recognizable bundles—Gestalts, configurations—are what the animal is looking for; if no recognizable bundle is present, something else that might, by its appearance, play the same role may be tested. In "scanning" the environment, movements will be random (so that the whole territory may be covered), but "trials" will be instituted on the basis of tentatively assumed sign meanings rather than in completely random fashion. There is very little opportunity in nature to institute a trial on encountering some pure, simple, "atomic" stimulus associated in the past with a series of satisfactory responses, for such combinations, commonplace in the laboratory, hardly occur in nature.

In the natural process of learning sign meanings, an initial series of reliable need-satisfactions is crucial; but this series does not consist in the administration of a single stimulus, characterized by an "index," together with the satisfaction. The series is that of sheltered childhood, in which a familiar individual organism or group of organisms, the "parents," play the central role as sources of satisfaction (and frustration). The parent-organism is not a stimulus event characterized by observational indices but a unique Gestalt; the point of the distinction is that an "index" is part of a continuum of indices functionally connected with others, whereas a unique, familiar Gestalt is set off against all other Gestalts, none of which can substitute for it. In the first series of satisfactions and frustrations which is the basis of all later adaptive processes, the central source is nothing "fungible," like a stimulus. We cannot even begin to probe into adaptive behavior without understanding the role of the unique, nonfungible, nongeneralizable biographic phase from which it starts.

Ability to learn and a "sheltered" childhood are intimately linked together. "Plastic" behavior, characterized by a great propensity to act upon learned meanings, is predominantly found in species in which care of the young is present. Where this is not found, the "preferred" routes leading to satisfaction are largely based on an instinctual endowment. (Not that no learning whatsoever occurs in the latter species; nor is instinctual behavior absent in the former. But the ratio of the two types of behavior is vastly different in the two classes of species.) If we study learning behavior in adult specimens, we are dealing with a fragment of behavior that cannot "explain" anything. In order to elucidate behavior, we must see it as a whole; and we must, above all, look at the beginnings, where the original stock of meanings has been set up, including not only the initial sequence of tense and satisfied states but also the basic "background" characters of familiarity and strangeness, security and anxiety.

Nor shall we be able to construct anything like a theory of behavior if we focus merely upon situations in which one acute and tyrannical need, such as hunger, may be assuaged by just one specific response. What about exploration, playing, fighting, "comfortable" resting? There are good reasons why *these* phases of animal behavior have not been explored much by the experimental method: they cannot be controlled by generating "calibrated" states of need imperiously calling for just one response. We can "control" the hunger of animals; we cannot "control" their curiosity and their playfulness. Of course, we can experiment only on what we can control. But what we cannot control exists nevertheless.

There are, of course, some other good reasons why behavior studies have stressed learning in "calibrated" need-situations above everything else. It is not only that behavior can be "controlled" by frustrating and satisfying needs; another reason for taking this approach is that animal behavior is not being studied for its own sake. What researchers really "mean" to study when they observe rats in mazes is man; the rats are merely substituted for man, because human solidarity forbids the "controlling" of human behavior by inflicting crucial deprivations. It is hoped that, once we develop a "theory" of how learning takes place in animals, we shall also know something about the "choice" cycle, the "need-reduction" cycle of human behavior. This knowledge may then be used to eliminate the ugly and undesirable features of the cycle.

Is this hope well founded? To my mind, this would not be the case even if the study of animal behavior in terms of observational indices could really tell us something about adaptive *animal* behavior; for, as we mentioned above, adaptation to "typical" sign events is not what is most characteristic of human behavior. Human meanings are, on the whole, "contextual" rather than "typical." Hence what we have to explain is something not found in rats. We cannot make a single step toward elucidation of human choice behavior without looking at "contextual" situations.

The students of behavior know, of course, that white mice are not humans and that the latter have "higher" and more abstractly organized cycles of behavior. Here, however, behavior research has met with what seems to be an incredible stroke of luck: "higher" behavior and verbal intelligence, it appears, can be "controlled" as much as we please and can be studied experimentally without mobilizing needs and inflicting pangs of frustration. Thus the "earthly" part of human behavior, the one concerned with satisfaction of animal urges, can be studied in rats and dogs, while the "nobler" part of man's endowment will be elucidated by making him learn nonsense syllables at a minimal cost in suffering. It sounds almost too good to be true.

But, unfortunately, it is still not good enough; for the essential point in "contextual" behavior is the integration of the "higher," communicative, and information cycle with the "baser," need-reduction cycle.

We cannot neatly carve up human behavior into a rats-in-mazes part and a students-at-desks part. Unfortunately, both rats and human beings carry their whole biography with them, and their world is a whole, "one world." For all, it all began at the beginning, when they were born of a mother; and, for man, in the beginning was the Word —not that symbol behavior originates immediately after birth, but in the sense that the symbol cycle is not superadded to a closed and finished behavior cycle. Symbol behavior arises in connection with the first real exploration of the environment; it is one of the original modes of enriching familiarity with the surrounding world. For man there is no familiar environment without word meanings; it is the name of things that first makes them really familiar. The human world is a symbol world, a contextual world, and not a need-reduction world to which word tags are attached externally. Hence it seems that a behavior system lacking symbols and contextuality cannot portray or duplicate a part of human behavior. It is a complete whole in itself: rats are not fragmentary men. Nor is symbol behavior in man ever supererogatory.

Does all this mean that there can be no "theory" of behavior? By no means. It means only that, at least for the time being, we cannot account for behavior in terms of a theory involving only event-indices as values of its functions. Even for a theory of noncontextual, animal behavior we need "Gestalt" functions rather than functions with arguments representing single observational data that can be varied in some purely quantitative sense. And, in addition to such Gestalt functions, we also need concepts like "need," "demand," and "familiarity," which seem to presuppose some implicit "interpretation." To say that the interpretation is only "implicit" means that we need no "meaning" relationships as variables in our theory: we simply take those relationships for granted as constants or boundary conditions. Nevertheless, a methodological analysis of the theory cannot neglect them.

When it comes to analyzing human contextual behavior, purely "factual" or "event"-like variables are still less adequate for explanation and theoretical analysis. This is the more startling, because symbols, in fact, serve to a great extent to designate and describe events. Could we not say, then, that the choice of symbols for the purpose of a given communication could itself be derived, "explained," and "predicted" from purely factual and descriptive variables, along the lines of Carnap's *Der logische Aufbau der Welt?*

The hypothesis that all symbol behavior can be "explained" and "predicted" by means of a theory using only "descriptive" variables means the following: In explaining and predicting "speech events," that is, actual instances of communications by symbol, we can do so entirely without using interpretive concepts—concepts specifying the "meaning" of the symbols used. Is this hypothesis valid?

Let us consider an explanation which *does* make use of interpretive concepts. The "speech event" we want to explain consists in someone speaking the words: "This curtain is red." Explanation in terms of interpretive concepts requires that we look at the same object and describe it in our own language. We then explain the speech event as follows: "X said 'this curtain is red' because he observed the color of this object and wanted to make a report on his observation." Similarly, prediction in terms of interpretive concepts requires that we produce a speech event that would fit the situation. We then predict that the sentence we are about to hear will be, if not exactly similar to the one we formulated, at least similar to it in "meaning." ("Meaning" can be defined in this context as that which remains constant when a communication is translated from one language into another or if individual terms contained in it are replaced by their synonyms in the same language.)

On the other hand, explanations and predictions which make no use of interpretive concepts consist in the deduction of the physical characteristics ("indices") of a speech event from other indices, without referring to "similarity of meaning" or "synonymy."

Now my feeling is that, for the time being at least, interpretive explanations and predictions, though by no means sufficient or complete in any instance, are indispensable. Many speech events are such that we could not explain or predict them at all without using interpretive concepts.

To summarize:

a) Facts are classes of signs.

b) They enter into the contextual interpretation of situations in which meaning is determined on the basis of situation-class relationships.

c) On the animal or adaptive level a purely "factual" theory of behavior is possible, in the sense that no explicit interpretation or judgment is needed for making explanations or predictions. But interpretation of meaning will be concealed in the presuppositions (boundary conditions) of the theory; and the "facts" serving as variables in the theory cannot be analyzed down to homogeneous indices related to one another in quantitative fashion.

d) Specifically human, that is, contextual, behavior cannot be explained in purely factual, descriptive terms. Its theory must involve explicit "interpretation." The difference may be briefly characterized as follows: When we say that an animal "eats" or that it is "hungry" or that it "eats because it is hungry," we state *facts*. There are "meanings" involved in the animal's behavior, but the theorist may take them for granted as boundary conditions. However, when we say that "*A* utters a sentence in French," this is no mere fact statement, for it involves a judgment to the effect that *A*'s speech behavior conforms to *our* understanding of a set of rules of language.

e) That certain subjects entertain certain demands may be treated as a "mere" *fact*, if we choose to consider those demands as boundary conditions within our theory of the subject's behavior. But when the demands themselves are to be treated as variables in our theory, the theory itself must be an "interpretive" one.

3. PERSPECTIVES OF SITUATIONAL MEANING

We can deal far more briefly with another dimension in the analysis of situational meaning: that of the *point of view* from which meaning is being considered. We have seen that it is not only the organism itself that can interpret its own situation; an outside observer familiar with the organism's needs and capabilities can also make judgments about the "meaning" of the situation for the organism. Interpretation of the situation of organism *O* by observer *T* may serve different purposes and assume different forms. One difference hinges on the question of whether *T* is a *mere* observer of *O* and its situation or a partner involved in some way in a common situation with *O*.

Let us take pure observation first. In this role, *T* will simply look at the environment, as it were, with *O*'s eyes; he will, for instance, consider "events" as "sign correlates" for *O*. Given enough data about *O*'s needs and previous adaptive experiences, *T* may make *judgments* about the "meaning" of the signs for *O* and *forecasts* about *O*'s adaptive, scanning, or maladaptive behavior. If the situation is highly standardized and calibrated, *T* may break it down into "stimuli" and response-events; in this case, both *O*'s needs and his previous adaptive processes will be treated as "boundary conditions," the stimuli and response-events being the variables expressly considered. Otherwise, *T*

will have to exercise a certain empathy with O: he will have to cultivate his ability to recognize the sign Gestalts that are significant for O,
for otherwise no good anticipation will be possible.

It is also possible that T observes some act performed by O but does
not see any sign correlate to which it may be related. He may then
set out to solve this riddle; this problem may be designated as the problem of determining an "intent" behind an act. Therefore, T must form
certain hypotheses about the meaning of the act. If he knows enough
about O's habits and other behavior patterns, he may surmise the kind
of sign that may have prompted the act; in the end, he may discover
a relevant sign constellation or give up his attempt at explanation in
terms of intent: the act may have been a purely instinctual one or
simply a random response.

Now let us turn to the other kind of roles which T may play. He
now is a "partner" of O, that is, O's behavior and action have direct
significance for him. In such a situation questions about "intent" will
be paramount. O's intent will have to be determined, not only for
reasons of curiosity but as a matter of finding the correct response to
O's behavior. The neutral observer will study his object in terms of
intent (that is, start from the response and look for a sign accounting
for it) only if he sees O behave oddly or unexpectedly. But in the nonneutral situation the question of intent will come up, even if O's behavior is seemingly fully accounted for by the available sign events.
This is the most characteristic form of intent analysis, rather than the
neutral one: in addition to the *ostensible* meaning of O's situation,
find an occult (and more "real") meaning to it. Such problems will
arise, of course, in general only with highly "intelligent" partners
(higher animals or men) who are capable of insightful and deceptive
behavior. Symbol behavior, which is exclusively human, lends itself
particularly well to deception and therefore to analysis in terms of
"intent."

Finally, I may interpret O's behavior (O being a "partner" in the
situation) in terms of the latter's behavioral *symptoms*. A "symptom"
may also be described as a response with a double-meaning reference,
but not in the sense of a hidden (particularly deceptive) *intent*. In the
case of a behavioral symptom, O is aware of one sign constellation
which accounts for the response but may feel that the response is
somehow incongruous and fails to bring real satisfaction. Then O may
turn to T to "explain" the symptom and help in overcoming it. T's

problem, then, goes beyond empathy; the entire evolutionary process leading to the symptom must be laid bare, and the hidden meaning which accounts for it must be uncovered.

Behavioral symptoms present an interesting methodological problem, for they exhibit a degenerate form of "meaning." They are not characterized by the plasticity and flexibility of normal adaptation; they are comparatively rigid and stereotyped. The hidden "second" or "real" meaning accounting for the symptom is considered by psychoanalysis to be particularly rigidly "dynamic," the manifestation of a force rather than the solicitation of a sign. Yet it has enough characteristics of the meaning relationship to be included among the categories of meaning. It certainly has a "demand" structure: a response is good if . . . ; it certainly calls for interpretation.

The interpretation and analysis of symptoms involves observation by T of O's situation in terms of meanings that are in no way entertained by O or interpretable by him. This is the difference between interpretation of "intent" and interpretation of "symptom." (In the general or medical sense, too, a "symptom" is a sign the meaning of which is, in general, not clear to the patient. The perceived meaning is only that the patient suffers and has to seek medical advice; a more useful and explicit interpretation can be supplied only by the physician.)

CHAPTER II

STANDARDS OF MEANING

1. RELEVANCE AND ORDER

WE SAID that every meaning determines a "good" response —"good" in terms of satisfaction according to some standard. We also indicated that there are various kinds of standards by which meanings are determined. Now we shall try to make a preliminary survey of some of the most important "working" standards, that is to say, standards toward which actual behavior is found to be oriented. Certain standards, as we shall see, are found on the human level only; others on the animal level as well.

We shall begin with standards underlying *situational* meaning.

The most fundamental of these standards are given by nature. They are needs and urges of the organism, directed toward its well-being. For this group of standards of meaning, we shall use the general name "relevance." Anything that satisfies an urge or need of an organism, or frustrates such an urge or need, is to that extent "relevant" to the organism; this "relevance" determines whether the response to a sign constellation is "good" or "bad."

Although the well-being of the individual organism is the core of relevance, it should not be assumed that relevance is always rigorously self-centered and that each organism has its own set of relevant meanings, sharply set off against those of every other one. On the contrary, as we shall see later, organisms may share in one another's relevances; their behavior may be oriented toward a relevance which, in fact, embodies the well-being of the group or species rather than merely their individual well-being. On the other hand, one organism's relevance may conflict with that of another. Such combinations of relevance may give rise to various relationships.

Relevance, the most primitive standard of meaning, is found on the level of meaning-in-behavior, without reflective consciousness. Certain other standards, on the other hand, may require conscious manipulation.

In contrast to relevance which is given by nature, we may distinguish purely "artificial" standards, such as *conventions* and *rules of games*. There are also standards of *cultural* origin: rules and patterns of behavior enforced by the group. Such standards usually have a bearing on the "relevance" of the group and its members; in that sense, they are not wholly artificial. Whether artificial or not, however, every standard somehow is connected with the basic stratum, that of relevance, even without being completely reducible to it. One of the objectives of our inquiry is to find out how artificial or social standards are related to the fundamental stratum of relevance.

But let us first consider relevance itself.

"From within," that is to say, from the perspective of the organism whose well-being is at stake, relevance is experienced as a tension which is reduced as the meaning of the situation consummates and thereby transcends itself. In the tense, relevant situation the life of the organism is like a stream which flows in one direction, away from fear, need, and pain and toward safety, satisfaction, and enjoyment. Relevant meaning is a vector in a field of behavior. The field has a negative and a positive pole; the "good" response is one by which the organism gets nearer to the positive pole.

The relevant standards of meaning, as manipulated by the organism itself, are frankly hedonistic. The organism primarily interprets its own situation in terms of gain of pleasure and enjoyment and release from pain and suffering. Phenomenally, relevant meanings always present themselves under the color of pleasure or pain (tension or relief, fear or safety, etc.). But in itself relevance reaches beyond the phenomenal, hedonistic perspective. Pleasure and pain, for instance, are not ends in themselves; they are subservient to something that does not reveal itself in phenomenal experience, namely, life itself: the life of the individual or that of the group or species.

Looking at the situation of the organism from the perspective of the outside observer, we may ask what promotes and protects life, regardless of whether it is pleasurable or painful. Doing this, we apply a new relevant standard: that of biological, vital advantage. This standard somehow expresses the essence of relevance more "objectively" than the phenomenal, hedonistic standards, but it cannot be applied naïvely; it presupposes reflection, looking at the situation from the outside.

The biological standard is that of health: the harmonious, undisturbed flow of the life-process. In normal cases behavior naïvely controlled by hedonistic standards of relevance will also be appropriate from the viewpoint of health; in exceptional and critical cases, however, the two standards may conflict—e.g., painful processes will be necessary to restore health, etc.

There is one striking difference between the hedonistic and the biological standard. The sole judge of hedonistic appropriateness is the organism itself. It is the subject that speaks the last word; its decision admits of no critique; pain, pleasure, and the other hedonistic features of the situation are present to the subject (and directly to it alone) in its actual experience. Meanings related to the "biological" standard, on the other hand, are not experienced with such immediacy. They are not given in a single throb of experience but embrace long sequences of situations. This is why the individual organism cannot apply the biological standard, as it can the hedonistic one, naïvely and without reflection. While the hedonistic standard is part and parcel of the organism's private world, the biological standard belongs to the public world which the subject shares with outside observers.

The separation of the two worlds is not an absolute one, of course. The public and private worlds are interconnected. It is true that A alone can experience his own pleasure or pain or fear or relief directly. But his experience will also somehow belong to the public world, since it will manifest itself by a kind of typical behavior. These symptoms of relevant experience will enable the outside observer to recognize its character; they will also generate currents of sympathy in others.

On the other hand, there may be a certain discrepancy between meanings in the public and private worlds. Symptoms of hedonistically relevant experience may be simulated; hence they cannot always be taken at face vaule but must be critically evaluated. Or the hedonistic "meaning" of a response may differ from its "true" meaning, as interpreted by the outside observer. The insects which lay their eggs in substances on which the larvae will feed are not aware of this "objective" purpose or meaning of their behavior; we may assume that this response has a phenomenal, subjective meaning to the insect itself, but one different from the "objective" biological meaning.

The urges and needs which underlie relevance are manifold. Some exhibit a periodic rhythm, such as hunger; others, such as flight impulses, display no such rhythmical pattern but assert themselves in accordance with the hazards of the outside situation. But in any case the same object may or may not carry relevant meaning, depending on the context. For the hungry animal the sight of food is pregnant with relevant meaning and hence colors the situation accordingly; to the satisfied animal the same spectacle will be a matter of indifference. If the chick is far from its mother, the presence of an enemy will spell the relevant meaning of danger; to the chick under the hen's wing the same object will be harmless.

But the distribution of relevance among the objects of the environment is in no way rigid. Relevance has what we may call "inductiveness": anything not relevant in itself may become relevant if it is somehow integrated into a relevant context. Instruments, tools, and safeguarding and protecting devices are cases in point. An animal which is not hungry may hoard food as a precaution for periods of scarcity; defense mechanisms may be developed and maintained, even though no actual menace prevails.

This inductiveness of relevance is a "dialectical" feature, since it implies transition from nonrelevance to relevance. The realm of relevance as a whole displays dialectical character; this is shown by the possible conflict between different standards, such as the hedonistic and the biological. Immediate hedonistic relevance may also conflict with future hedonistic relevance. Where standards conflict with one another, the decision requires conscious manipulation of standards.

It seems to me, in fact, that reflective consciousness is a product of the "dialectical" conflicts of relevance; these are the primary field of activity to which consciousness addresses itself. Reflective consciousness presupposes a separation of an "outside" and an "inner" world. This separation emerges, I suggest, as a result of conflicts and contradictions in the handling of relevant meanings. These contradictions cannot be resolved without a disruption of the harmonious flow, of the continuity of meaning-in-behavior. They necessitate an interruption of the "rapport" between the subject and the world; this leads to the adoption of the outside observer's attitude toward one's own situation.

We shall now turn to the examination of another group of standards of meaning: those of "order."

Standards of meaning other than relevance may inform the situation of an organism when vital tension is quiescent. All urgent needs are satisfied, all imminent threats are met. Such saturation and quiescence, of course, has its own relevance; it also opens a perspective upon other meanings.

In a quiescent situation, organisms may play; human beings also may use the lull to take stock of their situation and resort to tasks of classification. Accordingly, we have two types of meaning corresponding to these types of situation: rules of games, on the one hand; rules of classification, on the other. Both together make up the field of "order."

Standards of order determine definite tasks, just as standards of relevance do; in other words, an "order" meaning also defines sets of "good" and "bad" responses. But in their case the "good" response is not the one in terms of some enjoyment or gain of well-being. The rules of games usually define a winner and a loser, but the satisfaction of winning and the annoyance of losing are encompassed within the universe of meaning of the game. More tangible, relevant rewards may also be added later on; they may add to the attraction of the game (although it is the importance of playing and winning the game that motivates the offer of a reward, and not the attractiveness of the reward which motivates the playing of the game). The rules of classification also are self-centered: the solving of a problem of this kind does not in itself result in a gain of vital satisfaction. Indirectly, however, classificatory tasks do serve "useful" purposes; they contribute to man's mastery over his world.

All standards of order—rules of games and rules of classification—have this in common, that they are not wholly given by nature but presuppose an artificially ordered universe. This artificial order itself is nondialectical: rules of "order" must be free from contradiction. No game can be played if its rules are self-contradictory; no task of classification can be carried out if its rules are marred by ambiguity or contradiction. The artificially ordered universe of the game or of the classificatory pattern has, moreover, a hierarchical structure: there are basic alternatives underlying the order pattern and subordinate differences which follow from them under the rules. On the other hand, differences which have no bearing on the rules of the game must be neglected.

Each order pattern, then, involves a hierarchical system of responses. We may distinguish two types of such hierarchical systems, differing in complexity. The first type of order pattern presupposes only a few elementary operations; all the configurations possible within the pattern can be brought about and identified by repeating and combining a small number of primitive operations. Order of this type will be called "formal." Examples of formal order are: "number" as underlying the "game" of arithmetic; geometrical configuration; musical pitch. The other type of order requires many independent basic operations for producing and identifying its possible cases; this type of order will be called "intuitive." Examples of intuitive order are: color; natural species; nomenclature; classification of instruments; classification of relevant situations and responses; group games.

Formal order proceeds from initial configurations of great simplicity to configurations of increasing complexity, which can be obtained by the repetition and combination of the elementary operations. The initial application of intuitive-order standards is far more complex, but this level of complexity is not surpassed, since no new configurations can be created by merely repeating and combining elementary operations.

Sometimes the same objects may be approached from a formal as well as from an intuitive viewpoint. Thus each musical interval may be conceived as the result of the repeated execution of the same elementary step; but intervals also have their intuitive, unique "Gestalts." Conversely, we usually identify colors by intuitive operations: there is no such thing as the generation of "green" by proceeding from "red" to "orange" and then repeating the same operation. The physicist, however, can represent colors by means of a purely formal, metrical scale, by ordering them according to their wave lengths.

It is characteristic of *formal* order that it can be represented by symbols alone. The basic operations of each formal-order pattern can be performed on symbols as well as on things (thus we may count things as well as symbols). The symbolic representation of any formal-order configuration will exhibit the same order; it will not only "represent" but "be" the same order configuration. A symbolic representation of *intuitive* order, on the other hand, will not "be" the same configuration.

Formal order may be grasped by every individual who is capable of distinguishing symbols and performing operations on them. In principle, every normal human individual has this capacity, but only in so far as the elementary operations are concerned. After a certain number of repetitions and combinations of original steps, configurations may reach a baffling degree of complexity which only a special kind of intuition or insight can unravel.

Order as such is, as we said, "nondialectical"; in principle, it should permit a clear-cut decision in any case. In actual fact, however, order patterns, as applied to things of the world, often fall short of this requirement. The patterns have "vague" regions of transition between clearly defined loci—the vague region between blue and green, for example. Intuitive order, which can never be completely represented by symbols, is seldom clear-cut enough to avoid such vagueness. But formal order, if applied to things rather than to symbols, also has areas of vagueness. Measurement, for instance, is a formal operation performed upon things in the world: and measurement is necessarily vague, since there is no one-to-one correspondence between real numbers and the positions of a pointer on a dial, so that the same datum can be expressed by several different and mutually incompatible numerical expressions. The counting of objects, another formal operation, yields precise results only if the objects have clear-cut individual limits; but we need intuitive operations to distinguish individuals as such.

It is therefore wholly unjustified to extol formal order as essentially precise and deprecate intuitive order as essentially vague. No intuitive order can reach the degree of precision attainable in formal operations performed upon symbols, but it is an illusion to believe that formal operations still retain the same precision when performed upon things in the world. When it comes to such application, each order pattern will suffer from a certain vagueness. In individual cases precision can be increased by substituting formal for intuitive order, but vagueness cannot be wholly eliminated so long as we are dealing with things in the world. We can attain complete precision only in "analytic" discourse.

All standards, in fact, have an "analytic" structure; from a logical point of view, they can be considered as "definitions." A standard of relevance *defines* a kind of situational satisfaction; a standard of order defines winning or losing in a game or the correct or incorrect way of performing some kind of ordering operation. We can apply these standards to judge actual situations or operations; but we can also talk about what is implied in the standards themselves, regardless of how any actual piece of reality looks in the light of some standard. We can disinguish these two types of discourse as "analytic," and "nonanalytic," or "a priori" and "a posteriori." When we discourse in an "analytic" or "a priori" vein, we say things which apply to any actual state of the world and, hence, need not be confirmed by any actual experience.[1]

Such analyticity is not confined to "formal" order, although it is true that rich analytic structures (such as those of logic an mathematics) are found only in this realm. To say that food is desirable to the hungry man is just as "analytically" true as to say that two and

---

1. Cf. Rudolf Carnap, *Meaning and Necessity* (Chicago: University of Chicago Press, 1947), pp. 9 ff.

two are four; and intuitive order also gives rise to analytically true statements. This is the kind of analyticity studied by "phenomenology."[2] An example of "intuitive" analyticity is Russell's statement: "Blue and green are more similar than blue and yellow."[3] To say that such statements are "analytic" means that they can be understood to be true without any "knowledge of the world," that is, without knowing which particular objects are blue, green, and yellow. To say that "two and two are four" is analytic means to say that, without knowing about any collection of objects actually having two or four members, we know that a collection of four members contains exactly as many individual members as a collection consisting of two pairs of individuals. In this sense, all analytic statements are "a priori," that is, their truth or falsehood can be determined without ascertaining anything about actual objects to which the terms we use might be descriptively applicable.

But "a priori"-ness in this sense should not be taken literally; the distinction between "analytic" and "nonanalytic" is not an absolute one. It is not the case, even ideally, that we need no knowledge of the world whatsoever to generate all the analytic knowledge of mankind, as it were, within ourselves. We have to have a minimum stock of experience in order to "define" anything, and there can be no definition without some actual experience of the "possible" cases we define. The statement we made about a hungry man is "analytical," that is, no experience is needed to prove its truth and no experience can disprove it; but this means only that, when we know what hunger is, we can characterize it in terms of "desirability of food" without knowing who in the world is hungry or even whether at a given moment there is any hungry individual at all. We obviously could not make such an analytic statement about hunger without having experienced hunger or without having isolated a complex that is characteristic of "hungry" behavior. This is obvious with reference to all "definitions" (e.g., classificatory definitions) of actual things, such as types of experience or types (species) of organisms. We can make the statement "All crows are black" analytical[4] by deciding not to apply the term "crow" to any bird that is not black (even if it is hatched from crow

2. Cf. Edmund Husserl, *Ideen zu einer reinen Phänomenologie,* I (3d ed.; Halle, 1928), 95 ff.

3. In *Proceedings of the Aristotelian Society* (1936), p. 40.

4. On this type of analyticity cf. C. I. Lewis, *An Analysis of Knowledge and Valuation* (La Salle, Ill.: Open Court Publishing Co., 1946), p. 125.

eggs); but, obviously, we could not have adopted such a definition without having become acquainted with crows. Similarly, we must have become confronted with *some* blue, green, and yellow objects before we could make an analytic statement about the relationship between the colors as such.

But it is not only "intuitive order" and "relevance" which depend on experience for objects that exemplify the analytic relationship involved in them. Formal order, too, needs such "paradigmatic" objects and experiences. Someone who had never actually manipulated countable objects and never experienced "yes-no" situations could not understand arithmetic and logic. The distinction between analytic and nonanalytic statements means merely that there is a difference between specifying what we "commit ourselves to" when we decide to make judgments in terms of some standard and making the judgments themselves. No actual judgments are needed or helpful in any way when we merely spell out our commitments, for obviously the commitments must be clear if any judgment based on them is to be valid. But actual judgments are both needed and helpful when we deal with a different type of question, namely, whether it makes sense to act on a certain commitment in a certain type of situation. Euclidean geometry, for instance, commits us to recognizing as plain triangles only figures with three sides whose angles add up to 180°. When this commitment is accepted, it is still questionable whether any figure observed in nature—such as a triangle formed by three stars we observe—falls under this definition. We may find that the commitments implied in Euclidean geometry embroil us in difficulties when we try to judge such observed triangles; thus we may be led to develop a different set of commitments.

Our commitments are "a priori" in relation to the judgments we make on their basis. Definitions and rules of games are "a priori" in this sense. But they are not a priori in an absolute sense, as things actually created in complete ignorance of any state of things in the world.[5] When someone invents rules for a ball game, he is certainly ignorant of any actual instance of the game; he cannot even know whether the game will ever be played. But he cannot be ignorant of certain facts involving the existence of balls and boys. What distinguishes the inventor of the game from the empirical fact-finder

5. Cf. W. V. Quine's critique of the "absolute" distinction made between the analytic and the nonanalytic in "Two Dogmas of Empiricism," *Philosophical Review*, Vol. LX, No. 1 (January, 1951).

about balls and boys is that, for the former, the things he knows merely serve for mapping possibilities for the future; and he must be particularly careful to avoid contradictions, that is, commitments that cannot be lived up to in *any* state of the world.

A meaning predicated upon mere "order" can be interpreted and acted upon without urgent, vital organismic needs being affected. This, of course, is not possible with meanings based on relevance. Order may be generated and observed in a purely "contemplative" way, in a kind of neutral universe.

We now turn to "communicative" standards. More complicated "situational" standards will be taken up afterward, in Part IV (dealing with values).

2. RULES OF LANGUAGE

The "standards of meaning" in terms of which responses to communicative meaning may be said to be "good" or "bad" are rules of language.[6] "Responses" include those of the author as well as those of the receiver of the communication. The choice of the right expression and the correct understanding of the sense of the message are "good" responses; mistakes in choosing symbols and in interpreting them are "bad" responses. Whether a language response is "good" or "bad" in this sense can be determined only with reference to a linguistic convention; in order to master a linguistic convention, however, one must also be familiar with extra-linguistic, "situational" meanings. After all, one can choose the right expression and interpret it correctly only if one is familiar with the "properties" which those symbols designate. Part of the rules of language, at least, will concern the correspondence between symbols and "situational" meanings.

Not all rules of language are in this class, however. We have to distinguish several sets of language rules, i.e., rules which merely concern mutual relations between the symbols as such and rules which refer to extra-linguistic, situational factors.

This distinction corresponds to a well-known classification of the sciences dealing with meaning and interpretation, proposed by Charles Morris. According to him, the science dealing with interpretation (that is, interpretation of communications by means of a language)—semiotic—has three branches, each dealing with a separate problem of interpretation of meaning. One of these branches—syntax—examines relations between the various expressions of a language, regardless of

6. Cf. K. Ajdukiewicz, "Sprache und Sinn," *Erkenntnis*, IV (1934), 100 ff.

their designata; the second—semantics—discusses expressions and their "designata"; the third—pragmatics—deals with relations between expressions, on the one hand, and the intentions, motives, and other behavioral and mental processes of the users of language, on the other.[7]

Syntax, of course, can be studied without reference to situational meaning or other "extra-linguistic" categories, since it concerns only ways in which symbols of the same language are related to one another, e.g., ways in which "valid" and "countervalid" sentences can be formed in a language, regardless of what the various symbols designate. This is the traditional problem of logic—an analytical problem. But what about semantics and pragmatics?

According to Rudolf Carnap,[8] a semantical rule can be formulated in the following way: First, we have to choose a "metalanguage" in which we want to formulate the semantical rules of the language we study, the "object language." A statement specifying that a term t of the object language L has the same designatum as the term t' of the metalanguage L' will be a semantical rule for L. Proficiency in using the metalanguage (i.e., applying its terms to extra-linguistic objects) is presupposed in this connection; semantics deals only with identity of designation between symbols of different languages and not with the application of symbols to something extra-linguistic. The "designata" of symbols are treated through the medium of a metalanguage. This has prompted a criticism according to which semantics, as conceived by Carnap, is caught in a "linguistic predicament": it can speak only of relations between languages but fails to elucidate the operation of "designation" of extra-linguistic referents.[9] It is quite true that "designation" in this sense it not treated by Carnapian semantics; but then the clearly defined purpose of "semantics" in Carnap's sense is something entirely different. The relation of "designation" primarily serves to permit definition of nonanalytical "truth," as contrasted with purely syntactical "validity."[10]

7. Charles W. Morris, *Foundations of the Theory of Signs* (*International Encyclopedia of Unified Science*, I, No. 2 [2d ed.; Chicago: University of Chicago Press, 1940]), pp. 6 ff.

8. *Introduction to Semantics* (Cambridge: Harvard University Press, 1942), pp. 3 ff.; on the conception of "metalanguage" cf. also Alfred Tarski, "Der Wahrheitsbegriff in den formalisierten Sprachen," in *Studia philosophica* (Lemberg and Lwow, 1935), p. 282.

9. Everett W. Hall, "The Extra-linguistic Reference of Language. II," *Mind*, LIII (1944), 25–47.

10. Cf. Gustav Bergmann, "Pure Semantics, Sentences, and Propositions," *Mind*, LIII (1944), 238–57.

Semantics, then, does not deal with extra-linguistic referents. Should rules which link the use of language symbols to extra-linguistic, situational meanings belong to the field of *pragmatics*? According to Morris' definition, pragmatics studies the *user* of language, his intentions and motives, as well as the effects produced by communications. But we have already seen that a study of *intentions* and *effects* is something different from the study of *meanings*. Pragmatics is not a normative science; it examines actual language behavior rather than the rules underlying it.

Carnap also defines pragmatics as a purely empirical science. Not that it has nothing to do with the rules of language; rather, "pragmatics is the basis for all linguistics,"[11] meaning that the study of actual language behavior alone enables the student to ascertain the rules governing language behavior. But the rules themselves—and this is the main point—are either syntactical or semantical ones and hence can be formulated with reference to symbols alone, without taking extra-linguistic referents into account.

Incidentally, it seems to me that the pure description of behavior as such never warrants conclusions concerning linguistic rules. For instance, from findings of the type, "The inhabitants of S form the sound 'chaise' in the presence of chairs," we cannot conclude that, "in the language of the inhabitants of S, 'chaise' *means* chair." Such a conclusion is justified only if we can be sure that the categoreal system of the inhabitants of S corresponds to ours, in that it is based on the same basic classificatory and other responses and that a given sound-pattern fulfils just this categoreal function. What the basic categoreal system of a linguistic group is, however, cannot be derived from purely descriptive, physical findings; on the contrary, these findings are themselves based upon a categoreal system. Although pragmatics pretends to be a purely empirical science, it seems to me that the pragmatic analysis of language behavior—if it is successful—surreptitiously makes use of the student's *normative* knowledge of rules.

Our problem can be formulated as follows: as long as we retain the Carnapian approach to semantics, we have to use a *metalanguage* if we want to indicate what the designatum of a symbol is. To answer the same question with regard to a metalanguage, we have to adopt a meta-metalanguage, and so on ad infinitum.[12] The ultimate expla-

11. *Introduction to Semantics*, p. 13.
12. On this *regressus ad infinitum*, cf. Bergmann, *op. cit.*, p. 240.

nation of meanings presupposes a language which is already under-stood. What we would like to know, however, is precisely how to make explicit the rules which the users of the *metalanguage* follow in talking about things. What happens when people who *know* a language communicate by means of it? Obviously, they apply rules which fix the use of words in terms of nonlinguistic operations, e.g., classificatory ones. For instance, in order to use color adjectives correctly, one must be able correctly to tag or classify things according to their color. The rule we have in mind, the one determining the correct use of words like 'red' and 'green,' presupposes, and in a way appeals to, this ability. The question is how to formulate such a rule, co-ordinating symbolic with nonsymbolic operations.

Carnap holds that this problem is nonexistent, since, try as we may, we cannot explain the use of a symbol except by using other symbols. "The interpretation of a language can be given in a completely formal manner."[13] That is to say: If a term is definable, its "meaning" can be indicated by a definition; if it is undefinable, its "meaning" cannot be explained in the same language but can be conveyed by giving its translation in a metalanguage which is understood.

Obviously, this metalanguage method does not serve us here. Our problem is, for instance, how the meaning of the word 'red' should be explained to a child who cannot yet use this adjective. We solve this problem by pointing to an instance of red and saying, 'This is red.' But —Carnap would say—this is also a sentence; even the demonstrative gesture which accompanies the sentence can be replaced by words, e.g., by giving time and space co-ordinates. Consequently, "even if we define the meaning of a term by a demonstrative gesture, in reality we define symbols by symbols rather than by extra-linguistical objects."[14] The "definition" by means of a demonstrative gesture has been translated into a purely formal "definition":

$$\text{Red} =_{Df} \text{Col}\,(x,\ y,\ z,\ t)\,.$$

But is this analysis correct? Was the demonstrative gesture a "definition," and was it replaced by a purely formal "definition"? I doubt it. The gesture was, in fact, no definition: it did not state any synonymity, its burden was not that, under the rules of the language, the word 'red' and a certain expression referring to one space-time instant

13. R. Carnap, *Logische Syntax der Sprache* (Vienna, 1934), p. 182.
14. *Ibid.*, p. 71.

can be used interchangeably. And the same is true of the formal expression which replaces the gesture.

What we wanted to do was, after all, not to supply our pupil with an expression synonymous with 'red' but to give him a rule, a direction concerning the use of the word, which he could remember and put to use on future occasions. The all-important thing is that the pupil should grasp the nature of the connection between the word and the patch of color we pointed out to him. He must understand, if the instruction is to succeed, that the red patch is an illustration, valid for an indefinite number of "similar" cases. He must know what kind of "similarity" is meant—that is, not the outline of the patch but its color, and not its exact shade but only its redness. He must know how to attend to this similarity and how to disregard dissimilarities which are "allowed" by the rule. In other words, it is not sufficient for the understanding of the rule that the pupil should know the meaning of the *symbols* used: the demonstrative gesture as such or the co-ordinate expressions. Something more is required: the mastery of an extra-linguistic operation.

There is, it seems, a kind of language rule that cannot be conveyed in a purely formal way. We shall call such rules "deictic" rules, "deictic" being that branch of semiotic which deals with the connection between symbols and extra-linguistic referents. We hold that any language in which fact statements can be made must have deictic rules; only purely fomalized languages can do without them.

There is no possible one-to-one correspondence between signs and situations, on the one hand, and symbols, on the other; this is why we need deictic rules. Such a rule specifies a range of signs and situations to which a symbol corresponds. As we have seen above (chap. i), such a range is a property. A deictic rule is one which correlates a symbol with a property which it designates; the rule has to be conveyed by means of an illustration which can be understood only by those who are capable of carrying out the basic response corresponding to the property.

Proper names are also governed by deictic rules: the basic response involved is the recognition of an individual. This is, in fact, only a special case of the recognition of a property: the "property" is "being the individual *A*."

While properties and individuals can have names, single signs and situations cannot. This has far-reaching consequences in connection with the linguistic expression of facts which involve one definite situation. As we shall see later (chap. vi), such facts cannot be completely represented by linguistic means.

Apart from this restriction, the field of deictic rules is universal: it takes in the whole realm of situational meaning, standards of relevance as well as standards of order. Language is universal in the sense that language symbols can be assigned to any distinguishable kind of meaning.

Operations pertaining to the use of language as such carry a situational meaning which itself is governed by standards of "order": the understanding of a symbol is based primarily on classificatory operations. But the classificatory operations underlying the use and understanding of language include the classification of relevant responses, too: a pattern of order is superimposed upon the realm of relevance. Language has a bearing on relevant meanings in still another sense: communications as such are always parts of a situation and carry a relevant sign meaning. At this point however, we are concerned only with the rules of language as such and not with the possible sign meaning of communications.

We have seen that deictic rules cover all sets of identifiable responses of which the "normal" subject, as user of the language, is capable. Who is, however, a normal subject? When it comes to identifying colors, some subjects are "normal"; others are not, although they can be, of course, perfectly normal with regard to other operations. Symbols designating properties which certain subjects cannot identify cannot, of course, form part of a truly universal language. If we want to construct a really universal language, we must be careful not to include any symbols the understanding of which presupposes some differential ability, one in respect to which not all men are equal. Symbols designating formal-order properties seem to satisfy this requirement; an important group of these symbols is metrical expressions. Hence the proposal that the universal language of science should be more and more limited to metrical predicates; differential sensory abilities will certainly not affect the universal usability of these predicates, since, as Carnap pointed out,[15] the ascertainment of a metrical datum does not presuppose the use of any specific sense organ but may be carried out through the medium of any of the senses.

I doubt, however, that a purely metrical—"physicalistic"—language could suffice, even for the purpose of "exact" scientific discourse.

15. *Erkenntnis*, II, 443 ff.

Even an operation of measurement involves more than a reading of dials. Before we can read the dial, we must, in many cases, isolate the object which is to be measured; this necessitates a nonmetrical, "intuitive" response. The identification of the measuring apparatus also is necessarily an "intuitive" operation.

The deictic rules of proper names also necessarily refer to intuitive operations. Let us try, indeed, to substitute for a proper name a complete description of the individual for which it stands—a description containing only "metrical" terms. Can we consider this description as synonymous with the name? Certainly not, since the name is supposed to remain applicable to the individual even after many of his metrical properties have undergone more or less drastic changes. A description which would really be synonymous with a name would have to allow for all the changes that the description of the individual goes through during his lifetime; but it is entirely impossible to replace a symbol by a comprehensive law of this sort. Communication by symbols would be pointless, as well as impossible, if mastery of the *vocabulary* presupposed the complete knowledge of the *facts of the world* which we want to describe by means of the vocabulary.

There is another consideration which is pertinent to the question of the adoption of a purely metrical language. When we substitute metrical terms for intuitive ones in science, it is in order to insure the universal intelligibility of our language. Obviously, many uncertainties can be eliminated by the adoption of precise, metrical (or statistical) instead of intuitive terms. But if we ruled the latter out altogether, we would sacrifice the universality of our language in another sense; we would render it incapable of expressing the greater part of the things which fill our life and which should not be inaccessible and indifferent to science. We need a precise and universally intelligible language, but our language should also be universal in the sense of being able to express all the moods and states of mind which make a difference to us. Consequently, we cannot do without intuitive terms.

And, as we said, these intuitive terms cannot be beyond the pale of science. The science of human behavior, for instance, must be able to interpret all these terms; their meaning, however, would be hopelessly falsified if they were translated into metrical terms, so as to give them "precision."

Apart from this, we have to consider certain psychological factors affecting the use of scientific language. As is well known, scientific phraseology cannot be handled by every "normal" individual of a language community; as a rule, only specialists are able to communicate by means of it. This is true of analytical as well as of empirical sciences. In the case of the former, the difficulty for the layman is not that he cannot understand the meaning of the basic terms and the way derivative terms are generated; given sufficient time, he could be led to grasp the meaning of every mathematical proposition. The difficulty is that the layman lacks the concentration necessary to grasp the meaning of these propositions quickly enough. As for the empirical sciences, on the other hand, the specialists who familiarize themselves with a field develop sign responses which normal subjects who lack the requisite training cannot perform; the specialized language of the experts is based on these responses. A large part of these specialized responses is "intuitive." With regard to such a language with its specialized deictic rules, only the specially trained subjects are "normal"; the others cannot use the language. At a certain level of the evolution of science, such specialization seems to be inevitable.

The universality of the *results* of scientific investigation is by no means impaired by the fact that the language by which the investigators communicate is a specialized one. The results may be called "universal," first, because the findings can be applied to natural or artificial (laboratory) situations of the average individual and, second, because the specialized groups are not closed; anyone with a normal ability can master the requisite elementary operations upon which the specialized language of the science in question is based.

There is no rigid alternative, such that language either must be universally usable and understandable by every subject or arbitrary and unsuitable for the formulation of decidable sentences. Verifiable truth concerning a great many matters is accessible only to those who have gone through a certain special training. Even such truth, however, is not the exclusive possession of those who, by virtue of their training, are alone able to discover it; the application of scientific truth is universal without qualification.

3. Meaningless Expressions and Philosophy

We have said that, if a person to whom a communication is addressed is not conversant with the rules of the language in question, he will miss the meaning of the communication; his response will be "inadequate" in terms of the rules of the language as standards of meaning. But it may also happen that the author of the communication violates a rule of the language. In this case the communication itself will be meaningless; it will not lend itself to interpretation as communication in a certain language.

According to our definition, the meaning of a declarative sentence is that it asserts a fact, i.e., that it is true if the fact is the case. When an expression is meaningless, it asserts no fact; it is not either true or false. Such an expression may look more or less superficially like a sentence, but it is no sentence of the language whose rules it violates. Such "meaninglessness" is not a third possibility besides truth and falsehood of which sentences may partake; an expression is a "sentence" only if it has meaning, that is, if it is either true or false. To say of an expression of superficially assertive form that it is "meaningless" is, then, tantamount to saying that it is a sentence only in appearance but not in fact.[16] Of course, if an expression has no sentential meaning, i.e., is neither true nor false, it may still be meaningful as an exclamation or exhortation, etc.; in that case it must satisfy a different set of rules of meaning. For instance, an expression which superficially looks like an exclamation may be meaningless as an exclamation, e.g., if there is a sharp clash between the emotional tone conveyed by different parts of the expression and if the emotional contrast is not accounted for in any way. Since such an expression does not convey an emotional state that can be shared by empathy, it cannot be asked whether it is "sincere" or "adequate" under any other standard; in this sense it is meaningless.

There are several kinds or forms of meaninglessness, according to what kinds of rules of language have been violated. Let us consider, for instance, syntactical rules. If rules of logical syntax are violated, the resulting expressions are not meaningless but contradictory. On the other hand, we may also speak of grammatical syntax, i.e., of the set of rules which specify what kind of words in what sequence will form a "sentence" or any other meaningful expression of the language. One of such rules is, for instance, that a sentence must have a predicate. The expression "yesterday red and" is meaningless in terms of this rule. Certain other "grammatical" rules have a *semantical* import. Let us consider, for instance, the expression "prime numbers are blue." This sentence is defective because its predicate, "blue," is a predicate of the first level: it designates a property of individual things and can therefore be asserted only of such things. Numbers, on the other hand, as "classes of classes," belong to level 2; hence the predicate of a sen-

16. Cf. L. von Wittgenstein, *Tractatus logico-philosophicus* (London, 1922), propositions 4.022, 4.024, and 4.064.

tence in which the subject is the name of a number must have a predicate of level 3. These are "semantical" considerations.[17]

Now what if a *deictic* rule is violated? In general, the result then will be a false sentence, provided that syntactical rules are not violated. If someone says of a red object that it is blue, he utters a falsehood. (From the psychological point of view, of course, it makes a difference whether the falsehood is deliberate or not. It may be that a person says 'blue' instead of 'red' deliberately, in order to induce a false belief in the existence of a red object; of it may be that he says 'blue' instead of 'red' because he is not conversant with the language. In terms of the conventions of the English language, of course, both cases result in false sentences.)

We may obtain meaningless expressions by incorporating false sentences in our assertions. Let us suppose, for instance, that a dishonest art dealer, talking to a customer, says of a recent factory product, "This is a Ming vase." Here we have violation of a deictic rule, as well as a false sentence. But suppose that the buyer says later, "I have paid a thousand dollars for this Ming vase." Then he will be talking nonsense, for there never was a Ming vase to begin with. In order to obtain a meaningful sentence—one which may be true or false—the phrase uttered by the buyer must be transformed, e.g., by making it read thus: "This is a Ming vase, and I have paid one thousand dollars for it." The first component sentence of this assertion will be false but meaningful.

This is the kind of transformation discussed in the chapter dealing with descriptions in *Principia mathematica*.[18] A "description" is an expression which designates a unique object not by its proper name but by identifying it as the only object which satisfies a "propositional function," say, ϕ. Such a description can be null, e.g., if no object satisfies ϕ or if ϕ is satisfied by more than one object. Can an expression containing a null description be true or false? If the description were a name, according to *Principia mathematica*, such an expression would be meaningless; but the description is not a proper name, and it is always possible to transform the expression so that it will contain no description. So transformed, the expression will be meaningful. The well-known example illustrating the concept of "description" in *Principia mathematica* is "The author of 'Waverley' was a Scotchman."

17. Cf. Carnap, *Introduction to Semantics*, p. 16.

18. A. N. Whitehead and B. Russell, *Principia mathematica* (2d ed.; Cambridge, England, 1925), pp. 66 ff.

This description is not null, since there was one and only one person who wrote *Waverley*. But, in any case, we can eliminate the description by saying, "There was one and only one person who wrote *Waverley*, and he was a Scotchman." In this form, the sentence would be meaningful—and, of course, false—even if the description were null; since the description is not null, the first component part of the amplified sentence is not only meaningful but also true.

There is no doubt that, if we transcribe an expression containing a null description in amplified form according to the prescription given above, we always obtain a meaningful sentence. But is this transformation a legitimate one? Does the amplified sentence express what the original expression tried to express? I doubt it. The amplified expression is an existential sentence; it asserts that a thing having certain properties exists. The original assertion, however, was not one about existence but about a thing having a certain property. The existence was merely implied. But it seems to me that existence is similarly implied when I use a name and that the same transformation is possible in the case of expressions containing not null descriptions but null names. It seems to me that both expressions are meaningless as far as they go but that we can obtain meaningful sentences if we amplify them in existential form.

A. Tarski pointed out that expressions which contain only free variables coupled with a predicate are meaningless:

> In view of the fact that variables do not have a meaning by themselves, such phrases as: "x is an integer" are not sentences, although they have the grammatical form of sentences; they do not express a definite expression and can be neither confirmed nor refuted. From the expression: "x is an integer" we only obtain a sentence when we replace "x" in it by a constant denoting a definite number; thus, for instance, if "x" is replaced by the symbol "1," the result is a true sentence, whereas a false sentence arises on replacing "x" by "$\frac{1}{2}$."[19]

It cannot be denied that such a variable expression has no sentential meaning, since it does not assert anything and cannot be either true or false. As a symbol, however, it is by no means "meaningless"; it has a well-defined meaning, which consists in the fact that it can be transformed into a sentence by a substitution of the kind mentioned. In our terminology, words also have meaning, though, of course, no sentential meaning (since they assert no fact). *Their* meaning is that they can contribute in a certain way to the assertion of facts.

According to B. Russell, since nonsensical expressions are neither

19. *Introduction to Logic and the Methodology of Deductive Sciences* (New York, 1941), pp. 4 ff.

true nor false, the predicate "false," when applied to sentences, is not synonymous with "not true," for a nonsensical sentence is not true, but it is also not false. "We must, therefore, if S is a nonsensical sentence, distinguish between 'S is false' and 'S is not true.' The latter will be true, but not the former."[20]

It is difficult to accept this proposition, because it implies that there is a difference between asserting a sentence 'p' and asserting that the sentence 'p' is true. This, however, contradicts the fundamental semantical principle according to which the assertion "The sentence 'p' is true" or "it is true that 'p' " is the same assertion as the assertion of 'p' itself.[21] For this reason, we cannot think that the expression "It is not true that 'p,' where 'p' is meaningless, can itself be meaningful. If 'p' is meaningless, we can assert only that it is not a sentence in the language in question; it is quite true, but redundant, to say that it is not a *true* sentence in the language, but it is equally true that it is not a *false* sentence either. The semantical predicates 'true' and 'false,' 'not true' and 'not false,' can be applied only to sentences, i.e., to meaningful sentences.

There remains to be examined one more class of expressions which are often called "meaningless": undecidable statements. According to logical positivism, expressions which have the grammatical form of declarative sentences but state neither analytical truths nor analytical contradictions nor empirically verifiable facts are meaningless.[22] The adjective 'metaphysical' is often used to characterize—and to disparage—these "meaningless" expressions.

Here we have to do with a specific case of meaninglessness. It obviously does not result from the violation of a syntactical or semantical or deictic rule of language. What is asserted is not that language is used in a defective way but that the language which the "metaphysicians" try to use is itself defective and unsuitable for communication. Its defect is that its deictic rules are too vague to allow any clear-cut use, any decisive test whereby the truth or falsehood of any of the expressions of the language could be established to the satisfaction of all. This language, it is charged, is so contrived that it allows the formulation of more or less emphatic beliefs, carrying an emotional charge of more or less suggestive power, but excludes that kind of consensus

20. *An Inquiry into Meaning and Truth* (New York: W. W. Norton & Co., 1940), p. 216.

21. Cf. Carnap, *Introduction to Semantics*, p. 26.

22. Cf. A. J. Ayer, *Language, Truth, and Logic* (London, 1936), p. 19.

which can be achieved in empirical discourse. The defectiveness of the language, it is added, does not reside in the fact as such that its expressions are emotional ones and do not allow for interpersonal decision but that, this being the case, the expressions of the metaphysical language still masquerade as declarative sentences. This pretense, the proponents of this thesis argue, should be abandoned; traditional philosophy should give up its claim to be considered a science, a pursuit of objective truth. Part of the traditional subject matter of philosophy (logic) should be taken over by mathematics, another part by the empirical sciences; the rest should be treated as the expression of personal preferences, allowing for no rational discussion.

At first glance, the thesis seems unanswerable. In the sciences no question is discussed unless all disputants agree that such and such a crucial test will be accepted by all as settling the question. This permits, in the sciences, if no "eternal" truths, at least ordered progress, with a certain guaranty against unnecessary loss of time. Why, then, allow philosophers to discuss the same questions over and over again, without even knowing that consensus can be reached?[23] Is such a loss of time and energy over irrelevancies and insoluble questions not an insult to the principle of rationality in the management of human affairs?

Well, upon closer scrutiny, I would be tempted to answer No. I do not deny that philosophical discussions are often inconclusive, whereas controversies over empirical matters can always be settled, at least in principle. What I deny is that the conclusion drawn from this state of things concerning the rational management of human affairs is correct.

I think there is a definite conception of the best, or most rational, management of human affairs which underlies the logical-positivist thesis. According to this conception, it is not only possible but desirable so to organize human affairs that every question which is not amenable either to analytical proof or to empirical verification is declared to be strictly arbitrary in the sense that no argument concerning it is to be allowed. Obviously, there can be no guaranty against inconclusive debates, unless we adopt this decision. But is it rational? Is it safe to adopt it?

23. Cf. F. W. Bridgman, "The Prospect for Intelligence," *Yale Review*, XXXIV, No. 3 (March, 1945), 444–61: "it [*sic*] no less than an intellectual scandal that much of philosophy in its present form, particularly the parts dealing with theology and metaphysics, exist today. After thousands of years of discussion, philosophers still argue the same old questions, without even being able to agree as to whether agreement should be possible . . ." (p. 454).

It seems to me that such a decision may be considered safe and reasonable only if either of two assumptions is correct—namely, either if it is possible to organize peaceful and civilized society by allowing each individual to proceed arbitrarily concerning any matter which cannot be settled by analytical or empirical methods or if such a society can be organized by using coercion and suggestion to decide questions which cannot be solved by analytical or empirical methods.

I think both assumptions are open to strong objections. The first assumption implies that society can remain at peace if only scientific consensus about empirical and analytical questions is being cultivated. In other words, the only source of conflict that society needs to bother about is disagreement about purely logical and empirically verifiable matters. I thing everybody will agree that this assumption is preposterous, since this kind of disagreement is socially the least dangerous. Hence the foes of "inconclusive" discussions must fall back upon the second assumption, namely, that group problems which cannot be settled by analytical or empirical investigations must be solved by coercion or suggestion. There is no doubt that such a society is possible, but I see little reason to consider it the prototype of *rational* social organization. To me it looks rather like the contrary.

Group life cannot be ordered by empirical and analytical science alone. We may admit also that it cannot be ordered entirely without resorting to compulsion and suggestion. The question is, however, whether all we can do with the residual problems—those which cannot be settled by scientific methods—is necessarily either nonintervention or compulsion or suggestion. To accept this, it seems to me, is tantamount to condemning society to swing back and forth between the extremes of anarchy and totalitarianism. It is quite possible that alternation between anarchy and totalitarianism is the fate which is in store for us. But, as long as we still can search for a rational way to organize our society, such a search, I think, means precisely that we are looking for a *third* possibility besides anarchy and totalitarianism. This hinges upon some method of rationally treating problems which fall outside the scope of empirical and formal science. Even if this "rational" treatment lacks the conclusiveness of empirical and analytical methods, it may still be better than nothing or than coercion or suggestion.

That such imperfect but rational modes of discussion are necessary in human affairs is evident from the fact that both analytical and empirical methods are applicable to specialized types of problems only within narrow limits. Obviously, analytical science can help us only if our problem is to find out what follows from certain assumptions; it cannot help us decide whether the assumptions are right. Empirical science, on the other hand, can solve only a type of problem which can be stated in terms of "facts," that is, of properties present in situations or sets of situations.

As we have seen above (chap. i), factual information deals with *classes* or class relationships of situations; its actual use is a contextual problem: it involves a judgment about what we had better do, "the facts being such and such." The answer to questions of this kind depends crucially on value standards, particularly standards of relevance. We cannot postulate that questions of the sort "What is the best way of acting, the facts being such and such?" always answer themselves when the facts are filled in. We cannot even expect automatic consensus about what facts are relevant to the determination of the best way of acting in a certain situation.

The logical-positivist thesis implies either that there can be no disagreement among humans concerning the facts upon which decisions are to be based or that, once some agreement about this has been reached (in whatever way), a decision acceptable to all will be revealed by the facts or, finally, that we can always safely agree to disagree if neither of the first two conditions is satisfied. I think that all three presuppositions are completely gratuitous.

I hope it will be clear from the preceding that I am not trying to depreciate the role of factual information in the making of human decisions. On the contrary, I have stressed the capacity of behaving "contextually," that is, the capacity of basing decisions upon "information," as a primary distinguishing mark of specifically human behavior. It is precisely one of the main points emphasized in this analysis that the capacity to act upon factual information not only is "useful" to man but is essential to his dignity, to his being human. But this does not mean that we can overlook the *other* pole of the "contextual" situation—the way in which the cycle of "information" is integrated into the cycle of "need-reduction." Questions which concern this fitting of the facts into the situation involve interpretation and judgment.

Every "contextual" judgment involves both ascertainment of facts and application of a standard of "good" response. The elimination of all nonanalytic and nonfactual statements from rational discourse means that we are ready to leave the second component in the judging operation to the individuals concerned, without making any systematic effort—comparable to that devoted to the discovery of facts and their

functional relationships—to educate and improve it. This looks superficially like the only "democratic" attitude; for, indeed, it seems implied
in the principle of democracy that one should not interfere with people's value standards but let everyone work out his own decisions,
once the facts are in. It can be shown, however, that this view rests
upon a complete misunderstanding of the democratic principle and of
its implications.

Attempts to influence people's value judgments and attitudes by
coercion and suggestion are, indeed, undemocratic; and it is understood that, in trying to improve and co-ordinate the value process,
such methods should not be applied. But it does not follow from this
that the only avenue toward such improvement that is consistent with
democratic respect for individual freedom is the presentation of a reliable factual background. On the contrary, it is positively dangerous
to democracy to accept the dogma that "mere" factual information is
a form of influencing thinking that is always legitimate and always
respectful of the autonomy of the human personality. Once this is
generally admitted, those who want to influence the value process will
do so by selecting those facts which are favorable to their goals; control of the channels of information will thus be a major stake in the
social and political struggle, and the result will be either that one group
will have a monopoly over information or that various channels will
exist, each characterized by a systematic bias in selection. No doubt, it
is also thinkable that the channel of information will be controlled by
perfectly disinterested scholars and that the selection of facts presented
to the public will be both complete and unbiased. But this outcome is
hardly possible in any real society, for it really implies that those who
control the channels of information are both all-powerful (since they
can resist all attempts at biasing the channel) and completely disinterested in power (since they introduce no bias themselves). This is
precisely the utopia conceived by Plato in his *Republic*; to say that
this is the prevailing order of things means to say that the perfect society, a society ruled by totally disinterested philosophers, has been
achieved. I think ideas about the management of human affairs which
presuppose the attainment of ideal perfection are without practical
value.

Furthermore, the utopia itself has, to me at least, some unattractive
features. It seems that, if we retain only the presentation of facts as
our tool used in influencing attitudes and eliminate appeals to general
moral principles and to the conscience of the individual, we pave the

way for a completely manipulative society. Indeed, I can see in such a situation no room for an autonomous decision at all. For the *major* element of the decision process upon which all attention will be focused will be the "scientifically established factual background," and this is something the nonexpert (that is, practically everybody) will have to accept on faith. At least, the overwhelming majority will not be able to grasp the rationale of the statements by which his decisions are supposed to be swayed. I grant that this faith will not be entirely irrational and mystical, since the experts—the controllers of information—will be able to point to the visible applications of scientific knowledge in every field of technology. But such appeals to success by no means represent true rationality if they are used to bolster the authority of the scientist in nontechnological matters. I see both moral callousness and logical sloppiness in the argument that, if someone makes the trains run on time, he is entitled to run society on *his* schedule.

In all this, a basic misunderstanding of the nature of "freedom" and of "free decision" seems to be involved. This misunderstanding consists in considering a decision "free" if the judgment upon which it is based is (*a*) influenced by facts presented as such and (*b*) not influenced by anything else but determined by the individual as a self-contained unit in all its nonfactual "goal" aspects. This doctrine seems to me theoretically false and morally pernicious; for it cuts off all person-to-person intercourse in matters of right and wrong, in matters of the conscience, while, on the other hand, it implies manipulation of persons by the control of information. This is not the way of utilizing information "contextually," a thing here recognized to be one of the marks of the essential dignity of man.

Information can play its role in the "contextual" decision process only if certain essential conditions besides the mere transmission of the factual information as such are fulfilled. First and foremost, there must be confidence in the source of the information; confidence based not upon suggestion and blind faith but upon "interpretation" getting at the meaning, the rationale of the partner's attitude and behavior. If there is no moral rapport between informant and recipient of information, there can be no true contextual use of information either. If we consider man morally as an "island entire in itself," beholden to no one but himself as far as his goals and values are concerned, we also deny him the capacity of true contextual use of information.

The idea that communication—in so far as it is recognized as a legitimate means of influencing the decision process—must be limited to "factual" matters breaks down because factual communication is lifeless and meaningless without communication in terms of values. It is a complete mistake to believe that "freedom" of decision is predicated upon complete absence of moral persuasion and moral influence. No man can make a free decision without having a moral rationale in mind (that is, some idea of right or wrong), and no man can develop such ideas without being educated in them and exposed to communications revolving around these basic ideas. This "ethical" dimension of conduct—the right-wrong dimension—will be discussed in detail when we come to the topic of values; at this point, we stress only that these communications have a full-fledged rationale of their own; they are real communications in the sense of a full give-and-take, of mutual concern with a commonly felt problem, rather than merely egocentric statements of preferences of the isolated subject as such.

It seems, then, that the sweeping logical-positivist principle of denying all rationality to discourse other than analytic and factual must be rejected. I do not think that logical positivism is a "dangerous" doctrine, one that favors totalitarianism or moral nihilism—but only because this principle, which might lead to such results if really acted upon, is pathetically impracticable. Man will simply not renounce his search for rational answers to value problems, because this search is part of his life; the logical positivists themselves are witness to this, since their own pleas, bolstered with earnest conviction and considerable virtuosity in argumentation, aim at nothing but the rational justification of a preference in nonanalytic and nonfactual terms. If all traditional philosophy is bad, it is certainly not bad because it contains statements which are neither analytic nor factual nor blandly and groundlessly preferential.

Upon reflection, a logical positivist might admit all this, without altering his basic attitude toward "philosophy" in the traditional sense. He might agree that some kind of "rational" discussion of moral values and ends, which is not wholly reducible either to logic or to natural science, could be unavoidable and possibly fruitful. But then, he would add, this is certainly not what makes up the bulk of all traditional philosophy. The trouble with traditional philosophy is precisely that it does *not* limit itself to the comparatively pedestrian task of examining the nature of "reasonable" preferences and the ways of determining them. Instead, the philosophers have been talking about God and the world, the absolute and the relative, essences and substances, the nature of reality and of the *ens realissimum*, the mind and its role in "creating" the world, ideas subsisting in a realm beyond the heavens, and similar preposterous nonsense. What sane men could have any other wish than to take a broom and sweep all this out? If we *must* have philosophy (that is, discourse that pretends to have intersubjective validity but is neither wholly analytic nor wholly factual), then at least it should clearly limit itself to a meaningful subject matter and, above all, maintain the closest possible contact with logical analysis and scientific research. If, after extracting everything that can be extracted from these sources, some questions of "principle" still remain that can be discussed fruitfully, let philosophy discuss them; but its every step must be carefully controlled, lest it again stray into metaphysics, irresponsible speculation, and meaningless mumbo jumbo.

This logical-positivist critique of philosophy deserves serious attention, unlike the self-defeating attempt to kill philosophy by banishing from discourse all terms by which *any* position (including the logical-positivist one) could be justified. I shall try to answer it briefly before going on with the analysis of "meanings."

The broad subject matter of philosophy is the rationale of all human beliefs—beliefs about "facts" as well as beliefs about "values." We shall miss the point of this philosophical endeavor if we try to commit the philosopher to the role of determining *what* "beliefs" are true or "warranted." In so far as beliefs about matters of fact are concerned, it is obviously science which will best determine which are true and which are false; and as regards beliefs about values (right and wrong, for instance), the determination of the "moral truth" or rightness of any such belief is a matter for the codifier, for society as a whole, and for the autonomous conscience of each of us, acting in constant, tense, and intimate intercourse. The business of philosophy is not to pass upon individual beliefs but to elucidate the rationale of the operation of distinguishing between the true and the false ones. It deals with the principles underlying such choices. To hold that this endeavor is always and necessarily a waste of time means to hold that the problem does not exist: as long as we admittedly have people who, singly and collectively, are capable of selecting the best-warranted beliefs, nobody should worry about the principles upon which the selection is based. I hold, as against this, that, even if the "fact-finders" and the "value judges" never needed to turn their attention to the rationale of what they are doing but always could proceed instinctively in the right direction, it would make a great difference to the others—those who are supposed to *accept* the "best beliefs" so arrived at—to know something about the rationale of their derivation. Actually, of course, the process of selecting the "best" beliefs never takes place in a completely instinctive and intuitive fashion; both the scientist, the legislator, and the ethical subject must have their explicit "philosophy." What might be asked is only whether the philosophical endeavor should be carried on merely as a part-time occupation of those who grapple with the factual and moral issues in hand or whether it is legitimate for some people to devote their main effort to the philosophical problems (problems of principle) involved in choices among beliefs.

For the early periods of intellectual development the problem does not arise, because the early philosophers were also scientists, legislators, and statesmen. *As* scientists and legislators, they propounded factual beliefs and material value judgments; at the same time, *as* philosophers, they explicitly spelled out the principles upon which they based their choice of beliefs. It is only in modern times that an issue exists at all, and it is a difficult one; for if clarification of the underlying principles were left only to the fact-finders and the decision-makers, we should have only a multitude of specialized statements of principle and method without the possibility of integration; but if we invite some people to carry out the task of integration, we shall risk getting integrative statements very far removed from what any of the specialists is actually doing. Both the scientists and the decision-makers will then feel that the philosophers add nothing of value to their endeavors. The logical-positivist thesis in its "moderate" version that I am discussing now is really dictated by the desire to make philosophy worth while to people who are supposed to "act" upon its findings. This is, in fact, a compliment to philosophy, and an undeserved one; it is based upon a misconception of the true role of the philosopher.

My own belief is that in well-developed sciences the scientists themselves can and should be their own philosophers, in so far as the rationale of the process of fact-finding and theory-construction (i.e., methodology) is concerned. No outsider can explain the procedure followed by scientists in the past and open new paths as well as the creative scientist can, if there is a fully developed basic theory of the field. In two other areas, however, I think society needs philosophers who are not at the same time specialists. One is the area of sciences lacking a "mature," fully developed theoretical framework; the other is the "contextual" realm of exploiting factual information for determining the best course of action. In the field of nonmature sciences, philosophical analysis conducted from a point of view different from that of the specialist will be of value to the latter, because philosophical reflection may produce fruitful over-all considerations, guesses, and criticisms. In the "contextual" field the philosopher is needed to perform a similar function: that of injecting into the never ending debate about "what should be done" considerations not bound to sectional viewpoints. It is to be noted that *the philosopher is in neither case a specialist, expert, or technician who "advises" a lay public on the best course to be taken.* When the philosopher's job is done, every question is undecided, and the groups and individuals addressed by the philosopher must make up their minds and decide for themselves. The philosopher can only hope that he has helped some people make a better decision, owing to their having adopted a broader point of view. Precisely because the philosopher's subject matter is the contextual problem—the problem of decision itself—his contribution cannot be of the same nature as the expert's. The latter can "solve" a part of the decision problem: he can provide the factual "constraints" upon which the decision is predicated. The philosopher, however, supplies no "constraints"; what he does consists rather in a *shaking-loose* than in a pinning-down. He does not produce "findings" to be "acted" upon, but only interpretations which may enrich the contextual process.

Yes, but what has all this to do with the traditional subject matter of philosophy, such as "substance" and "essence," the "absolute," "mind and reality," and the like? The answer is that all these terms which today arouse the scorn and indignation of undergraduates of all ages have been selected, at one time or another, to differentiate "warranted" beliefs from "nonwarranted" ones. All efforts to define "reality" as distinguished from "appearance" have been undertaken in the presence of a body of current beliefs, in order to answer the question of how one might distinguish the well-warranted ones from the less well-warranted. This is a "perennial" problem, but obviously one that cannot be solved once and for all; in every age, having its current beliefs and generally adopted warrants, it must be faced anew. This is why philosophical discussion must always return to the same problems, without the possibility of building upon earlier findings and gradually correcting them on the basis of new evidence. There are no philosophical findings; there are only philosophical judgments and interpretations.

To understand these judgments and interpretations, we must relate them to the intellectual background of "current" beliefs and methods which they codify and criticize. But this does not mean that the validity or value of a philosophical judgment is limited to just one stage of the intellectual development. For the *problem* of distinguishing well-founded beliefs from less well-founded ones is in a way the same, whatever body of beliefs is examined as the currently dominant one; and the really great philosopher is one who discovers a type of warrant that will prove valid, in one guise or another, throughout the ages. The great philosophers are those whose interpretations enrich the contextual activities of their own and many successive generations. Their prototype is Plato.

It is fashionable nowadays to counterpose "Platonism" to every sound canon of scientific thinking and research. Plato is always referred to as a classic example of the irresponsible metaphysician who tries to answer all questions by inventing a priori entities not related to actual experience. This conception of Plato as the archetype of the aprioristic thinker perpetuates itself in its turn in an a priori fashion, through failure to inspect the empirical evidence—Plato's own writings. The evidence, however, is clear enough; Plato has coined the concept of "idea" to put into relief the particular type of *cogency* attaching to mathematical reasoning. A Platonic "idea" is any entity about which exact reasoning is possible—in particular, a mathematical entity. This distinction between "idealized" concepts and "empirical" data, which Plato enunciated for the first time, is as valid today as it was in his own time. That Plato characterized the "ideas" as having *real* subsistence and as being in a sense more "real" than sense data may sound scandalous today, but the thought itself is by no means foolish if we remember what Plato meant by "degrees" of reality. These he conceived as corresponding to the degrees of cogency of reasoning that an object allows. It is quite true that on this definition the most "real" entities are those of mathematics. Another strange feature of the Platonic concept of "idea" is that he ascribed "ideal" status (that is, the highest degree of reality in the sense of cognitive cogency) to moral as well as mathematical entities. This was, I think, due to an "irradiation" effect accompanying the discovery of the specific cogency of mathematical reasoning. Since the intuitive concepts of ordinary experience, such as those of various shapes, can be reduced to an exact deductive framework, is the hope not warranted that the intuitive concepts of moral experience, such as "virtue" and "the good," can also be shown to have this degree of "reality"? I think this hope was bound to be disappointed, but it was neither gratuitous nor foolish. On the contrary, real progress in moral thinking was possible only on the basis of postulating a rationale behind it; and even today we can proceed only on this basis, although we must abandon a *literal* interpretation of the isomorphism of the moral and the geometrical.

All this, however, by no means exhausts the decisive "perennial" significance of Platonic philosophy. The point is that Plato was not content with distinguishing between the "cogency" of mathematical reasoning (διάνοια) and the "vagueness" of sense-impressions and ordinary everyday intuition (πιστίς and δόξα); he also proclaimed that knowledge of the experiential world can be made "scientific" by discovering the geometrical and numerical relationships among and "behind" phenomena. The concept of "science" as a rigorous deductive discipline somehow related to observation is a Platonic one; it is the gist of Plato's theoretical philosophy. Not only are the Platonic "ideas" *separated* from the world of sense-experience; the latter also *participates* in them and is scientifically knowable to the extent that it does. The fundamental idea underlying Western science—that of the interlocking of mathematical deduction and empirical observation— goes back to Plato.

It is a myth that Plato was not interested in studying empirical phenomena. The business of the Academy was in part such a study; for instance, one of the tasks Plato set his students was the development of an astronomical theory of the solar system. Even some of the dialogues (which do not, on the whole, reflect the curriculum of the Academy) afford some glimpses of this scientific work; in the *Sophist* we see an application of a technique of classification, a taxonomic method, that apparently was practiced there; and in the *Timaeus* Plato presents a full-fledged theory of atomistic physics on a geometrical basis. Considered as science, all these efforts, except those devoted to harmonics and astronomy, were very faulty; Plato never found the secret of effecting the junction between deduction and observation in terrestrial physics. But it was he who created the concept of "science" in our sense: the central driving force of the intellectual conscience of the West. This is far more significant than the fact that his own attempts at building up physics went wrong and that his own logical reasoning was often faulty. There are only a few inexcusable mistakes in Plato's theoretical philosophy—not his alleged apriorism or his fanciful atomistic speculations but, for instance, his dogma that heavenly bodies—since they move in orbits describable in terms of mathematical equations—must themselves be alive and intelligent. This way of reasoning was characteristically Greek; it was inevitable, once one had accepted the fundamental principle of early Greek logic, formulated by Parmenides as the postulate of the identity of Thinking and Being (that is, the identity of the thinker and the content of his thought). Plato did not challenge this prejudice as he did other Greek prejudices.

In moral and political philosophy, too, some of Plato's ideas became organic components of the entire Western way of life. I do not refer primarily to his championing of the autonomous conscience and of an absolute standard of right and wrong; there are many who regret this contribution and would prefer the relativism of the Sophists. This will have to be discussed later. What should be mentioned here is the Platonic origin of some of the basic components of Western institutional life.

When Plato's contribution to political thought is discussed, most people think of the *Republic*—that is, utopianism, communism, and the rule of the wise. And it is fashionable to interpret this utopia as a totalitarian one, a charge which I do not consider justified. But, although I think the spirit of Plato's utopia is not totalitarian, I regret the extraordinary fascination which the *Republic* has exercised throughout the ages, for I consider the idea of a "perfect" ("perfectly" just, "perfectly" happy) society pernicious—not because of its totalitarian features, if any, but *particularly* if the content of the utopia is wholly "angelic." Mankind is not served by giving it the task of realizing the perfect society. Nor do I think that Plato meant the *Republic* to be read in this vein; the modern fascination with utopias for their own sake would probably have repelled his Greek mind. I think Plato was wholly serious only about the ethical and epistemological ideas developed in the *Republic* but presented the political utopia in it with tongue in cheek. But be this as it may, all his later political thinking was predicated upon the impossibility of any utopian, perfect society, and it was the nonutopian element in Plato's political thinking which proved decisive for later Western history. For, just as he was the first to formulate the concept of science as a rigorous deductive discipline, so he was also the first to formulate the concept of *law* as an impartial form of social control. Plato's essential political philosophy may be summarized thus: Barring a society directly controlled by gods or godlike individuals, the way to achieve a form of social control that is worthy of man is to establish rule by law. Rome was the first actual commonwealth that embodied the rule of law, but it was Plato who first enunciated the concept of law as impartial rule, as distinct from the earlier Greek concept of law as mere convention (and also from oriental conceptions of law as a sacred directive).

It would be possible, I think, to examine the writings of other great philosophers, too, and show that their speculations about "metaphysical" entities were perfectly meaningful and sometimes decisive for intellectual progress. This cannot be attempted here even in the sketchy form in which it was done for Plato; suffice it to say that the meaning of philosophical discourse may always be made clear if we refer it, first, to the intellectual background (the current body of beliefs, the warrants for which have to be examined) and, second, to the particular role of the philosopher, who does not furnish facts to be acted upon but interpretive patterns which one may use in judging about facts and values.

Just as this function should not be confused with that of the "expert adviser," so it should also be distinguished from that of the purely emotional exhorter. It is a complete misunderstanding to attribute to "metaphysics" and other branches of philosophy an "emotional" function. Interpretation is not a matter of emotion, although it *is* a matter of value and choice. The emotional raptures that one may feel in connection with "beautiful" metaphysical theories do not differ in kind from similar responses to "beautiful" mathematical proofs or empirical discoveries. The real question is whether the interpretation pattern actually works: whether it enriches the contextual process; whether it makes a better integration of "facts" and "choices" possible. The philosopher contributes to this process, not by actually "interpreting" situations (and still less by presenting facts), but by providing patterns of interpretation beyond the accepted routine. This alone is philosophy. Philosophy may be briefly defined as a breaking-up of routines in thinking.

The proposal to limit philosophy to questions of scientific methodology, in full co-operation with the specialists of the various sciences, is based upon a misunderstanding of the essential function of philosophy. To be sure, methodology, as the elucidation and enrichment of the rationale underlying the "choices" made by scientists, is a philosophical task, and an important one; but it cannot be the only one. For, in so far as the theoretically well-developed sciences are concerned, the really philosophical task—that of breaking new ground in methodology—will be performed by the creative scientists themselves; in this field the contribution of the "professional" philosopher will be the *least* philosophical one. Where the latter can make a significant contribution is in a different field: the uncharted region of undeveloped sciences and, above all, of the human choices that have to be made in view of all the needs felt and all the facts known.

I think it is time to challenge the belief, current in a part of the philosophical community today, that the main task of philosophy is to protect the purity and orthodoxy of "empiricism." The battle cry of "empiricism" implies the following: Unless we are ever vigilant in banishing from nonanalytical discourse every statement that is neither scientifically verifiable nor purely and simply preferential, we open the door to irresponsible "apriorism." Now I certainly do not want to defend apriorism, if by this term is meant the doctrine that pure "thinking," without experience, can discover truths—or the truth—about man, life, and the world. But I do not think that the way to avoid apriorism is to insist upon "factual evidence" for any statement that is not an arbitrary demand and to prescribe complete abstention from assent and dissent in the presence of every statement that cannot be bolstered by factual evidence. For this program itself is unworkable; whenever we make a judgment (and we must *always* judge, even when we talk about purely empirical matters), we must always commit ourselves to a "definitional" rule as well as to a factual assertion. We cannot split our discourse into an entirely arbitrary "definitional" part and an entirely "constrained" nondefinitional one. Our definitions always have a stubborn residue of factuality, and our fact statements always have a stubborn residue of "definitionality." Hence, if we consider philosophy to be a guardian of the rationality of discourse, we cannot define its task as being confined to maintaining an anxious watch over the adequacy of evidence for fact statements. This may be a very necessary task at times. When the empiricist movement started, it performed the truly "philosophical" function of disturbing and shaking up the routine into which academic philosophical idealism had fallen. But today empiricism itself threatens to settle down into a mechanical routine; it is becoming apparent that the time has come to turn our attention toward problems of the rationality of discourse which concern its "definitional" rather than its "evidential" aspects. If philosophers neglect the real intellectual need that must be satisfied in this connection, time will by-pass them, and the problem of interpretation and judgment will be solved "empirically" along lines in which the empiricists themselves as "empirical" persons will find little comfort. If the philosophers neglect their task of loosening and vitalizing the process of judgment, there will be others who will make every effort to mechanize and banalize it.

To repeat: this is no plea for apriorism. In fact, it seems to me that apriorism and empiricism both share in the same error. Their common presupposition is that one *can* separate the factual from the definitional. If, acting on this faulty presupposition, we choose the empiricist side, we risk neglecting the task of attending to the rationality of our principles of action and of thinking. If we choose the apriorist side, we risk making our principles irrelevant to our actual thinking and acting. The "contextualist" position taken here[24] calls for looking at the factual and the definitional together—for recognizing judgment and interpretation as a part of human experience, not as something freely floating beside it.

24. The designation "contextualism" has been used by Lewis E. Hahn to identify his philosophical position (see *A Contextualistic Theory of Perception* [Berkeley, Calif., 1942]). I have developed the position outlined here without being aware of Professor Hahn's work; my concept of "context" and "contextual" behavior is more specific than his and refers to symbol-using behavior rather than to perception and behavior in general.

II. MEANING AND BEHAVIOR

CHAPTER III

MEANING AND CONSCIOUSNESS

IN THE preceding sections "meaning" has been defined with little reference to "thoughts," "beliefs," and other mental occurrences. The basic pattern which we have chosen to illustrate our conception of meaning, namely, meaning-in-behavior, involves no thoughts or conscious reflection in any way. The interpretation of situational meaning "from the outside," as well as that of communicative meaning, does involve thought-processes; but we have been careful to avoid confusion between the meaning of the sign or communication which is interpreted and the thoughts involved in the interpretation. Meanings for us are relations between organisms, situations, signs, and responses or between symbols, properties, and sets of situations, or situations; they are not mental processes either experienced by a subject or communicated by him to a partner.

This approach differs considerably from the usual one. As a rule, the meaning of a sign is defined either as a state of mind of its author or as a state of mind that it generates in its interpreter.[1] Thus, Bertrand Russell says: "The 'significance' of a sentence is what it expresses."[2] He explains that the "state of the speaker" which an assertion "expresses" is a "belief," adding that beliefs may exist without words "and even in animals and infants who do not possess language."[3] Russell says further, in discussing significant statements, that they produce effects in the hearer which are different from those produced by meaningless statements;[4] these effects, according to him, constitute the meaning of signs. "Since a significant sentence may be false," he says, "it is clear that the significance of a sentence cannot be the fact that makes it true (or false). It must therefore be something in the person who believes the sentence, not in the object to which the sentence refers."[5]

1. It is to be noted, however, that Morris rejects this "mentalistic" approach (see *Signs, Language, and Behavior* [New York: Prentice-Hall, 1946], pp. 49 ff.).

2. *An Inquiry into Meaning and Truth* (New York: W. W. Norton & Co., 1940), p. 215.

3. *Ibid.*, p. 214.   4. *Ibid.*, p. 215.   5. *Ibid.*, p. 229.

It appears from what we said above that, according to our definition too, the meaning of a sentence is not a fact which makes it true and that the meaning is not "something in the object to which it refers." But it does not follow, in our opinion, that it must therefore be "something in the person who believes the sentence"; just as the sentence can be significant, although there is no fact in the real world which "corresponds" to it, so it can be significant even if nobody believes it. The mental processes taking place in the consciousness of a person who hears a sentence and believes it cannot be the meaning of that sentence, since these processes always contain much material that is extraneous to the meaning of the sentence as such.[6] The actual reaction to a message depends not only on the meaning of the message but also on the hearer's ability to understand it and on the entire situation on which the message impinges. This is a matter of the hearer's personal history, his established routes of association, his level of performance, and also of the whole context in which the message happens to be delivered. We may add that, on the author's side, the actual intention prompting the message also depends on similar subjective factors and on the situational context. Both the intention behind the message and the reaction to the message go beyond the meaning as such. The meaning is nothing that can be identified as one of the actual events found in the "stream of consciousness" of a person or in a behavior sequence.

Meanings are communicated, but such actual mental events or behavior elements are not. The communication of a message has nothing to do with the transference of a "thought" from one consciousness to another. When we hear a message and understand it, we do not reproduce a thought which has been entertained by someone else; rather than make a mental copy of a thought, we always "jump to conclusions." When hearing, "The house is on fire," we do not think, "the house is on fire," but "let's get out." When hearing, "Smith's house is on fire," we do not think, "Smith's house is on fire," but something like, "Poor fellow, Smith, that's bad for him," or "Now he's going to collect insurance." We reproduce communications only if we do not understand them. But all this goes beyond communicative meaning and its straight interpretation. The communicative meaning itself is an invariant of a wide range of actual responses. Its

6. Cf. Peirce on this distinction: "Now the logical comprehension of a thought is usually said to consist of the thoughts contained in it; but thoughts are events, acts of the mind . . . " (*Collected Papers* [Cambridge: Harvard University Press, 1935], V, 171 f.).

correct interpretation presupposes familiarity with a linguistic convention; but this, in turn, presupposes familiarity with certain properties or sets of possible sign meanings. The communicative meaning
as interpreted is neither "in the speaker" nor "in the hearer"—neither
is it something "in the objective facts referred to." It is a relation
which involves a linguistic convention and the presence or non-
presence of certain properties in certain situations or sets of situations.

Similarly, a situational meaning (sign meaning) also is different
from the actual reaction to a sign. The actual reaction may or may
not be the "good" one; the sign meaning is a relation by virtue of
which a response is "good" if it satisfies certain conditions.

That meanings have a relational character has often been noted.
Meaning is frequently defined as a relation. Morris' definition of
"sign"[7] belongs to this group; see also the following tentative definition of truth proposed by Russell: "A sentential sign present to an
organism O is *true* when, *as sign*, it promotes behaviour which would
have been promoted by a situation that exists, if that situation had
been present to the organism."[8] Similarly, according to Ogden and
Richards, the meaning of a sign is that it produces in a hearer thoughts
which are "similar in certain respects" to the thoughts which have
been caused "to occur to the speaker by some object or referent."[9]
These relations, however, have nothing to do with meanings.

We need not attach too much weight to a difficulty which arises in
connection with Ogden and Richards' formulation but is avoided by
Morris and Russell, namely, that the similarity of thoughts occurring
to people is not open to observation, so that "meaning" would be based
on something pretty occult. This difficulty is not decisive, because it
can be surmounted by a behavioristic analysis of the concept of
"thought."[10] Whether we speak of "thoughts" or of "overt" features
of behavior, however, we are not dealing with meanings as long as

7. Cf. the following two definitions given by Morris: "If something, A, controls
behavior towards a goal in a way similar to (but not identical with) the
way something else, B, would control behavior with respect to that goal in a situation in which it were observed, then A is a sign"; and: "If anything, A, is a
preparatory-stimulus which in the absence of stimulus-objects initiating response-
sequences of a certain behavior-family causes a disposition in some organism to
respond under certain conditions by response-sequences of this behavior-family, then
A is a sign" (*op. cit.*, pp. 7 and 10).

8. *Op. cit.*, p. 235.

9. C. K. Ogden and I. A. Richards, *The Meaning of Meaning* (London, 1930),
pp. 54, 10.

10. Cf. Karl Britton, *Communication* (London, 1939), p. 14.

we concentrate upon the *effects* of signs upon interpreters and the similarity of these effects to those produced by other objects.

Russell's analysis of "the meaning of a sentence" will make this clearer. Someone hears the sentence, "Caesar has crossed the Rubicon." The hearer's reaction to the sentence may be different from that of an actual eyewitness of the crossing of the Rubicon, but the two reactions have one element in common: the belief that Caesar crossed the Rubicon.[11] No matter how the actual reactions differ otherwise, the belief as such is the same belief.

To this we would reply that the belief is "the same" only in the sense that it is belief in the same fact. What is really meant by saying that two persons—the eyewitness and the recipient of a message—have "the same belief" is merely that they believe the same thing to be the case. It is true, but tautological, that all those persons who believe a sentence to be true, whether on the basis of personal observation or not, believe the same thing to be the case and, in this sense, have the same belief. What matters is, however, that their beliefs will be totally different from another point of view: as actual mental occurrences, they will differ completely from one another. The person who comes to believe that something is the case because he sees it happen does not make the same response as the person who comes to believe the same thing because he gives credence to a message asserting it. What the eyewitness does has to do with properties present in his situation, i.e., among other things, with his own situational meaning, from which he may effect a transition to communicative meaning by formulating his findings according to a linguistic convention. The recipient of the report, on the other hand, will at first have to interpret communicative meaning—an act of interpretation which in itself is neutral toward belief or unbelief; then he will have to interpret the message "situationally," so as to determine its trustworthiness. Thus the message does not elicit "the same belief" that the actual experience does, in the same way; and if, in the end, the recipient holds the same belief, this is not merely a matter of the communicative meaning of the message. Ultimately, belief in either case is based on the evaluation of the situational context, but this is entirely different for the observer and for the recipient of a message, respectively.

Similar considerations hold for sign meanings. The view that the sign causes thoughts to occur which are identical with, or similar to, thoughts caused by the thing signified may be dismissed as an over-

11. *Op. cit.*, p. 224.

simplification; after all, the response to a sign is usually different from the response to a "correlate."[12] But, quite apart from this, the question of what behavior is elicited by the sign is different from the question of what the meaning of the sign is.

The main defect of the approach which identifies the function of signifying with that of eliciting a certain kind of behavior or "pre-paratory-behavior" (Morris) is that it makes no distinction between the actual response to the sign and the "good" response. This distinction, however, is absolutely vital to a correct interpretation of meaning. The meaning of a sign is not determined by how organisms actually respond to it; in any individual case the response may be "good" as well as "bad." The meaning of the sign cannot be the fact that it elicits behavior related in a definite way to the signified object, because signs of the same meaning may actually elicit behavior related to the signified object in different ways or even behavior entirely un-related to that object. What the response will actually be does not depend on the meaning as such alone but on the degree of adaptation, the level of performance of the organism, and possibly also on chance features of the situation. The meaning of the sign, its signifying function, is not that it will lead to a certain response but only that, *if* such and such a response takes place, it will be good in terms of some standard. It is perfectly true that we may conceive of standards defined by actual responses—e.g., those found to occur in the majority of cases among a certain species—and it certainly would be absurd to adopt a standard to which no actual response could be equal. But it would likewise be absurd to let our standards of meaning coincide with each actual response. If we are interested only in the actual responses as such, we do not need the category of meaning—but then such categories as that of "sign" and "signifying function" also become super-fluous. The category of meaning and such related categories as "sign" and "signifying function" are needed only for the analysis of cases in which the distinction between "good" and "bad" responses is relevant.

For declarative sentences and situational signs we have shown that the meaning of symbols or signs is something different from the re-sponses they elicit. But what about nonsentential and nondeclarative expressions, such as questions, exclamations, commands, and the like (cf., for instance, "appraisors" and "prescriptors" in Morris' termi-nology)? In the case of declarative sentences and situational signs we could think of standards that were neutral toward the actual response

12. Cf. Morris, *op. cit.*, pp. 6 ff.

performed by the interpreter. Nondeclarative expressions, however, seem to be addressed to an interpreter in a far more intimate way, and their meaning somehow seems to involve the actual response of the interpreter. The meaning of the command "Come here," addressed by *A* to *B*, seems to be somehow that *B* should go to *A*. A command is "meant to be obeyed."

Nevertheless, I would maintain that in the case of nondeclarative expressions, too, the meaning must be distinguished from the actual response. The order "Come here" has the same meaning, whether it is obeyed or not and even whether the author of the command sincerely wishes it to be obeyed or not. In other words, a command or exclamation may be "misleading" just as a declarative sentence can, and the interpreter may refuse to go along with it, as he may refuse to believe a declarative sentence.

Obviously, the meaning of nondeclarative expressions cannot be defined in the same way as that of declarative sentences (the meaning of a sentence is that it is true if such and such is the case). An exclamation or a command cannot be "true" or "false." Both, however, involve a linguistic convention, and both can be related to certain standards of meaning under that linguistic convention. An exclamation, for instance, may be judged as to whether it is sincere or not; its meaning is that it is sincere if its author really experiences the emotion, the expression of which is the exclamation, under a linguistic convention. Commands may be interpreted in a similar fashion; we may define the meaning of a command by saying that it is sincerely meant if its author really wishes the addressee to act in a certain way. We can say that a command is "effective" if the addressee acts in a certain way; that it is "appropriate" if the addressee may be expected to obey it; otherwise it is "preposterous."

Symbols in general have a strong suggestive power; declarative sentences frequently are believed almost automatically; commands also tend to be obeyed automatically. Yet, their meaning as such is not that they are so believed or obeyed. Symbols may be used to control the behavior of partners, but their meaning is independent of their success as instruments of control.[13]

13. This conclusion is directed against Alan H. Gardiner's interpretation of language symbols: "they are primarily instrumental . . . their function is to force or cajole the listener into looking at certain things" (*The Theory of Speech and Language* [Oxford, 1932], p. 33). What I deny is not that symbols have instrumental uses but that their meaning is their instrumental use.

CHAPTER IV

LEARNING AND FREEDOM

1. Meaning and Representation

THE "meaning relationship," as we have tried to characterize it, lacks the feature most prominent in the customary analysis of meaning: the one-to-one correspondence between the "sign" and that which is "designated" by it. This is inevitable, since we have started from the examination of "good" choices; and in these no such clear-cut separation between the manifest "sign" and something non-manifest but "indicated" by the sign can be spelled out. When the animal reacts to something in the environment that appears to be "edible," it does not isolate completely manifest surface features as set off against something equally clear-cut but not immediately present. We cannot draw the line separating the manifestly given from the "inferred," potential sequel. The point is precisely that anything that is "given" is given as a vehicle of meaning, that is, of potential satisfaction. The organism does not *infer* the potential sequel from some brute datum, meaningless in itself.[1] Whatever is identified is identified as a "such-and-such" related to some meaning-oriented activity. What we call "sign" (a meaningful, interpretable datum) is not a sign "of" something not in the data but a patterning or structuring of the prevailing situation. Nothing can be definitely identified in the environment except in terms of such a structuring or patterning. Nothing is perceived as a mere datum; what is perceived is always perceived-in-a-role.

To consider a sign as essentially a "representation" of something other than itself means to break down this unity of the "role" in which

1. Cf. Ernest R. Hilgard, *Theories of Learning* (New York: Appleton-Century-Crofts, 1948), p. 332. Hilgard emphasizes in this connection that the "meanings" are attributed to the "percepts" on the basis of previous learning or experience. This may be true in every case, although Gestalt psychologists stress the "innate" character of many meaning attributions. Our point is that, when the "percepts" get endowed with "meaning" in the course of experience, it is not a clearly isolated "pure percept" which gradually acquires "meanings" but that either the percept becomes isolated as an identifiable object *pari passu* with a "meaning" being attributed to it, or a percept-with-meaning acquires additional meanings.

things are perceived. It would indeed seem indispensable for scientific analysis to separate the truly "given" from the "role" aspects of the percept; how else could we overcome the essentially subjective nature of role attributions? The unfortunate thing is only that, whatever conceptual framework we adopt for identifying the "truly given," we still proceed in terms of role attributions. The datum considered "merely" as that which affects measuring devices in a certain way is also identified in terms of a "role." Has subjectivity been overcome? In a sense, yes; for measuring devices are incapable of learning —their reactions oscillate around some mean value but do not get "better" with repetition. A measuring "error" is not a learning "error" or malfunction which we may hope to eliminate. Since measuring lacks the progressive and flexible nature of learning, we can say that the "role" that the datum plays as a purely measurable entity is a standardized role—a role neutral with regard to any "demand" imposed upon the environment. But we cannot say that, if we cast the items of our environment in such standardized roles, we get hold of their "real" nature, whereas the attribution of other roles through interpretation-in-behavior gives us only "relative" and "subjective" knowledge. For one thing, "objective" or "neutral" roles are also roles predicated upon interaction between the environmental item and some measuring device or sense organ. For another, it would seem hazardous to identify the "reality" or "real nature" of things solely with their interactions with mechanisms which do not "learn." If the objects we study do not themselves exhibit "learning" on the basis of demands (as inanimate things in nature as a rule do not), this identification of their "real" nature with their interaction with similarly non-learning devices will not lead us astray.[2] But what about objects whose behavior is flexible and involves learning? I think that in their case the identification of "reality" with what is recorded by measuring devices leads to faulty models.

Defining signs as entities "representing" something clearly separated from them is characteristic of such models. A model of this kind explains learning behavior in this way: Let us assume a set of items A to which the organism reacts in a satisfactory way instinctively, without any learning—or at least without need for any *further* learning. In addition, let us consider another set of items S to which no such

2. When, as in quantum physics, the interaction between the measuring device and the measured object affects the latter's behavior and something like "learning" emerges on both sides, the contention that the measuring devices give us the "real" essence" or "real nature" of the object is immediately subverted.

"unconditioned" response takes place. Initially, the A's have a perceived value or attractiveness; the S's have none. Now, however, some S is being presented every time an A is about to emerge. This near-simultaneity causes the organism to "learn" to consider an S as a "sign" for an A, that is, to respond to it as it originally had responded to A. By virtue of proximity, the response to A has been grafted onto the originally neutral S. This is the schema of "stimulus-response" learning (Thorndike, Guthrie).

This schema might be refined to eliminate the obvious objection that an organism is far from always responding to the "sign" as it does to the "signified" event. According to the revised model, the originally meaningless S's, if presented together with the A's for a long time, will not necessarily evolve the response which A always evokes without "learning," but some "preparatory" response (Morris). For instance, the presence of S will lead them to "expect" A, or they will scan their environment for S in order to be guided toward A.

It seems to me that this model does not represent the learning process correctly, for it presupposes that there are, for the organism, clearly identified S's before any "association" between the S's and the A's is set up. Both before and after, S is the same object, the only difference being that it becomes "associated with" something nonneutral, something attractive in itself. Also, A remains what it always has been; it is not A's "attractiveness" that is learned but merely the route to be followed to get to A. I do not deny that much sign learning exhibits this character: something fully identified in itself becomes endowed with additional "meaning" by becoming associated with a presently or potentially available object or mode of satisfaction. But it seems doubtful to me that *all* learning takes place exclusively in this fashion. Sometimes, I believe, an object which lacks any particular "meaning" as sign correlate is tentatively seized in scanning the environment and is found to conceal a present possibility of enjoyment. Then the object which originally meant "nothing in particular" becomes meaningful in retrospect—not as a "sign" fully distinct from something "signified" but as a correlate. Or it may happen that a correlate functioning in a certain role reveals itself as also being capable of playing another role. In this case the correlate itself becomes transformed: it becomes identifiable (or interpretable-in-behavior) in terms of its new role rather than in a mere "signifying" role.

There are, to be sure, situations in which a perceived event is, in a real sense, a "sign" *for* another event, as, for instance, smoke is a sign for fire burning somewhere or a dark cloud is a sign of impending rain. In these cases we can clearly distinguish something manifest from another thing not yet actually manifest, the former being "neutral" in those respects in which the nonmanifest thing heralded by it is not neutral. A smoke without fire does not burn me, and a cloud without rain does not drench me, but both indicate the existence or the advent of some *other* thing that might have such an effect. Such sign functions, as we see, approximate the "association" model of learned meanings fairly well. In fact, these are the only cases in which we really can observe something like "*A* representing *B*" in actual life. But this does not mean that the process in which the significance of smoke as an indicator of fire is learned actually follows the associationist schema. I suppose that, if organisms ever arrive at perceiving such sign relationships by pure "learning" (that is, without receiving information and without engaging in goal-directed operations of causal analysis), they will proceed by "dissociation" rather than by "association." That is, having perceived *A* and *B* together, they may learn to respond to *A* alone and to *B* alone in a different way than to *A*+*B*. To "learn" to see smoke as a sign of fire means to discover a *different* way of responding to "smoke alone" than to "smoke plus fire," this different reaction being somehow related to the smoke-plus-fire reaction. I do not believe that even higher animals will be able to learn to dissociate smoke alone from fire plus smoke in this way, although they might. But they certainly learn other sign relationships in this dissociatory way. Thus, for a dog, "master plus stick" will certainly elicit a different response from "master alone" and "stick alone." The response to "master alone" will be marked by trust and obedience, that to "stick alone" possibly by some vague apprehension (I have known cats always to keep at a respectful distance from brooms), and to master plus stick by sheer abject terror. The "stick," then, is certainly a sign of an imminent beating; *A* represents *B*. And, once this sign function is set up, the stick will be identified as a more or less "neutral" object when it is perceived alone, while it will function as a "sign" in the master's hand. But the sign function has not been "learned" by having the stick, as a clearly identified neutral object, become gradually meaningful by being associated with the experience of beating. On the contrary, it was suddenly discovered as a source of pain and became more "neutral" as a result of dissociation.

2. Conditioning and Learning

The case of a "conditioned response"[3] is another illustration of the way in which A may be said to "represent" B. In this case the "associationist" schema is precisely followed: A kind of stimulus which originally elicits no particular response is repeatedly presented together with another type of stimulus which—being the "correlate" of some significant experience, either of satisfactory or of frustrating character—always evokes a specific response. This will have the result that after some time the associated, formerly neutral, stimulus, if presented alone, will for a while "automatically" call forth the specific response which the organism had always performed in the presence of the "significant" stimulus. Here "representation" has a fairly literal meaning: the formerly neutral or "conditioned" stimulus acts like a "representative" or proxy for the significant or "unconditioned" stimulus. The organism does not respond to the former as a "sign" of the latter but, in a way, treats the conditioned stimulus as if it were the "correlate" itself. This has little to do with sign learning, such as the learning of the "rewarding" route—when a route becomes stabilized, the signs or "guideposts" which the organism learns are by no means treated as proxies of the "correlate" of the satisfactory experience but simply as guideposts, as signals for going straight ahead, or turning right, or pulling a lever, etc. In the conditioned response case, what happens is not this incorporation of meanings into a behavior sequence but the appropriation of the correlate role by something which is not the correlate.

Actually, of course, such "appropriation of the correlate role" by a "proxy stimulus" never takes place in a full and literal sense. For the organism duped by the conditioned stimulus never performs the *full* response evoked by the unconditioned "correlate." It performs only part of the response, or rather it performs nothing at all; something happens to it. The prototype of the "conditioned response" is the secretion of saliva which occurs in hungry dogs when they hear a whistling sound that had previously accompanied or preceded their dinner. Now I submit that salivating is no "behavior," just as blushing and squirming are not; we should have the "same" response to the

3. Cf. I. P. Pavlov, *Conditioned Reflexes* (London: Oxford University Press, 1927); Ernest L. Hilgard and Donald G. Marquis, *Conditioning and Learning* (New York and London: D. Appleton–Century Co., 1940); Clark Leonard Hull, *Principles of Behavior* (New York and London: D. Appleton–Century Co., 1943); Gregory H. S. Razran, "Conditioned Responses," *Archives of Psychology*, No. 191 (1935).

whistling sound as to the food if the dogs also ate the former, which they most certainly never do. How an occurrence which is no response at all in the behavioral sense can be thought of as the basic phenomenon in the learning of new ways of behaving is incomprehensible to me.

This is not said to belittle the importance of the discovery of "conditioned responses." To be sure, it is interesting to know that sensory stimuli which "in themselves" affect only sense organs will set secretory glands in motion, if they are of a kind which previously had been presented in conjunction with other stimuli that had activated those glands. It is certainly legitimate to deduce from this, as Pavlov did, that the entire organism is an integrated whole and that stimulation of sense organs has consequences going far beyond the possible generation of voluntary muscle movements. And if salivation in itself is not a "response" or a way of "behavior," it is, of course, not irrelevant to behavior. Secretory processes of all kinds accompany or stimulate many "behavorial" responses, and it is certainly important to study secretory phenomena associated with various types and phases of behavior. What seems to me unjustified is merely to confuse categories, and to say that, if stimulus S_1 and stimulus S_2 result in the occurrence of the same secretory process, we are in the presence of an identical "response" to S_1 and S_2. That a new kind of response is learned in the way that an already established response is "transferred" from one stimulus to the other because they occur together is precisely what the conditioned response experiments do *not* show.

We may call a *learned* response (turning right in the maze, pulling a lever) a "conditioned" response, and it is certainly true that such a "conditioned" response will become stabilized if and as long as it "works," that is, if and as long as it is rewarded. But the word "conditioned" does not mean the same thing when we use it to refer to "rewarded response" as when we use it to refer to a secretory process activated by a sensory stimulus. When we talk about a response which becomes stabilized because it is reliably rewarded, we refer to a choice from among available possible responses, none of which is the response performed in the presence of the reward itself. When we talk about the secretory process or "reflex," we do not refer to "behavior," that is, to an interaction between an organism and its environment in which some pattern or structure is projected onto the external environment. We deal merely with processes within the "internal environment" of the organism. There is the formal simi-

larity between the two kinds of processes that show both "reinforcement" if they are followed by a reward and "extinction" if no reward
follows. But there is also a formal difference: in the case of response
learning, the response that is so "reinforced" or "extinguished" is a
choice among environmental routes which does not form part of the
"unconditioned" response, whereas, in the case of reflex-conditioning,
the event which is "reinforced" and "extinguished" is also part of the
"unconditioned" response.[4] Obviously, behavioral learning cannot be
explained in terms of reflex-conditioning, for the phenomenon to be
explained is the appearance and stabilization of a new type of response
rather than the association of an already existing type of response with
a new stimulus.

In the reflex case the "conditioned" response occurs automatically
when it takes place the first time and then tapers off if it is not accompanied by a reward. In the case of behavioral learning, neither the
first occurrence of the "conditioned" response nor its stabilization is
"automatic" in the same sense. This point needs some more detailed
discussion.

Hull says: "We must regard the processes of learning as wholly
automatic," explaining this to mean that "the learning must result
from the mere interaction between the organism, including its equip-
ment of action tendencies at the moment, and its environment, internal as well as external."[5] But on this definition of "automatic," all
behavior, even that involving choice and deliberation, would be
automatic; in fact, this is what Hull seems to mean, for "nonautomatic" behavior, according to him, would be one guided by some
occult, outside agency which is distinct from the "action tendencies"
of the organism and the impulses coming from the "internal and external" environment. I believe, however, that we can distinguish
"nonautomatic" from "automatic" behavior in accordance with generally accepted usage, without having to appeal to "occult" agencies.

To clarify the problem, we must first distinguish between two
types of response which a system may perform, both of which may
be described as "automatic" but which differ essentially between
themselves.

The first type of automatic response is that of the automaton: this
is a system constructed in such a way that, when a specific impulse

4. The difference between these two types of learning is stressed by B. F. Skinner,
The Behavior of Organisms (New York, 1938).

5. *Op. cit.,* p. 69.

reaches it, it "cannot help" reacting by a specific sequence of motions, prescribed by the arrangement of its parts. This type of "automatic" response may show a considerable degree of adaptivity and flexibility; if the construction of the automaton includes a feed-back circuit, it may in a way modify the impulses it will admit and thus respond differently and "adaptively," according to the way in which the impulse (or, as we may say, "input") affects it. In any case, however, the response is determined by the nature of the input and the construction of a mechanism—it is "specific" to both.

Organisms, of course, often perform such "automatic" responses; many of the processes going on in their "internal environment" are automatic in this sense. In addition to this, organisms also perform random movements (Hull's "oscillations"). These may, of course, also be considered "automatic," but not in the sense of a *specific* automatic response, determined by the input and the structure of the internal environment. Now which kind of automatism is meant when we say that the learning process is "automatic"?

"Specific" automatism with a "feed-back" feature is found in the case of reflex-conditioning. But in behavioral, trial-and-error learning, we see something different. There is no *specific* automatic response to begin with; instead, we start with a more or less "random" sequence of responses, and the learning process consists in reducing the randomness. Some of the responses available to the organism are singled out and come to be performed exclusively; the others gradually disappear. The end-result is that a certain response singled out from among a number of others will become "habitual" whenever a stimulus is presented (provided that it is rewarded). This habitual occurrence of the learned response looks like a "specific" automatism. Thus we might try to characterize trial-and-error learning as a kind of process in which an initial "nonspecific" or "random" type of functioning is supplanted by a "specific" automatism. If this process is, as Hull says, an "automatic" one, it represents a *third* type of automatism—neither "random" nor "specific" but a combination of the two. It seems to me that a term which has three such completely different meanings is not very useful; in any case, whenever the term is used, it should be made clear in which of the three senses it is meant. I would add that, while "specific" and "random" automatisms seem to be clear-cut, "real" entities, the third type is a rather hypothetical one, much in need of clarification.

But can a habitual response be conceived as a specific automatism? In other words: Does the acquisition of a "rewarded" behavioral route mean that a response is performed unfailingly upon presentation of a stimulus, and not at all when the stimulus is absent? Experimental evidence shows that this is not the case. It seems, in fact, that when animals have learned to perform a response in a satisfactory way, they have learned *more* than muscular habits; they have learned "meanings" imbedded in a behavioral "map." Tolman and his associates demonstrated this theme in a number of experiments. In one series of experiments about "place learning," they modified the routes available to rats in getting at food, without displacing the food box itself. The rats then preferred that route which was best under the new circumstances, although these routes had not been learned (or even identified) in the original situation.[6] Tolman speaks of "insight" in characterizing this mode of behavior, and I do not see how one can avoid such a characterization.

But even when no insight is involved, the concept of "specific" automatism does not seem to fit in well with what we see in behavioral learning. There is not just one input which enforces a response, given a pre-existent arrangement of the parts of the system which is being stimulated. Rather, the system itself gropes its way toward coping with the inputs; it summons certain organizational principles available to it to this end. Of course, these organizational principles and this readiness to adapt behavior to the environment are somehow inherent in the organism; they represent no outside

6. Cf. Hilgard, *op. cit.*, pp. 268 ff. Hilgard comments: "The experiment shows rather clearly that the animal is oriented in space, that it 'knows its way around.' It has learned not just how to run along a path, but where the goal is in the experimental room. It is important to remark . . . that such a demonstration, while it accords fully with Tolman's theory, does not necessarily exclude alternative explanations. Hull, for example, has attempted to deduce just such behavior upon the basis of habit-family hierarchies built up through experience in free space. . . . The conception of a habit-family is so much like that of cognitive structure that it might be argued that Hull has in fact capitulated to Tolman's theory, although Hull believes himself to have deduced it from more elementary principles." It seems to me that on Hull's hypothesis, whenever a response is learned, the way in which the response should be varied under altered circumstances is learned right along with it. This principle is certainly valid within a given range: pure mechanical repetition of the same reponse would be both terribly inadaptive and impracticable. The learning of a response, then, would seem to imply some "generalization," e.g., in terms of preserving the same "Gestalt" in differently structured action fields. But this principle does not seem to account for cases in which the Gestalt of the response itself is lost. Then, it seems to me, we can no longer speak of acting within the framework of a "response-family."

occult agencies. But they also lack the passivity which seems to me to be implied in the concept of automatism. The "learned" response is not an "enforced" response.

True specific automatism, I think, never characterizes full responses learned in a trial-and-error fashion. They may be habitual and thus superficially resemble specific automatism; but if the situation in which they occur is varied, it will be possible to see that more than specific automatism is involved. Paradoxically enough, however, it seems that in other, "higher," types of learning, specific automatisms *in fact* are being set up.

Let us take human learning involving "symbols" and their "meanings," such as learning to read. This is a type of learning different from the trial-and-error type; for the association of the "correct" response with the stimuli that are "learned" is not based on any "reward," needs no " reinforcement," and does not get "extinguished" if it is not "reinforced." The solving of the task (which is "understood" to begin with) is, in a sense, its own reward. (Of course, rewards may stimulate the learning process in this case, too; the letters the child learns may be made of marzipan, to be eaten when they are mastered. But the child does not learn *that* the letter A is something made of marzipan that it can eat upon performing the conditioned stimulus of uttering an "a" sound. In fact, the whole purpose of learning the ABC's would be defeated if such disastrous beliefs were implanted.) Now what occurs in learning the ABC's is something remarkable indeed: after a series of goal-directed, deliberate efforts, the "reading" of letters and words will become an "automatic" process. And this will be a true, specific automatism, characterized, to be sure, by "generalization" in terms of Gestalt but without depending on any "reinforcing" feedback. The letter and word "Gestalt" will be true automatic "inputs" (we have called these "instructions") such that a specific kind of response ("reading" with understanding) will be performed unfailingly upon presenting the stimulus. Once one has learned to read, he will *have to* read whatever written text is presented at a suitable distance. No deliberate effort will be able to suppress the response—this is very different in the case of learned adaptive "habits," which can be interdicted if one tries deliberately to deviate from them or is punished for following them. Such learned "reading" skills can be forgotten if not practiced for a long time; but they need no specific reinforcement to remain stable, and they cannot be shut off at will. Nor can anybody who knows how to read be "untaught" by administering painful stimuli whenever he reads. He may forego the *habit* of reading, but he will not lose the ability or rather the automatic performance of the response when the stimulus is presented. Reading, then, is very much like a conditioned reflex, except that it is not "conditioned" by rewards and not "extinguished" by their absence. We may call it a "learned neural reflex."

But, although the result of learning may be the acquisition of a quasi-automatic habit or a genuinely automatic neural reflex, it cannot be said that behavior based upon learning is always either habitual or reflexive. Organisms perform "habitual" actions on the basis of learning as long as their environment remains standardized. When the behavioral field is "turned around," the *same* learning may lead to behavior which is not habitual but must be "figured out," for the way to the rewarding "food box" must now be found from a different point of departure. If the chickens are always fed in front of the porch and the porch is opposite the coop, the chickens will run straight ahead from the coop, expecting to be fed. But when the coop is moved toward the left, the chickens will not run straight ahead—they will run slantwise toward the poch. Habitual responses can in this way be modified in accordance with the situation. (This is also the point of Tolman's "place-learning" experiments mentioned above.)

What happens here? I think that, when a learned habitual response is not or "would not be" rewarding, the organism will perform a new "scanning"—but this will no longer be a perfectly random scanning of the environment. The scanning will have a "goal": the discovery of a familiar sign object, the significance of which has been learned. When the sign object comes into sight and is identified, it will repattern the behavioral field and define the new "good" route.

What trial-and-error learning gives rise to, then, is not necessarily habitual behavior but a behavior in which goal-directed scanning alternates with goal-directed choice. (We may call this the "modulation" of the habit.) Behavior is habitual, that is, quasi-automatic, as long as it is not "modulated," i.e., not punctuated by new scanning-and-choice sequences. It is usually possible to distinguish clearly between the "habitual" and the "modulational" cycle.

In this respect, too, "rule" learning (such as the learning of the alphabet) shows a striking difference from trial-and-error learning. In this case we see practically no quasi-automatic habit being set up, possibly to be "modulated" by goal-directed scanning. Instead of habits, we find true reflexes, immediately grafted onto an entirely non-habitual way of functioning. When we read a text, the neural reflex is, of course, not *all* that happens; it is never the *full* response, except when we do not want to read "for information" but just look idly at some written text. Usually, we *do* read for information, however; we "interpret" our text in a contextual way. But this is never a matter of habit. If I read in the newspaper about the latest goings-on in Washington and incorporate this information into my understanding of what the state of things is, I am not performing something habitual—it is not a "habit" of mine to take cognizance of what Senator X said yesterday. Or let us consider the learning of the rules of a game. To be sure, the rules become automatized; in chess, I "cannot help" seeing the knight as knight and the bishop as bishop. But when I move them in play, the individual moves are not determined "by habit" (except, perhaps, in so far as the choice of an opening is concerned; but such "conventional" action could still be differentiated from habit acquired *by* learning). The beauty of games is precisely that "habitual" action is not rewarded but penalized.[7] One learns to play a game by automatizing the rule; one learns to play it well by getting rid of habits that one may have acquired.

The way the game is played is never a matter of "habit"; in the game situation every constellation which arises has to be met on its merits. The play of the game involves a rapid sequence of "goal-directed" scanning responses alternating with decisions. Formalized games like chess and card games do not, however, represent really "contextual" behavior. Everything that happens must, and can, be interpreted in the light of the "rules of the game" alone; reality outside the game situation exerts no influence upon the process. It seems to me that there is considerable difference, in this respect, between "completely formalized" and "incompletely formalized" games—the former being those which require no umpire, and the latter those which do. In a game which is not completely formalized, the actual moves are not reliably limited to the alternatives foreseen by the rules. In order to "interpret" a move in the light of a rule, one must judge some "state of the world" contextually. The difference between the two types of games means that, while one might construct an automaton that would play chess, no automaton could play baseball, one of the reasons being that it could not argue its case with the umpire.

What is involved in specifically human, that is, true contextual, behavior? It exhibits, first of all, the "broken sequence" with which we are already familiar—alternation between "goal-directed scanning" and "choice." In contextual behavior, however, the "choices" are based not only on "interpretation-in-behavior" and not only on interpretation in terms of "rules" alone but also on explicit "judgment." This means that, in order to make a choice, the subject has to determine the existing state of the world and judge it in terms of rules and standards. In this process a prevailing situation must be related to classes of situations in the light of factual information. Here we are in a region beyond "habit" and beyond specific automatism.

It seems to me that it is meaningful to speak of "automatism," both with reference to some specific automatism and with reference to "scanning" behavior. Further, we can attribute "quasi-automatic" character to behavior based on acquired habits. All these forms of automatic or quasi-automatic behavior can show great flexibility, adaptiveness, and intelligence; and human behavior has its share of all such forms of automatic and quasi-automatic functioning. Its truly contextual sequences, however, do not fall under any description of either full automatism or quasi-automatism. They are not instances of the former, because they cannot be elicited by "inputs" in the form of "instructions"; and they are not instances of the latter, because they do not occur from "habit." They must, then, be termed "free."

3. Freedom

What is this "freedom"? Is it sheer "unpredictability"? It is not, for random scanning behavior is also unpredictable without being "free." Is it self-determination? It is not, for the choice characterizing contextual behavior need in no way be "gratuitous." Is it "acting according to a rule"? It is not, for man's world is not limited to alternatives foreseen by his rules. Is it "power"? It is not, for goals may be reached by automatic functioning too, while, on the other hand, freedom may manifest itself in a renunciation of goals. Freedom, I think, contains all these ingredients, but its own essence is elusive and mysterious. Freedom itself is free; it brooks no confinement within formulas.

Free contextual action certainly has an element of unpredictability. Even with maximum knowledge of a human being's predispositions, goals, and standards, we cannot foresee his judgment and his choice in every constellation of circumstances that may arise. This is not merely a matter of the practical difficulty of anticipating every possible future constellation of circumstances and of projecting the individual's pattern of goals and standards onto the future. To do the latter, we must reckon with the fact that individual goals and standards change during the adaptive process; thus, if we want to predict future choices, it is not enough to know what the individual's present goals and standards are; we must also know how these standards will be modified in the future. This is difficult to achieve; but let us suppose that all these practical and theoretical difficulties are overcome. Even then we shall still be far from our goal of complete prediction, for we shall have attained only maximum predictability in terms of "meaning." This is not enough, for acts and choices depend also on "meaning-free" causal factors; and the trouble is that it seems impossible to embrace "meaningful" and "meaning-free" factors in one single theory. Because of this, complete prediction of behavior seems to me infeasible on principle.

I do not think, however, that "freedom" is the same as unpredictability. Free, truly contextual choice may be *more* predictable than an automatic response. Interpretive concepts give us a basis for predictions where mere descriptive concepts or indices are relatively barren of predictive value. In a game situation, for instance, we cannot foresee with complete certainty every move that the individual players will make; but if we know the rules of the game and interpret the situation in their light, our predictions will be better than they would be otherwise.

Free behavior also has an element of self-determination: the ultimate choices are not fully "constrained" by extraneous factors. The process of self-determination, however, as a rule presupposes person-to-person interaction. Its prototype is the "educational" situation in which a personality ideal is chosen on the basis of identification. It is not the isolated individual who determines himself in a perfectly gratuitous way; he achieves his autonomy by being "educated."

Acting according to an internalized rule is likewise an ingredient of free behavior. One could not act contextually without observing the rules of the game. All information has to be evaluated in terms of rules. But the rules never completely determine a contextual choice. To derive their implications with regard to the situational problem at hand, a judgment must be made.

Finally, an element of power is essential to free behavior. Freedom implies a capacity to say No, to resist both urges and habits, on the one hand, and "instructions," on the other. But we cannot say that we are "free" only to the extent that we are *resisting* some outside agency or some inner urge. For a compulsion to say "No" would make us just as dependent as a compulsion to say "Yes." Free behavior may manifest itself in co-operation and voluntary self-subordination as well as in resistance, rebellion, and protest. The exercise of power, on the other hand, need not be a mark of "freedom." Brute forces may crush free man; and groups can maximize their power by abolishing freedom within themselves.

If contextual behavior is essentially "free," how can we hope ever to construct a theory that will account for it? It seems to me that it would be just as wrong to renounce all theorizing about contextual behavior as to aim at a theory that would enable us to "explain" and to "predict' all that may happen in the process of free, interpersonal intercourse. At best, our theory of free behavior will give us partial explanations and partial prediction. The question is which type of "partially" explanatory and predictive theory will serve us best.

One type of such "partially" explanatory and predictive theory would be a *statistical* theory of behavior. Suppose that in every situation a certain number of choices is available to each subject, and we may observe the frequency with which each of these choices is made; and we can establish various probability patterns, showing how certain frequencies of choices are "clustered" together.[8] This will give us hypotheses about "latent" attitude groups or "latent" personality factors. It is important to realize, however, that the establishment of a latent structure is not yet a theory—it is not even an "incomplete" theory in the sense that it will provide us with a basis for explanations and predictions of a "probabilistic" nature. For in each case the "meaning" of the latent factors or structures has to be "interpreted," either with reference to a more comprehensive *theory* of the group under consideration or with reference to the value standards and attitudes underlying the choices we are studying. The "best" theory of free behavior we may hope to develop will include "interpretation" as well as statistical analysis.

8. For techniques of the statistical analysis of attitudes and choices see S. Stouffer (ed.), *Measurement and Prediction* ("Studies in Social Psychology in World War II," Vol. IV [Princeton, 1950]).

III. MEANING AND LANGUAGE

CHAPTER V

SYMBOLS

1. THE MEANING OF NAMES

IN ANALYZING the role of "signs" and "meanings" in behavior, we have found that the schema "*A* represents *B*" does not fit the process of interpreting the meaning of signs in the situation. An isolated event may serve as an "indication" for another, if we know that they are causally connected; but this causal analysis in itself is no "interpretation" of "meaning."

Let us now turn to communicative meanings. Is such separation possible in *their* case? In other words, can we characterize the "meaning" of a symbol, or of a symbolic expression, by means of a two-termed relation in which one thing—a word or an expression—"means" or "represents" or "designates" another? And what is this "naming" or "designating" relation in itself?

Of course, we can in a way distinguish "names" from the entities which they name. Persons have proper names, and the name, while it is something quite distinct from the person, in some way "represents" him. But in what way? It is obvious that the name is not a "sign" for the person or a "representative" of the person in a situation. We cannot say that the "proper" or "good" response for the name, whenever the name occurs in a communication, is a "proper" response in the presence of the bearer of the name. Nor does the occurrence of the name in general herald the presence of the bearer or "structure" the situation in such a way as to define "good" responses toward the bearer as a correlate. But all this merely amounts to saying that a proper name is a "symbol" and not a "sign." The question is: What kind of symbol?

We said that the meaning of a symbol is given by the rules of a language. But it appears that the "meaning" of a proper name is not in any essential sense part of the rules of any language. To be sure, some proper names have different versions in different languages—the name of the Matterhorn is "Cervin" in French, and the name of London is "Londres"; we have to learn such conventions when we learn French. But such conventions are not essential to the rules of the different languages; in a sense, proper names are untranslatable, and we learn their "meaning" in a different way than we learn the "meaning" of nouns. We can (to speak only about essentials) know and correctly apply all the rules of a language without learning any proper name. Proper names, then, are symbols not belonging to any single language: they are an alien body in all languages. Or we might say that, besides language proper or "word-language," we also use a different kind of language: a "name-language."

All word-languages are almost complete in themselves: we could refer to every object by using only words rather than names, provided only that, in addition to the words, we also adopt a convention establishing a co-ordinate system for common reference. In a maximally pure word-language, the only "proper name" would be that of the origin of the co-ordinate system. All references to individual objects could then be made in terms of co-ordinate values, which would be "words," not names. We may say, in this sense, that, while it is possible (according to *Principia mathematica*) to replace all "descriptions" by "names," it is also possible to replace all "names" by "descriptions." This latter procedure would, of course, be suicidal for formalized languages in which "names" are considered to be the values for all nonpredicate variables occurring in sentential functions. But our actual languages are not of this kind; *their* nonpredicate variables do not take names as their values according to a rule specified for the language. An actual language cannot be analyzed by enumerating, say, its nonpredicate variables and then giving all the "names" which can be the values of these variables. To learn the meaning of the word '*homme*' in French does not imply the learning of any rule by which a French sentence in which the variable *homme* is bound could be translated into another, enumerating all the names of the individuals falling into the domain over which the variable is bound. If we want to replace the bound variable by an enumeration of individual names, we can do so, but, in doing this, we no longer apply a substitution rule within the French language.

Most words in actual languages refer to kinds of things such that the individual objects falling under them "have" no proper names. It would be a senseless undertaking, in actual speech, to replace descriptions by names; there are simply not enough names to go around, and communication would be impossible if we tried to refer to each individual object by a proper name. The "co-ordinate numbers" which we *might* use to identify individual objects are not "names" in the *Principia mathematica* sense but genuine *descriptions*; $P_{x, y, z}$ means *that* P which has such and such a position "in relation to" the origin of the co-ordinate system in which x, y, and z are defined. Now my position is that, for communication among the members of a language community, it would not be sufficient to use only such "descriptions"; other expressions, consisting of words only, are also necessary. But it would also be impracticable to use only "names" instead of "words." Names in a nonformalized language are exceptional cases; they are not the fundamental components of such languages.

The reason for this is easy to see. The "fundamental" components of a language are those symbols which are sufficiently well understood by all members of the language community to enable any individual member to "interpret" any communication containing them. But proper names can have no such unlimited currency throughout a language community. For a communication containing a proper name can be interpreted only by those who are aware of some set of circumstances characterizing the individual object designated by the name; personal "acquaintance" with the object is one type of "awareness" of this kind, though by no means the only one. This requisite knowledge about individual objects is, of necessity, unevenly distributed in any language community. We can require of all members of a language community that they be familiar with all the different properties and clusters of properties which recur in the situation common to all of them and which are differentiated by words; and these requirements are embodied in the "deictic rules" of the language. But we cannot require of all members of a language community that they be able to identify by name all the individual objects which "have" names in the community. We may say, in this sense, that names have more or less limited currency in actual language communities; the "name-languages" are sublanguages restricted to "name-language communities"—communities including those, and only those, to whom a certain name "means something." Such a "name-language community" could be defined for each name; and the boundaries of the name-language communities are constantly in flux. For some names the name-language community overlaps with the word-language community.

In an actual language community, only few objects can be dignified with names of their own. There are certain conventions governing the conferring of proper names. The objects which "should" have names of their own are those having some unique importance, such that singling them out from all others is a matter of actual concern for some and is potentially a matter of concern to the community at large. Thus the "naming" function (whatever it is) involves more than mere symbol reference; it involves the conferring of some exceptional rank or dignity. The "named" object is one for which no other object could be substituted in certain respects of more or less public import. Naming involves a hierarchical relationship. Among inanimate objects, only prominent features of the celestial or terrestrial landscape have proper names; among living beings, only men and such individual animals or plants as have some unique relationship to the users of the name. There is a certain flexibility in this matter of conferring names; members of a family may single out domestic animals by name, and such names will have no currency outside the family group. But geographical, astronomical, and personal names are "public" names. This does not mean that their name-language communities embrace the entire public; it means only that they may be used in communications of public importance, such as scientific or legal communications.

We have seen that individual objects may be referred to in communications either by a "description" or by a "name." Each name is —to use Quine's terminology—"cognitively synonymous" with any of a set of word descriptions phrased in *some* word-language; these word descriptions can be broken down into a "word part," on the one hand, and a "name of reference," on the other. The name of reference may be, as we said above, that of the origin of a co-ordinate system. Now what is the "communicative meaning" of descriptions and of names? We may try to analyze these meanings in terms of "extension" and "intension." The "extension" of any term is the actual set of objects to which it may be applied; and to say that two terms are "cognitively synonymous" means that they have the same "extension." They apply to the same objects; hence, if any one of a set of cognitively synonymous terms is replaced in a sentence by any other, the truth value of the sentence will not be altered. But this does not mean that such cognitively synonymous terms have the same "meaning," for their "intensional" meaning may be different, even if their "extension" (or "extensional" meaning) is the same.

It is comparatively easy to give an idea about the "intension" or "intensional meaning" of a description. The intensional meaning of a description consists in specifying one definite operation by which an individual object can be "singled out" among all the individual objects of the world.[1] It is obvious that, for each object, indefinitely many descriptions could be used, since there are many different operations by which we can single out one and the same object from among others. We can, for instance, "describe" New York at will in terms of the interval separating it from any other city of the globe that we may happen to choose as our point of reference. Each of these descriptions specifies a different operation, and each results in singling out the same city—the "extension" of all descriptions is the same, while their "intension" is different. (We see that "intension" has nothing to do with subjective associations or actual thought contents "evoked" by an expression; it is a rule-specifying-a-good-response, like all "meanings.")

But what is the "intensional meaning" of a name? Proper names obviously "single out" an individual object from among all objects of the world; but they do not specify any definite operation by which this singling-out can be effected. We may say in this sense that, while the "extensional" meaning of a name is clear-cut (there is just one object to which it may be properly applied), its "intensional meaning" is indefinite (the name as such leaves open the way in which the actual identification might be performed). Thus any description gives at least a hint concerning the way in which one might go about seeking out the object to which it refers: they can be "understood," in a way, without the object to which they refer being known. But a "mere" name is a blank; it "means nothing" to someone who knows none of the descriptions that "go with it."[2]

We may also say, alternatively, that the "intensional meaning" of the name is the class of the descriptions "cognitively" (or "extensionally") synonymous with it. This does not mean, of course, that the

1. This definition of "intensional meaning" corresponds to what C. I. Lewis calls the "signification" of a term. "Intension," in Lewis' terminology, is "the conjunction of all terms each of which must be applicable to anything to which the given term would be correctly applicable" (*An Analysis of Knowledge and Valuation* [La Salle, Ill.: Open Court Publishing Co., 1946], p. 39).

2. Of course, "descriptions" contain *names* as terms of reference: "Mr. Smith's cow," or "the city which lies at thirty miles due west from New York." And to someone not familiar with the object *named* in the description as term of reference, the name as such is a blank, and therefore such a person could not identify the object described with the help of the description alone. But at least he will have some idea about how the object could be singled out, once the term of reference was known. Part of the identifying operation at least is defined. The name alone, however, offers not even a partial clue; to identify the object named, a search (or scanning operation) must be instituted from scratch.

name must be a "blank" unless one knows *all* the descriptions referring to the same object; nobody can know every possible description of an object (that is, every single operation by which it might be sought out and identified). To know a "class" of descriptions, it is sufficient to know a member of the class; once that is given, the class as such is defined. The name will cease to be a blank (it will acquire meaning) by providing one of the descriptions that go with it; one must make sure only that the clarifying description contains no name as term of reference which is in its turn a blank.

One way of clarifying a name consists, of course, in introducing— or pointing out—the bearer of the name in person. This operation is logically tantamount to supplying one of the extensionally synonymous descriptions: if Mr. Smith is once identified as "this person," he acquires a description: "the person of such-and-such appearance whom I met on such and such a day." It is the introduction, the face-to-face familiarity, which enables me to "single out" Mr. Smith on future occasions. To define a "name" in this way means to provide a "deictic" rule for its use.

This is all we need to say about the "meaning" of a name from a purely logical (or semantical) point of view. Considered in terms of its intension (communicative meaning), a name is simply a blank, unless and until a description referring to the same object is supplied. From that point on, the name itself has a meaning, and sentences in which it occurs will be "understood." But this is not all there is to the meaning of names. Considered in terms of "situational" (or "contextual") interpretation, names have, as we pointed out above, a "valuational" aspect. In conferring a name upon an object, the community does not merely provide a "blank" which is capable of acquiring meaning by associating with it a specifically defined "singling-out" operation. A name could be conferred upon every distinguishable object in this fashion; actually, however, only few objects are given names, and still fewer are given "public" names (names used in communications of public import). To have a name means to be an "equal" (or "fully valued") member of the community. It means a high standing in the hierarchy of objects.

All this, however, is still not sufficient to characterize the hierarchical nature of names and naming. For among the "objects highest in the hierarchy of individual things"—human beings—there is a further hierarchical graduation, and the use, currency, and understanding of names reflect this hierarchy. Some names are "obscure"; others are "illustrious." In our terminology, the name-language communities may vary in extent. In old societies, names implied social classifications: there were "clan" names, "aristocratic" names of greater or less prominence in the community, "bourgeois" names, "peasant" names, and "slave" names. Some names of illustrious individuals are household words in the community—indeed, they may become "words." The hierarchical "rank" of a name affects the way in which the "descriptions" clarifying the name are selected. The names of "ordinary" persons are blanks to everybody except those who know them personally; usually, with such names, the description clarifying them is supplied by face-to-face introduction. But "illustrious" names are not "blanks" to anybody in the community; everybody knows how to "identify" their bearers—not necessarily in the sense that one can actually single out any one person from among any given group of individuals (although even this capacity is widespread in our age of the ubiquitousness of the pictures of celebrities) but in the sense that he can characterize the bearers of the names by various "descriptions," ranging from the enumeration of the functions and achievements of the illustrious person to the ability to point out his dwelling and favorite haunts.

Names, it appears, are not only language symbols in the sense in which we defined "symbol," that is, as neutral vehicles of communications from person to person, serving to transmit information or verbal "demands" or "judgments." They have a "situational" function *in themselves, as* names; this is another aspect of the peculiarity of names which we noted at the outset, namely, that they are not properly part of the various "languages." Names structure the social world, they organize the ways in which men form associations among themselves. Each group engaged in a common endeavor has its "illustrious" names, its eponymous heroes—living leaders or models and long-dead, sacral, or traditional hero-figures. There are names revered among "the faithful" of a church and among other communities—those of the sciences and arts, business and sports, politics and warfare, fashion and dandyism, down to neighborhood communities, on the one hand, and underworld communities, on the other. Pure "language" symbols are not "signs" in themselves: their sign meanings vary and must be established contextually in each case. A name, however, has an invariant contextual meaning.

This hierarchical function of names is by no means an anachronism: it has nothing to do with the aristocratic or democratic nature of societies. A democratic society, no less than an aristocratic one, acknowledges a hierarchy among men, reflected in the distinction between more or less "illustrious" names. In no democracy, either actual or ideal, could all men be equal in the sense that all names would be equally private or equally illustrious in their currency. No society could function on either basis. The difference between aristocracies, democracies, and totalitarian regimes concerns rather the *grounds* on which names become "illustrious."

In the eighteenth century the "illustrious" names par excellence were those of the great aristocratic houses. Theirs was a closed circle of eminence; one either belonged or not, and whether one belonged or not depended solely on one's name. We have already forgotten the connotations of such expressions as the French '*un homme de qualité*' or the English 'person of rank.' The distinction implied was independent of the actual power wielded or the recognition won for purely human "qualities." Of course, there was also eminence of other sorts; both rich people and those brilliant in some human field of activity were known and valued; they could "make names" for themselves. But their names were "illustrious" only by metaphor. The *genuinely* illustrious names were those of the great families. The bearers of the illustrious names often picked their company among those who "made names" for themselves; and in England, where the magic of the aristocratic names still persists, names of the *aristocratic* kind of distinction are conferred upon deserving persons as a reward of their merit. This reward is, indeed, of incomparable value; for no distinction can be transmitted to one's descendants unless it is contained in the name as such, divorced from any personal merit.

A democratic society differs from an aristocratic one in that no name can become "illustrious" except by public recognition. Behind the name recognized as belonging to the "public" domain, there must be some reason for admiration other than the name itself. These reasons may be, from the point of view of the idealist or theoretician of the "good" society, good or bad, valid or paltry; but they are reasons. In a democracy a man may become illustrious because he has become very rich (in whatever manner) or because he excels in some sport or because he has maneuvered himself (again in whatever manner) into a politically eminent position. For names recognized as prominent in a democracy, the "descriptions" that go with them (and specify the basis on which the individual so named may be singled out from all others) ascribe to them "qualities" which nobody else has but which all "could" have in principle. This, at least, is true of the American type of democracy. I do not believe that the "hierarchy" founded upon such principles is the best that one could desire. For it might be argued that society would be better off—spiritually and culturally— if the "communities" making it up admired and respected certain individuals *without* the proviso that, with sufficient luck or application, "anybody" could be in their place. A society could still be democratic if its component communities recognized eminence of a unique, personal kind, residing in the substance—the heart and the mind—of the "illustrious" person rather than in his more or less fortuitous circumstances. I know that this sounds like a plea for hero worship and that societies which worship heroes will both generate and court disaster. But what I mean is something radically different from idolization and hero worship; it is the recognition of genuine moral or intellectual or spiritual authority. What is characteristic of the free recognition of authority is neither highly charged emotional identification nor unconditional subordination. It is, rather, genuine respect—whether one actually "agrees" or "disagrees," "concurs" or "dissents." Genuine respect based on fully internalized, autonomous value judgments is necessary for the moral health of the community.

Such respect is freely granted on a differential basis; it cannot be "shared equally" by all. Such theorists of democracy as Lasswell are certainly right in stressing that equal sharing of "respect" in a sense is essential to democracy; but I would add that this "equalized" respect is a "nonfunctional" kind of respect; it need not be "earned," since everybody is entitled to it. The type of respect I am discussing here is, however, functional and earned; it confers a distinction upon some individuals. Distinction is, by definition, something that cannot be equally shared by everybody; and it would be a mistake to believe that a democratic society is one which recognizes no distinction. No society can do without conferring some differential distinction upon some of its members. While distinction must and may be granted for various reasons and on various grounds, I think the moral and spiritual health of the community requires that *some* distinction be based on genuine respect for moral or intellectual authority. This is particularly needed in democratic societies in which distinction must be maximally "functional."

What is the basis of moral authority that members of a community may confer upon some of their fellows? It is not, to my mind, achievement and success—certainly not achievement and success alone. An in-

dividual may be acclaimed and honored for his achievement and success alone, and his community may be proud of him for this reason;
but that does not make him a moral authority within the community.
Moral authority can accrue to the eminent and successful only in the
measure that they appear devoted to the ideal, or code of value, under
which their activities stand. Devotion to such ideals is different from
striving toward success, and its acid test is readiness to forego success
if it could be attained only by compromising the code of values. It is
these things for which the "true sportsman" or the "uncompromising
artist" or the "honorable businessman" or the "genuine scholar" may
be *respected*, and not their competitive success as such.

It is my feeling that competitive achievement counts for too much
in the public recognition and acclaim granted to individuals in American society and that moral authority counts for too little. Too few
men are "influential" in this society because of their moral standing
in the community. The reason for this is not that we lack individuals
deserving respect for living up to the "codes of value" under which
their activities stand; it is, rather, that the community does not feel the
need to accord respect to moral (or intellectual or spiritual) leaders.
The feeling is widespread that by acknowledging respect, one would
either renounce his freedom or deny the essential equality of all human beings. Hence "eminence" is readily recognized when it can be
justified on the basis of "undeniable" facts involving success measured
by some neutral, factual, numerical standard of comparison. It is felt
that individuals can be set apart and covered with acclaim or oppro-
brium if their positive or negative distinction rests either on some
numerical criterion or on the findings of some formally constituted
authority; but positive or negative distinction granted on the basis of
spontaneous, personal judgments is considered suspect—it is held to
express either unseemly subordination and allegiance or intolerant and
dogmatic self-righteousness. That all judgment involves such dangers
is undeniable. Yet I believe that the general attitude I have outlined is
based on a profound misunderstanding. For one may let his essential
freedom lapse in many ways; and one of these ways consists precisely
in surrendering one's valuations of other persons to the impersonal
machinery of success and of formal, institutional authority.

One cannot be truly free without being able to feel genuine respect.
"Authorities" in the sense of arbiters of fashion and dictators of morality are not needed; but all societies, and democratic societies in particular, need the capacity to recognize as "moral authorities" persons

whose claim to distinction rests on disinterested service of a code of values which all are pledged to uphold to the best of their ability. Such distinction can be recognized only by judgment based on personal conviction; it cannot be formalized; for, if it were, it would become a competitive affair.

It is not enough for the moral and spiritual health of a society to feel respect only for institutions in the abstract, while denying it to all persons who represent those institutions. In the long run, no institutional system can be respected if a claim to respect—moral authority —is not operative in selecting its representative personnel. On the other hand, a free society also needs moral authority divorced from official standing in the institutional system. "Opinion leaders" who express only their own personal views without fear or favor are needed, because official power-holders, no matter how high-minded, are always committed to serve vested interests and to temper their convictions with expediency. The community needs people who speak for all because they speak only "for themselves." But neither the moral authority of people in official positions nor that of free agents outside government implies that all should defer to their judgment unconditionally; that would make them arbiters and dictators rather than leaders. Neither the recognition of authority in the moral or intellectual sense nor respect based on this recognition excludes independent judgment and possible dissent.

In moral matters, "inner-directed"[3] conscience should have the last word rather than deference to any authority; but this does not exclude moral *influence* from person to person and the readiness freely to acknowledge moral examples and moral arguments that help us to shed limitations in our position and to grow to fuller stature. Being shut off from moral "influences" is not autonomy; nobody has ever lost his freedom and autonomy by being exposed to words or deeds from a higher moral plane that pierced his heart and shattered his pride.

In intellectual matters, on the other hand, the last word must very often rest with the "expert." We must often defer to him without the possibility of an autonomous judgment (whereas in moral matters we always judge the matter in hand ourselves, even if the words or deeds of others *convince* us of what is right or wrong). Our theme here is, of course, moral rather than intellectual authority as such; but it may

3. See on this D. Riesman and Associates, *The Lonely Crowd: A Study in the Changing American Character* (New Haven: Yale University Press, 1950), pp. 13 ff.

be said about deference to the "expert" that it, too, should be based on at least some insight into the reasons *why* his expertness ought to be recognized; and "moral" respect for the "expert's" single-minded service of the code of fact-finding plays a crucial role in this.

All these matters are seemingly far removed from our theme, the discussion of the "meaning" of names; but, actually, these problems are intimately connected with the "name-language communities" and with the way in which social intercourse is structured by publicly significant names. The understanding of a name always involves more than simple singling-out or identification of an individual object. Just as we perceive "things" in a role they play, so we identify individual objects in terms of the function they perform or the position they occupy as individuals—and the "position" occupied by human beings is a person-to-person or person-to-group position.

So far, we have been discussing "names" in the proper sense, that is, individual names. We have seen that these do not form part of the word-language, they are not learned as words are, in the course of learning a language. Names are added to one's vocabulary one by one, as he gets "acquainted" with more and more individual objects, or they are added to the public vocabulary as individuals acquire new public roles. With words it is different: a word vocabulary must be acquired in its completeness before one can communicate in a language.

All this points to a clear-cut difference between the "word-language" and the "name-language." Upon closer inspection, however, it will appear that the word vocabulary is not so neatly separated from the name vocabulary as one might think. There are some intermediary types of symbols which are like names in certain respects and like words in others. We have already alluded to such intermediary expressions—the individual "descriptions." These are like names, in that they have unique reference: their understanding (or interpretation) presupposes following a rule by which one individual object can be singled out from among all others. In other respects, descriptions belong, in part at least, to the word-language. There are, however, other types of symbols, too, which occupy an intermediary position between names and words.

In fact, we use in everyday and scientific communication certain symbols which might be called "generic" names—the "brand names" of trade and the "taxonomic names" of science. We may consider such generic names as synonymous with words; a brand name or taxonomic name might be looked upon as a coined word, designating the members of a species of objects. Sometimes a brand name becomes a word, like 'aspirin' or 'cellophane.' Yet in some important respects the generic names are not like words at all but rather like names. This will become clearer as we analyze the vocabulary meaning of words.

2. THE MEANING OF WORDS

We now turn to a different class of symbols—"words" the meaning of which is defined by the rules of a word-language; that is, the "learning" of such meanings is what is involved in "learning a language." (The name-language is not "learned" as a language is; names are added to one's vocabulary one by one.)

There are different classes of words; some "designate" things, or properties, activities, rules, and values; others "designate" nothing but are needed to articulate assertions, such as connectives, prepositions, and the like. We shall examine first the words which designate something: thing-words. Other kinds of words will be taken up afterward.

a) THING-WORDS AND NOMINALISM

Here again the first question that arises is whether the "meaning" of a word can be characterized by the schema "*A* represents *B*," where *A* is a symbol and *B* some object or property or event. The schema suggests that the word 'cat,' for instance, in some way "represents" a *real* cat. From our earlier analyses it is clear that the word is in no way a *sign* for the occurrence, presence, or impending arrival of any real cat; whatever the meaning of the word as such is, it is communicative and not situational meaning. In what way can we understand such communicative meaning to be the "representation" of something by something else? Surely not in the sense that the word "evokes" the "thought" of a cat; many things can make me think of cats, and the word 'cat' may make me think of many things besides cats. The meaning of the word is, rather, some rule we have to observe if our communications are to be "right" within a language. The rule for 'cat,' and for any other English word, says something like this: "If you want to make an assertion that is to be acceptable or understandable as the assertion of such and such a fact (and here we may point to a "deictic" example to make the rule clear), you have to use the word 'cat' rather than 'dog' at such and such a place in the sentence schema." As we see, the meaning of words is defined with reference to *asser-*

tions, so that we cannot really characterize it without specifying what the meaning of assertions is. This, however, will be dealt with in more detail in the next section; at this point we shall take it for granted that words (as well as names) are essentially part of assertions or other fully meaningful expressions, such as demands, and we shall proceed to say something on the "vocabulary meaning" of the word.

This "vocabulary meaning," the one that has to be learned in order to enable us to form "understandable" sentences, must be distinguished from "naming." The word is not a name, for its understanding (in the vocabulary sense) does not enable us to single out an individual object from all other individual objects in the world. Its reference is rather "generic"; 'cat' somehow refers to a biological species. But it is not the "name" of the species 'cat'; it is not a taxonomic name.

What is the difference? We may say that understanding of the meaning of a thing-word presupposes only the ability to perform certain classificatory operations upon objects or images of objects that may be present. We possess the "meaning" of the English word 'cat' to the extent that we can say truthfully, in the presence of a certain animal, "This is a cat." Such meanings are vocabulary rules, involving some "standard of order," and the vocabulary rules of ordinary languages are so framed that the standards of order on which their application depends are operatively shared by all normal members of the language community. The vocabulary meanings of words point to some acts of classification by which the different "roles" that objects may play can be easily identified. These meanings presuppose only the ability to distinguish ubiquitously recurrent properties, or clusters of properties, which the things encountered in the situational field may exhibit.

It would seem, at first glance, that this is precisely what taxonomic names are all about, with the only difference that they specify the underlying acts of classification more rigorously than ordinary speech does. In ordinary parlance, eel, lamprey, and snake may be more or less the same thing, whereas cat and tiger, dog and wolf, are very different things; in taxonomic parlance an eel is not a lamprey, let alone a snake, whereas a tiger is a cat. But it seems to me that there is more to the difference between taxonomic names and words than this matter of precision. A taxonomic name calls for identification not only in terms of recurrent properties but also in terms of "position." It designates not only a thing having such-and-such properties (which is essentially what a thing-word does) but also a thing having such-and-such a unique position in relation to other things, or groups of things, in a positional scheme. *Felis domestica* is not a mere translation of 'cat' into Latin; it is an untranslatable "name" of something (though, of course, not a "proper" name, since it lacks individual reference). The "name" character of the expression stems from the fact that it involves a positional element in a unique array and not merely a constellation or cluster of recurrent, classifiable *properties*.

This is still more pronounced in the case of the taxonomic names of chemistry. The *word* 'iron' refers to a familiar kind of substance: heavy, malleable, and used to manufacture certain objects. But the taxonomic name 'Fe' is defined in terms of position within a table or array of elements and covers a large variety of phenomenal appearances—such as spectrum lines—which do not enter into the "familiar" meaning of the word 'iron.' Taxonomic names are conventionalized for all languages; this is why they are given in Latin, Greek, or pseudo-Latin and Greek. But they are also like words: the taxonomic name-language is learned like the word-language, prior to use; they form a common vocabulary, unlike the proper names.

Brand names also exhibit this dual character. The name 'Chevrolet' does not refer to a "kind" of car; succeeding types of Chevrolets vary greatly as to their properties—and brand names are, in this respect, closer to proper names than taxonomic names are, for the latter *are* defined in terms of an unvarying configuration of properties. The brand name 'Chevrolet' designates not a car having such-and-such properties but a car manufactured by a certain individual firm. On the other hand, of course, the brand name is not a proper name, for its reference is generic, and it also implies uniformity of the *properties* of the objects falling under it, if we disregard successive changes in design.

Thing-words, then, have something in common with taxonomic names and brand names: generic rather than individual reference, and meaning defined in terms of classification by properties or clusters of properties. This is what we have to consider now.

To what does the "generic reference" refer? Can we say that symbols of the kind now considered refer to "kinds" or "species" of objects, as "real" entities? This interpretation of the meaning of words was held, in the course of the history of thought, by the philosophical school of "realism" as against "nominalism." The realist position is that the "generic reference" of the thing-words is to something having "real being," in some sense of "real being" as distinguished from the mode of being of a mere mental object, abstraction, or construct. The nominalist position is that only the individual things coming under the "generic reference" defining the meaning of the thing-word are "real existents," while the class or species to which they belong "exists" only in the sense of being their collection.

Now in so far as the meaning of "thing-words" is concerned, it clearly calls for a "nominalistic" explication. The thing-word is not the "name" of a species, and it is not used to "refer" to the species as such. When we *use* such a word (in contradistinction to the cases when we merely *define* it), we make reference not to all the *possible* objects that could be designated by it, taken as one class or collection, but to some or all *actual* (or imaginary) instances in which the term is applicable. When I say that a chair is something to sit on, I certainly speak of all "possible" instances in which the word can be used correctly—but then I merely *define* 'chair.' When I make an *assertion* about a chair or some chairs or all chairs, then the truth or falsehood of my assertion can be ascertained only by examining actual "things" which come under the designation 'chair.' When my assertion is merely an imaginative one, then one must *imagine* an actual thing, a chair, to understand my fictitious statement. To be sure, I must be conversant with the "definition" of a thing-word in order to use and understand it correctly, and this presupposes familiarity with the "property" of "being a chair" rather than with its actual instances. But the word does not "refer" to the property; it "refers" to individual things which are instances of the property.

When we say that the "word" refers to the "thing," we should not personify this relationship as an actual operation performed by the word, or by its user, upon the thing. "Referring" is not "pointing out" something as being present here and now; it is not an operation performed upon a thing. We can try to characterize it, rather, as a complex relationship of this form: "To say that the word W, used in a communication, 'refers' to an object of the kind P means that, when the communication is fitted contextually into an actually prevailing situation, an object of the kind P will be found to characterize, in a specified way, one of the situation-classes to which that situation belongs, provided that the communication is true." This interpretation of "reference" is nominalistic, since it admits only sign correlates, that is, concrete things present in a situation, as the real "referents" of a thing-word.

All this is not controversial; few people would defend the Platonic ontology according to which the class or property which "defines" the correct application of a thing-word is a more genuinely "real" existent than the concrete instances which exhibit that property. We can understand how Plato came to lay down this ontological principle; he defined as "having real being" those entities about which clear, scientific, provable knowledge is attainable, and it was evident to him that our scientific knowledge is knowledge of classes of things rather than of individuals. Now we certainly cannot quarrel with the latter statement: scientific knowledge, in the sense of the content of a scientific theory, certainly is "about" classes of things rather than about individual instances. It is only that, for us, the "data" upon which a scientific theory is based and to which it can be applied are more "real" than the *content* of the theories as such. We define as "having real being" that which can serve as a *datum* to be accounted for by a theory. We are still Platonists in the sense that, for us too, the the possibility of "clear," "warranted" knowledge is a mark of reality; we have merely shifted the emphasis from the theoretical expression of knowledge to the *data* belonging to its field of application. But when we say that the really existing things are data, we still think of the data as related to some actual or possible theory. This, at least, is the prevalent ontology of present-day scientific nominalism.

The "real reference" of more "abstract" words is conceived of in our scientific ontology in the same way. Thing-words "refer" to concrete things; this means that a thing-word 'T' can be the predicate of an "elementary sentence" of the form "This thing here is a T,"[4] and it is the thing pointed out that represents the only "real" term involved in this relationship. "Property words," on the other hand, cannot be the predicates of sentences of this form; the word 'blue' cannot be the predicate of a sentence of the form "This thing here is a blue." Only thing-words are such that we can point out instances of the kind of thing the word refers to; when it comes to property words, we can only point out instances of things which "have" rather than "are" the property. But in this case, too, the "real" component of the reference of the word is the concrete instance that exhibits the property and not the property as such.

Now it might be suggested that the nominalistic ontology which is dominant today is both ill-defined and too narrow. It is ill-defined, because, if we say that the "real" entities of the world are "data" within the context of a scientific theory, we cannot really indicate what a

4. On elementary sentences see the following chapter.

"datum" contains and what its boundaries are. Is the "datum" a complete singularity, a time-space instant characterized by a set of observational indices? If we look at it this way, we can hardly maintain that we have expressed what we really have meant to express. For we have rejected the Platonic ontology because it contradicted our feeling that only the concrete, stubborn, resistant items of our environment can be real—those which force themselves upon us, those which we cannot ignore. But the "data" characterized in the above way do not answer this specification. For one thing, they are extremely transitory and fleeting; they do not abide with us. For another, they are, in fact, "created" by us: the "observational indices" which define a datum point to a theory in the context of which we conduct our observations; with a different theory in mind, we would make other observations and obtain other indices.

The dominant ontology is also too narrow—for it denies contact with "real being" to everbody except the scientific observer. This conception of reality is, it seems, too "unrealistic." As living beings, in prescientfiic intercourse with our environment, we are certainly in touch with reality; at least, our immediate experience gives us the only feeling of reality we can have, and it was this prescientific, everyday feeling of things "obtruding" upon us and preventing us from "ignoring" them that induced us to reject the too rarefied Platonic ontology. From the point of view of common sense, there is not much to choose between the Platonic "hypostatization" of mathematical objects as the only fully "real" entities and the modern scientific "hypostatization" of the data characterized merely by indices as values of theoretical variables. I think a satisfactory ontology should do better justice to our ordinary, instinctive feeling of reality.

It looks as if nominalism, born of the wish to acknowledge the reality of the concrete and incontrovertibly given, had played a trick upon itself by trying to assure itself of contact with undeniable reality by focusing upon the absolute singularity of the "real" object. We do not and cannot live with absolute singularity; what is real "for us" must have a certain stubbornness and durability, a permanent role within our field of behavior—in one word, "thingness." It is a paradoxical thing for a doctrine called "nominalism" that it ends up with ultimate entities which it cannot even name or refer to by any symbol, except by tying them surreptitiously to some abstract theoretical framework. Moreover, this atomizing tendency turns out to be inadequate even for scientific description; for the "Gestalt" characteristics of many physical objects and systems can be neither ignored nor deduced from simple, elementary data. A scientific ontology which recognizes only elementary particles as "real" things seems to be too narrow.

We cannot attempt to outline an ontological theory here that would satisfy both the requirements of scientific theory construction and the feeling of reality which we have within our own experience. It is probably impossible so to define "real being," as distinguished both from mere "appearance" and "construct," that we can use the same concept in all the varying contexts in which a distinction between the real and the nonreal must be made. There are many facets to our obscure and vague idea of "reality," and it seems that we inevitably have to stress now one and then another of these facets, depending on the problem at hand. Sometimes we have to emphasize the *situational* aspect of our vague idea of reality and focus upon the incisive difference which things make in our life, in trying to distinguish the real from the nonreal. This is the pragmatic and existentialist approach, and, in a sense, it is incontrovertible; for no matter how we try, we cannot characterize *known* reality except in terms of some difference it makes in our experience. But our unanalyzed idea of reality has also an objective, factual side: something that is real must, we feel, impress its existence and its "being what it is" upon its environment, regardless of the difference it makes to the "situation" of living beings. Both the situational and the factual must have a place in our ontology; all we can do is to correct the excesses to which one-sided emphasis upon the one or the other aspect might lead. Thus, if we tried to label as "real" all those things, and only those things, which have a well-defined situational relevance and meaning for us, we would build a myth of a completely transparent and rational universe, only to find that this transparence and rationality depend to a large extent on acts of judgment which are often essentially controversial. Thus a reliable common measure would be lost. But if we restricted our concept of "real being" only to data which are recorded impartially by standardized instruments, we should again deceive ourselves, for we should find that the mere record provided by the instruments must be supplemented with connecting links and meaningful frameworks to be intelligible. Thus we must try to balance the two aspects and look at reality "contextually": that is, admit that we can never get out of a situation and therefore never establish contact with "pure being" without situational links; but admit also that we need not be *dominated* by our prevailing situation but can "break it up" and analyze it in terms of situation-class relationships. Not to get away from "subjectivity" to this extent would be unwise; to go farther toward "objectivity" is impossible.

The individual "thing" to which the thing-word refers (in the sense outlined above) is more than a mere datum and even more than an assemblage of data; it has a "role" which represents a "meaningful framework" giving unity to the data with which the thing may be associated. Can we say that things in their "role," rather than only the data associated with the things, are part of "reality"? It seems that we cannot do otherwise; for the absolutely singular data, deprived of all companionship with others in the unity of a "role," are nothing of which we can intelligibly say that "it is there." That somehow the isolated datum *was* there we know only from the trace it left on an instrument which we must use in its "thing-role." If no "thing" in its "role" is real, then we are in the peculiar situation that only the testimony of nonreal things can give us any inkling of reality. If, on the other hand, measuring instruments are "real," then other things-in-roles cannot be denied this status.

This does not mean that everything for which we have a thing-word is "real," that is, "real" in the role which the thing-word attributes to it. There are fairly deceptive words like 'rainbow' or 'wave': they refer to "something colored up there" or "something like a wall moving toward us," while "in reality" the colored thing out there and the moving wall do not "exist." We discover this when we "break up" the immediately experienced situation and try to construct situation classes in which the rainbow and the wave appear as invariant components. Other "thing-word" referents, however, resist such "factual" analysis pretty well.

b) ABSTRACT WORDS

We encounter real difficulties in trying to analyze the "reference" function of words designating large collectivities. What "in reality" do we refer to when we speak of a "group," of a "society," of a "nation"? Similar difficulties arise in connection with words specifying rules of behavior or values. What "in reality" do we refer to when we speak of an "institution," a "political system," or a "law"?

According to the positivist doctrine, words like 'nation' and 'law' have, as their "real" referents, individual human beings living in a certain place and acting in certain ways under specified circum-

SYMBOLS 145

stances. Neither the collectivity as such nor the rule or prescription as such should be regarded as part of "reality." This way of construing the "reality" behind these words, however, encounters great difficulties. While it is true that no group would "exist" without its members, it is also true that individuals acting within a group are a different "real thing" from the individuals taken in isolation. The "pair" is a part of reality *as pair;* and there is no reason left for denying it real status, once we have recognized that reality cannot be broken down into absolute singularities anyway. Furthermore, even individual human beings are not "absolute" singularities; if they may be considered "real," other segments of the universe consisting of parts may also be considered "real."

Shall we say that the "reality" to which we refer when we speak of "nations" or "laws" is that of concrete events in time and space— events participated in by individuals and also by "real" groups of individuals? Collectivities can certainly be described as "events" of more or less considerable dimensions in space and time. But the question is, In terms of what features can we delimit and characterize an "event" such as a nation-group in its continuous, historic existence? To characterize a group, we must specify criteria for membership. Without such criteria, the group as such would not "exist" as a real group; and we may specify, for any number of individuals, different "real groups" in which they may hold membership. For any of the groups, some roles defining "membership" are crucial. And we cannot distil these roles from the observed movements of the members; the attribution of the crucial "membership" role involves judgment.

The same applies to the "real" content of concepts of social "laws" or "rules." It cannot be said that the "reality" to which these concepts refer consists entirely in bits of actual behavior which somehow embody or illustrate the "rule." Concepts of rules and laws would certainly be devoid of real reference if no actual behavior exemplifying their application could be specified. But the "law" is not a mere summation of actual occurrences, forming a set all by themselves. No matter how we collect our behavioral data illustrating the concept of "law," we must make a judgment to make sure whether a certain behavioral datum belongs to the set, and this judgment will also have to determine the more or less correct or defective way in which the behavior item under consideration embodies the meaning of the law.

We see, then, that in a number of cases the "real events" which correspond to words we use form sets which we can delimit against other parts of a universe only by making explicit judgments. This runs the risk of making the application of these words an arbitrary or subjective affair; and the nominalistic or positivistic views we have alluded to are inspired by the wish to make "judgments" superfluous in discourse. According to these views, we refer to "reality" only when we can specify the object of our discourse without "judgment," without any possible controversy that might arise from a diversity of standards. The position taken here, however, is that, even in the most factual parts of our discourse, we cannot dispense with judgments altogether, because, in order to talk about things, we must imply a role which they play. The difference between "factual" and "evaluative" discourse is one only of degree; "purely" factual discourse does not exist.

To be sure, we may distinguish judgments according to whether they are inherently controversial or relatively standardized. Where no value conflicts are involved, it is possible to attribute a "role" to things which will be conceded them by everyone; and judgments about such roles may be made implicitly or taken for granted rather than stated expressly. It is certainly justifiable to strive for maximum objectivity or verifiability in our discourse—meaning thereby that we shall seek to rely on "judgment" only when judgments are not controversial and can be taken for granted, as it were, before the investigation begins. But it is illusory, in my opinion, to make every case for a controversial judgment disappear by reformulating every question calling for explicit judgment in terms of facts or noncontroversial, standardized judgments. It is quite true that whenever we try to answer directly the question of whether certain behavior is right or wrong, lawful or unlawful, we cannot guarantee agreement. It is also true that agreement will be generally attainable if we content ourselves with stating what certain individuals have *declared* to be right, lawful, or generally desirable. But statements of this second kind do not give us all we need to know in order to deal with questions of rightness or lawfulness. They would do this only if we surreptitiously endowed some of the individuals we study with implicit authority, by assuming that what *they* do and say is the "correct" standard for the value problem at hand. We might say, for instance, that no case need be controversial, once we decide that the majority view (which we can ascertain in a factual way) will always be taken to be the right view. But this is an *explicit judgment*, no mere statement of fact, and it is a judgment which in many cases needs qualification and correction. The majority judgment is not necessarily the "best" judgment; all we can say is that in political matters, for instance, it will be best for society to accept the majority view, provided that it does not dictate a course of action which will exclude future consultations, possibly reversing today's decision. There are some valid reasons why the majority view must be endowed with authority in certain matters. In other matters we may have good reasons for accepting other judgments as authoritative. But in all such cases the assignment of authority is a matter of explicit judgments; and we cannot assume that we can preassign decisive authority to settle a controversy in *every* case. *Some* matters must be left to be judged freely, and, in these, what we need is not the transformation of value questions into questions of fact but an improvement in the process of judgment itself. Exclusive concern with a mechanical guaranty for eliminating controversy will not enable us to dispense with judgment altogether; it will merely deteriorate our process of judgment.

The meaning of law words and rule words has, of course, a purely "ideal" component, in that they imply some standard we have to apply in judging cases that come under them. A standard as such is not part of "reality." But an act of judgment is a "real" event, and when we say of a law or rule that it is being applied in a group, we say something about reality. Law words or rule words have "real" reference in this sense. In my view this "real" reference is not to a purely factual behavioral substratum, one we can identify without making a judgment; the "real" instances, those which make law a social "reality," are not pieces of behavior to be described without reference to standards requiring judgment. Law becomes part of reality precisely because some instances of actual behavior may be *judged* in legal terms. It is quite true to say that law as part of reality is made up of actual instances of law-related or law-oriented behavior, but we cannot delimit this sector of reality without recourse to ideal standards of judgment.

A last question we shall briefly discuss in connection with word meanings concerns words without "reference," such as connectives and "logical constants"—words like 'if' and 'or.' Morris discusses such words under the heading "formators."[5] True to his leading principle, he seeks to establish the "meaning" of these words by ascertaining what difference it makes to behavior whether the words are used and understood or not. To this end, Morris compares behavior prompted

5. *Signs, Language, and Behavior* (New York: Prentice-Hall, 1946), pp. 86 f.

by two sentences, both of which contain the same thing-words and property-words but only one of which combines these with a "formator." The difference between the two behaviors is the "meaning" of the "formator."

Here, as elsewhere, focusing upon the behavior actually prompted by different configurations of symbols tends to obscure rather than to clarify the problem of "meaning." It is true that *actual* behavior which reflects "understanding" of a symbol differs from actual behavior which is not informed by such understanding. But, in order to say that a certain behavior is the one which corresponds to the "meaning" of a word, it is not enough for me to know that such behavior followed after the symbol was perceived; I also have to make a judgment about whether or not the behavior was appropriate.

In addition to this, it seems somewhat questionable to me whether the meaning of "formators" ("logical constants") can be fully demonstrated by isolated behavioral tests. Morris describes an imaginary experiment in which dogs are first trained to look for food in different boxes upon hearing different sounds and then to try "one or the other" of a pair of boxes upon hearing a new kind of sound. If the dogs can be taught to do this, he says, this shows that they acquire some understanding of the formator "or." This, however, is doubtful. The dogs' behavior, it seems to me, would actually reflect understanding of the logical constant "or" only if they always indulged in such "alternative" explorations whenever the "or" sound is administered—that is, if they acted as if to them the "or" sound were a signal indifferently for "this box or that box," " the ball or the stick," "left or right," and so on. There is a difference between modes of behavior somehow corresponding to the meaning of a formator and modes of behavior in which the formator is being interpreted as such. Behavior sequences do have a logical form. Take, for instance, a kind of behavior we might describe as "if" behavior. In fact, all habitual responses, whether learned or instinctive, exhibit an "if" structure. "If" the dog hears a whistle, he runs toward his master; "if" he sees the stick thrown, he runs for it. But in such sequences of behavior, there is no "stimulus" which plays the role of the logical formator itself.

Also, a dog can easily learn the meaning of "No," a typical "formator," in the sense that he will stop whatever he is about to do upon hearing "No." But what he learns, then, is still a no-signal rather than a true formator, a no-symbol. We should be in presence of signal behavior approximating true "symbol behavior" only if the dog were taught to obey different signals and also to do the exact opposite when the no-signal is given together with any of the other signals. Such a logically proficient dog would also have to be able to "go in reverse" without specific learning whenever any *new* command he learns is given together with the no-signal. I imagine that it would be hard to train dogs to perform in this way.

The meaning of logical constants, as symbols, is different from sign meanings occurring in situations to which the logical form specified by the constant somehow applies. It is, in the first place, communicative rather than situational meaning. The meaning of "if" as a symbol is definable only with reference to communications in which it may occur; or, rather, it *would* be so definable if logical constants of this generality could be defined at all. Actually, it seems that *all* definition of meaning must contain an "if": to define the meaning of any *x*, we have to say that "if *x* is present or forms part of an expression, then. . . ." *Some* logical constants must, it seems, be considered as primitive, undefinable parts of discourse. It is true that their meaning has to be taught and learned, but it must be taught and learned "deictically," and this means that, in order to teach it, we must make appeal to already existing behavioral capacities. The pupil learning a "deictic" rule must discover the "point" of the rule in terms of some meaningful performance of which he is already capable. The understanding of formators in this sense presupposes some logical ability which seems to be essential to the characteristic human capacity for "contextual" behavior.

CHAPTER VI

SENTENCES

1. ELEMENTARY SENTENCES

THE meaning of any sentence can be traced back to that of simple or "elementary" ("molecular") sentences. As Wittgenstein says: "It is obvious that in the analysis of propositions we must come to elementary propositions, which consist of names in immediate combination."[1] These "names" designate objects which are absolutely "simple,"[2] and an elementary sentence consequently asserts the existence of an "atomic fact."[3] Thus the elementary character of the sentence seems to be due to the fact that the designata of the symbols composing it are themselves "absolutely simple"—not sets or collections of individual objects or events.

It is obvious that the objects or events which make up atomic facts cannot be enduring "things" like the individual things we encounter in everyday life. They are absolutely "unique," while the individual "things" of ordinary experience can be broken down into simple parts or states.

Thus "elementary propositions" in Wittgenstein's sense are characterized by two things. They consist of "names," but the names are those of absolute singularities, not of enduring things.

We find a similar conception underlying Ayer's theory of "elementary" objects. After having explained that the names of ordinary things, such as "table," in reality stand for collectivities, he proposes to formulate really elementary sentences by replacing words such as "table" by symbols designating "sense-contents."[4] A sense-content in this sense is an absolute singularity; it is punctual, nonrecurrent, unique. Ayer's method, reminiscent of that of Wittgenstein, consists in obtaining elementary sentences by adopting symbols with unique referents.

1. *Tractatus logico-philosophicus* (London, 1922), proposition 4.221.
2. *Ibid.*, proposition 2.02.
3. *Ibid.*, proposition 4.21.
4. A. J. Ayer, *Language, Truth, and Logic* (London, 1936), p. 74.

Now it seems to me that this conception of "elementary" sentences is based on a misunderstanding of the nature and the functions of symbols. A symbol cannot serve for anything except for identifying an object or a property, which may be presented to any number of observers in various situations. Unless a symbol can be used for communication, it is no symbol, and it could not be used for communication if its referents were not common recurrent elements in the situations of a number of observers. There can be no symbol with an absolute singularity as referent.

Our actual situations are unique. We may point out something in a unique situation, and, in doing so, we may use symbols; but the symbols as such will not suffice to identify any unique referent; a nonsymbolic device must be added to accomplish this. Only non-symbolic devices can refer to unique objects. Unique, punctual objects can have no "proper names," nor can they be referents of "words."

What would happen, indeed, if we tried to follow Ayer's proposal and introduced "proper names" having one single sense-content as referent? Let us make 'FLA' the proper name of a flash of light seen by a certain person on a certain occasion. This proper name, I submit, could not become part of a language. After the flash is over, there will never occur a situation for which 'FLA' would fit. At most, the person who had the 'FLA'-experience could use the name to refer to it in remembering it; but, since the name refers to a singularity belonging to *his* stream of experience, it could not convey anything to other people.

A proper name which is part of a language does not designate a singularity but serves to identify something recurrent as "the same" object. This presupposes that certain collectivities, enduring in time, retain a certain individual identity. Such collectivities can have proper names, precisely because they are not singularities but are recurrently identifiable. The individual sense-contents into which we may try to analyze our experience of these collectivities, on the other hand, can have no proper names.

What, then, is an elementary sentence? It cannot be a sentence consisting of "elementary" symbols, meaning symbols designating absolute singularities, for there are no such symbols. Each symbol as such designates something recurrent. Yet an elementary sentence must be something asserting something unique. It must be a sentence pointing out, revealing, something about an actually prevailing situation. As we shall see, such sentences are possible, although the symbols contained in them as such stand for recurrent properties or collectivities or syntactical configurations.

The paradox of elementary sentences is that they assert an absolutely singular fact, without being able to specify it by means of the symbols they contain—their "text."

Let us see, first, in what the singularity of the "actually prevailing situation" consists. It has nothing to do with the uniqueness, the extensionless punctuality, of objects or occurrences. On the contrary, the situation as such, while unique, is not extensionless. Nor is it "unique" in the sense of being inclosed within one numerically singular consciousness. An actual situation may be shared by several partners; it is an extended "field" of responses. The possibility of communication is an essential feature of the actual situation. "Actuality" has nothing to do with atomic objects. It is a field character which involves some kind of structure and extension.

By "actually prevailing situation" I mean the field of responses, acts, and operations that may be performed by an organism on a given occasion. It is a set of ways in which a prevailing state of affairs may be rearranged or continued by the intervention of organisms. The subject grasps the meaning of the situation by "projecting" a response structure on it and by "anticipating" a certain continuation. The response structure may fit or not; the anticipation may be confirmed or not. In each situation there is an open alternative of adequate and inadequate responses. What the "real" meaning of the situation has been can be seen only afterward—that is, only after the situation ceased to be "actual."

An elementary sentence, then, is one which asserts something about the actual situation *qua* actual. What the sentence conveys is that a certain response, as performed here and now, would be adequate in terms of some standard. Our question is how a sentence consisting of symbols can convey this. The symbols as such designate recurrent elements of possible situations; the sentence must correlate the unique situation that prevails now with a recurrent structure of potentialities. This correlation is effected by pointing out one aspect or element of the situation as "this here," and identifying it as the possible correlate of a recurrent type of response.

The field of actually performable operations is extended, of course, and that part of this field which is pointed out as "this here" is no flash of experience, no extensionless atom. Nothing can be designated as "this here" unless it has some sort of public existence and enduring identity. If we point out something as "this," we imply a certain enduring law of its existence—an invariance persisting through a range of situations. If it is a momentary event, this enduring law concerns the traces it leaves, by which it can be identified as an object of discourse. That which is pointed out as "this" is no sheer actuality; it is actually given, but given as enduring beyond the prevailing situation.

The elementary sentence is no mere "tag" or counterpart of a momentary situation; on the contrary, the sentence attempts to elucidate the situation by projecting on it a pattern of responses (of identification, classification, etc.) which is always available. In the elementary sentence we may distinguish what we described above (pp. 41 f.) as the "recurrent" and "unique" pole of meaning. The pole of recurrence is represented by the various patterns of invariances entering into the meaning of the sentence, that is, not only the designata of the symbols as such but also the implied law of endurance by which the object designated as "this" can be identified in subsequent situations. All this is conveyed, or at least implied, by the "text" of the sentence. The nonrecurrent, unique pole of meaning is the fact that the sentence itself belongs to an actual context of events and responses. The "text" of the elementary sentence cannot convey this unique aspect of its meaning.

What do we understand, for instance, from the text of such a sentence as 'This is blue'? From the word 'this,' we understand that it is an elementary sentence, referring to a classificatory response as actually performable. From the other words of the sentence, we also know what that classificatory response is. Yet the full meaning of the sentence is not given by the text. Those who know the text alone—as quoted in this book—cannot know whether the sentence, as uttered in an actual situation, was true or false. To the extent that 'This is blue' may be a true or false sentence, it is more than a quotable text; its truth or falsehood depends on what is designated as 'this,' which may change while the text as such is unchanged.

If we substitute for 'this' a proper name, this anomaly will end, and the truth value of the sentence will be determined by its text. But, as we shall see, this transformation will not render elementary sentences superfluous. For certain purposes, sentences like the one containing a proper name instead of 'this' will suffice; but these are not elementary sentences. As for the sentences containing 'this' which are elementary, they are intelligible only to those who share in the situation in which they are uttered.

The unique, nonrecurrent pole of meaning of an elementary sentence is constituted by words such as 'this,' 'here,' 'now,' 'I,' 'you,' 'today,' 'ten weeks ago today,' etc.—words the actual meaning of which can be grasped only by those who share the speaker's situation and hence know what is pointed out as 'this,' etc.

I believe that elementary sentences are only those which contain such variable words or analogous syntactical features, such as tenses. No other kind of sentence can express ultimate, elementary, sentential meaning, namely, the response structure that fits the actually prevailing situation. If we substitute a proper name for a variable word, we are left with only potential instead of actual meaning, because the sentence then merely says what kind of response may be adequate *if* a certain kind of situation prevails. 'This is green' conveys a definite meaning; it formulates the claim that, in the situation now prevailing, a classificatory operation is adequate if it proceeds along such and such lines. But 'Alfred's hat is green' merely says that, in a situation in which it is correct to say 'This is Alfred's hat,' it is also correct to say 'This is green.' In order to translate the sentence into actual terms, we still have to resort to the use of the variable words. This is what we mean by saying that what symbols can designate constitutes only potential meaning.

2. Occasional Functions

That words such as 'this,' 'here,' 'now,' 'I,' and the like consitute a class apart from other words has been variously noted by linguists. Thus, Brugmann has called attention to "deixis" as a special mode of communication in which "the meaning of an utterance is derived from the context of the situation in which the utterance is made, that is to say, from the place where the conversation takes place as well as the surrounding objects."[5] Taking up this hint, Buehler distinguishes two "fields" corresponding to different modes of communication by language, namely, the "field of designation" (Zeigfeld) and the "field of symbolic representation" (Symbolfeld). He says: "What 'here' and 'there' is varies with the position of the speaker, just as the reference of 'I' and 'you' alternates between two partners according to

---

5. Cf. Karl Brugmann, "Die Demonstrativpronomina der indogermanischen Sprachen," *Abhandlungen der sächsischen Gesellschaft der Wissenschaften*, Vol. XXII (1904), quoted by Karl Buehler, *Sprachtheorie* (Jena, 1934), p. 81.

whether they are assuming the role of sender or receiver."[6] For Buehler, "demonstrative" words such as 'here' and 'now' are not symbols at all, since a symbol, by definition, has invariable reference. This invariability of reference, according to Buehler, makes symbols logically superior to variable demonstrative expressions. Logical operations, it seems, can be carried out only on fully "symbolic" sentences; in fact, if we admitted sentences containing variable expressions in logic, we could not avoid contradictions. 'This is green' may be true or false, according to the situation. 'All violets are blue' is contradicted by 'All violets are red,' but 'This is blue' is not contradicted by 'This is red.' There is contradiction only if 'this' refers to the same object at the same time in both cases, but the text does not show this; in fact, the proper function of the word 'this' is to designate different objects. Hence, according to Buehler, words such as 'this' logically disqualify the sentence in which they occur.[7]

It would follow from this that a logically well-constructed language would not contain expressions such as 'this,' 'here,' and 'now.' Buehler does not countenance the proposal that all such expressions should be banished from language altogether,[8] but he would restrict them to "everyday speech" in contrast to the "language of science."[9]

Russell[10] calls these expressions "egocentric particulars" and maintains that they "are not needed in any part of the description of the world, whether physical or psychological."[11]

In so far as the language of scientific propositions is concerned, it is true, I think, that such variable expressions have no place in it. The reason for this, however, is not some logical deficiency from which the variable words suffer but because scientific propositions do not need such words. 'This,' 'now,' and the rest represent *actual* meaning, whereas scientific propositions convey only *potential* meaning. A scientific proposition is not addressed to one group of partners in a definite situation; it contains information destined for *any* student in *any* situation. This does not mean, however, that we can do without actual meaning and its indicators, the variable words, either in "everyday life" or in cultivating science. For when a scientific proposition is

---

6. Buehler, *op. cit.*, pp. 80 ff.
7. *Ibid.*, pp. 103 ff.
8. Cf. E. Zilsel, *Erkenntnis*, III (1932), 143 ff.; O. Neurath, *Erkenntnis*, III (1932), 208.
9. *Op. cit.*, p. 105.
10. *An Inquiry into Meaning and Truth* (New York: W. W. Norton & Co., 1940), pp. 134 ff.
11. *Ibid.*, p. 143.

tested—an operation which is vital to scientific practice—we have to say what the result of the test is 'here' and 'now.' In the test situation we are confronted with actual meaning. And it seems to me that the meaning of each scientific proposition can be made explicit only by testing or illustrating it in the actual situation. If a proposition does not mean anything in terms of 'here' and 'now,' it means nothing. Potential meaning can be made explicit only by actual meaning. Hence, great as the logical anomalies besetting variable expressions admittedly are, it seems to me that they have a definite logical function in testing nonvariable expressions. Instead of relegating them to some inferior "everyday speech" or banishing them altogether, we should find a way to use them in logically unobjectionable fashion.

I shall call variable words such as 'here,' 'now,' 'this,' 'I,' etc., "occasional functions." One particular "here" and "now," as referred to by an occasional function, is a "value" of the function. A sentence containing an occasional function the value of which is determined is an "occasional sentence." The mere *text* of an occasional sentence—that is to say, its words, including the variable word without any clue as to its referent—does not constitute a sentence but only a sentential function. Sentences not containing any occasional function will be called "transoccasional sentences."

General (universal) sentences, such as the formal implication: '$(x).fx \supset gx$,' are, of course, transoccasional. But there are also sentences which are transoccasional without being universal, for instance, existential sentences like '$\exists x.fx$,' and individual sentences such as '$f(A)$,' which ascribe a property (f) to an individual (A).

Occasional sentences may be transformed into transoccasional ones and vice versa. For instance, we can transform the occasional sentence 'This box is green' into a transoccasional one by omitting the occasional function 'this' and replacing it by an existential or all-operator: 'A box is green' ('There is a green box') or 'All boxes are green.' One transformation consists in replacing the occasional function by an expression, containing dates or other co-ordinate values, which identifies the value of the occasional function: 'The box seen by Peter on Tuesday is green.' We shall call such transoccasional sentences "dated accounts." A dated account is logically equivalent to the occasional sentence to which it corresponds, that is to say, neither can be true (or false) without the other also being true (or false). Their meaning, nevertheless, is different. The other transformations we have mentioned are not equivalent: if, on a certain occasion, it is true that 'This box is green,' the existential proposition 'There is a green box' is true, but not inversely; the existential proposition may be true, while the corresponding occasional sentence is false. Conversely, if it is true that 'All boxes are green,' then 'This box is green' will be true in every case; but, if 'This box is green' is true, it does not follow that 'All boxes are green' is true.

It is easy to see that these transformations from the occasional into the transoccasional form, and vice versa, are vitally important.

Let us take, for instance, a universal transoccasional sentence: 'Water freezes at 32° F.' This, as we have seen, represents only "potential" meaning; it is merely "abstract" knowledge which comes alive only when we are able to point out a case in which it is realized. This happens when we are able to point out a 'this,' 'here,' 'now,' which is water and freezes.

'This is water and freezes at 32° F.' is an occasional "illustration" of the transoccasional sentence 'Water freezes at 32° F.' We obtain such an "illustration" by ascribing a definite value of an occasional function to the "properties" designated by the symbols contained in the transoccasional sentence. A transoccasional sentence is meaningful only if it has meaningful illustrations. It is tested by means of its illustrations. We shall see later the logical laws underlying this testing. At this point we mention ony that a true illustration is a confirmatory instance of the transoccasional sentence to which it corresponds, while a false illustration is a contrary instance, and that the illustrations are logically independent of the transoccasional sentences to which they correspond (they cannot be deduced from them alone).

Let us now consider the inverse transformation: from the occasional into the transoccasional language. From an occasional sentence of the form 'This is an x,' an existential transoccasional sentence, 'There is an x,' follows directly. A universal sentence of the form 'All x's are f,' however, does not follow from the occasional sentence. 'This x is f.' The problem of induction is to find out under what circumstances it is justifiable to conclude from a number of instances in which occasional sentences of the form 'This x is f' are true that the all-sentence, 'All x's are f,' is true.

We have already mentioned another transformation of this kind: the transformation of an occasional sentence into a dated account. Since this transformation is "logically equivalent," it is understandable that the proposal has been made that all occasional sentences should be replaced by the corresponding dated accounts. This proposal, however, overlooks the fact that the dated account, precisely because it is transoccasional, cannot render the specific service which the occasional sentence can render. The mere knowledge that 'The hat Peter saw on Tuesday is green' does not help me in any way to size up my own situation here and now. In spite of the logical "equivalence" between the occasional sentence and the dated account, they are logically "independent" in the sense that neither can be deduced from the other alone.

The other transformations (either from the occasional into the transoccasional or from the transoccasional into the occasional form) are nonequivalent. Obviously, an illustration is not equivalent with the all-sentence it illustrates; we may try to exhaust the meaning of the all-sentence by conceiving the logical product of all its illustrations; but this logical product cannot be formulated on any one occasion, since it would have to contain all values of an occasional function, whereas we can "mobilize" only the contemporary values of any occasional function at a time. The logical product of the illustrations which would be equivalent to the all-sentence could unfold itself only *pari passu* with the series of situations; it could never be completely given.

We have to mention a certain difficulty in connection with our thesis that transoccasional sentences are meaningful only if they have meaningful illustrations. Obviously, there are symbols to whose designata we cannot simply ascribe a value of an occasional function. Symbols designating large geographical units or large collectivities or objects of higher "level" are cases in point. Sentences containing such symbols cannot be illustrated directly; we can give only indirect illustrations for them, e.g., by pointing out instances. Sentences dealing with the past can be illustrated only by referring to *traces* of past events.

"Formal" sentences—such as sentences dealing with sentences, numbers, etc.—can be indirectly illustrated simply by pointing out the symbols ("sign events" in Carnap's language) representing them. This is possible because operations upon the numbers, sentences, etc., are isomorphous with operations we can perform upon the symbols. It follows from this that "formal" sentences can be illustrated on every occasion, since symbols are ubiquitous: I can produce them at will.

Nonformal transoccasional sentences are, of course, different in this respect. In certain situations, illustrations for them will be available, but not in others. For some sentences, dealing with practically ubiquitous objects, we can produce illustrations almost at will. In other cases we have to wait until nature provides illustrating instances. Organic processes, for instance, have their own rhythm, and they occur only in very specific milieus.

We may mention, in this connection, the case of statistical laws. They are transoccasional sentences which cannot be illustrated by occasional sentences containing only one value of an occasional function. They can be illustrated only by occasional sentences of a more complicated character, extending over a range of values of an occasional function. Sometimes seemingly "straight" laws reveal their statistical character when we try to illustrate them in a certain fashion.

We have said above that no transoccasional sentence is meaningful if it has no meaningful illustrations. Now we have to add that these meaningful illustrations must be obtainable in every "normal" situation. Ideally, illustrations should be ubiquitous and capable of being produced at will. This ideal, however, is literally fulfilled only in the case of formal sentences, because only symbols are ubiquitous and can be produced at will. In so far as nonformal sentences are concerned, we have to declare ourselves satisfied if the instances illustrating them can be found or produced by every normal individual under well-defined conditions realizable in principle in every situation. The propositions of physics satisfy this condition.

It seems to me, however, that this requirement of meaningfulness goes too far. What it stipulates is that illustrations should be provided by experimental, laboratory methods. These methods, however, cannot be applied unreservedly where human lives, impulses, and interests are involved. On the other hand, we cannot admit that sentences dealing with such matters are necessarily meaningless. Hence it is necessary to liberalize the criteria we lay down for the meaningfulness of nonformal sentences. In addition to illustrations which can be produced at will in the framework of laboratory experiments, we also have to admit illustrations provided by "life" itself. We cannot control these illustrations as we would like to; either we have to wait for them, or they thrust themselves upon us when we are least prepared. The more uncontrollable the illustrations for a certain piece of knowledge are, the less it is a matter of exact science, and the more it calls for wisdom.

It seems to me that this "wisdom knowledge" is no less universal than "science knowledge," although it is less manageable. Universality is not the same thing as humdrum ubiquity. Sometimes the deepest and most universal meaning—universal because it illuminates vast stretches of human experience—becomes visible to us in rare moments which we know we cannot reproduce at will. Great works of art also embody such "universal" meaning. We should lose the real "universality" of our concept of meaning if we admitted as meaningful only those sentences which could be illustrated by laboratory methods. We may well insist that a sentence or concept is meaningful only if it has meaningful illustrations; but we have to admit that the context determines the kind of illustration that will be acceptable. In many cases insistence upon rigorously controllable illustrations will be justified. But these cases do not exhaust the whole realm of meaning. It would be especially erroneous to believe that sentences for which no rigorously controllable illustrations can be given are necessarily epistemologically arbitrary. This belief can be explained only as a naïve anthropomorphism of a laboratory scientist who attributes to reality itself criteria which are determined merely by his own possibilities of exercising control over things.

However, the question may be asked at this point whether it is possible to distinguish knowledge from idle speculation if we admit noncontrollable illustrations. If such evidence is admitted, then, it might be argued, even the most fantastic speculations cannot be thrown out of court; some illustration might turn out for them. And whose judgment will be competent where strict control is impossible? We have appealed to wisdom; but how is it possible to recognize it?

The answer is that in these matters no safety is attainable. There is no easy and reliable test for wisdom; and yet we cannot do without it. We know that the true universality of our concept of meaning would be lost if we restricted meaningfulness to controllable illustrations or even to a wider group of illustrations which, if they are not strictly controllable, are at least reliably and "intersubjectively" decidable. On the other hand, we also know that we run the risk of allowing for arbitrary speculation if we admit illustrations which are neither controllable nor even reliably decidable. This is a dilemma we have to face. We must find some optimum course, permitting us to obtain a maximum of insight with a minimum of arbitrariness. Within science, of course, we can admit only controllable knowledge, with a marginal element of wisdom and judgment in the background. Outside scientific theory, however, we need reasonable judgment, which has to discipline itself in the absence of safe, sure, reliable tests. This discipline of judgment is a matter no less important than the scientist's discipline of method.

It is not surprising, I think, that we encountered a dilemma in discussing the occasional "illustrations" of communicative meaning. The whole realm of meaning, indeed, is profoundly problematic. It is only by interpreting meanings that we can illuminate our situations, but there is no way of excluding interpretive error a priori. Especially the grasping of "actual" meaning, as exemplified by occasional "illustrations" of transoccasional sentences, is always an adventure; it cannot be made secure by anchoring it in logical generalities. This will be further elaborated in the next section.

3. LOGICAL OPERATIONS ON OCCASIONAL AND TRANSOCCASIONAL SENTENCES

In order to examine in greater detail the logical relations holding between occasional sentences, on the one hand, and their transoccasional "transformations"—i.e., transoccasional sentences containing the same invariable symbols—on the other, it is necessary at first to adopt a convenient notation for occasional sentences.

I shall use the letter 'h' to represent an occasional function. In this notation, 'h' may stand for words like 'here,' 'now,' 'this,' etc.; '$h.fx$' stands for: 'this x has the property f.'

But '$h.fx$' is not an occasional sentence. It is merely the text of an occasional sentence, that is, according to what we have said, a sentential function. It is obvious that a genuine occasional sentence cannot be rendered by any notation, except in a few exceptional cases, because an enduring written or printed symbol does not, in general, retain the same value as an occasional function throughout its existence. (An exception is the expression 'this book' printed in a book and referring to the same.) Thus our notation will not enable us to write occasional sentences; it will merely facilitate our discussion by enabling us to specify that we mean an occasional sentence. For this purpose, we shall introduce the symbol '$h!$'; where this symbol stands, the reader has to supply a definitive value of an occasional function. The expression '$h!fx$' stands for an occasional sentence, not merely for its text, which is nothing but a sentential function. Logical operations in which occasional sentences figure will be illustrated with such shorthand expressions, which indicate that the operation in question will be performable upon an occasional sentence, or a number of occasional sentences, with the understanding that the value of the occasional function remains the same throughout the operation.

Let '$(x).fx{\supset}gx$' be a transoccasional sentence. We may distinguish three "occasional transformations" of this sentence. The first is an "illustration": '$h!:fx.gx$.' The second transformation is an "implicative occasional transformation": '$h!.fx{\supset}gx$.' The third transformation is the "occasional extension" of the sentence, written '$(h,x)\ fx{\supset}gx$,' meaning that the implication '$fx{\supset}gx$' is true of all values of the occasional function 'h' ascribed to any x. This is not an occasional sentence, since it says something about every 'here' and 'now' rather than of a definite 'here' and 'now.'

In order to carry out logical operations in deducing occasional conclusions from transoccasional premises or vice versa, we need certain axioms.

Our first axiom is the "axiom of extension." It asserts equivalence between a formal implication and its occasional extension:

$$(x).fx{\supset}gx = (h,x)\ fx{\supset}gx . \tag{I}$$

The second axiom is that of "exemplification"; it asserts that the occasional extension of a formal implication implies the implicative occasional transformation of the formal implication:

$$(h,x)\ fx{\supset}gx : {\supset} : h!.fx{\supset}gx . \tag{II}$$

With the help of these two axioms, we can deduce occasional sentences (or "diagnoses," as we shall sometimes call occasional sentences for the sake of brevity) from a formal implication and a diagnosis. Thus, '$h!g$' can be deduced from '$(x)\ fx{\supset}gx$' and '$h!fx$' with the help of Axioms I and II. This is, indeed, the only way to deduce a simple or "molecular" occasional sentence; no 'straight" occasional sentence can be deduced from transoccasional premises alone. Actual meaning can be deduced only from actual meaning. An "occasional implication" may, indeed, be deduced from a transoccasional, formal implication alone, without an occasional premise being needed. But an implication—even if formulated in occasional language—expresses no actual meaning.

Besides deducing occasional sentences from occasional and transoccasional premises, we can also form them directly, by stating the outcome of an observation. We may ascertain directly whether an object x, present in the actual situation, does or does not exhibit the property g; in order to do this, we need only know the deictic rules governing the use of the symbol 'g.' Having obtained a diagnosis directly in this fashion, we may confront it with a corresponding diagnosis (i.e., a diagnosis containing the same value of an occasional function and the same invariable symbol or symbols) deduced from transoccasional and occasional premises. The directly obtained diagnosis may be identical with the deduced one or may be its contradictory.

Let us suppose that we obtain contradictory diagnoses from our direct inspection and from deductions: while the deduction gives '$h!g$,' direct observation gives '$-h!g$.' From this state of affairs we may draw conclusions as to the validity of the transoccasional premise; this is what we mean by saying that we "test" a universal sentence (hypothesis) by confronting it with a direct observation.

Naturally, it cannot be said that the transoccasional premise must be false whenever the directly obtained diagnosis contradicts the deduced one. There are, rather, *three* possibilities when this occurs: (1) the transoccasional premise is false; (2) the occasional premise ('$h!f$') is false; (3) the directly obtained diagnosis '$-h!g$' is false. Each of these possibilities must be carefully scrutinized in each case before we can draw a final conclusion. We can speak of a conclusive "test," invalidating the transoccasional premise, only if we can be sure that both our diagnoses are correct.

"Testing" means that transoccasional conclusions are deduced from occasional premises. For this kind of conclusion, a third axiom is valid:

$$h!fx \supset (\exists x (fx . \qquad \text{(III)}$$

This axiom asserts that each diagnosis implies a transoccasional sentence: not a formal implication, to be sure, but an existential sentence. From 'This is green' it follows that 'Something is green.' Actual meaning obviously implies potential meaning. We could not assert of anything that it is green if we did not possess a pattern of classification, foreseeing 'green' as one of its potentialities.

We can use this axiom to illustrate one of the most frequently followed lines of reasoning in the "testing" of hypotheses, although the same result could also be obtained by Axioms I and II alone.

Let us suppose that we have two diagnoses in conjunction, the one affirmative, the other negative:

$$h!fx . - gx . \qquad (a)$$

From this follows, by Axiom III,

$$(\exists x) fx . - gx . \qquad (b)$$

Now (*b*) is nothing but the negation of the formal implication '*x.fx⊃gx*.' In other words: a directly obtained conjunction of diagnoses of the form (*a*) may be used to disprove or "falsify" a formal implication. As we said, it is not necessary to use Axiom III for this purpose, since Axioms I and II are sufficient. What we need Axiom III for is rather the verification of existential propositions. In science, of course, formal implications (hypotheses) are far more important than existential propositions; and, while our Axiom III permits us to verify an existential proposition, none of our axioms enables us to verify a formal implication. If we start from occasional premises, we can only falsify formal implications but cannot verify them.

In other words, no amount of concrete, singular data may prove with strict logical certainty the truth of a nonanalytical formal implication, while a single instance may disprove it. This point has been put forcefully by Karl Popper. He concludes from this[12] that "falsifiability" rather than "verifiability" should be taken as the decisive criterion by which we can tell whether a sentence is epistemologically meaningful or not. According to him, the only really meaningful or "empirical" sentences are those which can be falsified (but not verified), whereas all sentences which are not falsifiable are "metaphysical."

This, however, does not seem to me to be convincing. Why should falsification have methodological superiority over verification? The two operations, after all, are equivalent: if I have "falsified" a proposition, I have "verified" its contradictory, and vice versa. It is quite true that the only finite, empirical operation by which we can determine the truth value of a formal implication is its falsification (and the verification of its contradictory); as long as we cannot falsify a sentence of this form, it must remain in suspense, but it cannot be verified conclusively. And we may add that the same is true of a negative existential proposition. That there is no such thing as *S* may never be completely established by experience, but it may be disproved, namely, if a specimen of *S* is shown to exist. The same operation, of course, will verify an affirmative existential proposition.

As we see, the scope of "conclusive" empirical tests, determining the truth value of transoccasional sentences by confronting them with diagnoses, is limited. In some cases, only falsifying tests are possible, and in others, only verifying ones.

It is possible to deny, of course, that *any* empirical test can be con-

12. Karl Popper, *Logik der Forschung* (Vienna, 1935), pp. 12 ff.

clusive, even with these limitations. As R. B. Braithwaite says: "It is now generally agreed that . . . propositions [about material objects] are neither completely verifiable nor completely falsifiable."[13] He probably means here that no "crucial" diagnosis—which *would* falsify a formal implication if it were accepted unconditionally—can be considered as entirely conclusive. But, if this is so, our perplexity can certainly not be removed by the method which Braithwaite proposes in order to obtain completely verifiable sentences. This method consists in substituting for an empirical sentence 'p,' asserting that 'There is not a cat under the table,' a disjunction '$p \lor q$,' where 'q' says that 'The experience conveying the supposed fact that there is no cat under the table is unreliable.'[14] That the disjunction will always be true cannot be denied, since its terms are, in fact, contradictory; but for this very reason it is not a "completely verified empirical sentence" but a tautology.

Instead of trying to design methods for obtaining "completely verifiable" empirical sentences, we shall admit that no empirical tests are absolutely conclusive; we can never be absolutely sure that subsequent tests will not induce us to question the outcome of a crucial test. Nevertheless, we shall continue to speak of conclusive, crucial tests in a relative sense. A test is relatively conclusive if it leads to the establishment of the truth value of a transoccasional sentence on the strength of a diagnosis which cannot be doubted without questioning the reliability of direct observation, carried out with every precaution characterizing the best available observational technique. The certainty of such diagnoses is not absolute; it is possible to doubt them and to assume that a recheck would invalidate them. To consider any one observation, or series of observations, as a "conclusive" test of a transoccasional hypothesis is a *decision*, although, of course, no *arbitrary* decision. We are justified in considering such tests as conclusive, because this is the only way in which it is possible to preserve the logical coherence of our knowledge without severing our contact with reality. To refuse to recognize the decisiveness of diagnoses in testing hypotheses would be tantamount to denying the supremacy of actual over potential meaning—a source of grave aberrations.

If we admit "conclusive" tests in this relative sense, we may say that we have two classes of transoccasional sentences which can be conclusively falsified but not verified and two other classes which can be

13. In *Erkenntnis*, VII (1937), 281.
14. *Ibid.*, p. 286.

conclusively verified but not falsified. The former are affirmative formal implications and negative existential sentences; the latter, negative formal implications and affirmative existential sentences. That a thing of a certain kind exists and that not all specimens of a certain class of things exhibit a certain property may be shown by finite experience (since one single instance will corroborate it); but it cannot be refuted by finite experience. I confess I do not see the slightest reason why sentences of this kind should be considered "metaphysical," as Popper suggests. It would seem better to reserve depreciating adjectives, suggesting epistemological meaninglessness, for sentences (or, rather, sentence-like expressions) not admitting of any conclusive test of their truth value—either verification or falsification. Since no empirical transoccasional sentence admits of both, we cannot consider it a defect of meaning if a sentence fails to lend itself to one of these operations.

Meaningful transoccasional empirical sentences are of two kinds: either verifiable but not falsifiable or falsifiable but not verifiable. We may designate sentences of the first kind as the "V" class, and those of the second kind as the "F" class of transoccasional empirical sentences. "V" sentences are, as we have seen, either affirmative existential sentences or negative formal implications; "F" sentences are affirmative formal implications or negative existential sentences. A "V" sentence must be left in suspense until it is verified; an "F" sentence must be left in suspense until it is falsified.

There is, however, an important difference between "V" and "F" sentences which concerns precisely this "being left in suspense." To be "verifiable but not verified" is something very much different from being "falsifiable but not falsified." In the former case it appears that we have tried to verify a sentence but did not succeed; in the latter, that we have tried to falsify it but did not succeed. Now an unsuccessful attempt at verification is unmitigated failure, but an unsuccessful attempt at falsification is, in a way, a success. Only "F" sentences can be tested with a measure of success without being either conclusively verified or disproved. For "V" sentences the only successful confirmation is complete verification.

In testing a transoccasional sentence, we confront it with an actual situation. To this end, we may do one of two things. First, we may deduce a diagnosis from the transoccasional sentence which is to be tested and from another, independently obtained, diagnosis and confront the *deduced* diagnosis with one obtained through the direct inspection of the situation. Second, we may proceed in the inverse way: that is, we deduce from a diagnosis obtained through direct inspection a transoccasional sentence and then compare the deduced transoccasional sentence with the one which is to be tested. If there is coincidence between the deduced and the directly obtained diagnosis or between the deduced and the examined transoccasional sentence, the situation may be said to be "consonant" with the transoccasional sentence under test; otherwise, the situation is "not consonant" with the sentence.

That in a specific instance the situation is found "consonant" or "not consonant" with a transoccasional sentence does not necessarily determine the latter's truth value. If, for instance, nothing is found consonant with a "V" sentence, it does not mean that the sentence is disproved; all such tests are, in fact, inconclusive. Conversely, if a situation is found to be "consonant" with an "F" sentence, this again means only that the test is inconclusive rather than that the sentence is verified. But let us suppose that the series of inconclusive tests is indefinitely prolonged in both cases. In the case of the "V" sentence, this would mean that nothing consonant with it would be found, no matter how long we continued the series of our tests; the limit toward which the series converges is disproof. In the case of the "F" sentences, on the other hand, the indefinite prolongation of the series of inconclusive tests would mean that, as far as we can go, we would encounter only situations consonant with our hypothesis; this series of inconclusive tests converges toward verification.

We cannot, of course, continue any series of tests indefinitely; we have to stop at a point. When a critical point is reached, we "extrapolate" and "go to the limit," that is to say, we declare our "V" sentence falsified and our "F" sentence verified. This kind of "extrapolatory" verification and falsification may be called "inductive" verification and "elimination," respectively.

In actual practice, of course, there is more to inductive verification and elimination than just extrapolation from an unfinished series of tests. What the scientist is actually doing is not merely to repeat the same crucial experiment again and again until he reaches the point where he convinces himself that it is safe to "extrapolate," i.e., to assume that further tests would have the same result. This does happen, of course, but this pattern fits rather the necessary rechecking of an observation than the inductive confirmation of a hypothesis. In the latter, mechanical repetition is less important than the building-up of a kind of "reticular" pattern in which new theories are derived from experiments and new experiments are postulated on the basis of theories. The whole pattern, which straddles the "actual" and "potential" poles of meaning, must be kept in constant equilibrium. Ideally, one single crucial experiment is often considered sufficient confirmation of a hypothesis. Whether one experiment is sufficient or a long series is needed depends on the logical structure of each individual case.

Real scientific procedure also differs from this rigid schema, in that one contrary instance does not lead necessarily and automatically to the dismissal of a hypothesis. Rather, it does not seem to make much difference whether the one crucial experiment whose outcome is to be accepted as decisive points toward confirmation or toward disproof. In both cases the decisiveness of the experiment depends on the logical structure of the situation. And, even when a hypothesis has to be abandoned on the strength of an unfavorable crucial test, it seldom happens that one isolated implication is expunged from the scientific universe, with the rest unaffected. In other words, the question is not whether sentences as isolated entities should be saved or dismissed but rather how the entire system of scientific propositions should be altered to account for all crucial tests while remaining coherent.

If we look at sentences in isolation, the distinction between "V" and "F" sentences remains valid, and, according to the type of sentence at hand, the determination of truth values will require either one crucial test or an open series of tests. The accompanying table shows these relationships at a single glance.

Determination of the Truth Value of		Finite	Indefinite
"V" sentences	Affirmative existential sentences Negative formal implications	Straight verification	Elimination
"F" sentences	Negative existential sentences Affirmative formal implications	Falsification	Inductive verification

This table, however, should not be interpreted as illustrating actual procedures in scientific inquiry. In particular, it should not mislead us into believing that scientific hypotheses derive their strength merely from not being falsified. If a hypothesis is successful, it is not merely that each situation that has been investigated has turned out to be consonant with it; in addition to that, the hypothesis must also represent the best logical link between observational data, on the one hand, and other theoretical assumptions, on the other. There is more to the existence of a scientific hypothesis than waiting until just one contrary instance knocks it down. If it is a good hypothesis, it will not only jibe with observations but also lead to further fruitful hypotheses. These are essential to its being "verified." And the logical center of gravity of a hypothesis is still verification, not falsification.

CHAPTER VII

THE LANGUAGE OF EMPIRICAL SCIENCE

1. Scientific Propositions

THE propositions constituting the body of any science are transoccasional. Only transoccasional sentences can be formulated once and for all, passed on to the next generation of students, tested, and revised. Hence we may say that science as a system of propositions conveys only potential meaning. Potential meaning, however, is the potentiality of actual meaning; if scientific propositions are meaningful at all, it is because they can be confronted with actual situations, because we can see what difference they make to this or that actual situation. But there are certain differences in this respect between propositions occurring in different sciences.

So far, we have discussed two types of transoccasional sentences, namely, formal implications (all-sentences) and existential propositions. These two types of sentence constitute a class in itself. Logically, they are equivalent; the negation of a formal implication can be stated as an existential sentence, and vice versa. Such sentences will be designated as "sentences of unlimited generality."

It is characteristic of a "sentence of unlimited generality" that it may be exemplified in any situation; the sentence itself does not restrict possible actualization to a set of situations, defined by a value or a range of values, of an occasional function. Natural laws, for instance, are formulated in a language of "unlimited generality."

We may, however, speak of transoccasional sentences of "limited generality." These play an important role in certain sciences. Such sentences are "individual sentences," on the one hand, and "historical sentences" or "dated accounts," on the other.

Let us take, for instance, the individual sentence '$f(A)$,' where 'A' is a proper name and 'f' designates a property. The sentence asserts that the individual object A has the property f. Now we have seen that a proper name does not designate an absolute singularity; the individual object for which it stands may be broken down into a collectivity of individual instances. But if this is so, could we not try to formulate our individual sentence as a formal implication? We might, for instance, define an individual sentence as follows:

$$f(A) =_{\text{Df}} (x) : x = A . \supset . fx .$$

In other words: to assert that an object A has the property f means to assert that, if any given object is identical with the individual A, it has the property f. The latter assertion is one of "unlimited generality," and, if an individual sentence were nothing more than such an assertion, it also would have "unlimited generality." It seems to me, however, that the above definition does not render full justice to the meaning of the individual sentence.

The point is that "being identical with A" is not simply a recurrent property, like a color, for example. When we say of a thing that 'this is A,' we mean not only that one of the things present in our situation exhibits the recurrent property of 'being identical with A,' but that A itself is present—that very thing which in other situations may be pointed out as A. To use our terminology: 'A' is defined by a certain value of the occasional function 'this,' which is itself invariant with regard to a certain (indeterminate) range of the occasional functions 'here' and 'now.' Thus the individual sentence as such is transoccasional, but one of its invariable symbols—the proper name—is defined by a value of an occasional function. This is not made apparent by the above definition.

The use of a proper name presupposes that there is an enduring object, conserving its identity throughout its life-history, to which the name can be applied. This object corresponds to a value of the occasional function 'this'; all the values of the occasional functions 'here' and 'now' which are satisfied when this value of the occasional function 'this' is satisfied are arranged along a historical route, which must be considered continuous and along which the genetic identity[1] of the object is maintained. Such a route can be represented by co-ordinate values. The *different* values of the occasional function 'this,' on the other hand, cannot be so represented: they cannot be derived from one another. We may call occasional functions of this kind "noncoordinated," to be distinguished from "co-ordinated" functions such as 'here' and 'now.' For example, 'I' is a nonco-ordinated occasional function, like 'this.' The values of such occasional functions are enduring individual objects which may be "present in" a situation and

1. Cf. Kurt Lewin, *Der Begriff der Genese in Physik, Biologie und Entwicklungsgeschichte* (Berlin, 1922).

upon which operations may be performed.

Now let us turn to "historical sentences" or "dated accounts." Such sentences may be written in the form: '$h_{m,n}P$,' meaning that the event P took place on an occasion when the value of the occasional function 'h,' expressed in terms of certain co-ordinates, was $m,n,\ldots$, etc. Because the value of 'h' is not pointed out directly but is expressed by means of co-ordinates, this is a transoccasional sentence. But it is not one of "unlimited generality."

The attempt could be made to define a "historical sentence" or "dated account" as an existential sentence:

$$h_{m,n}P =_{Df} \exists x : x = P.h =_{m,n}.$$

In words: to assert that the event P took place on the occasion characterized by the co-ordinate values m, n of the occasional function 'h' means to assert that the totality of all events contains one having the characteristic 'P' and corresponding to the 'dating' co-ordinate values m and n.

This definition, however, does not do justice to the real meaning of the "dated account." The definiens does not indicate that anything different from recurrent properties is involved. In other words, nothing suggests that m and n, the "dates," are values in a unique co-ordinate system in which the recurrence of the same value on various occasions is excluded or at least limited. Temporal dates, for instance, are definitely nonrecurrent; 'now' can never again have the same value that it had on a past date. The definiens equally fails to point out that 'm' and 'n,' though possibly nonrecurrent, are related to the present values of 'h' by a definite "interval." What the dated account asserts, therefore, is not only that the event of which certain things may truthfully be said is (or has been) a real one but also that the values of certain occasional functions corresponding to that event are linked by certain intervals to their present values.

This is important, because it concerns the actualization of the meaning of a dated account. Since the dated account is satisfied only by one definite value of an occasional function, it cannot be directly "illustrated" by any '$h!$' sentence. This does not mean, however, that its meaning is incapable of "actualization," i.e., has no bearing on the actual situation in any case. Its bearing on the present situation can be expressed by means of the "interval" which exists between the present value of 'h' on the one hand, and 'm,n,' on the other. Thus the actual illustration of a dated account will be a sentence of the form '$h! P_{\text{int } m,n}$,' meaning that the event P is separated from 'here' and 'now' by the interval which is that separating the actual dates from 'm' and 'n.'

Obviously, the interval as such is not given "here" and "now." It is only inferable from things present here and now, such as milestones, calendars, records, and traces. Sentences of the form 'h! $P_{\text{int } m,n}$' are not, as a rule, obtained through direct inspection; they must be deduced from occasional and transoccasional premises. The calendar of Robinson Crusoe, in which each day was represented by a notch, always enabled him to tell at a glance the number of days elapsed since his arrival on the island, because he knew he had made just one notch every day. But in most cases the determination of the interval is less simple than that. It may be that we possess one apparently contemporary record which gives the date in terms intelligible to us, i.e., translatable into the language of our own calendar. But historical evidence may also be incomplete, unclear, or contradictory. The date may be lacking altogether or may be given in terms of a calendar unfamiliar to us. One set of records may also contradict another. It may be that, in the absence of reliable contemporary records, we must content ourselves with more or less precarious indirect evidence. Then it may happen that certain data suggest that the event under examination is fictitious, whereas other data seem to prove that it is real. The historian's task is to evaluate all data in such a way as to arrive at warranted conclusions concerning past events. In this endeavor he will have to rely mainly on enduring objects connected, as traces or records, with a certain locus of space-time. The evidence for historical sentences rests on these objects; it is similar to the evidence for individual sentences. We may say, in this sense, that historical sentences have "limited generality."

All this should not be taken to mean, however, that physical sciences are interested only in "general laws," and historical sciences only in "individual cases."[2] Such a dichotomy, in fact, says nothing at all. Ultimately, no sentence has meaning except in so far as it bears on individual situations; but it could have no bearing on the actual situation unless it referred to something potentially recurring in many situations. The "individual cases" illustrating physical laws are just as indispensable to physics as the "general laws" explaining individual incidents are to history. It is true, however, that the body of physical theory contains no reference to any one of the individual cases in

2. Cf. Heinrich Rickert, *Grenzen der naturwissenschaftlichen Begriffsbildung* (3d ed.; Tübingen, 1921).

which this or that physical law has an actual bearing on the situation. The "incidence" of a physical law is not dealt with in the proposition expounding the law. The historian, on the other hand, deals precisely with the "incidence" of laws which are formulated in part by non-historical disciplines.

If we define a "theory" as an attempt to formulate a mass of available evidence in a manner free from contradiction, we may say that historians as well as physicists are engaged in establishing "theories." The difference between the kinds of theory cultivated by the historian and the physicist, respectively, is that, in order to illustrate the physicist's theory, we may use examples available, as it were, at any time and everywhere, whereas the historian's theory can be illustrated only if certain objects (or copies thereof) are present.

In both cases theories must satisfy a number of conditions. They must account for all individual illustrations and possibly even lead to correct predictions of new kinds of illustrations; they must also be consistent with other established theories. Within this general framework, however, there are considerable differences between "historical" and "nonhistorical" theories.

Let us examine historical theories first. "History" may be defined as the systematic study of the *incidence* of laws, including laws established by other sciences. The emphasis is on "systematic." An isolated diagnosis which points out the incidence of some law here and now is no part of historic "theory," although it may be raw material for history.

Any systematic study of the incidences of certain laws—e.g., the laws of heredity as impinging upon a certain population—would be "history." History, however, is not written to record the incidence of each and every natural law. "Incidences" of laws, in fact, are studied only if and because they are important in themselves. They are studied for their own sake, not merely as "illustrations" of general laws. The mere description of historical events in itself is sometimes an important goal of the efforts of historians, even if it is impossible to specify any laws of which those events are the "incidences," although the ultimate goal of the historian is to pass from description to explanation. In general, we may say that we want to "explain" events and sequences of events which interest us in themselves. This applies, for instance, to the historic route by which our own society has reached its present state.

The laws which we can use best for the purposes of such explanation are not the general laws of physics. Nothing would be gained for the understanding of the historical evolution of our society if we recorded the history of how gravitation affected each point of the territory. The laws we need are those governing the behavior of groups and individuals. These laws, however, differ in an important respect from those of physical reality; they can be formulated only by explicit reference to sets of their incidences. We shall call such laws "historic," to be distinguished from the ordinary (nonhistorical) type of law.

A nonhistorical causal law is an invariant of all its incidences. Such laws assert that a certain system S, characterized by the properties p_1, p_2, . . . , etc., will undergo such and such changes under such and such circumstances, no matter what had happened before. Now it will be found that in some cases we encounter systems whose behavior on future occasions will be different form their past behavior under analogous circumstances, if in the meantime they have experienced certain influences. This will prevent us from formulating a law describing the behavior of the system regardless of what has happened before. In order to be able to predict how these systems will behave on a certain occasion, we must know the historical route they have traversed. In other words, the law characterizing their behavior must take its own incidence into account. There are examples of such systems in the inanimate world; magnetization is a case in point. But it is in the realm of life that this kind of law becomes predominant. As a rule, we cannot predict how an organism will behave, "regardless of what happened before." In many cases the organism will react in a way determined by its history; different historical routes lead to different reactions. The law characterizing the behavior of the organism must be stated in terms of its own incidences. We may say in this sense that an organism is a "historical" being.

Laws expressed in terms of their incidences can be applied only if the incidences are known. If an observer knows such a law and knows the present state of a system but is ignorant of the past incidences of the law, he is in a condition which may be described as "historical perplexity." As long as the perplexity persists, the behavior of the system remains unpredictable.

"Historical perplexity" could never be overcome, short of the reconstruction of the entire historical route of the system (which, however, is often impracticable), if the *entire* historical route were uniformly relevant and each variation in the historical route made a difference to the system's way of reacting to external impulses. If this were the case, however, not only would there be insuperable "perplexity" concerning the application of the law, but there would be no law at all. We can formulate laws concerning the behavior of "historical" beings only because many different historical routes are "equivalent" as to the way in which they modify behavior.

If external influences have induced an organism to change its behavior in a certain sense, the new way of behaving can often be determined by certain tests. In other words, the new kind of behavior can be inferred from certain "properties" of the system which can be ascertained in a nonhistorical way. In so far as an "acquired" way of behaving can be ascertained by means of tests, we can say that the behavior in question has a certain "level." We may say that the way in which organisms will react to definite stimuli depends, in many respects, not so much on the entire historical route in its individual concreteness as on the "level" that has been reached by that route. Skills such as "speaking a language," etc., are good examples of "levels." Obviously, "levels" characterize a behavior only in a rough way; the knowledge of certain concrete details of the route is required if we want to account for certain reactions.

In practice, our aim is to foresee as much as possible of the future behavior of the system by means of the "level" of its behavior. In other words, we seek to replace historical laws by nonhistorical ones. This is how we try to overcome "historical perplexity." Once a "level of behavior" is ascertained, it can be used as a nonhistorical datum. To return to the example of magnetization, the mere macroscopic inspection of a piece of iron leaves us in a state of "historical perplexity": we do not know how it will behave if we do not know whether it has been magnetized. But this perplexity is easily overcome; we may ascertain the "level of behavior" of the piece of iron by seeing whether it will attract another piece of iron, or we may examine its molecular structure and draw our conclusions from it. Where the historical route changes the behavior of a system by modifying its morphology, the change can be described in nonhistorical terms.

The morphological properties—"instincts," etc.—of organisms are like "levels," in that they enable us to predict certain phases of their behavior regardless of historical routes. "Historical perplexity" comes in when we are dealing with acquired, learned behavior patterns. This historical perplexity is mitigated only by the fact that adaptation often is progressive, passing through certain typical "levels"; a certain type of behavior corresponds to each "level" (of skill, etc.).

Organisms, which are historical beings, may be treated on a par with nonhistorical beings, inasmuch as their behavior is situated on a certain level—with an important exception with which we shall deal later. Transitions between levels, however, must be treated "historically."

We may consider types of behavior, starting with those of non-historical physical systems and proceeding toward "historical" patterns of lower and higher organisms, as displaying a hierarchy of "levels." Systems which have reached a higher level in this hierarchy remain subject to the laws of lower levels. Ontogenetic adaptation does not eliminate the "instincts."

Ascent from the lower to the higher levels in this hierarchy is the proper field of history; levels which have been surpassed in the hierarchy constitute the sphere of "nonhistorical" laws.

The highest level reached thus far—that of meaning-oriented contextual behavior—is characterized by the fact that its historicity is insurmountable. On this level, historical perplexity cannot be overcome by the knowledge of the level as such, and behavior cannot be treated in nonhistorical terms (this is the exception to which we alluded above). Historical theories accounting for behavior on this level must take meanings into account; that is to say, they have to reckon with factors which influence behavior without determining it. This means that these theories cannot be completely deterministic; they must leave a certain scope for "freedom." This "freedom," however, is not *lack* of determination; it stems rather from the fact that there are two sorts of affective causal factors: meanings and "brute" factors, the one superposed on the other.

Now to turn to nonhistorical sciences: we may say, in the first place, that they have greater (less limited) "generality" than historical sciences, because their illustrations are not limited to definite values of occasional functions. Moreover, they can state most of their propositions without taking their incidences into account. Therefore, the structure of nonhistorical theories is less complicated than that of historical ones.

Because of their greater "generality," nonhistorical sciences are further removed from concrete, unique situations than historical ones. (That even the most concrete historical sentences are "transoccasional," and hence infinitely removed from the *really* unique and concrete, we have seen.)

Transoccasional sentences of unlimited generality may differ among themselves as regards their degree of abstraction. We may say of a formal implication, '$(x)\ fx \supset gx$,' that it has a low degree of abstraction if 'f' and 'g' stand for isolated, concrete properties, identifiable by direct inspection based upon intuition: 'Oak leaves are green.' To the scientific temper, such laws are too concrete; we are striving for more abstract, more universal laws, i.e., laws which can be applied to as many (superficially different) phenomena as possible. Hence we seek to establish laws referring not to isolated concrete properties but to functions covering a wide range of possible properties. Metrical functions satisfy this requirement. They satisfy it because they are "formal" in the sense that any value of a metrical function may be obtained by repeating a few elementary operations. Physical theory deals mostly with such functions.

Metrical functions, however, do not represent the only type of law occurring in physical theory. There are phenomena which require statistical treatment, combined with metrical functions. Also, the metric itself which we have to apply to physical phenomena is rather problematic. Thus we have, besides ordinary "metrical" physics, statistical physics, on the one hand, and the more speculative physics of space (of the Einsteinian type), on the other. Each of these varieties of physical laws, however, strives for comprehensiveness. There is no part of the universe which could not be described in terms of some physical theory. Yet, as we have seen, physics does not account for every type of occurrence, especially the higher "levels" of organic life.

Thus, if we compare "historical" and "nonhistorical" theories, we shall find that, while the latter are far more comprehensive, the former are able to deal with phenomena which have a closer bearing on our own problems. Not that the physical universe is a matter of indifference to us—quite the contrary. Nothing has changed human life more fundamentally than the discoveries made during the last few centuries concerning the physical universe. This transformation, however, has been brought about not by the physical phenomena themselves but by man exploiting them for his own ends. We can understand the impact of physical science upon human life only with the help of a theory of behavior. This theory, however, deals with a sphere of "insurmountable historicity." The impact of physical science upon life cannot be explained by a science of the same structural type as physics.

So much for the scientific theories themselves—the "transoccasional" propositions of science. In order to make our survey of the language of science more complete, we also have to deal with "occasional" sentences formulated in scientific language. First of all, we shall consider the "application" of scientific theories.

To "apply" a scientific theory to a situation means to deduce a predictive diagnosis from a theory and from a descriptive diagnosis, obtained through direct inspection. The person who is able to formulate correct predictive diagnoses in this fashion is the "expert." We must distinguish the role of the expert from that of the scientist proper: the builder of theories. Obviously, both roles may be played by the same person, but the roles as such are different. Theory proper has precedence over the expert's work, inasmuch as the latter would not be possible without the former; but, from another viewpoint, we may also say that the scientist exists for the sake of the expert: his work acquires meaning by being "applied."

Let us examine the expert's procedure a little more closely. First, he has to isolate a feature of the situation which can be subsumed under a scientific theory; then he must work out the subsumption and draw the correct inferences. In this procedure, observation and deduction lead to anticipation. The first stage consists in operations upon things; the second, in operations upon symbols; the third again turns toward the things. Both the operations upon things and the operations upon symbols must be so devised that they can interlock.

This is most remarkably insured in the case of so-called "formal" laws and operations, those in which every possibility in the universe of discourse can be obtained by repeating a few primitive steps. A formal operation, performed upon symbols, is "calculation"; performed upon things, it is "measurement." Although the materials used in performing these operations are quite different, they structurally correspond to each other. Calculation and measurement can interlock. A diagnosis obtained by calculation can be direcly confronted with one based upon measurement.

In the case of nonformal ("intuitive") laws, such structural correspondence does not exist. In making anticipations, the expert must rely on memory and imagination: he will expect to happen what he has seen happening. Yet, even where it is impossible to attain complete structural correspondence between the observational and the deductive phase of the expert's work, it is possible to approximate it by the systematization of experience.

The fascination of "formal" laws consists in the fact that the result of calculations, although these have an independent meaning of their own as symbolic operations, can be immediately "translated" into observational terms. Calculations have a "systematic" meaning, whereas "nonformal" laws are only "empirically" meaningful: they have no meaning apart from the possibility of application. Compared to the elegance of formal laws, they represent a phase of knowledge that Plato would dismiss as mere ἐμπειρία καὶ τριβή.

2. PROTOCOL SENTENCES

Scientific theory in the making necessitates interlocking operations of calculation, observation, and anticipation that are closely related to the expert's activities as described above. In testing theories, the scientist also must form predictive diagnoses on the basis of theories and observations. To a theory in the making, the confirmation of such predictive diagnoses is somehow crucial.

The Vienna circle has studied the role of observational records in testing hypotheses under the heading of "protocol sentences."[3] In these studies the protocol sentences are not characterized as occasional sentences; they are, in fact, "dated accounts," formulating the results of an observation in historical form, identifying the value of the occasional functions corresponding to the situation in the form of dates. It is obvious, however, that the protocol sentences are meant to transcribe actual experience: they are based upon 'h!'-sentences, and their epistemological value (as crucial evidence) is based upon this fact. Thus, from the "T-protocol" (a protocol written down in transoccasional language, as a dated account), we may distinguish the "O-protocol," comprising the original occasional diagnosis upon which it is based. The T-protocols are handed down to posterity and may be used as documents, whereas the O-protocols perish with the situation. Yet the meaning of the T-protocol is that it preserves the O-protocol.

What is the logical and epistemological character of protocol sentences? It is obvious, in the first place, that they cannot be deduced from other propositions; they are obtained through direct observation.

---

3. Cf. R. Carnap, *Erkenntnis*, II (1931), 219 ff., 432 ff.; III (1932), 177 ff., 215 ff.; E. Zilsel, *Erkenntnis*, III (1932), 143 ff.; O. Neurath, *Erkenntnis*, III (1932), 204 ff.; K. Popper, *Logik der Forschung* (Vienna, 1935), pp. 55 ff.; R. Carnap, *Logische Syntax der Sprache* (Vienna, 1934), p. 244.

What kind of sentences are they, then? Is it possible to ascribe a definite truth value to them?

Sentences which cannot be deduced from other sentences may be (*a*) fundamental principles, (*b*) axioms, (*c*) "conventions," such as definitions, and (*d*) "decisions."

Sentences of the first group—fundamental principles—have a definite truth value; basic logical principles, for instance, may be considered as true propositions.

Axioms, on the other hand, are not "true" or "false." They specify certain conditions, referring to a set of propositions, such that certain conclusions follow if the conditions are satisfied. Changing the conditions, we obtain a different axiomatic system, but there is no way of telling which axiomatic system is "more true" than another one.

Conventions also are neither true nor false. From a strictly logical point of view, they are arbitrary. Still, it makes a difference, even to logic, what conventions we adopt. Rules of games, for instance, are conventions. We may create games and specify any rule we wish, but only within certain limits. The rules, for instance, must not be either ambiguous or contradictory; otherwise, it would be impossible to play the game in an ordered fashion. Or let us take definitions. A definition is not an assertion, it is not true or false; yet it is possible to distinguish "good" and "bad" definitions.

It is customary to distinguish "verbal" and "real" definitions. Let us consider first the one kind, then the other.

A verbal definition is a rule introducing a new, simple expression as a complete equivalent of a composite expression consisting of symbols already understood. From a logical viewpoint we are free to introduce as many verbal definitions as we wish, although for psychological reasons it is advisable not to enlarge the vocabulary of our language beyond a certain limit. We are also free to "coin" the new terms we define. But, even from the point of view of logic, there is a limit to the arbitrariness of verbal definitions—that is, the *definientia*, the expressions we replace by new terms, must be "understood." They must not, for instance, be contradictory; otherwise, all expressions containing the *definienda* would be meaningless.

A real definition is an expression analyzing a deictic rule (cf. p. 75, above). For instance, if we define a "shrew" as "a certain small, mouselike animal," we mean that the deictic rule governing the correct use of the word "shrew" can be broken down into a number of deictic rules. Although itself conventional, the real definition implies assertions of fact: that is, that there are real objects corresponding to a certain combination of deictic rules. Thus there are certain limits to our freedom in introducing definitions.

Now it is obvious that protocol sentences are neither fundamental principles nor axioms nor definitions. This leaves us only one possibility in terms of our enumeration: they must be a kind of "decision." This does not necessarily mean that we must consider them as "arbitrary" from a logical point of view; as we have seen, the other types of nondeducible expressions also are not wholly arbitrary. However, the question confronting us is not whether protocol sentences as "decisions" are *wholly* arbitrary or not, but whether they should be treated as sentences. Should we treat them as either true or false or as expressions having no definite truth value?

Popper and Carnap adopt the latter approach. Popper, who calls protocol sentences "basic sentences" (*Basissätze*), declares that their adoption is based upon a "decision" which is not subject to the jurisdiction of logic. The "experiences" upon which basic sentences are grounded are not instances of logical proof. There are reasons impelling the observer to adopt a "basic sentence," but this motivation concerns psychology rather than logic; "from the point of view of logic, the adoption of a basic sentence is an arbitrary decision."[4]

Carnap expounds a similar view: "From the viewpoint of logic," he says, "every conceivable set of protocol sentences is equally justifiable."[5] The question of why a protocol sentence is adopted, according to Carnap, is meaningless; he considers protocol sentences as data which the scientist subjects to analysis rather than as parts of scientific discourse.

It seems to me that Carnap's interpretation is more consistent with the view that protocol sentences are wholly arbitrary than is Popper's theory. If the protocol sentences are really *Sätze*, they must be considered as either true or false; but then the decision by virtue of which we ascribe a certain truth value to them cannot be logically neutral. In a sense, of course, the reasons for which we ascribe truth value to a protocol sentence are "extra-logical": we cannot logically prove it, since it is neither an analytical truth nor deducible within the framework of an axiomatic system. Nevertheless, if we ascribe truth value to a sentence within a scientific system, our reasons must be distinguishable from psychological urges which are neutral toward the

4. *Op. cit.*, p. 65.
5. *Erkenntnis*, II (1931), 179.

quest of truth. The question is how a decision concerning the acceptance or rejection of a sentence can be scientifically "right" in the absence of logical proof. It seems to me that the only possible answer is that such a decision must be "meaning-oriented," that is, governed not only by "brute" psychological factors but also by "meanings." If the admission of a protocol sentence is a scientific decision, it cannot be logically arbitrary.

For Carnap, this difficulty does not arise, for he sees that, if protocol sentences are wholly arbitrary, they cannot be genuine sentences. According to him, protocol sentences must be treated like "signals" devoid of any linguistic meaning.[6] A "language" is to be constructed by endowing the signals with meaning. Thus if we notice that certain protocols contain the letter combination 'snow,' we may find, upon analyzing the situations in which the protocols have originated, that the letter combination is a "signal" for the presence of the substance we call "snow." This interpretation itself must be considered a hypothesis; further analysis of the protocols may suggest a different interpretation.

The logical meaning of Carnap's view of protocol sentences is this: If there is apparent contradiction between two protocols, it does not follow that one must be false ("principle of tolerance"). The apparent contradiction may always be removed by finding a suitable new interpretation for one or both protocols; thus any set of protocols may be made consistent.

This approach toward protocol sentences, no doubt, is logically possible. However, we need another interpretation of protocol sentences if we want to use them in testing transoccasional hypotheses. Protocols can function as controls for scientific assertions only if they have a definite linguistic meaning. As long as we consider a protocol as variably interpretable, we can conclude nothing from the fact that the protocol coincides with, or contradicts, a diagnosis deduced from the hypothesis we want to test and another observational (protocol) diagnosis. A protocol which is still to be interpreted cannot be used in verifying or disproving transoccasional sentences.

Hence we shall consider protocol sentences as expressions having a definite linguistic meaning. We shall also assume that to adopt a protocol sentence means to consider it as a "true" sentence. Our question, then, concerns the nature of the "decision" which underlies the acceptance of protocol sentences.

6. *Erkenntnis*, III (1932), 216 ff.

This question has considerable cultural importance; its implications are momentous. Much depends, indeed, on the way we answer the question of whether *all* decisions are basically of the same kind—logically arbitrary, subject only to "brute" influences—or whether some decisions differ from others in this respect. The alternative is between cultural "decisionism" and "rationalism."

Let us consider first some admittedly arbitrary and logically neutral decisions.

If, for instance, a question of interest and advantage may be settled "by decision," this means that there is a person who has the power to disregard and overrule all wishes and interests contrary to his. Such is "arbitrary" power.

Another case of "arbitrary" decision may concern a problem which, on the contrary, does not affect *any* wish or interest whatsoever. Let us suppose that a certain task can be fulfilled in several possible ways which exclude one another, but none of these specific ways makes any difference either to the successful accomplishment of the task or to any conceivable personal interest one may have in the matter. For instance, the task at hand may be to hang a map on a wall. The job can be done in four different ways, with north, east, south, or west as the upper side. A choice between these possibilities can be made only by arbitrary decision; the decision must be arbitrary precisely because "it makes no difference" how we decide.

It appears, now, that the decision to adopt or reject a protocol sentence cannot be arbitrary in either of these senses. It would be palpably absurd to consider the matter of the acceptance of protocol sentences as subject to decision by force. But the acceptance of protocol sentences cannot be an "arbitrary" decision in the other sense, either. It could be that only if it made no difference to the task at hand —the testing of scientific propositions—which of possible, and mutually contradictory, sets of protocol sentences we accept. But this is clearly not the case; the outcome of the test will be different according to whether we accept or reject a crucial protocol sentence. The problem differs from that of establishing conventions concerning indifferent matters.

If protocol sentences are not "arbitrary" decisions in either of these senses, there must be reasons for adopting or rejecting them. We can agree with Popper to the extent that these reasons are not "logical" in the sense of a logical proof. But the reasons cannot, I think, be extraneous to the task at hand: the establishment of scientific truth. In other words, they cannot be merely "psychological" or "sociological" factors. If they were, there could be no choice between contradictory decisions based upon objective criteria; contradictory protocols would simply have to be attributed to a difference in psychological and sociological backgrounds, and science, as a result, would become a mere function of psychological and sociological factors. This view, in fact, follows from the principle of "decisionism," which fails to recognize a difference between rationally founded scientific decisions ("judgments") and nonrational decisions merely depending on psychological and sociological factors.

On the rationalistic view, which is the one adopted here, decisions concerning protocol sentences are "meaning-oriented." Above all, they are oriented toward the "deictic rules" governing the use of terms employed in formulating observations. It may always be asked whether a protocol is "correct" or not; to ask this means to inquire whether the account of an observation is correct in terms of certain deictic rules.

If we are satisfied that a protocol as such is correct, we can use it in testing a hypothesis. We have repeatedly alluded to the procedure followed in carrying out these tests: the deduction of a diagnosis, and its confrontation with a diagnosis, containing the same invariable term or terms obtained through direct observation. The crucial question is whether the deduced and the directly obtained diagnosis coincide or are mutually contradictory.

Let us suppose that the latter case arises. From the hypothesis which is to be tested and from a directly observed datum, we deduced the diagnosis '$h!f$'; through direct observation we get its contradictory, '$-h!f$.' In this case, we may draw one of the following four conclusions:

1. '$h!f$' really follows from the hypothesis which is to be tested and from the pertinent data of the situation. On the other hand, '$-h!f$' is a correct description of the prevailing situation; that is, the property 'f,' so called in the same language as the one used by the authors of the hypothesis, is not present in the situation. This means that there is contradiction between the protocol and the hypothesis; if the test is accepted as crucial, the hypothesis must be discarded.

2. '$h!f$' follows from the hypothesis and the pertinent occasional data, but there is no real contradiction with the protocol '$-h!f$,' because the protocol is not couched in the same language as the hypothesis. In order to obtain a conclusive test, we have to reinterpret the

protocol, that is, make sure that the same deictic rules are observed throughout the test.

3. The same linguistic usage is observed throughout, but the situation has changed with regard to the conditions for the presence of 'ƒ' asserted by the hypothesis. If this is the case, 'h!ƒ' does not follow from the hypothesis and the pertinent observational data, and there is no contradiction with the protocol '—h!ƒ.'

4. There is no workable "deictic rule" corresponding to the property 'ƒ,' that is, there is no operation by which the presence or absence of 'ƒ' could be reliably established in any situation. This means that 'ƒ' is meaningless, and so are all the hypotheses and diagnoses in which it occurs. Of course, meaningless hypotheses cannot be tested by any protocol.

Which of these four cases prevails can be determined only by the careful analysis of the situation. If two diagnoses appear contradictory, we may conclude either that there is contradiction between two empirical assertions or that the divergence is one of linguistic usage. Carnap's "principle of tolerance" points in the latter direction; it maintains that each case of apparent contradiction may be treated as a case of our second alternative and that the contradiction may be removed by reinterpretation. I cannot agree that this is the *only* method by which *every* case of apparent contradiction must be treated; our aim, after all, is not to make all protocols consistent but to know when a protocol contradicts our hypothesis and when it does not. Certain cases, however, are conceivable in which the discrepancy of our data compels us to resort to reinterpretation and to analyze protocols in terms of linguistic usage rather than of the objective data to which they seem to refer.

As long as questions of interpretation do not arise, we apply our "deictic rules," as it were, naïvely, instinctively, without paying any attention to the rules as such and how they have to be applied. As long as we do this, our discourse may be said to be in the "empirical" mode. When, on the other hand, we try to eliminate discrepancies by assuming possible differences in "usage" and possible violations of deictic rules, our attitude is no longer purely empirical. Then we no longer merely ask what the facts are but also how the facts can be "correctly" described in terms of a linguistic convention. A linguistic convention cannot be described in purely empirical terms, since the meaning of the convention cannot be exhausted by the description of the behavior of the linguistic community.

In this connection we must pay particular attention to the *fourth* alternative described above. This is the case in which we conclude from the analysis of a test that the terms used are meaningless. Such a conclusion can never be reached by purely "empirical" methods. It does not concern facts alone, but the possibility of establishing facts. Obviously, we can speak of facts only if—and as far as—our categoreal apparatus, the deictic rules we apply, render consistency possible. If we discover discrepancies indicating that our categoreal apparatus may be faulty, we have to correct the deficiency of the categoreal apparatus before we can again attend to the facts.

This does not mean that questions of "meaningfulness" and "consistency" can be completely divorced from empirical questions. As a rule, the decision about such matters will hinge on empirical data, and the account we give of "conventions" and the like must square itself with the observed facts. What is asserted here is simply that questions concerning meanings cannot be decided *merely* by reference to facts.

This has an important bearing upon our problem: the nature of the "decision" by virtue of which observational diagnoses (O-protocols) are accepted. The *contents* of such diagnoses are purely empirical. But the meaning toward which the observational act is oriented is no purely empirical matter: it is bound up with a set of standards (deictic rules). This is why I cannot accept the "decisionism" which holds that the acceptance of crucial observational diagnoses is wholly gratuitous, or at most is determined by "brute" sociological and psychological factors. On the contrary, I hold that adoption of such diagnoses, although it is a "decision" from a purely *logical* viewpoint, has a meaning proper to it, in terms of which it can be analyzed.

Making these "decisions" dependent on psychological and sociological factors would, I think, only confuse the matter. After all, the scientific "decision" involved in the adoption of a protocol is an indispensable step in the genesis of *all* scientific knowledge. An impossible circle would result if we were obliged to possess psychological or sociological knowledge before being able to account for it. Clearly, we have to do with a problem which belongs within the jurisdiction of philosophy, whose subject matter traditionally includes the possibility of knowledge.

CHAPTER VIII

THE LANGUAGE OF INTERPRETATION

1. VALUE-LANGUAGES

ALL use of language involves interpretation, just as all "meaningful" choice behavior does. That is, in all our symbol behavior, as well as in all choice behavior, we let ourselves be guided by some standard of meaning. In the cases we have examined so far, however, we had to do with the straight or "naïve" application of standards that the situation might impose. We have been using terms like "meaning" and "interpretation," but we have not yet explored the meaning of *these* terms. Our discussion of symbols and sentences has been largely confined to the analysis of symbols with empirical reference and with empirical sentences; the assertions we have been dealing with were assertions of "brute fact." Now we shall turn to the examination of assertions which not only are "interpretable" in themselves but directly refer to some act of interpretation or to some other meaningful act qua meaningful.

What is the status of these assertions? Can they be considered as objectively valid and confirmable? And, further, can they be used only in extra-scientific, everyday, or "philosophical" language, or can we also make scientific use of them?

a) THE LANGUAGE OF CONVENTION

Let us consider, first, "rules of language" from this point of view. Our interpretive statements, referring to communications, always involve an explicit judgment; a specimen statement of this kind is, for instance, "Jones has just uttered a sentence correct in the English language." Whenever one makes an assertion of fact about some state of the world, such a judgment is implicit; some clause, such as "This communication is to be interpreted in accordance with the rules of the language *L*," must be understood as implied in every communication that is to be accepted as meaningful. But this "implicit" judgment is something different from an explicit statement that, indeed, the rules of *L* have been applied and that they have been applied correctly.

Suppose that Jones's sentence was an empirical one, asserting the existence of some state of the world. Our question is: Is the "judgment" about the linguistic correctness of the sentence also an empirical assertion?

It seems that it is not, at least not entirely. For, in order to decide whether the judgment about the "correctness" of Jones's sentence is itself correct or not, it is not enough to make observations about facts. Part of our business, to be sure, will consist in just this; we shall, for instance, look at the observational material that Jones's sentence (we suppose) referred to; and in case of doubt we may look up a word in a dictionary or ask members of the language community as to what their understanding of the agreed-upon usage in this case is. But when all these observations have been made, something remains to be done; we have to decide whether the verdict of the sources we consulted was really to be accepted as binding for us. This decision is something additional to the observations we make, and, in our case, this additional decision is indispensable. We *may* say beforehand, of course, that the verdict of the dictionary will settle the matter; but, if we say so, it is because we have decided that it is to be accepted as authoritative. The "observation" (looking up a word in a book) clinches the matter by virtue of a decision made prior to the observation: *this* decision is, in any case, additional to the observation itself, and not the *outcome* of the observation.

This is something entirely different from the case of a "crucial" observation or experiment. In this latter case we start with some belief and discover, merely by analyzing that belief, that it cannot be true unless some observation turns out in a certain way. There is no special "authority" that we ascribe to the clinching observation; all that we say is that our belief implies it, regardless of what any authority says. But our "belief" about the correctness of Jones's sentence is of a different kind. It is not a belief implying that a certain sentence will be found printed on a certain page in a certain book. We may only *decide* to accept such an implication, depending on whether we do or do not accept a certain dictionary as authority. And, even so, the "verdict" will not hinge entirely upon what we observe on the page in question; we shall feel vindicated not by the presence of such and such observable printed marks but by *any* combination of marks which—"according to the rules of the language we apply"—are consonant with our judgment. On the other hand, we shall not feel refuted, even though the entry in question turns out to be different from what we expected it to be, e.g., if it is apparent that the discrepancy is due to a typographical error.

This may be made clearer by an example. A belief we try to validate may be: West wind always brings rain. We observe that the wind is from the west; unless it starts raining within a short time, our belief cannot be true. This conclusion has been arrived at merely by analyzing the belief: the only finding we need to invalidate our assumption is "The west wind has blown, but there is no rain." Now let us take the belief that Jones has "correctly" described a flower as a lilac. We may agree that this belief will be vindicated if the illustration in Webster's dictionary, under "lilac," resembles the flower we see; but, to do this, we need a decision to the effect that "questions about correct usage in English will be decided by reference to Webster's dictionary." This has to be our *definition* of what we mean by "correct" usage, if consultation of the dictionary is to settle the matter. In this way the validation of our belief depends on a definition, and not *merely* on an observation. There is no such definitional intermediary link in the case of the west wind and the rain. Of course, in the latter case, too, we must know how "west wind" and "rain" are defined, that is, we must know what observational indices call for the use of these words; but it would be absurd to say, in this case, that the validation or nonvalidation of our belief depends on the choice of a definition. In the "west wind" case the acceptance of the definitions (rules of language) which govern our choice of terms is taken for granted; in the "lilac" case we must make explicit the basis on which we choose a word. This calls for a decision, and not merely for an observation.

Now, of course, such decisions as that to consult the dictionary are themselves fully observable, empirical events. The "validity" of such a decision, however, is not observed; it is not a matter of observation but of adhesion. What we observe is merely that someone says, "Let's consult the dictionary; that will settle the matter." We may then be ready to go along with the suggestion or not; we shall concur if we share the speaker's attitude toward the dictionary as an arbiter. The question is whether we ourselves are ready to incorporate a rule into our behavior. In the "west wind" case no such question came up for consideration; the rules to which our language behavior was supposed to conform were taken for granted.

One might suggest, in order to prove the fully empirical character of the judgments we are discussing, that all the "decisions" we are talking about may be arrived at by observing the behavior of people who use correctly the language we want to apply. This demonstration, however, cannot be successful. In order to derive "correct" usage from observed behavior, it is not enough to observe; we must also participate in the communication process. We must ourselves *do* what the subjects we observe are doing.

This is, generally speaking, the way in which conventions, such as rules of a language, are handed down to new generations of language-users. Children or pupils do not *observe* what their parents and teachers are doing; they *identify* with them. Without such identification, the rule would not be appropriated and incorporated into behavior. This distinguishes "conventional" rule-learning from other kinds of learning. One can "learn" about things of the environment without identification; thus identification plays no role in becoming "familiar" with this or that feature of our environment. And, in learning "rules" which are not merely conventional, identification with the teacher might be dispensed with—a pupil with superior intelligence might discover the same rules by himself, as Pascal is said to have rediscovered the proofs of Euclidean geometry. But no degree of intelligence would enable anyone to discover language conventions; these can be taken over only from models considered to be authoritative.

The scientist, making supposedly purely empirical observations about the language behavior of a people he studies, must also abandon his role of "outsider" when he makes his reports about the language as a system of rules. Then he cannot remain detached; he must become a participant in the communication process. A report to the effect that certain members of a tribe made such and such sounds on a certain day is not a report about language behavior, although it will obviously be *part* of such a report. To give us information about language behavior as such, the scientist must provide a translation; he must engage in language behavior himself.

This entire predicament has been forced upon our scientist because of the particular nature of the object of his study. He had to report about behavior subject to rules; and it turned out that he could not make his report without using expressions such as "use of words correct in *L*." Such words are value words; they stamp the language in which they occur as a value-language or judgment-language. Value-languages differ from pure fact-languages in that their deictic rules refer not merely to acts of "ordering" and "classification" but also to acts of valuation and identification. Every fact-language implies a value-language, since, as a system of "correct" communication, it *consists* of rules; but we are asking now about the rules of this implied rule-language itself. It seems that they are not addressed to a pupil who wants merely to play the "role" of a detached, empirical observer who is content with giving "correct" reports about his findings; they are addressed to a pupil who is anxious to learn how and with whom to identify, and on what basis. For our first pupil—the pure empiricist—this was no problem; he performed the identification with his teacher naïvely, he accepted the teacher's authority, and all he was concerned with was how to apply correctly the rules he had accepted. But our second pupil, who wants to learn the rules of the value-language, is more sophisticated. He asks us: "What do we mean by saying that a certain behavior—in this case, language behavior—is 'correct'? What kind of test exists for determining correctness in this instance?"

This question may be answered in two ways. First, we may focus upon the behavioral result which conduct conforming to the rules is supposed to bring about; in this case, successful communication. Second, we may consider the nature of the criterion by which we distinguish "correct" from "incorrect" conduct. The first type of answer, however, is irrelevant to the question we are dealing with now. It is concerned with the reasons we may have for adhering to certain rules and conventions rather than with the explication of the rules of our value-language. "Reasonableness" is a value predicate, too, and we shall have to consider it in connection with the value-language to which *it* belongs; but at present our concern is with the value-language whose predicates are "correct" and "incorrect," as applied to language behavior. What criterion do we apply in assigning these predicates to individual bits of behavior? The criterion is not behavioral success in a situational context as such; for faulty communications may be quite effective. The criterion is, rather, whether a certain act—consisting in the formation of some sound pattern—is a good imitation of some model, accepted as authoritative. It is impossible to explicate the rule for correct sound formation without indicating some model with which one has to identify.

This is generally the way in which the meaning of "conventional" value predicates have to be explicated. If the value ("correctness") is defined by convention, the rule for applying the value predicate must specify models whose behavior embodies the rule. Of course, one may decide to follow or defy the convention; that is, whether one "identi-fies" with the models or not may be decided on the basis of some other value criterion. Whether to identify or not may be controversial. For instance, conforming to certain conventions may seem to be just unnecessary trouble, and one may decide to disregard the convention. In the case of language conventions, however, such questions do not arise. For, first, one's own language is learned when identification with the parents is beyond question; and, second, communication with others would quickly break down if one decided to disregard the convention. We may say, in this sense, that the rules of the linguistic value-language (comprising the predicates "linguistically correct" and "incorrect," as applied to utterances) are both conventional and un-controversial. This, at least, is the case with regard to all completely homogeneous language groups. In these, all language behavior is per-fectly "natural"; there are no discussions as to whether one "should" express something in one way or another.

In nonhomogeneous language groups, where different conventions are followed by different classes, the "correctness" of certain utter-ances may be controversial—the subject may be faced with the decision to identify with one model rather than with another, and the result may be stilted attempts to use the "King's English" (or "literate speech") rather than dialect or "colloquial" speech. Resort may also be taken to recognized authorities, such as dictionaries. In some language com-munities nonhomogeneity may be extreme, and colloquial language may be an entirely different language from the literate one (as in modern Greek). Finally, there is, in every language community, non-homogeneity in the temporal direction: although each succeeding gen-eration acquires its speech by imitating the parent-generation, the imitation becomes relaxed in some details, and small deviations may add up to considerable shifts over a number of generations.

Such shifts seem to occur in the way that subgroups adopt new "models" of correct speech behavior; the homogeneity of the lan-guage group is broken up. At first, we observe local fads or jargons; later these fads may disappear, to be replaced by others, or they may be stabilized in subgroups, or, finally, they may become a generally adopted convention in the over-all community. Sublanguages tend to show great fluidity: each generation develops its own distinctive sublanguage or "argot."

The quickest and most comprehensive changes in language behavior seem to occur when a literary or literate language is developed; this is usually the work of a single generation of legislators. After this legislatory period, fluidity will decrease: speech becomes standardized.

b) THE LANGUAGE OF IMMEDIATELY FELT RELEVANCE

So much for the "value-language" of correctness of speech. We shall now turn to another value-language the rules of which are not conventional; the language of "good and bad" in terms of a standard of biological "relevance" (see chap. ii).

What kinds of value predicates do we have here? There are predicates in this language designating immediately felt pleasure and pain and predicates designating fear, apprehension, and anxiety, as well as confidence and security. The criteria for the applicability of these predicates are to be found in immediate experience. The criterion as to whether "correct" is to be applied to an utterance in a language is: "Does this utterance imitate an accepted model?" The criterion as to whether the predicate "painful" applies to an experience is: "Do I feel pain?" In this case the standard of value is given in the subject's own experience; we say in this sense that the standard is not conventional. The judgment expressed is wholly an affair of the individual subject; there is no appeal to any authority or model.

Of course, the value predicates of the linguistic value-language may be applied to every utterance, and we may ask whether a statement someone made about the pain he felt was expressed ungrammatically or not. But the language we are considering now is that of pain predicates and pleasure predicates; and what we are saying is that the standards governing the ascription of these predicates to the things to which they are supposed to apply are "subjective" ones: it is the subject's immediate experience alone that has to be consulted. This "subjectivity" is not the same thing as "arbitrariness"; it does not mean that there is no rule at all to be followed in assigning the value predicates but only that, in applying it, only one present, immediate experience has to be consulted; there is no need either for controlled observation, as in the case of empirical fact predicates, or for confrontation with authorities, as in the case of conventional value predicates.

c) THE LANGUAGE OF UTILITY

The foregoing applies, however, only to part of the language of "relevance" values: that part which consists of "good-bad" predicates referring to immediately felt experiences. These, however, do not form a self-contained universe. For some of the immediately felt experiences are anticipations: fears, hopes, desires, and the like. *Whether* an individual is fearful, apprehensive, reassured, or hopeful is something he feels immediately; but when he is in such a state, the "meaning" of his situation may be that he would like to get out of this state or avoid a frustrating sequel to it. Consequently, he will be looking around for signs or information that would be of help; and in this sense factual knowledge is what will make the greatest difference to him. This leads us to another set of value predicates—predicates which will classify things as "good" or "bad," not in terms of some immediately felt experience, but in terms of some factually warranted knowledge about how "good" immediate experience could be acquired and "bad" immediate experience avoided. We shall call these predicates, in accordance with our earlier considerations (see chap. ii), "utility" predicates. They will be represented by the pair "useful-harmful." The assignment of these predicates will require analysis and controlled observation—somehow combined with attention to immediate experience.

What is required in this connection is in part causal, factual analysis; in this way the utility-value-language is closely linked to the fact-language. To be able to determine what is "useful" and "harmful," one needs, first of all, knowledge of facts. In this context, however, factual knowledge merely provides premises—the conclusions have to be judgments into which considerations of immediately felt "relevance" enter. The judgments are of the following form: P is useful, because among its consequences is Q, which is an immediately felt "good"; or R is harmful, because among its consequences is S, which is an immediately felt "evil." The P-Q and R-S chains are causal chains, to be determined by causal analysis.

Analysis, however, is needed not only to discover such chains but also to "compare" the immediately relevant end-states of the chains. P may be "useful" in terms of an immediately felt pleasure or satisfaction, Q; but it may also be harmful in terms of another consequence, the immediately felt displeasure S. To decide whether P should be judged useful or harmful, Q and S must be compared: a conflict of goals must be resolved. The analysis of utilities requires a "hierarchy" of values ("relevances"). This hierarchy must be based on some standard, and these standards, too, are among the rules of the utility-value-language.

Standards underlying a ranking of values may be called "principles." In order to assess utilities, we need not only factual knowledge but also principles of ranking. The principles involved in the utility-value-language are in part "subjective," just as the judgments about the pleasurable or painful character of immediate experiences are, but only in part. The individual who "ranks" his goals is not the sole judge of the correctness of the ranking.

When it comes to comparing the attractiveness of two mutually exclusive goals, preference between them is a subjective matter, in so far as the question is merely whether to choose Q_1 or Q_2, all other things being equal—for instance, if the future consequences are about the same in either case. But if, for instance, Q_1 leads to seriously painful consequences in the future, whereas Q_2 avoids them, it is "foolish" to choose Q_1. In general, we consider any preference of "less good and more evil in the long run" over "more good and less evil in the long run" foolish.[1] We do not say that if a subject prefers more present pleasure to more pleasure in the long run, it is his affair; if we feel any solidarity with that subject, we shall interfere with his choice. We shall not dispute his judgment that his immediately preferred goal would indeed be pleasurable or that it would be painful to give it up; what we say is that foregoing the pleasure would be worth while in his own interest.

Some ranking principles are culturally approved maxims. In our culture, for instance, health ranks as preferable to illness, even if the subject's own comparison in terms of immediately felt pleasure and pain would favor illness. Longer life also is considered absolutely preferable to a shorter one, even if it implies more pain without more pleasure. Whenever subjects act on different ranking principles, society tends to interfere. Such interference is not always based on "ethical" norms—the latter, of course, form part of a different "value-language," the "right-wrong" language, which we shall consider separately. Suicide may be considered "wrong" and condemned on an ethical basis. But doing things which are injurious to one's health is not necessarily termed "wrong"; it may be interfered with by members of the group because it is "foolish," even if the subject prefers it.

It appears, then, that in judging the "usefulness" or "harmfulness" of things, the subject may conduct a debate with himself—he will play several roles. The participants in such a debate are, so to speak, different egos—the ego swayed by an urge and the ego guided by "reason." The latter is not indifferent to, or neutral toward, the former;

1. The "summation" of values over time is forcefully brought out by C. I. Lewis, *An Analysis of Knowledge and Valuation* (La Salle, Ill.: Open Court Publishing Co., 1946), pp. 503 ff.

in fact, in this context, "being reasonable" means so arranging one's conduct that the urges one has will be maximally gratified in the long run. The urge-dominated ego will be curbed by the "reasonable" ego, not because the latter has goals higher than, and preferable to, urge satisfaction, but because the "reasonable" ego at time t_1 may consider the urge-dominated ego at time t_1 to be the enemy of the urge-dominated ego at times t_2, t_3, . . . , and so on. Those who interfere with the satisfaction of a subject's urges out of solidarity with him put themselves in the place of that subject's "reasonable" ego.

The "reasonable" ego analyzes experience; he compares the consequences of alternative courses of action in terms of the quantity of urge satisfaction they may be expected to bring about. This presupposes, of course, that we may have accurate expectations concerning the character of our immediate experience under foreseeable circumstances. Is this presupposition justified?

Each organism discovers, by learning, recurrent sets of circumstances which reliably lead to one familiar type of pleasure or displeasure—a favorite food will always taste good if we are hungry, and fire will always burn us. On the other hand, utility judgments need not refer to such learned, reliable sequences. We may judge a thing useful without specifying a familiar type of satisfaction among its consequences. In fact, some of the things we deem most useful are prized, not because we can know and specify what kind of satisfaction they will bring within reach, but because we know they will help us, in a generalized way, to get what we may want. Money, for instance, is such a "generalized" instrument. Everybody would like to have "lots of money" to do with as he pleases, without necessarily being able to specify what he would do with it, and without being able to foresee accurately the real consequences which riches bring in their wake.

Furthermore, one may aim at tasting pleasures that are unfamiliar and novel, and one may flee dangers that are nonspecific and undefinable. Also, there are pleasurable experiences such that novelty and unpredictability is an essential element of their charm; what we can anticipate about them is only that they will surprise us in a pleasant way. It might be argued that, even when we arrange things so as to have a familiar pleasure, we expect to experience the familiar in some novel way. A repeated experience of familiar pleasures involves not only recognition but also fresh discovery. When we contemplate a familiar landscape and enjoy its beauty, we have the feeling that, although we have known all this, we did not really know how beautiful it was. And likewise with the avoidance of familiar dangers and hurts: when we perceive the threat or feel the pain, we always discover it anew.

We have to say, therefore, that the "reasonable" analysis on which we base utility judgments does not tell the whole story; it focuses only upon the "familiar" element in the immediately relevant experience but has no hold on its element of novelty. "Reason," in this way, may lead us astray. It may induce us to direct our efforts to getting pleasures that pall or to avoid dangers and hurts that could be conquered.

The reasonable assessment of utilities is most reliable with reference to causal chains leading to major, radical consequences affecting the health and well-being of the organism. Its guidance is far less sure when it comes to arranging for experiences satisfactory "in themselves." Too much comparison and calculation in this context is liable to spoil the pleasure; this is why the planned euphorias dispensed by the amusement industry are often so frustrating. The euphoria has been produced reliably, but it does not add up to happiness; one has had a "wonderful time" but cannot say: "I had no idea how wonderful it would be."

d) THE LANGUAGE OF "HIGHER" VALUES

It remains for us to examine one more class of predicates—those expressing ethical, aesthetic, and other "higher" value judgments. Examples of these are "right" and "wrong," "great" and "poor" (as applied to works of art); this "value-language" comprises all those predicates which ascribe to an object some "meritorious" quality or the lack of it. Their common characteristic is that they express approval or disapproval in terms of some standard that is taken to be "objective" in a sense. Our question is again: What are the "rules" governing the assignment of these predicates? What experiential test is supposed to determine, for a subject, whether one of these predicates applies?

Thus far, we have seen three types of "experiential tests": conventional ones, involving imitation of a model; immediately introspective ones, consisting in paying attention to some felt relevance; and causal ones, concerned with the establishment of linkages among factual states of things and immediate experiences. These tests correspond to three modes of judging: conventional, introspective, and factually "reasonable." Our question is now: Is the "mode of judgment" appropriate to these "higher" values one of the above-mentioned three? Or is it a combination of some or all of them? Or, finally, is it an additional "mode," related to the others but emergent with regard to them?

In the discussion about the problem of value, we encounter views reducing the "mode of judgment" in ethics or aesthetics to one or the other of the three modes mentioned. Some authors consider these "higher" values as essentially conventional; others, as essentially "subjective"; and yet others, as essentially "factual." We may call these schools the "conventionalist," the "intuitionist," and the "empiricist" school, respectively. In addition to these three groups, we also find "pluralists," who see all three modes combined in "higher" value judgments, and "emergentists," who consider "higher" value judgments to be based on a different "mode," specific to them.

Conventionalism stresses the element of authority and identification in the development of moral or aesthetic, etc., judgment. Elitist theories (e.g., Pareto) belong in this group; and psychoanalytic doctrine also corresponds to this general characterization. A point of view common to the representatives of conventionalism is that so-called "higher" value judgments are not autonomous; they are imposed upon the subject just as conventions are imposed, from without. A conventionalist may admit that the subjects who make such judgments are under the impression that they judge "autonomously." This, however, merely means, according to this school, that the subjects have "internalized" the rules inculcated by authority: they have developed a "superego" as the representative of authority within their own personality; or they may have accepted a "derivation" (Pareto) which makes the dictate of authority appear as if it were an autonomous motive of the subject. The autonomy of judgment thus emerges as fiction; heteronomy is the reality behind "higher" value judgments. The assignment of utility predicates alone is an "autonomous" process.

Intuitionism (Scheler, Moore),[2] on the other hand, stresses the autonomy of higher value judgments. According to this view, there is a close parallelism between judgments about immediately felt "relevance" and "higher" value judgments. The "moral good," for instance, is essentially a quality to be grasped in an intuitive act, just

2. Cf. Max Scheler, Der Formalismus in der Ethik und die materiale Wertethik (Halle: Niemeyer, 1927), p. 11; George E. Moore, Principia ethica (3d ed.; Cambridge: At the University Press, 1929), pp. 7, 10.

like any other experienced value. The subject's own intuitive experience is the basis for making the judgment. This, however, does not mean that the "higher" value categories are essentially subjective or impressionistic. For the qualities to which the judgments point are not immediately visible to every subject; they become visible only if a particular attitude or role is adopted, or, alternatively, they can be seen only by the "good man." One may ask, of course, how the "moral" attitude is learned or how one becomes a "good man." The intuitionist answer minimizes the roles of authority in this; it invokes, rather, some innate moral sense, akin to other fundamental capacities of discrimination.

"Empiricist" theories (Dewey, C. I. Lewis) explicate "higher" value judgments after the pattern of utility judgments. Lewis, for instance, states that "evaluations are a form of empirical knowledge, not fundamentally different in what determines their truth and falsity, and what determines their validity or justification, from other kinds of empirical knowledge." And he explains this by pointing out that value "judgments," properly so called, do not merely express some immediately felt quality of experience; they are "cognitive" because they essentially involve prediction. Value judgments are essentially "predictions of goodness or badness which will be disclosed in experience under certain circumstances and on particular occasions"; as such, they "are either true or false, and are capable of verification in the same manner as other terminating judgments, which predict accrual of other qualities than value."[3] This analysis follows closely the schema we have assumed to underlie "utility judgments."

For Dewey, too, evaluation is largely a cognitive matter, except that for him cognition in itself is always part of a goal-oriented process and, as such, conceptually inseparable from evaluation. The point is, however, that value judgments are concerned with the way of resolving some existing quandary, of attaining some "end-in-view." "Ends as objective termini or as fulfilments function in judgment as representative of modes of operation that will resolve the doubtful situation which evokes and demands judgment. . . . The business of inquiry is to determine that mode of operation which will resolve the predicament in which the agent finds himself involved, in correspondence with the observations which determine just what the facts of the predicament are."[4] It is common to theories of this type that they

3. Lewis, *op. cit.,* p. 365.
4. John Dewey, *Logic: A Theory of Inquiry* (New York: Henry Holt & Co., 1938), pp. 167 f.

see the function of judgment as related to the determination of conditions of satisfaction rather than to the characterization of the satisfaction as such.

The prototype of the "emergent" theory of higher value judgments is formalism (e.g., Kant).[5] Formalism draws a sharp line between the higher value judgment (e.g., moral judgment), on the one hand, and judgments about satisfaction, utility, and conventional "correctness," on the other. The judging subject, according to this view, neither follows the dictate of an authority, expresses some immediate experience of satisfaction, nor determines factual conditions for the attainment of immediate satisfaction. His problem is to determine that conduct which satisfies the formal conditions defined by the concept of "right." The definition itself is an ultimately apprehended postulate; it does not subserve any of the empirically felt needs of either the individual or the group but has to be recognized as right "in itself."

Like intuitionism, formalism considers judgments of value to be autonomous, that is, based on the subject's own insight into the matter rather than on his following a dictate or his identification with a model. The difference between the two views is that for intuitionism this insight is unanalyzable, while for formalism it can be accounted for in terms of a judgmental schema that can be applied to many experiences differing in their "material" aspects. For intuitionism, insight into a "value state" or "value configuration" (Scheler's *Wertverhalt*) is like the recognition of a color, while for formalism it is more akin to a logical deduction. The intuitionist's "mode of judgment" is an undefinable act, prescribed by the "nature" of the object with which the judger is in intimate communion; the formalist's "mode of judgment" involves, basically, operations upon symbols and relationships among symbols which parallel the "structure" of the value experience but do not reflect its unique, concrete "nature."

Empiricism may lead to either a heteronomous or an autonomous interpretation of the value judgment. In so far as value judgments are "cognitive," they are autonomous; for empiricism, it is the "knowing" subject that is the really autonomous subject. The noncognitive elements in judging, however, are not truly autonomous according to this view. They may be imposed by the group, by the culture, or by instinct; as such, they are impervious to "insight."

Our own explication of "higher" value judgments is a "pluralistic"

5. Cf. Immanuel Kant, *Kritik der praktischen Vernuft*, ed. B. Kellermann (Berlin: Cassirer, 1922), p. 31.

one, and this for two reasons. For one thing, the so-called "higher" (ethical, aesthetic, etc.) judgments deal with heterogeneous matters: it is not one "value-language" which deals with all of them but several value-languages, the predicates of which require different "modes of judgment." For another, the judging process in these fields appears in a different light, according as we look at it from a genetic point of view or from the point of view of the mature subject. Thus judging will be seen to involve identification with models, intuition, factual knowledge, and a specific formalism, depending on the kind of value and on the specific phase of the value-learning process we are looking at.

At this point we are not discussing the different "higher values" as such; they will be taken up in the concluding part of this study. In this preliminary analysis we are concerned only with the "value-language," with the "meaning" of the different types of value predicates which occur in judgments. Two questions arise in this connection: What kind of operation underlies the assignment of these predicates? And how are these operations learned?

Let us begin with one pair of predicates—the "right-wrong" dichotomy. These predicates express approval and disapproval; and these types of judgment must, I think, be sharply separated from expressions of "likes and dislikes," "preference and repugnance." To say "You are wrong to do this" means to say something different from "I wish you would not do this." The difference is that in the former case we appeal to some principle to which every man's conduct "ought to" conform, whatever his likes and dislikes are, whereas in the latter no such supposedly objective principle is invoked. Nor can we say that, in approval or disapproval, the underlying principle to which appeal is made is meant merely to specify the kind of conduct that the judging subject would "prefer" to have prevail among mankind. A general principle such as "It is wrong to tell lies" says something different from the preference statement, "I wish people wouldn't lie."

This much will probably not be seriously questioned by anyone; but disagreement is possible about the question of whether, and to what extent, the distinction should be taken seriously. Granted that the judgments and principles in question *purport* to express something different from mere egocentric preferences, it is still possible to maintain that analysis will reveal that some egocentric preference is, at bottom, responsible for the judgments. An empiricist, for instance, may argue that an "approval" can be considered true or false only to the extent that it truthfully labels a type of conduct desirable or undesirable, depending on whether such conduct will factually lead to consequences consonant or incompatible with some preference which can and need not be analyzed further. To say that lying is wrong is not the same thing as to say that nonlying is preferred; but the only difference is that, when we express a disapproval, we imply something about the consequences of lying as they would affect our preferences, while in the other case we merely state our ultimate conclusion without implying any reasons. A conventionalist also may conclude that right-wrong judgments ultimately express, or hinge upon, preferences—not, to be sure, those of an individual subject but those of a model or of an elite. "Right" merely stands for whatever is preferred by leaders, legislators, or parents, for whatever reason. In both views it is a mistake to believe that right-wrong judgments are, in fact, based upon some valid objective criterion independent of *all* preferences.

As against this, intuitionists and formalists maintain that the differentiation between preference statements and judgments about right and wrong (approvals and disapprovals) has a basis in truth. The subject who approves or disapproves actually judges about things on the basis of a criterion neutral toward *all* personal preferences. The question is: Do such independent criteria exist, or are they merely illusory rationalizations of individual and group preferences?

I think we may dismiss the ultra-individualistic version of the empiricist interpretation, according to which approvals and disapprovals deal with nothing but the consequences of the conduct under judgment as they affect the egocentric goals of the subject. Without denying that "right" and "wrong" predicates refer to many different things in the same culture, and still more so in different cultures, we can maintain, I think, that all such predicates somehow prescribe a "mode of judgment" based on a neutral, detached, critical, or possibly hostile attitude toward the subject's own egocentric preferences. If a language contains right-wrong predicates, this means, I think, that the members of the language group intend to communicate about matters of individual conduct in terms permitting commendation or rejection from a point of view independent of the agent's own preferences. This prescribed point of view is more "independent" of the felt urge than the "point of view" of the "reasonable" ego we discussed above; the basis on which the felt urge is supposed to be resisted is not *merely* that "it will be better for you in the long run" to forego satisfaction now. If this is so, we are left with two possibilities: the "point of view" involved in making right-wrong judgments either reflects some preference other than that of the individual subject or is independent of all egocentric preferences.

Let us consider the first view. "Right" and "wrong" predicates, one may hold, reflect what is conducive to, or destructive of, "group survival." Here we have an "egocentric" preference at bottom—"egocentric," of course, not from the point of view of the individual but from that of the group. In judging about "right" and "wrong," the individual must learn how to subordinate his own urges to rules of conduct best suited to insure group survival. This interpretation, too, is "empiricist" in character: the dominant category here, too, is "usefulness," to be determined by factual investigation. It is also possible to combine this interpretation with the ultra-individualist "utilitarian" one we have rejected in its pure or all-or-nothing form. Granted that the individual must sometimes sacrifice his interests, or even his life, for the sake of the group's survival, the general relationship between group and individual interests, by and large, may still be harmony rather than conflict. By doing what is "right," the individual will also obtain advantages for himself; if "right" conduct is good for the group, it cannot be bad for the individuals taken singly. This is how an empiricist would explicate "right" and "wrong" in terms of group preferences; that is, he would specify a "rational" criterion for "right" and "wrong," but not a preference-neutral one.

Conventionalists may go along with this explication to some extent; but they would argue that it is too rational. A group, they would say, cannot judge what is good for its survival. First, "survival" itself is too vague a term. What does it really mean? Does it mean that *all* individual members are to survive? No, because *some* individuals may have to be sacrificed to the group's survival. Does it mean that the number of those lost should be as small as possible? No, because "survival" involves more than numbers. What seems to matter is that the group itself should preserve its distinct identity, its own patterns of co-ordination, its "meaning" to its members. "Right-wrong" predicates are concerned with the maintenance of a group structure, a way of life, rather than with mere survival. They protect stability of organization rather than only continued physical life. But this means that they cannot be analyzed in a purely rational manner. For "right" conduct, if we look at it in this light, is not "right" *because* it maximizes some desired end, such as survival; it maximizes the group's chances to remain integrated because it is deemed "right," and, if other rules were considered the "right" ones, they would be just as effective in insuring the same result. This conventionalist analysis stresses the arbitrariness of "right-wrong" rule; it implies that the existence of a firmly established code is more important than its content.

The conventionalist view favors conservatism: it is the stability of right-wrong judgments which makes them "adaptive"; any attempt to improve upon the rules would merely weaken the cohesion and vitality of the group. The empiricist concept, on the other hand, leads to progressive conclusions. A set of rules which is good for "group survival" at one time may become inadaptive and harmful when conditions change; hence groups should always be ready to change their rules of conduct.

Formalism and intuitionism maintain, as against both views, that "right-wrong" judgments, properly speaking, cannot be reduced to any egocentric preference, whether of individuals, elites, or groups; for such judgments, in their essential purity, require a universal frame of reference. The criterion of rightness and wrongness, according to these schools, cannot be the maximization of the self-centered goals of any empirical group. The criterion of group welfare, however defined, can lead only to in-group morality; but this is not what we "mean" when we appprove of a type of conduct as such. Even the maximization of the welfare of mankind as a whole would not represent a proper criterion. For, in thinking about principles of right and wrong, we do not have those things in mind which contribute most to the increase of human welfare as such; technological improvements, for instance, are not the prototype of "right" action. Approval and disapproval are concerned with intentions rather than results: they presuppose criteria for judging intentions which are independent of *all* interests, even the interests of mankind. What these criteria are, however, is a question answered differently by formalism and by intuitionism. According to the former, the criterion is essentially a rational one: whether an action or a way of acting is right or wrong can be determined by confronting it with a self-evident, rational principle. According to the latter, no such rational over-all criterion of rightness and wrongness exists; each field of action has its own basic ethical values which the subject can discover by inspection rather than by rational analysis. Because of its stress upon rationality, formalism tends to exclude from "ethical" consideration proper the more "irrational" approvals or disapprovals, such as those involved in sexual morality; it concentrates, rather, on universal categories like justice, humanity, or truthfulness. The intuitionist, on the other hand, is not troubled by the "irrational" nature of sexual codes; he can "inspect" the intuitive value content of such standards as chastity, marital fidelity, or saintliness.

Having surveyed this array of conflicting interpretations, we feel that this divergence of views may be explained, in part, by the fact that the predicates "right" and "wrong," and others somehow related to them, do not belong to just one value-language but to a number of value-languages used alternately, depending on the context; and it also seems to us that different cultures use these different value-languages in varying combinations and proportions. All genuine approval and disapproval imply, in our view, "detachment" from egocentric interests and drives. But there are many different types of approval and disapproval—some more and some less universalistic and also some more and some less rational. In other words, in learning to distinguish between right and wrong in whatever culture, the individual must learn how to discipline his own egocentric urges; but this is not all he learns; he must also learn to distinguish various kinds of objects that take precedence over his urges, and these range from "irrational" taboos to fully universalistic, rational, and impersonal principles of conduct.

In one sense it seems that the formalistic analysis succeeds best in doing justice to what is essential to right-wrong judgments. For we can see that some commands recognized as valid in a culture have a large admixture of "irrationality" and arbitrariness, while others prescribe little more than preference-neutrality or "fairness" as such. There is no need for supernatural sanctions or subservience to external authority to recognize the "rightness" of fair dealing and justice, while some other principles of right and wrong conduct stand and fall with the assumption of such sanctions or with identification with a concrete group or authority. It is clear that the value predicates used in these two classes of judgment belong to different value-languages; and, while the predicates of the second language define principles of conduct which may be necessary to insure social cohesion or survival, they do not correspond to our idea of what is "right in itself," that is, of what deserves approval under all circumstances. The formalist—whose "value-language" is of the first type mentioned above—need not reject "irrational" commands and group-centered values, just as he need not reject egocentric strivings if they do not violate the principles of justice and fair dealing. He will merely insist that it is the principle of fair dealing and justice as such which defines "rightness," rather than these other more irrational and contingent demands. To him, such goals as welfare and happiness, both for the group and for the individual, are neither immoral nor irrelevant to morality; on the contrary, "fairness" means that every individual and group must be given a fair chance to attain such goals. It is only that no conduct is right *solely* because it promotes individual or group welfare. In trying to determine whether an action is "right," the point to bear in mind is not whether it has or has not promoted the happiness, cohesion, and power of a group but whether, in doing so, it has or has not unfairly slighted other groups. And while the formalist agrees that any action promoting the welfare of mankind is *ipso facto* right, he will add that it is right not because it promotes *welfare* but because it promotes the welfare of all human beings *indiscriminately*. In this way the formal principle of justice becomes the supreme criterion by which other value criteria will be judged. This approach will not make other standards—whether intuitive, conventionalist, or empirical—superfluous but will enable us to focus upon what is the most "rational" and "universal" in a value-language suitable for autonomous judgment.

Our position, then, is that, while actions may be approved or disapproved for a variety of reasons, including group welfare or respect for authority, one set of reasons—those defined by the principle of impartiality and preference-neutrality itself—occupy a position apart and may be used critically to test the validity of the others. This does not mean that, whenever justice conflicts with group welfare, justice must take precedence—*fiat justitia et pereat mundus*. Certainly, no matter how "right" the condemnation of social injustice is, it would not be "right" to use wholesale violence and cause death and destruction to eliminate injustice. My reason for saying this is not that I consider peace, comfort, and life as "higher" values than justice; fortunately, this issue need not be settled. It is enough to reflect that a violent and destructive propagation of justice is likely to destroy not only life, comfort, and property but also justice and fairness itself. The only way to propagate justice is to practice it one's self in action as in judgment; if one cannot move the conscience of others in this way, justice cannot be served by fighting. It is unjust to propagate justice by violence.

On the other hand, of course, it is not unjust to resist by violence an unjust and violent attack. In this case, however, the violence employed in the just cause should not be considered a means of realizing justice but merely a means of preventing injustice from achieving dominance; the positive task of creating a just order can be attempted only when it is no longer necessary to rely on wholesale, acute violence.

The value-language of "right and wrong" in the sense of justice and impartiality provides, it seems to me, the chief criteria for "autonomous" ethical judgment. But this does not mean that this language is acquired, historically and genetically, in a completely "autonomous" fashion. In "learning" the autonomous language, identification with authoritative figures seems to be necessary. Nobody is born with a motivation for impartiality; this motivation can be acquired only in and through a process of education. This, I think, is the part of truth in the "conventionalist" theories of the right-wrong language. Without identification, no motive for curbing directly felt urges could be developed, either in the sense of egocentric "reasonableness" or in that of obedience to authority; in the sense of the service of group welfare; or, finally, in the sense of the application of a principle of impartiality. To be sure, identification with the early authoritative figures must be relaxed if autonomy is to emerge; identification need not be static at all: it is, rather, in dynamic cultures a dynamic concept, pointing to growth. Growth toward maturity involves not only questioning of the self from the point of view of an authority with which one identifies but also, eventually, questioning of the authority itself.

With this, we may leave the subject of the language of right and wrong, adding only that there is more to moral life and ethics than this dichotomy. Love, sympathy, and harmony, although they are outside the domain of "right-wrong" dichotomies, are also essential moral phenomena and will be considered in connection with the ethical values.

We must, however, take up briefly the value-language of aesthetics. The predicates I shall consider are not "beautiful" and "ugly," for these predicates express immediate, subjective experience which belongs rather under the category of "relevance" than under that of "higher" values. The predicates I want to discuss are "great" and "poor" as applied to works of art. On the basis of what criteria are these predicates supposed to be assigned to objects?

In this field, too, we encounter the four types of interpretation which we met with in ethics. For the conventionalist, "great" and "poor" works of art are those which conform, or fail to conform, to models accepted as authoritative. For the intuitionist, the greatness or poorness of a work of art is apprehended immediately by the subject who adopts the aesthetic attitude. For the empiricist, the two predicates refer to the causal efficacy of the works in question in producing immediate experiences of rapture or repulsion. Finally, the formalist seeks to specify formal conditions which all great art satisfies.

Here, too, my own position combines some of the elements of these divergent views. Essentially, intuitionism seems to be closest to the truth of the matter: the experience of great art or poor art is an intuitive one, and neither formal nor causal analysis can fully account for it. Moreover, the judgments in question should be considered autonomous rather than as merely reflecting the point of view of a model or authority. Formalism can say very little about great art beyond a few generalities; when it tries to be specific, its conclusions become questionable. Empiricism, on the other hand, is better able to analyze the psychological background of the creative and appreciative experience than it is to analyze the experience itself and the object around which it is centered.

But the "intuition" of aesthetic "greatness" again is not an inborn capacity, arising spontaneously, although it probably has instinctual bases. The sense of the aesthetically great must be cultivated, and it can be developed only by familiarity and identification with a historic heritage of art. This again points to an element of truth in conventionalist analysis. A sense of "greatness" in art can be developed only in a historic context: criteria of greatness cannot be deduced from timeless, abstract principles. Further, the secret of artistic creation is handed down from masters to pupils. Here, too, the "educational" relationship—a person-to-person relationship based on identification—is essential. The road to autonomy leads through identification, beginning with the learning of rules and ending with their internalization and autonomous application. To the mature artist or connoisseur of art, the masters and models may be a source of inspiration without representing procedural models to be followed literally in new creation. Learning from them is not the same thing as imitating their practice. Creative art is both essentially traditional and essentially revolutionary; neither the iconoclast nor the imitator is a true artist.

2. Science and Interpretation

We shall now consider the question of whether the value-languages we have discussed can be used in scientific discourse or whether their use must be confined to extra-scientific communication. To this question several answers are possible, ranging from one extreme view to another. One extreme is represented by the conception that each value-language has a "science" of its own, that is, a "normative" science, such as scientific grammar (in the normative sense), scientific ethics, and scientific aesthetics. The other extreme is held by those who not only reject the idea of a normative science as such but also hold that value predicates have no place in the vocabulary of science in any manner. Intermediate positions also are possible. For instance, one may hold that, although a scientific theory as such is never "normative," scientific knowledge, to be applicable to the solution of practical problems, must be so framed as to allow value conclusions to be derived from factual scientific premises. Another intermediate view holds that, although a scientific theory neither contains value judgments nor provides guidance for the deduction of value judgments, it nevertheless may go beyond pure factual description in the sense that it will account for certain facts—such as the facts of human behavior—in *interpretive* rather than in purely descriptive terms. The scientist studying behavior will, on this view, abstain from making judgments but will *interpret* the judgments made by others.

The basic question underlying the debate among these various schools of thought is that concerning the nature and conditions of scientific objectivity. We all agree that scientific assertions must be formulated in an "objective" language. This means, among other things, that no predicate P can form part of a scientific language unless there is an objective test, performable at will by everyone, by which it can always be determined whether P applies to a thing or not. Clearly, a normative science could be constructed over a set of value predicates if these predicates were objective in this sense, that is, if it were always possible to determine by tests which are not controversial in themselves whether the predicates apply or not. The upholders of a "scientific" ethics or aesthetics maintain, in fact, that one can define basic ethical or aesthetic predicates that do lend themselves to such unequivocal and uncontroversial tests. Those who range themselves with the opposite extreme deny not only the possibility of objective value judgments but also that of objective fact statements which depend on interpretation. These latter would exclude from science not only statements like "An action is morally right if it has the characteristics $P_1, P_2, \ldots$, etc.," but also statements of the form "An action of the subject S may be accounted for by assuming that his motives, or standards, are such and such." According to this group, science can "account" for any happening only on the basis of purely descriptive indices, calling for no interpretation of meaning. We shall label the former group the "normativists" and the latter the "descriptivists."

The normativists seem to me to be in a strong position in so far as purely logical values, such as consistency, are concerned. For, indeed, there are objective and unproblematical tests by which it can always be shown whether an inference is logically valid or not. We can say, in this sense, that logic is a normative science. In the case of purely conventional norms, it is also possible to determine in an uncontroversial fashion whether an actual piece of behavior conforms to them. A "normative" grammar thus must be recognized as having objective validity. Whether such a grammar would be a "science," however, is doubtful; for mere objectivity does not suffice to stamp a group of statements as "scientific." Science is defined not only by its use of "objective" predicates but also by its more or less systematic form. A scientific theory is not merely a collection of objectively true statements; it also exhibits an organic structure and hierarchy such that, once we are in possession of a fundamental law or a basic hypothesis, we can deduce any number of fact statements of lesser generality which are deducible from the law or hypothesis. "Normative" grammar lacks this feature. Unlike logic, it does not specify fundamental laws (principles and axioms) which determine in each case what does or does not conform to the "norm" involved. There is a grammatical code which is valid for each homogeneous language community, but it is not a systematic or scientific code. "Scientific" grammar, a part of linguistics, is not a normative but a historical science.

On the other hand, the normativist position appears to me weak in so far as ethical or aesthetic values are concerned. I cannot imagine scientific tests by which questions of right or wrong or questions of artistic greatness could be settled. Some actions, of course, will be generally acclaimed or condemned; some works of art will be generally praised or rejected. But such occurrences are not "objective tests." The normativist position in ethics and aesthetics would be well founded only if we had reliable scientific procedures that we could use in answering such questions as "Is this action right?" or "Is this work of art great?" I think the "reliable scientific procedures" we possess—those of logical and mathematical reasoning and those of laboratory experimentation, observation, and analysis—do not afford answers to such questions.

It is believed by some that observation and experiment can, indeed, settle value questions about ethical or aesthetic matters objectively. For can we not ascertain people's *responses* to actions or to works of art by observation and experimentation? Indeed we can; but what we obtain by such means is not an answer to the ethical and aesthetic value questions themselves. The observation and analysis of actual value responses can give us factual knowledge about people's attitudes but no normative knowledge about values. It is important not to confuse these two problem areas.

The differences I have in mind will be clear if we return for a moment to the "normative" science of logic. The logician has indeed a procedure by which he can establish whether a line of reasoning is logically valid or not. He thus answers the value question himself, and his science is in this sense a normative one. But the logician is not concerned with the actual response of people to pieces of reasoning; nor would he admit that these responses are relevant to the value problem he can and does solve by his methods. On the contrary, he would say that, if a psychologist collects data about people's responses to actual sequences of reasoning, he, the logician, should be consulted on the question of whether these responses do or do not depart from the logical norm. Under no circumstances could he be prevailed upon to alter *his* criteria so as to make them correspond to the outcome of the "tests."

Now one might say the following: Since there are no "objective" methods of normative value finding in ethics and aesthetics, the only "objective" data we are left with *are* the actual responses. With these science can deal; but, then, would we not be justified in developing such an observational science and calling it the "science of ethics and aesthetics"? No misunderstanding would be involved in the development of such a "scientific" ethical and aesthetic inquiry, if it were clearly understood that the science so constructed is not a "normative" science and does not settle questions of value. It would, however, be a misunderstanding if one were to assume that such empirical sciences about ethical and aesthetic responses are substitutes for the traditional disciplines of ethics and aesthetics, as if we now could forget about the traditional disciplines which cannot be made scientific, since we have a legitimate science about these matters. For the normative problems—what "is" right in action and what "is" great in art—are still with us and will not be answered by the new science.

The predicates of the new observational science refer to frequencies of certain types of responses; "approved with such and such a frequency" and "rejected with such and such a frequency" are examples of such predicates. My position is that these predicates cannot "replace" the old value predicates "right" and "great" and cannot be considered as providing a scientific "definition" or "explication" for them. In judging an action or a work of art, we use the old value-language. It now appears that this use of language cannot be scientific, since there is no normative science of ethics and aesthetics. Those who hold that scientific assertions alone are legitimate should then counsel and practice complete abstention of judgment about ethical and aesthetic matters, or at least a general admission that such judgments are purely arbitrary and not worth serious discussion. But they cannot say that objective findings about responses, with statistical tabulation, provide an objective basis for judgment.

The upshot of our discussion so far is: logical value terms belong in a scientific context; ethical and aesthetic value terms are limited to extra-scientific discourse, in so far as their "straight" applicability is concerned, whereas they may be used in scientific discourse on a different logical level, that is, if the scientist merely "quotes" them as being used by the subjects he observes, without in any way associating himself with the judgments which he quotes.

Here, however, objections will be raised from the "descriptivist" side. In order to gather findings about the relative frequency of value responses, we have to "interpret" the "meaning" of certain judgments. But even "interpretation" cannot be objective enough for the purposes of constructing a scientific theory, although it is perhaps less subjective than a "straight" judgment as such. For how can we know whether a subject "approves" or "disapproves" of something? All we have is a verbalization; but verbalizations are a poor indicator of actual attitudes. We would need a more "objective" index in order to explain or predict behavior.

To this objection, two answers may be made. First, we might defend the use of verbal data as follows: It is true that interpretation in general is not a valid scientific procedure. But, when we use verbal statements as data, we do not run a serious risk of being led astray by the "subjectivity" of all interpretation as such. For the chance that the experimental subjects will deliberately lie to us as to their preferences is small indeed; we can assume that they sincerely want to co-operate with the experimenter. Furthermore, the actual theory we construct will not involve any interpretation of meanings. We shall merely note the frequency of a few standard responses and observe correlations between such frequencies. The deductive framework that we obtain in this way is no longer concerned with goals, motives, and meanings entertained by the subject; neither does it presuppose any interpretive category which we ourselves apply in judging about things. What "interpretation" there is, is limited to the initial data. These, to be sure, are linguistic responses and must be interpreted according to the rules of a language. But, on the level on which we communicate with our subjects, communication is very reliable and uncontroversial; hence the objectivity of the whole inquiry is safeguarded.

The second answer to the "descriptivist" objection may run like this: The repudiation of "interpretation" as a method is itself unjustified. For, after all, we deal with human behavior; we want to account for it and, if possible, to predict it. Now it is by no means certain that noninterpretive, purely descriptive indices will give us a better chance of explanation and prediction than will interpretive indices. We may indeed look at behavior from two points of view: We may try to detect more or less "automatic" responses, responses the mechanism of which is not present to the subject's consciousness, and we may look at conscious, fully motivated choice responses. Both sets of data will enable us to make deductions about how the subject will behave in future situations. The first set of data—that consisting of automatic, unconscious responses—involves no interpretation; the second does, since we can assign a motive to a response only by judging a situation in terms of meanings and standards of value. And what differs in these two cases is not only our selection of initial data; the deductive frameworks we use in the two cases are also different. In the first case we look at behavior as shaped by unconscious mechanisms; in the second we look at it as organized by prevalent motives, goals, and the like. Incidentally, these two approaches can also be combined; this is the case in psychoanalysis, which operates by means of concepts of unconscious mechanisms which at the same time must be "interpreted" in a motivational sense. Now can we say that, in trying to account for human behavior, we can limit ourselves to the first method and discard the second one altogether? In other words, shall we assume that human behavior is basically controlled by unconscious

mechanisms not open to interpretation and that all motivation by goals
—conscious as well as unconscious—is merely an insignificant frothing
at the surface?

It seems to me that the first answer should satisfy the descriptivist;
in fact, no scientific study of human behavior would be possible if
verbal responses were ruled out. Nor would a study leaving communicative behavior out of account be particularly relevant to specifically
human behavior. The more important issue, however, is raised by the
second answer; when the problem is put in this way, the descriptivist
is not likely to give in.

The issue, indeed, touches upon fundamental convictions concerning the nature of science and the nature of man. The descriptivist rejection of interpretation as a method may be due either to insistence
upon the purity of scientific method or to a position held as regards
the metaphysical "essence" of man.

The methodological basis of descriptivism may be formulated as
follows: Science cannot well use interpretive concepts. Its aim is to
construct a deductive framework, allowing inferences to be made
from observational data to other data that may be observed at some
other time. Now the work of science can go on only if the "link"
among the data is completely well defined and unequivocal. This, in
general, can be assured only by quantitative data. The moment we
take "goals" and interpretable "motives" into account, we lose this
unequivocal linkage. For a motive is something plastic and flexible; it
is constantly re-evaluated; it cannot be taken as something given once
and for all. On the other hand, once we have established some reliable
quantitative, functional dependency among certain features of behavior, we are on firm ground. Then we can indeed make inferences.
We cannot be sure that human behavior can be successfully analyzed
in this fashion; up to now, in fact, nobody has produced a good enough
predictive schema based only on quantitative indices. But this means
only that we do not know whether a science of human behavior is
feasible. We do know, on the other hand, that no other predictive
schema can be scientific. Interpretive analysis may work within limits;
we can make shrewd guesses about human behavior, and we can produce convincing explanations in terms of motives. But all this is not
science. Those who are interested in scientific analysis must concentrate their efforts upon the development of quantitative inferential
frameworks; they cannot settle for less.

This methodological argument expresses well the prevalent scien-

tific temper of our day; but I think its value is largely psychological. What the argument really says is that the individuals who work
in the various fields of science are unhappy unless they can fall back
upon the unequivocal inferential linkages afforded by quantitative,
functional expressions. The task of science, however, is not to make
scientists happy but to discover the most powerful and essential truths
about the world of facts. We have no right to assume that the further-
ance of this task will always be best assured by methods most congenial to the prevalent scientific temper of an epoch. It may well be
that the object under examination is essentially refractory to the application of methods most congenial to scientists. Does this mean that
the scientist must withdraw from the field altogether? I think few
scientists would assume such a self-centered attitude. If the question
is put in this form, they will probably answer: We shall most certainly change our methods rather than withdraw, if we are satisfied
that human behavior is not amenable to our accustomed method. But
is this really the case? A change of method would really be indicated
only if it could be shown that those features of human behavior which
defy quantitative analysis are somehow real and essential rather than
merely superficial. This is the question we must settle somehow before
we make a methodological decision.

This confronts us with the metaphysical conception underlying the
descriptivist position. This metaphysical view holds that the quantitative method should be preferred, not because it suits the scientist,
but because it alone comes to grips with the real nature of all things,
including man and his behavior. Conversely, analysis in terms of goals
and meanings should be rejected, not because these concepts are un-
congenial to the scientist, but because they refer to unimportant surface phenomena. Men may believe that their activities are goal-directed
and meaningful, but this belief is an anthropocentric illusion, quite on
a par with earlier beliefs—now exploded by science—that processes in
inanimate nature are goal-directed and teleological. In fact, to think
otherwise amounts to setting up a dualistic partition wall between man
and nature. This attempt is incompatible with the spirit of science.
The scientific concept of the world stands and falls with "naturalism,"
that is, the idea that human events do not differ in kind from nonhuman events. Scientists hold this idea not as a matter of subjective
preference but as a deep metaphysical conviction. They are seriously
convinced that intellectual progress depends on driving teleological

concepts out of the analysis of human events. In this way alone can man get at the reality underlying his behavior.

As we see it, the issue is in reality a metaphysical one: it concerns the "real nature" of man. Is it possible to settle this issue? Clearly, a cogent proof cannot be provided by either side. The "descriptivists" (we shall henceforth use the label "naturalist" for this position) invoke in their favor the decisive progress made possible by the elimination of teleological concepts from natural science. They add that the human sciences in which teleological concepts have to some extent been retained have thus far failed to achieve comparable progress. But the opposing camp can also argue from experience. They can point out that attempts to construct purely quantitative theories of human behavior have not been lacking but that they have not succeeded in initiating an era of decisive discoveries, comparable to that of classical physics. The time lag between natural and social sciences can be interpreted in two ways. It may mean that social science will be as successful as physics when we learn how to apply purely causal, quantitative, and nonteleological concepts to human behavior; it may also mean that social science has remained backward because purely causal, quantitative, and nonteleological concepts cannot grasp the real essence of human behavior. On the one side, we have an unredeemed promise of decisive progress; on the other, an unproved belief that this progress cannot be achieved on the basis of the proposed method. The curious thing in this debate is that it is the naturalist side which argues from faith in simple analogy, not supported by factual evidence, while the antinaturalists rely on the immediate experience of goals and purposes. Thus nobody has an advantage in terms of hardheaded, empiricist toughness. In fact, it is the naturalists who seem to play the role of starry-eyed utopians, while the antinaturalists look like hidebound conservatives who believe only in what they actually see and experience. When the decisive progress in classical physics was initiated, the situation was different: all the accumulated evidence of the past did point to perfect regularity in the motion of heavenly bodies, and the hope that these motions could be explained by simple mathematical laws was entirely warranted by all that was previously known. With regard to human events, such a pre-existent knowledge is lacking. The advantage of the naturalists consists merely in this, that at least they promise something that is clear-cut—a future science for which we already have a model. It is only in this sense that the naturalist side can invoke past experience. In this respect the antinaturalists are at a disadvantage. They cannot specify the type of scientific theory they intend to develop. Otherwise, it is the antinaturalists who can marshal existing knowledge and accumulated experience as supporting their position.

If we define "reasonableness" in one's attitude as readiness to use past experience, the debate between naturalists and antinaturalists will appear in an anomalous light. For what is "reasonable" in terms of experience about the *subject matter* differs from what is "reasonable" in terms of experience with procedure and method. What we already know about man points in a different direction from what we already know about scientific method. We know a great deal about man as a being who communicates with his fellows by meaningful symbols and chooses what he thinks best on the basis of insight. We know practically nothing about man as a being whose various movements and responses can be predicted from quantitative indices alone. On the other hand, we have considerable familiarity with, and reliance on, scientific methods based on correlations among quantitative indices; we know little about what a science of meaningful variables as such could achieve.

The above statements will perhaps be challenged by adherents of naturalism and antinaturalism alike. The former may point to successes already achieved by the purely quantitative analysis of behavior; the latter may cite such impressive monumental studies, based upon an interpretive method, as Toynbee's *Study of History* or Max Weber's far-ranging researches into patterns of social and intellectual developments. Such examples, however, do not seem to me to invalidate the point I was trying to make. For it remains true, in spite of all the impressive work done by both schools, that the quantitative "laws" or regularities so far observed are of little help in dealing with actual behavior, either collective or individual, and also that it is entirely obscure how Toynbee's or Weber's methods could be used systematically by lesser minds to develop and apply in new fields the insights they have gained in theirs.

This being the situation, I think we have every reason not to adopt a dogmatic attitude either for or against naturalism. Should a Newton of social science arise, it is not to be feared that antinaturalist prejudice can prevail against him; if the laws found by such a genius account for human events as well as Newton's laws do for celestial events, it will be entirely impossible to argue against the naturalist position. If, on the other hand, someone develops a reliable method of using interpretive concepts in analyzing behavior, then this method will have to be recognized as legitimate and scientific, even though such concepts have no place in natural science. There should be no conflict among those who hold contrary preferences in this matter. Either naturalists or antinaturalists may feel, of course, that the other camp's efforts are wasted and that, if any funds are available for fundamental, methodological research, they should be withheld from the adversary. But this is hardly the spirit most conducive to scientific progress. Productive work can be based only on faith in one's position; and those who are inclined, say, in the naturalist direction cannot be expected to make a valuable contribution if they are forced to proceed in a direction not congenial to them. The same is true, of course, of antinaturalists. Since neither group can demonstrate that it, and it alone, will be able to develop a fruitful methodology of social science, the wisest course seems to be to let everyone explore all potentialities that seem promising to him.

The present study is based on the conviction that the naturalist metaphysic is wrong, not in the sense that human reality is outside and above nature but in the sense that the antiteleological principle of physical science is not fruitful when we deal with human reality. I do not hold this conviction with dogmatic rigidity. That is, I am ready to admit that I am wrong, as soon as someone produces a purely quantitative model from which all significant variations of human behavior can be deduced. All I am not ready to admit is that we should now act as if such a model were already available, or as if we knew that it would be available if we tried hard enough to produce it. We must, I think, reckon with the possibility that a model of this kind cannot be constructed.

Starting from this negative assumption, we may conclude either that a science of behavior may be impossible or that it may still be possible, once we learn how to build a theory utilizing interpretive, rather than purely quantitative, variables. We need not stipulate, of course, that this interpretive theory will make no use of quantitative (metrical or statistical) variables altogether or that it will be cast in a completely qualitative, nonmathematical language. All I mean is that the theory must provide for the use of interpretive concepts, in addition to purely descriptive, quantitative ones. I shall not attempt to construct a model of such a theory; the present study is designed merely to supply some preliminary considerations, classifying the problem of how to deal with human behavior scientifically.

What do we expect from scientific theory? A good working theory must, it seems to me, enable us to perform three types of operation, namely, explanation, prediction, and the practical application of knowledge. All three things will be possible if the theory provides a deductive fromework such that, if data are fed into it, other data can be deduced. If we use the theory to deduce from present data an antecedent constellation of data which accounts for the present observations, we engage in explanation. If we deduce a future constellation of data from those presently observed, we use the theory for predictive purposes. Finally, if we arrange our environment in such a way that we may expect, on the basis of our theory, some desired outcome, we apply the theory to practical ends.

Now it is important to realize that scientific theories in general need not be equally proficient on all three counts. Some theories yield excellent explanations but cannot be used with equal success for prediction. We can explain earthquakes after they have occurred, but we cannot predict them; our theory enables us only to specify those regions in which earthquakes are more likely to occur than in others. Similarly, we can explain the weather far better than we can predict it. The potentialities of these theories for practical application are also somewhat limited. Seismology does not tell us how to stop earthquakes; we can apply it only by taking the possibility of earthquakes into account in building houses in regions where earthquakes are frequent. Similarly, meteorology does not tell us how to stop rain or snow or whirlwinds (although it may help us to make it rain under certain conditions); we may apply meteorological knowledge, on the whole, by timing our projected activities in the light of expected weather conditions.

If we have a "good" theory in certain fields, this means that we can produce satisfactory explanations and predictions in many cases and can exploit our knowledge in many practical ways; but it does not mean that we can explain or predict anything that may happen and solve every practical problem that may face us. In general, all scientific explanation and prediction is true only conditionally. If we explain the event E in terms of the antecedent conditions $C_1, C_2, \ldots,$ and so on, all we can say is that these antecedent conditions *would* account for the event on the basis of the theory. In order to validate the explanation, we must produce evidence showing that C_1, C_2, etc., existed in reality. But we can never be quite sure that our explanation actually has specified all the relevant factors. The same applies to prediction. All we can deduce from a theory is that, if the conditions D_1, D_2, . . . , etc., are fulfilled, the outcome F may be expected to occur at a certain time t. But F will actually occur at t only if D_1, D_2, etc., are, in fact, the only factors on which occurrence at t depends. Sometimes we may indeed isolate all relevant factors on which the future outcome depends; but the situation is often too complicated to permit isolation and identification of all factors. That such a situation prevails does not mean that we have no good theory; it means only that we are prevented in practice from collecting all the evidence we would need to use the theory for explanatory or predictive purposes.

All this must be borne in mind if we want to formulate reasonable expectations as to what a good theory of human (individual or collective) behavior will accomplish. We are in no way justified in specifying that a theory of behavior must enable us to predict and explain everything, in addition to bringing the solution of every critical human and social problem within reach. It is entirely possible that some human actions are unpredictable in principle; some physical processes are also unpredictable, but this does not mean that there can be no physical theory. That an event is *unpredictable* in principle does not mean, in general, that it is *inexplicable*. We can explain the emission of a radioactive particle, although we cannot predict it. We may assume that a theory of human behavior (like seismology or the physics of radioactivity) will be better in explaining things than in predicting them; this need not be the fault of the theory at all. It is also quite possible that the practical application of a theory of behavior will be rather limited. To be able to account for human behavior is not the same thing as to be able to influence it in any desired direction. A good theory will always provide *some* possibility of practical application; but, in one case, science enables us to stamp out a disease altogether, while in another it merely helps us to take some precautions in case an earthquake occurs. We do not know what kind of application a science of behavior will allow for; I suspect it will be closer to the "earthquake" type than to the "disease" type. That a problem is grave and urgent does not mean that it "must" yield to scientific treatment. Biology has made very great progress and has helped in solving many urgent practical problems; but it has made no dent in the general law that all multicellular organisms must die, although this is surely a matter of grave concern to human beings, who alone among living things are aware of the prospect of death. It is entirely possible that some of the urgent social problems—such as the occurrence of violent conflict between organized groups—will prove equally refractory to social science. Only practice will show how far social science can progress in the field of explanation, prediction, and practical application; it would be unwise to commit it to an all-or-nothing program.

I have stated my belief that the "best" science of society and behavior we may hope to develop will have to use interpretive concepts, in addition to quantitative variables. But I do not mean to say by this that social science itself will furnish an "interpretation" of human situations or of history. Interpretation, properly speaking, is an extra-scientific operation; science deals only with facts, and its function is encompassed within the three operations I have mentioned, namely, explanation, prediction, and application. That science makes use of "interpretive" concepts means merely that either the interpretation of symbols or the interpretation of behavior will enter into the construction of the deductive framework of theory and will in this way contribute to factual explanation and prediction. Interpretation is, in this context, a method of gathering and organizing data; the ultimate purpose, however, is neither judgment nor interpretation, as such, but factual explanation and prediction (with possible practical application).

How far the scientist can adventure into the realm of interpretation is determined by the possibility of preserving scientific objectivity. This means that whenever the interpretive task incidental to the construction or testing of the theory requires judgment, the judgment must be a noncontroversial one. An example of noncontroversial judgment is that concerning the linguistic correctness of a communication. In using verbal data, the scientist participates in the communication process; this requires judgment, but there is no great risk of subjectivity involved in this, because language conventions and standards are stable and reliable. Another way of avoiding controversial judgment consists in "interpreting behavior" in terms of the standards underlying it, without identification with those standards. The scientist may, for instance, study choice behavior; in doing this, he must, if my thesis is correct, use concepts of goals and meanings, but he need not consider these goals and meanings as valid for him. He will find, for instance, that a certain cycle of behavior he observes is predicated upon certain standards of meaning. Such a finding cannot be made unless the scientist puts himself in the place of the organism which he is observing; but, in doing this, he does not give up his detachment entirely. He can report objectively about a preference scale that he is studying, without taking sides himself.

All these observations will concern not "meanings" as such but behavior as influenced and guided by meanings. In the introductory parts of this study, we emphasized the difference between the "meaning" of a sign and the actual response to the sign. The meaning of the sign, we said, is not the actual response it evokes but merely that the response is a "good" one *if* it takes place. We need not say more if we are interested merely in interpreting meanings as such; but if we want to study *actual* behavior, we do have to concern ourselves with the responses which actually occur. We said that the "good" response tends to occur if the organism is familiar with (or adapted to) the sign meaning in question and if the response is not inhibited by extraneous—meaningful or meaningless and unfamiliar—factors. The problem of interpreting behavior is precisely this: We want to ascertain how far "adaptation to" a set of meanings is responsible for actual behavior and how much of it is due to other factors.[6] We need concepts of "goal" and "meaning" in order to determine the role which adaptation, identification, experience, insight, and similar factors play in a certain sequence of behavior.

The scientist, then, does not "judge" a situation in his own name, but he must be able to say how the subjects whom he is studying "judge" their situations. An analysis in terms of meaning-oriented codes of behavior will, it seems to me, yield a more productive explanatory and predictive pattern than an analysis conducted *solely* in terms of quantitative variables could. This does not mean, however, that the use of such concepts will enable us to explain and predict everything. On the contrary, both the explanations and the predictions derived in this way will be tentative and provisional. We can only say: This choice is what we would have to expect, if we assumed that the standards of our subject are such and such and that he actually acted on the basis of these standards. But we obviously must allow for different outcomes in cases where disturbing factors enter the picture or adaptation breaks down for some reason.

How can we study "meaning-oriented" behavior? We must, first of all, learn to distinguish between the behavioral manifestations of different "standards" of meanings. For instance, play behavior is dif-

6. This method of following through the implications of a law involving one set of variables and allowing for the effects of a variable not belonging to the same set but characterized merely as a "disturbance" is reminiscent of the mathematical concept of "stochastic" relations. Cf. Kenneth Arrow, "Mathematical Models in the Social Sciences," in *The Policy Sciences*, ed. Daniel Lerner and Harold D. Lasswell (Stanford, Calif.: Stanford University Press, 1951), p. 151.

ferent from behavior oriented toward immediate "relevance"; and we must know how to distinguish the two, before we can try to discover the "rules of the game" or the "scales of preference" underlying the behavior. Further, it is necessary to distinguish between "conflict-free" situations and "conflict" situations, the latter being those in which behavior is influenced by conflicting standards, and the former, those in which this is not the case. Finally, if we conclude that the situation is characterized by a conflict of standards, we have to ask in which way the conflict is resolved—whether in autonomous or in heteronomous fashion. Behavior models, then, must allow for different types of standards of meaning and also for different modes of resolving conflicts; they must also leave room for meaning-free automatisms and other constraints upon behavior. This methodological principle I propose to call the "principle of multiplicity."

What the principle asserts is that, in trying to construct theoretical models of behavior, particularly of socially relevant behavior, we are faced with a double task. On the one hand, we must construct a theory which is not in itself a work of interpretation. In the social sciences, as elsewhere, a theory is a generalized statement of relationships obtaining among facts, enabling us to deduce predictions and explanations when we are presented with data that come under the theory. On the other hand, however, there is something specific to theories of human behavior, namely, that the variables entering into the theory and the data to which the theory can be applied can be "given" only by being interpreted in terms of some standard or other. The peculiar difficulty facing social science is how to combine interpretation (which we need in order to grasp our data) with the noninterpretive operation of theory-building proper.

Two circumstances combine to make the accomplishment of this task difficult. First, meaningful data can serve for the construction of a scientific theory only if their interpretation is highly reliable and noncontroversial. Second, in order to construct a theory upon "meaningful" materials, we need models showing how the "meaningful" enters into the fabric of the actual world.

How can we construct such models (to speak of this latter point first)? When we interpret a situation in terms of "meaning," we are noncommittal as to what is going to happen in reality. We merely say that, in the ideal case, something "should" happen and that there is a tendency to make it happen. Since the ideally "good" response, defined in terms of the meaning of the situation, occurs with much less than perfect regularity, we might decide that the thing to do is to treat actual responses in terms of their relative frequency or "probability." But it seems to me that this approach is unsatisfactory, for to say that meaning "tends to" evoke a certain response is precisely not to say that meaning is that which makes that response "most probable." What occurs most frequently is not necessarily the most adequate or the most insightful response. Meaning is not something that "loads the dice" in a certain way. In determining its causal import, then, we must combine different deductive patterns, some purely "ideal" and others possibly of a statistical nature. This is a difficult assignment, to be mastered, I think, only with a type of logic which is not yet developed.

The difficulty seems less great in so far as reliability of interpretation is concerned. There are various highly noncontroversial and reliable standards of interpretation, such as standards of communicative meaning, and also standards of elementary biological "relevance" and conventional "correctness." A scientific observer can interpret behavior in terms of such standards in a completely detached, relativistic fashion; the interpretive judgments he makes express not his own relevance or value attitudes but merely those of the individuals or groups he is studying. Restriction of all judgment to this "oblique" mode is known as the principle of "value neutrality" (*Wertfreiheit*), which was particularly stressed by Max Weber. This principle is often criticized as both impossible to achieve and involving moral nihilism. As to the first point, it is true that the theoretical scientist cannot be a completely value-indifferent person, since his own activities are based upon a specific theoretical ethos; Weber himself was quite emphatic in acknowledging this. For this and other reasons, no scientist can completely avoid all bias in describing, explaining, and evaluating behavior in his own or in alien cultures. But this does not mean that the scientist cannot at least strive to achieve as complete an avoidance of bias as possible; and the question is whether a conscious striving toward this minimization of asserting one's own value position does or does not amount to an advocacy of "nihilism" as part of the scientific attitude.

It seems to me that this accusation confuses a methodological principle, adopted by the scientist as scientist, with a metaphysical or ethical position of a comprehensive nature. "Nihilism" exists only where an assertion is made or implied to the effect that certain value concepts lack truth and validity, but not where a decision is made to abstain from a "straight" judgment in terms of these concepts for some specific reason, such as that abstention from judgment is necessary to realize the value of objective fact-finding. It may be argued, indeed, that Weber's own conception of the status of value concepts came close to nihilism, because he interpreted them in a purely decisionist sense. But this has nothing to do with his advocacy of a value-neutral attitude *within science*. We may reject the decisionist *philosophy* of values as nihilistic but still agree that, in pure theory, we have to seek to ascertain the facts, whatever our values are, just as in our thinking about values we must seek to judge what is right, whatever the facts are.

Weber's position is important to us, both because he emphasized the value-neutral, factual orientation of social science and because he postulated an "interpretive" theory of social reality. In the following section we shall briefly examine his position and confront it with that of another eminent sociologist, Vilfredo Pareto, who, in our opinion, tried unsuccessfully to develop a "meaning-free" deductive framework for social science.

3. MAX WEBER'S AND VILFREDO PARETO'S CONCEPTS OF SOCIOLOGY

Max Weber defines sociology as a science "which seeks to give a causal explanation of the course and of the effects of social action, by means of its interpretive understanding."[7] This, our author says, is not the only conceivable kind of sociology; in order to distinguish it from other sociologies, he calls *his* sociology "interpretive sociology" (*verstehende Soziologie*). It is, however, clear from the above definition that "interpretive sociology" is far from limiting itself to the *interpretation* of social action. It would be especially wrong to regard "interpretation" in Weber's sense as something opposed to "causal explanation." Sociology, as a science, seeks to give a causal explanation of the phenomena which it studies; in this respect there is no difference between Weber and sociologists of a more positivistic turn of mind. The difference is merely one of method. Social action, according to Weber, can best be explained "in its course and its effects" by "interpretive understanding"; the causal picture is deeply influenced by the *meanings* underlying social action.

Weber's concept of meaning (*Sinn*) does not fully coincide with the concept used in this study. According to him, the "meaning" of an action is what was subjectively intended by the agent, either an

7. Cf. Max Weber, *Wirtschaft und Gesellschaft* (Tübingen, 1922), p. 1.

actual person or a construct, a pure type representing an ideal group.[8] "Interpretive understanding" means, then, that the sociologist reconstructs the motives of which an agent engaged in social action was conscious. This, however, is possible only where the pattern of action is transparent to the sociologist studying it, e.g., where the sociologist can feel that he would act in the same way or can at least conceive that a person of different character would be impelled to act in a certain fashion. In order to achieve such interpretation, the sociologist has to rely on either of two methods: the rational analysis of action, on the one hand, and a kind of sympathetic intuition, on the other. The former is possible when one has to deal with action rationally adapted to an end; the latter comes in where one has to do with emotional responses of a familiar kind.

Social action as described by Weber, however, is far from being reducible to these two types. In many cases, neither rational nor emotional-empathic interpretation is possible: the pattern of action is opaque. The most important type of social action not open to interpretation is "traditional" action. One cannot establish the "intended meaning" or "purpose" of purely traditional action; one simply has to accept it as brute fact.

It follows that straight "interpretation," that is, the ascertainment of motives with which the observer can rationally or irrationally identify himself, is not the only method which the sociologist has to apply. In many cases he has to admit right at the outset that his data are not open to such interpretation. This does not mean, however, that the interpretive method has nothing to offer in these cases: Weber declares that the interpretive method should still be applied, but obliquely, in terms of a deficiency of interpretation.

Group behavior, for instance, often has to be analyzed and described as deviating from an ideally constructed, fully rational pattern.[9] First, we ascertain how people would act if their motives and modes of action were wholly rational. Then, seeing in what respect their actual behavior deviates from this rational pattern, we may look for the specific causes responsible for the deviation. Weber mentions the happenings during a Stock Exchange panic as an example.

In general, types of social action may be arranged along a scale, running from an "irrational" to a "rational" pole. Purely traditional action, for instance, is irrational; it occupies one extremity of the

8. *Ibid.*   9. *Ibid.*, p. 2.

scale. Rational business procedures, or those applied by a technological expert, represent the other pole.

Closer analysis shows that there are two different types of representative social behavior which defy straight interpretation—not only traditional but also "charismatic" action.[10] Certain remarks made by Weber suggest that these "irrational" types of action fall outside the scope of "interpretive" sociology; in actual fact, however, his description and analysis of social action, far from neglecting irrational types of behavior, stresses their importance in human history. Thus Weber distinguishes three types of legitimate authority: rational, traditional, and charismatic.[11] Of these, "rational" authority is the "purest" type: it has the maximum of efficiency. Analysis of the other two, however, also reveals elements of rationality, as well as certain transitions from irrationality to rationality.

This method of contrasting "rational" and "irrational" modes of behavior proved in Max Weber's hands a powerful instrument of historical analysis. Western history acquired depth in this way: it became three-dimensional. The specifically "modern" periods, characterized by "rationalistic" and "bureaucratic" techniques, were set off in sharp contrast against "pre-rationalistic" ages; they belonged to a different dimension. At the same time, Weber showed how rational techniques and modes of behavior *genetically* arose from irrational antecedents. Rational social systems emerge, not because they are conceived by rational thinkers, but because a certain constellation of irrational factors favors them. Although there is no plan or thinking behind history, a direction is still discernible—away from the irrational, toward the rational.

This view of history recalls Hegel's conception of the Idea which realizes itself through successive stages of decreasing irrationality. Weber's "rational," however, has little to do with Hegelian *Vernunft*. Its essence is not self-consciousness, self-realization, and sheer, actual substantiality, but effectiveness in the technical and economic sense. According to Weber, a social system is the more rational, the more certainly and economically the purposes recognized in it are achieved. What these purposes are is a question which has nothing to do with rationality as such. The antithesis between rationality and irrationality concerns merely the means-ends relationship, not the ends themselves; the ends are "random," they cannot be judged or analyzed in

---

10. *Ibid.*, p. 8.   11. *Ibid.*, p. 124.

terms of rationality. That human society is growing more "rational" does not mean, therefore, that man becomes wiser and more moral. It merely means that average, everyday human action becomes better adapted to its recognized ends, more regular, more predictable; this is entirely compatible with its becoming more destructive and immoral.

Sociology of Weber's type is especially interested in types of action which regularly occur and hence can be predicted, *because* they are "rational" in the sense of being effective in securing certain ends. To characterize predictable and interpretable phenomena of this sort, he has the quaint expression "adequate causation,"[12] as contrasted with "fortuitous" causation. Although the social scientist often must take cognizance of causal sequences of the latter sort, his own concern is with the former; he must rely on other sciences, geophysics, psychology, etc., in accounting for "fortuitous" causation of social action. In other words, "natural" causality does not interest social science: the latter's own field begins where the meaningful, the interpretable, and the rational also become causally effective.[13] This, as we have seen, does not mean that sociology examines only rationally "adequate" responses but merely that it elucidates irrational action by confronting it with a contrasting rational pattern, the "ideal" which it somehow does not attain.

This method does not produce a universally applicable theory of human society and group behavior. It does not give us indices which would enable us to make predictions wherever and whenever we observe them. The Weberian type of analysis starts from some unique, historical constellation of socially significant beliefs, motives, practices, and the like, and compares this constellation with others which are similar to it in some respects and dissimilar in others. The problem is to find that difference which will account for the most distinctive and significant historical line of development that we observe.

In other words, the Weberian type of analysis deals not with cultural uniformities but with cultural mutations. The cultural mutation which obsessed him was modern Western capitalism. Here, we have to do with a cultural process which is really "new" and unique. It originated in a narrowly circumscribed geographical area at a certain time when conditions were ripe. But conditions were "ripe" in many

12. Cf. *Gesammelte Aufsätze zur Wissenschaftslehre* (Tübingen, 1922), p. 280.
13. *Ibid.*, p. 408.

other cultures too, and yet the specific Western mutation, with its unparalleled dynamism, did not arise. What was the difference?

I shall not discuss the specific way in which Weber answers this question[14] but shall limit myself to a few remarks about the over-all principle which seems to have guided his procedure. His point of departure appears to have been an assessment of what was most significant in history, of what line of development was of the greatest moment. To be sure, the problem was to "explain" this line of development, to account for it scientifically. But scientific explanation could begin only after the question concerning significance had been answered.

By what standard does one judge the significance of a historic development? Weber's standard seems to have been dynamism and power. What distinguishes the Occident is, above all, its explosive, irresistible dynamism. But Weber is not interested in power as such. What fascinates him is rather the generation of new power, the chain reaction which sets new dynamic energies free. And, for Weber, the key factor which generates and multiplies power was rationality of action. Tradition binds energies; it prevents action from realizing all its potentialities. But where man cuts adrift from traditional limitations, where he chooses means exclusively in terms of their suitability to attain ends, a cultural mutation may set in.

This is the type of significant process which is to be explained; but in the course of the explanation itself, as Weber gives it, a curious twist occurs. For the process which is supremely significant because it gives free scope to rational choice—that process itself has not been inititiated as a result of rational choice and planning. Western culture stumbled into rationality because certain pre-rational motives and goals of Western man pulled in that direction. The process of cultural development may result in a maximization of means-ends rationality (*Zweckrationalität*); but this can happen only if, and because, something entirely different from this maximization is intended. In setting off the cultural mutation, certain absolute ends and "irrational" motives furnish the decisive impulse. As a *cause* rather than a result of the cultural mutation, the "rationality" of the absolute (*Wertrationalität*)[15] is more important than means-ends rationality.

14. Cf. Max Weber, *Gesammelte Aufsätze zur Religionssoziologie* (Tübingen, 1920–21); *The Religion of China*, trans. H. H. Gerth (Glencoe, Ill.: Free Press, 1952).

15. *Wirtschaft und Gesellschaft*, pp. 12 f.

As we see, Weber's analysis operates with a multiplicity of interpretive standards. Means-ends rationality is one of these; it is contrasted with others which are less transparent and require a greater effort to be grasped and applied in interpretation. In the framework of Weber's sociological analysis of culture, means-ends rationality is both the end-point and the explicandum. The other standards are in the background and provide the explanation.

All this gives Weber's perspective a certain ambiguity. In his choice of the "significant" segment of history, he is culturally egocentric like Hegel; but in his exploration of the background factors, he powerfully transcends cultural egocentricity. We have to understand ourselves, he seems to say, in terms of what is remote from us.

In our present context, Weber's method is important because it aims at a type of causal explanation which uses meaningful data, interpreted as such. But the question is whether the method can be used in dealing with other problems than that of the genesis of a particular cultural mutation. In sociology, grateful as we are for Weber's work, we would like to have laws of a higher generality.

Could such a generalizing type of sociology be developed without recurring to interpretive methods? We shall now examine briefly the way in which Pareto constructs a noninterpretive generalizing sociology.

Pareto proposes to examine social facts from a rigorously scientific point of view. He banishes from sociology all emotional as well as metaphysical elements. As a result, a large part of the usual explanations of group and individual behavior must go overboard; instead of "rationalizing" human behavior along traditional lines, we shall have to accept much of it as irrational and gratuitous.

For Pareto, too, some action is rational. One of his main distinctions is that between "logical" and "illogical" action. "Logical action" is, by definition, the only kind of action that can be justified on objective grounds, e.g., on the basis of scientific observation and experimentation. This is the kind of action the effects of which, on experimental evidence, may rightly be expected to turn out just as foreseen and desired. In this respect there is no difference between Pareto and Weber; both single out a kind of rational action, where means are adapted to ends; and for Pareto, too, the ends are beyond the realm of rationality: they have to be accepted as "brute facts," defying scientific analysis.[16] Weber and Pareto, however, differ sharply as

16. V. Pareto, *Traité de sociologie générale* (Paris, 1932), §§ 2112, 2143.

regards the status of "rational" or "logical" action in sociology. For Weber the proper, distinctive object of study of sociology is interpretable, rational action; for Pareto "logical" action is a marginal case which neither requires nor even admits analysis by methods proper to sociology.

"Logical action" in Pareto's sense is coextensive with rational, experimental techniques. It is characterized only by the fact that its subjectively envisaged and avowed aim tends to coincide with its actual outcome, or at least could so coincide in principle. This, however, is not the case with an important class of actions which Pareto calls "nonlogical." The point about nonlogical action is not that it misses its aim because the means employed are unsuitable; such inadequate action could still be "logical," at least in intention. What distinguishes "nonlogical" action is not the choice of means but the end. A "nonlogical action" in Pareto's sense is one that cannot even be discussed in "logical" terms—that is, in terms of the suitability of the means chosen—because its avowed aim is such that it could not be achieved by any rational, scientific technique. The observance of magical practices, taboos, and the like is a case in point. Actions of this kind have effects, to be sure, but the real effects are *necessarily* different from what the actors had in mind.

Failure to distinguish between logical and nonlogical action is, according to Pareto, the main fallacy barring the road to a scientific treatment of sociological problems. Sociology, he says, cannot be a science as long as every action is analyzed as if it were logical action.[17]

But there is more to the distinction between logical and nonlogical action than this contrast between scientifically and technically possible, realizable aims, on the one hand, and purely imaginary, "metaphysical," irrational ones, on the other. "Nonlogical action" is equated with the *permanent* and *invariant* part of human behavior, as opposed to its fleeting and variable elements, which for Pareto largely coincide with verbal justifications and rationalizations of action (*dérivations*). Social science, of course, is mainly concerned with the permanent element; its main aim is to disentangle the permanent from the variable. Thus "science versus metaphysics" has for Pareto a curiously twofold significance. On the one hand, only logical action can be scientifically *justified*, as its aims are within the orbit of experimental science. On the other hand, however, nonlogical action as such is the only proper *object* for scientific sociology. Not that Pareto denies

17. *Ibid.*, § 262.

the social importance of logical action. He stresses, on the contrary, that human behavior is to a considerable extent determined by "logical" motives.[18] This logical sector of behavior, however, does not call for treatment in sociological terms. It is largely made up of actions which represent the application of some scientific findings; there remains nothing here to be elucidated by sociology.

The main task of social science, in Pareto's conception, is to explode those theories which serve to explain and justify actions as appropriate to a rational end, when, in actual fact, no such means-ends relationship exists. According to this view, an explanation of action is specifically "sociological" if it traces an action back to a "nonlogical" source, exploding current explanations that give it a "logical" varnish. Thus, if an action can be understood as the application of a rational, scientific technique, it cannot be explained scientifically, as to its real motive. Causal explanation of behavior is possible only if we discard meanings; hence the interpretation of an action as a "logical" one is no causal explanation at all; it has nothing to do with sociological analysis.

If sociology has to go back to "nonlogical" ultimate motives in explaining behavior, then, Pareto concludes, utilitarianism as a theory explaining human behavior must be discarded. Utilitarianism assumes that moral codes, valuations, norms, laws, and the like can be effective only in so far as they coincide with each individual's pursuit of "pleasure" and avoidance of "pain," considered as the sole motive of action. Such a theory recognizes no other action than a "logical" one; it necessarily fails, therefore, says Pareto, "to remove the contradictions that may arise between the interests of the individual and the interests of collectivity."[19] If we assume, with Bentham, that every human action must and can be explained by the sole motive of seeking pleasure and avoiding pain, then we cannot see how the principle of the "greatest happiness of the greatest number," Bentham's main principle of ethics, can ever become effective in any society. After all, it is possible for an individual to increase his own pleasure by depriving others of pleasures and inflicting pain upon them, even to the point of reducing the total amount of happiness in the community;[20] there is no reason to assume that, if everyone is allowed fully to indulge in pleasure-seeking and pain-avoiding impulses, the amount of pleasure for all will be maximum, and that of pain minimum.

Pareto concludes that there is a discrepancy between ethical norms

18. *Ibid.*, § 152.   19. *Ibid.*, § 1479.   20. *Ibid.*, §§ 1487 ff.

and precepts, on the one hand, and the individual's hedonistic calculus, on the other. If, then, any ethical code—for instance, the Benthamite one, postulating the greatest happiness of the greatest number—is ever effective, it is because the actions of individuals are not exclusively motivated by their hedonistic calculus.

The essential feature of Pareto's interpretation of moral codes and behavior patterns is that he considers them rational from the viewpoint of society and irrational from the viewpoint of the individual.

For instance, in discussing the social effect of some line of action, Pareto speaks of its social "utility"; he means that the action of the individual may have utility for society as a whole, although its overt, conscious motive has nothing to do with such utility. This is how Pareto defines the "utility of a society" (as distinct from utility "for" a society, which we shall not discuss here): it is the sum total of all those changes whereby the individual "utilities" of the members of the society can be increased concurrently.[21] It is possible to effect changes of this kind up to a certain critical point. If the condition of society is changed further after that, only the "utilities" of certain members will be increased, while those of others will be reduced. That critical point, then, is the maximum utility *of* society.

Now Pareto's thesis is that, if the individuals are actuated only by their own interests and have perfect, "logical" knowledge of the means whereby those interests can be promoted, they will act regardless of the utility "of" their society, and the actual condition of society will move farther and farther away from the point of maximal utility. Society, however, seeks to maintain its condition at or about that point. How can this be achieved? The motives of the individuals are mainly self-seeking, and society cannot change that. The only way to make sure that the total outcome of individual actions will approximate the maximum utility of society consists, therefore, in eliminating the second condition formulated above: perfect logical knowledge of the results of every action. Society must, above all, prevent its members from knowing the ways in which their own happiness could be promoted.

If society wants to obtain from the individual the sacrifice of part of his happiness (that part which he could attain at the expense of the maximum utility of society), it must see to it that the behavior of the individual is "nonlogical" in some respects. "La plupart du temps, l'homme accomplit ce sacrifice par une action non-logique."[22]

21. *Ibid.*, §§ 2115, 2121.   22. *Ibid.*, § 2119.

There is, however, a certain oscillation in Pareto's thought with regard to nonlogical action. Especially in the first part of the *Traité*, "nonlogical" tends to coincide with "gratuitous";[23] nonlogical actions are performed in an entirely gratuitious way, without any conscious thought relating them to the actor's aims or interests, real or imaginary. Thus the passage quoted above continues: "... et les considérations subjectives d'utilité ne se font pas." Elsewhere, however, Pareto does not identify "nonlogical" with "gratuitious" action. Although irrational and ineffective in promoting the agent's true interests, nonlogical action is still motivated by the desire of promoting self-interest; the reason why it is led astray is that the agent has a subjective theory, not founded in fact, by which he justifies his action as being useful to him. The real, "nonlogical" motive is hidden from the individual; it is a "résidu," an unconscious urge. The pseudological theory by means of which the individual satisfies himself that he is promoting his own well-being is a "dérivation," that is to say, an illusion. Society makes use of "dérivations" in order to make its members act in accordance with "résidus."

It follows that moral codes, precepts, laws, religions, and the like constitute a kind of "pious fraud." "L'observation confirme," says Pareto, "... que les résidus existant dans une société lui sont en grande partie favorables. Il convient donc à la société que ni ces résidus ni les préceptes (dérivations) que les manifestent ne soient offusqués et amoindris. Mais le but est mieux atteint si l'individu estime, croit, s'imagine qu'en observant ces préceptes, en acceptant ces dérivations, il travaille à son propre bien."[24]

It will be especially useful for society if those who do not belong to the governing class imagine that they promote their own interest by complying with norms and precepts inspired by the interests of society as a whole and by the interests of the governing class in particular; this is why "nonlogical" thinking must be promoted.

But, when this conclusion is reached, it becomes apparent that the program of building a purely "scientific" theoretical system from which all categories of "meaning" are excluded could not be carried out. For the "nonlogical actions" and "résidus," which were originally introduced to provide a meaning-free theoretical framework, ultimately emerge as vehicles of meaning, interpreted from the point of view of the group rather than of the individual.

23. *Ibid.*, § 217.   24. *Ibid.*, § 1932.

IV. MEANING AND VALUE

CHAPTER IX

MOTIVES, NORMS, AND VALUES

1. The Concept of Value

THE problem of values occupied us repeatedly in the earlier parts of this study. We have seen that "standards" of "good" and "bad" are constituent parts of all meaning. Whatever is interpreted, either implicitly "within behavior" or explicitly in the process of communication, is interpreted in terms of one or several such standards. We have distinguished two main classes of standards—those of relevance and those of order; and we have seen that certain standards of meaning give rise to "value-languages" in which judgments of various types may be formulated. Now we shall ask the question: What are these "values," that is, the things asserted in value judgments? How are they related to standards of meaning?

We may define "value" as a kind of "property." That is, in our terminology, a "value" is neither a thing which is the object of some desire or striving nor a response or act of enjoyment, but primarily a property ascribed to something which is "evaluated" or "judged." But a value property is not a mere classificatory property, that is, one we ascribe to things in classifying them according to some standard of order. Accordingly, in evaluating things, we do not treat them as invariants or "classes" of situations. Evaluation is an act within the meaningful structure of a situation, and "value" is a situational category. A value accrues to an object as "correlate" of a meaningful response, and not as a situation class. In evaluating things, we take position, we perform a situational response. This is different from the ascertainment of a fact, an operation which requires a breaking-up of the meaningful structure of the actually prevailing situation. Nevertheless, evaluation is not a completely naïve and spontaneous response to a dominant sign or sign constellation as such. It also involves analysis and therefore a distance from immediately present sign meanings. In order to evaluate a thing, we must, first of all, isolate it as a correlate; thus, in evaluation, we have to single out a component of the meaningful situation and look at its particular role and merit within the context. In this way evaluation also breaks up the continuity of the cycle of interpretation-in-behavior, although in a less radical way than pure fact-finding and description do. In evaluating things, we do not step out of our role as agent, but we play that role self-consciously and critically, and we are concerned with the way in which that role as a whole is organized beyond the immediately prevailing situation. This "critical" role requires more than the mere isolation of a correlate; it involves looking at the correlate from different—actually or potentially conflicting—points of view.

Evaluation as a problem arises in connection with possible or actual conflicts among dominant sign meanings. No task of "judging" or "evaluating" things would emerge if dominant sign meanings never got in one another's way and never pointed in divergent directions within the situational map. We come to be interested in the "values" of things because we need some method enabling us to stand up to a dominant sign constellation and to pass it by in order to avoid conflict and disappointment. We have to distinguish in this sense between the nature of a sign correlate as "satisfying an urge" and its "value." In simple enjoyment we get urge satisfaction from a correlate, but we do not isolate it as a problematic element of the structure of our situation; we do not judge it explicitly. To judge a correlate involves not only enjoying its satisfactory nature but also taking position toward the satisfaction itself.

Hence we must make a distinction between "relevance" and "value." "Relevance" is the meaning of a situation by which a kind of "good" response is specified—"good" meaning "immediately satisfactory." "Value," on the other hand, is not this kind of experienced goodness as such, but a property by which the correlate-object of the experience and the experience itself are classified as not only satisfying now but also satisfying without counterindication. When we ascribe "goodness" to some correlate-object in the "value-language" of relevance (see chap. viii), what we attend to is the pure immediate experience of enjoyment; but this is not the whole story. The judgment of primary, immediate, relevant satisfaction says explicitly: "This is pleasurable," and implicitly: "and nothing else counts." The possibility that something else *might* count lurks in the background. In this way, we may conceive of judgments about "relevance" or urge satisfaction as the first link in a whole chain of types of judgment, generated in situations in which conflicts do arise—in which something else may count more than pleasure. We have already seen that this distance we take toward our own urges, this critical attitude toward the immediate impulse, is essential to the rules of value-languages other than that of pure "relevance." We can speak of relevance as a "value" only in the sense that it is a value with zero degree of conflict; this is what the judgment of relevance expresses. When we simply enjoy without judging, our situation has only "relevance" but no element of value or evaluation.

We have to look at values, then, as ordering possible goals or objects of desire in terms of possible conflicts among these desires. This definition of "value" differs radically from the usual one, typically represented by R. B. Perry's usage, according to which a "value" is that which is desired, in so far as it is desired.[1] It seems to me that this definition is sterile. Of course, no definition is true or false, and everyone is free to define his terms as he chooses. If "value for X" is defined as "that which X demands" or "that which X would like to get," a field of investigation is demarcated which is undeniably interesting and important. It is only that this definition does not give us a good perspective for the things we have in mind when we make value judgments. For what is the point of a judgment of value, such as "This is the decent thing to do, and I ought therefore to do it"? It is not that there is a strong, permanent, pre-existent "desire" for decency as something I should like to get as much of as possible: "decency" is not a goal in the same sense as, for instance, wealth or health is. If I attribute the character of "decency" to an action, I do not mean to say that there is something in that action which attracts me or strikes me as desirable to "have" or to "get." The character of "decency" is not something desirable in itself, regardless of everything else; it is, rather, a basis for preferring a certain way of behaving over something that might be satisfactory "in itself," if it were not for a conflict with certain conditions which we accept. "Decency," like other value terms on the basis of which judgments can be made, refers to a situation in which certain goals are or may be rejected in favor of others. Now the definition of "value" as "object of desire" would suggest that, when a goal is rejected for whatever reason, the reason can be stated as a desire for an object that is stronger than the desire for the thing we reject. But I maintain that, if the "reason" for rejecting one thing and choosing another is expressed by a value term, the term does not

1. Cf. Ralph Barton Perry, *General Theory of Value* (New York and London: Longmans, Green & Co., 1926). A concise statement of Perry's position is found on p. 115: "That which is an object of interest is *eo ipso* invested with value."

stand for the object of a strong desire but for some *relation* between objects or classes of desire; the term has no reference *outside* the conflict situation.

What I mean to say is *not* that the value term refers to some actually experienced "preference" or "preferability." In stating a preference *as such*, we compare desires or objects of desire; in order to do this, we must have properties in mind which can also be ascertained in themselves, outside the conflict situation. Such properties are properties of "relevance," not of "value," or, at most, values at zero-conflict level. A judgment of value which refers to such a property (a desirability simply experienced in itself) is not the type of judgment we need to explicate the meaning of value judgments in general, for their "zero-conflict-level" quality masks the *essential* function of value judgments. For instance, the judgment "Apples taste good" looks simple in structure; but, if I consider it as a value judgment, I must supplement it by some qualification: for instance, "Apples have a goodness we may enjoy when nothing else matters." The "higher"-value terms we examined in chapter viii, as well as terms of "utility," need no such supplement, for they explicitly imply a conflict level which is not zero. The term "decent" means "decent whether it is agreeable or not"; "useful" means "useful whether pleasant or not." Simple attributions of preference ("better than," "preferable to") do not have this structure of invariance-within-possible-conflict. "Better than" does not mean "better whether more pleasant or not."

Value terms refer to ways in which goal conflicts may be resolved, but they do not simply stand for an experienced preference. Preference as such need not involve a goal conflict. For instance, if we have free choice, we shall prefer a dish we like to one we do not like; there is no conflict whatever, and the preference is made on the "zero-conflict level." *This* act of preference, then, is based on relevance pure and simple. I think we may also speak of "zero-conflict" preference in cases where we prefer an enjoyment—say, a dish—to one we also like, but to a lesser extent; this also involves no conflict. Preferences determined in a conflict situation, on the other hand, involve a judgment of value. But the judgment is something different from the act of preference. The judgment of value expresses the *meaning* of the conflict situation, whereas the preference is the actual *response*. The two need not coincide—this much is clear from our previous analysis of meanings. In order to make preferences conforming to our value judgments, more than "judgment"—that is, grasp of the meaning of the conflict situation—is needed; there must also be sufficient motivation. The motivating agent is not the value as such; it also includes some desire which reinforces the value. But it would be wrong to say that the value—or "meaning"—plays *no* motivating role at all. Here, as elsewhere, "meanings" do not completely determine behavior, but they "shape" or "guide" it; behavior may be "oriented" toward them.

To return to the case of our honest man: he chose the course that appeared "decent" to him. Now "decency" as such was not his entire motivation; the actual impulse to "do the decent thing" was based on a variety of motives, partly conscious and partly unconscious. In the *motivation*, relevances—that is, things desired or feared "in themselves," regardless of conflict—have certainly played a major role. The motives underlying actual behavior may, in fact, be fruitfully analyzed in terms of what Perry calls "value": those things which are feared or desired, in so far as they are feared or desired. But we cannot analyze behavior in conflict situations properly if we look only at the motive which turns out to be the strongest, without asking how that motive came to be dominant. In answering this question, it is useful to assign a particular—though not necessarily dominant—role to "values" as interpreted "meanings" of the conflict situation. Sometimes interpretation in terms of value shapes the motivational structure; one may then "act" on a judgment. But the judging operation does not consist in simply *ascertaining* pre-existent motivations. Its function is, rather, to help one group of motives become dominant over others. If the judgment is not reinforced by a strong enough motive, the thing "judged" better will not be actually preferred. But if a motive is not shaped by a judgment, it may not come into play at all. A man will not act "reasonably," instead of impulsively, unless he has a strong enough *motive* to use reason; but he cannot act on such a motive unless he makes a judgment about what is most "useful" to him. The motive is something like the incentive or sanction behind the judgment; it is not the content of the judgment. That *content*, as distinct from the sanction associated with it, is the value asserted in the judgment.

In a conflict situation, what is in conflict is the various "motives"— urges, goals, desires—by which a person is swayed. The motives as such express "relevance"—they are not "values." We can speak of "value" where it is not the motive strength alone that decides the conflict but where some motive is helped or shaped by an interpretation of the conflict situation. A motive supported by a value judgment will not, by the same token, become dominant: one may succumb to temptation against his "better judgment." This does not mean that the "values" of the person in question are not those which he asserts in his judgment but those he expresses by his actions. On the contrary: we have to say, in such a case, that the actions of the person belie his values. This phraseology, I thing, does far better justice to the meaning of "value judgments" than the one which equates the actual decision with the "values" entertained by a person. For this reason, I think it is better not to define "value" as being "that which is desired or preferred." Nor can we simply equate the "norms" valid in a society with the actual behavior patterns followed by the society's members.

I believe, for instance, that a misunderstanding is involved in the following statement:

> Murdock points to the obvious discrepancy between sexual norms and sexual behavior. . . . The sexual norm of American culture, he points out, is pre-marital celibacy; but the actual behavior of many Americans is in direct violation of this norm. Kinsey's data, of course, have indicated how great the discrepancy actually is. But one is immediately led to ask: Does the sexual behavior of those who do not practice premarital celibacy constitute a violation of *their* norms? Is it not rather that their behavior is in accordance with their norms, and that their norms are in contradiction to the norms of other members of American society? . . . The fact is that most people in all societies do behave according to norms, and there is abundant clinical evidence that the rare person who chronically violates *his* norms pays the penalty of severe neurosis.[2]

The answer to the question raised by the author is that the actual behavior of a person may, but need not, be based on the norms acknowledged by him—norms which (as the author correctly says) in their turn may, but need not, be identical with those publicly proclaimed as valid. If a person does not practice premarital celibacy, this may mean, indeed, that he entertains norms deviant from the official code; but it may also be the case that the person in question recognizes the norm as valid but violates it in his behavior. In the former case, he will have a good conscience about what he is doing; in the latter, he will feel guilty. Presumably, conscious or unconscious guilt is very frequent in subjects engaging in officially disapproved behavior, even if they profess themselves to be too "enlightened" to recognize the validity of the official norm. It is by no means true to say that acting

2. Melford E. Spiro, "Culture and Personality," *Psychiatry*, XIV, No. 1 (February, 1951), 33. (Italics in original.)

counter to one's own norms always or almost always leads to neurosis. One might assume that neurosis develops even more easily in persons who *never* violate the moral code they recognize as valid but repress and frustrate some strong instinctual motive. A person who "succumbs to temptation," feels guilt, and then "purges himself" of his guilt in some reliable way (e.g., by confession) may achieve in this way a better balance, and be less neurotic, than a person who never violates his "norms" and never feels conscious guilt.

Particularly in the field of sexual morality, we find every possible combination between types of recognized codes and types of actual behavior. There are those who preach monogamy and practice promiscuousness; those who preach promiscuousness and practice monogamy; and those who both preach and practice either of the two. What they preach shows their "values"; what they practice reflects their "motivations."

That the "values of a person" are the values he "preaches" should be understood in a straight, rather than an ironical, sense: what we mean, obviously, is what a person seriously believes in rather than what he publicly proclaims. Values are a matter of conviction, conscience, and guilt, and not of overt (either purely verbal or actual) behavior. What a person's values are can be determined from how he feels about his own and other people's actions, not from what he says and what he does.

But then one may ask whether it is not possible to think of values objectively, rather than of the values "of" a person. What is right "for" *A* is what his conscience tells him is the right thing to do; but can we not ask what is right not "for" us but in itself? The answer is that everone's conscience puts the question in this form: the problem "for me" is not what is right "for me" but what is right "in itself." This is the sense in which value problems are considered in the actual process of judging. The value judgment refers to what is valuable "in itself." The expression "value of a person" belongs not to the value-language but to the scientific language. Behavior science does not ask and answer value questions, i.e., questions about what "is" right; it does ask and answer questions about what the values "of" individuals and groups are. Whether the value judgments have a kind of "objective" validity, or whether this claim is completely illusory, will be considered later.

2. Levels of Conflict

We shall now try to characterize the various "levels of conflict" among motives on which problems of value may originate. Thus far, we have referred only to the "zero level," on the one hand, and the nonzero levels, those involving actual conflict, on the other. Our present question is: Can we differentiate the various successive higher-than-zero levels, and how?

Since the "zero level" is that of simple, immediately experienced relevance for one subject, it seems natural to call level 1 that involving conflicts among relevances for the same person. There is no need for a detailed discussion of these problems; the cases are familiar. One would like to relax, but it is also desirable to earn money. A good meal is attractive, but it may endanger one's health. One would like to "tell off" a person, but his good will is indispensable. And so on. How are such conflicts resolved? One of the motives will, of course, prove stronger; when this happens without reflection—automatically, as it were—there is no acute conflict. But when one reflects about the choice to be made, what happens is not that he asks himself: "Now which of my two conflicting motives is stronger?" The question will, rather, assume the form of a value question: and the value standard appropriate to this level of conflict is "reasonableness." The person faced with a conflict of this nature will, if he wants to "reflect" rather than drift—that is, if he chooses to solve the conflict by a judgment of value—ask the question: What is the reasonable thing to do?

Let us note that this value question is still in a way self-centered. Only the relevance of one subject is at stake. But this is not entirely true: the "one" subject is in a sense several subjects, or at least several foci of relevance. The value question is directed toward selecting that "focus of relevance" which, in terms of the "meaning" of the conflict as one which should be resolved "reasonably," would have to be the dominant one. Usually, "rational" analysis favors the "ego" or "focus of relevance" which represents a more permanent interest. When we ask the question "What is reasonable?" the cards are stacked against the immediate urge in favor of more far-seeing expectations. No doubt, the conclusion may be that the fear of damaging one's health by indulging in a hearty meal is not "reasonable" or that there is no good reason why one might not risk incurring the ill-will of an obnoxious person. In such cases the ego interested in immediate indulgence will win, with the blessing of the "reasonable" ego. But when the danger to health or social position is recognized to be real, the value judgment will go against immediate indulgence. This does not mean that the subject will *act* reasonably but only that he will recognize that it *would* be reasonable to act along the lines of the value judgment.

The value term applied to the "correlate" of a reasonable choice is "useful," "economical," or some equivalent term. To judge a thing "useful" means that it is useful whether it is felt to be immediately satisfactory or not. Such a judgment, however, does not imply that in case of conflict the "useful" will be preferred over the "immediately satisfactory." This depends on the available strength of motivation on the side of the "reasonable" ego.

The subject that is making value judgments in terms of "reasonableness" of choice or "usefulness" of a correlate may be either an individual person or a collective subject. A group may, for instance, deliberate about what choice is most advantageous to the group as such, considering the group's abiding interests. Such a question is easily answered in cases in which the choices under consideration would be either uniformly beneficial or uniformly harmful to all individual members of the group, in so far as they take a "reasonable" attitude regarding their own interests. This case, however, does not always obtain. In general, any choice which a group may make will affect the interests of the various members differentially. When this is the case, value problems may arise which cannot be solved on conflict level 1. To solve these "higher" value problems, it is not enough to consider conflicts between the "fleeting" egocentric urges and the "permanent," "reasonable" interests of an individual or of an entirely homogeneous group. It will be necessary to invoke value standards of higher "level"—standards invariant toward *all* egocentric choices, whether based on an immediate urge or on a reasonable calculation.

On conflict level 2, we encounter what might be called "heteronomous" value standards—those by which the "correct" fulfilment of a convention or a norm "imposed" by authority is judged. The conventional rules of language which we examined above (chap. viii) belong in this group, and so do customary social rules of behavior, in so far as they involve no "autonomous" judgment. The formula characterizing a value of this type may be stated as follows: "A behavior type B is the correct one, whether it is immediately attractive or reasonable from some egocentric point of view, or not." This "middle" conflict level tends to be unstable, since judgments based on it may be challenged both from below and from above: if the judgment is reached on this level, it may be criticized and subverted either from the point of view of utility or from the point of view of an autonomous value standard (the last-named type of standard, belonging to level 3, will be considered in a moment). Conventions are likely to remain stable only if they are completely automatized, so that the underlying conflict of motivation does not enter consciousness at all, or if they do not run counter to first-level or third-level standards. A high degree of automatization, however, will protect conventions even against the conscious realization of their "unreasonable" nature. Many language conventions, for instance, are highly "unreasonable," in that they make communication unduly difficult; yet they cannot be changed in any radical fashion, because it is too difficult to replace a reliably working automatism by an equally reliable one, even if the latter were more "economical" or reasonable. Automatization means, of course, that the potential "conflict" to which the value term refers is not experienced as such. But this absence of conscious conflict should not be equated with the "zero-conflict level" on which immediate relevance is experienced. What it means is, above all, that in the normal course of things the value problem of "correctness" does not arise among mature individuals, i.e., those who have "learned" the convention. It also means that normally the value judgments of this level are not inherently controversial: debates can be settled by reference to a model or authority, as long as the convention is firm. When it begins to disintegrate, behavior problems will have to be settled by standards of a different level. In any case, when an *explicit* judgment about the "correctness" of an item of behavior is made, it is made on conflict level 2, that is, on the basis of invariance toward the lower-level standards.

The heteronomous value standards of level 2 do not yet, however, offer a method of dealing explicitly with the case we mentioned above, namely, that in which a choice made by a group would affect the interests of the various members differentially, if the supposition is made that all these conflicting interests may be legitimate. From the point of view of convention, every group must be considered as a homogeneous one, that is, one in which anything that is "good" or "bad" from the point of view of the group is, by the same token, to be accepted as "good" or "bad" by the various members. Many conventions, in fact, regulate conduct in interest-neutral fields. To consider language once more: every individual has an equal "interest" in

smooth and reliable communication. But where the settlement of conflicts of interest among members or subgroups of a group is regulated
heteronomously, by convention or authority, the conflict of interests
is negated; the members of the group have to act *as if* the "correct"
conduct were also one which satisfies *them*. A mechanism of this kind
may be necessary to maintain order within the group and prevent its
disruption. Conduct must be regulated in such a way that individuals
sometimes forego satisfactions they could obtain with the means at
their disposal. Such regulation, however, can be based on purely
heteronomous and conventional rules only as long as the group is
looked upon by all members as a homogeneous one. Then individuals
will reliably follow the prescriptions of custom and authority in their
mutual dealings, and cohesion and order in the group will be maintained.

Such homogeneity, however, cannot exist in very complex societies.
Certain primary groups of the "community" (*Gemeinschaft*) type do
show a high degree of homogeneity; in these, conduct may be regulated on the basis of automatically followed custom and unquestion-
ably accepted authority. But this state of things can prevail only if
life in the group follows a uniform pattern, with the same type of alternative of conduct being faced again and again. With high mobility
of individuals circulating among subgroups and a high rate of variation
in life-conditions and practices, homogeneity will be disrupted, and
conduct can no longer be regulated solely on the basis of stable conventions and stable authority. Some rules of conduct then will have
to be based on autonomous judgment: the participants in a group situation must have some way of determining by insight what decision is
required by the "meaning" of the group situation. For this, value
standards of conflict level 3 are needed; these are exemplified by such
value terms as "right." To judge a line of conduct "right" means to
judge it right whether it is attractive and useful, as well as "correct"
from the point of view of convention and authority, or not. Such
judgments refer to conduct within a nonhomogeneous group rather
than to choices affecting only the wishes and interests of one person
or one homogeneous group. They have no meaning apart from a
"conflict" situation in which the conflicting motives of an agent have
to be judged not from an egocentric, but from a nonegocentric, point
of view.

As we pointed out in the preceding chapter, no hard-and-fast classification of value terms into a purely autonomous and a purely heter-

onomous group is possible. Whether conduct of a certain kind is "right" may be judged in heteronomous or autonomous fashion; originally, every value term is "learned" on a heteronomous basis. Nor can we say that conduct in any group is regulated on a purely heteronomous or autonomous basis. Even in the most close-knit, tradition-bound, and "organic" group, there is some room for autonomous judgment; and even very complex nonauthoritarian groups must rely to some extent on tradition, convention, and stable authority. The distinction between levels of conflict does not mean that judgments about conduct are always made on the same level when a certain term is used. It means only that the value problem is articulated in either one way or another, that the problem has a different meaning, depending on the level of conflict.

3. Interpersonal Relationships

Before discussing higher-level values further, we shall consider the levels of conflict on which they arise from the point of view of motivation or relevance rather than of pure meaning or value.

What we have to bear in mind from the motivational point of view is that conduct cannot be guided by higher-level meanings, unless "all" self-centered demands of a person are taken together as a unit, or package, as it were, and set off against demands with a different, non-self-centered focus. We observe such motive structures, for instance, in interpersonal relationships, such that the egocentric demands of a person or homogeneous group are to be reasserted *en bloc* against, or subordinated to, or squared with, another "package" of egocentric demands. And likewise in person-group relationships: if the individual is motivated to achieve a certain standing within the group, he must learn to set off *all* his egocentric demands against this group-centered motive. It is clear that, if a person acts on a nonegocentric motive, the motive is still *his,* and the conflicts between the egocentric and the other-centered motives are still conflicts of motives within the same personality. Whichever of the conflicting motives is preferred, the choice indicates that alternative from which the agent derives greater satisfaction. What we assert, however, is that things may be preferred either on an egocentric or on a nonegocentric basis, depending on whether the stronger motive is a demand made by and on behalf of the self or a demand accepted by the self because of subordination to, or identification with, another subject. We shall briefly consider the ways in which such alien demand centers intrude into the motivational system of a person, beginning with interpersonal relationships. Person-group relationships will be considered in the next section.

Interpersonal relationships may be divided into two basic groups. The first is characterized by "conflicts of relevance" among two or more persons or homogeneous groups: any solution that would benefit the one would harm the other. The second group of interpersonal relationships includes relationships based on the (positive or negative) "appropriation" of one person's relevance by another, meaning that whatever is "relevant" to one member of the relationship becomes, by the same token, "relevant"—either with the same or with an opposite sign—to the other. "Appropriation of relevance" is familiar under the name of "love" and "hate." The difference between "conflict of relevance" and "appropriation of relevance" is easy to see. In the case of the former, there is some objective state of things such that there is no way of satisfying both A and B at the same time. If A is satisfied, B must remain dissatisfied; hence B is interested in seeing that A does not reach his goal. But this does not mean that A's satisfaction *in itself* detracts from B's happiness. If there were enough to go around, B would be happy to let A get everything he desires; their "conflict of relevance" results merely from extraneous circumstances. But if A "appropriates" B's relevance, either positively or negatively, this means that his happiness will depend on whether B is satisfied or frustrated, regardless of whether A himself is satisfied or frustrated in the same respect.

a) CONFLICTS OF RELEVANCE

We may speak of a "conflict of relevance" between individuals A and B if a situation common to both involves positive relevance for A and negative relevance for B, or vice versa.

In this type of situation various things may happen: First, there may be a violent solution: a trial of strength. A and B then try to force each other to yield or be annihilated.

Second, it may happen that one of the two parties, possibly in the light of earlier experience, renounces a trial of strength and defers to the other. This may give rise to lasting interpersonal relationships in which the will of one of the partners habitually yields to that of the other. This relationship will be termed "domination."

Another way of settling conflicts of relevance without resorting to violence consists in exercising *suggestion*. The use of suggestive devices has the result that the person who is made to yield does not become conscious of any *conflict* of relevance.

Finally, conflicts of relevance may be bridged over by compromise. In certain situations the contending parties are able to work out a solution without either violence or domination, each giving up some advantage in return for a gain. In an economic relationship it is possible to make the gain for each partner greater than the sacrifice made by him, so that the transaction is advantageous to both (although, of course, not so advantageous as a one-sided solution would be if any of the parties could impose it with impunity). The principle underlying this form of the settlement of conflicts of relevance will be called "interest."

Actual motivation of action, of course, never reflects these patterns in their abstract purity, with two isolated individuals left to themselves to work out their problems. In real life, conflicts of relevance always are decisively influenced by the attitude of third persons—ultimately, of society as a whole. Moreover, the above patterns are intermingled in the actual solution of conflicts. Domination is mitigated by interest; it is supported by violence, on the one hand, by suggestion, on the other; interest is tinged by both domination and suggestion.

The structure of societies depends to a very large extent on those interpersonal relationships which arise from the prevailing combination of patterns for the solution of conflicts of relevance. The patterns resulting from the exercise of violence, domination, and suggestion make up the distribution of *power*[3] in a society. Interest as such is neutral toward power, but in actual fact it is being practiced on the basis of a given distribution of power.

The various interpersonal relationships based on the solution of conflicts of relevance will now be surveyed one by one.

Violence.—Outside organized human society, two main types of violence occur: preying and rivalry.

Preying is a "radical" kind of trial of strength in which a member of a stronger species usually eliminates a member of a weaker one.

3. Cf. the following statement about power: "A person may be said to have *power* to the extent that he influences the behavior of others in accordance with his own intentions. Three major forms of power may be distinguished. . . . The power-holder exercises *force* when he influences behavior by a physical manipulation of the subordinated individual (assault, confinement, etc.); domination when he influences behavior by making explicit to others what he wants them to do (command, request, etc.); . . . and *manipulation* when he influences the behavior of others without making explicit the behavior which he thereby wants them to perform" (Herbert Goldhamer and Edward A. Shils, "Types of Power and Status," *American Journal of Sociology*, XLV, No. 2 [September, 1939], 171 f.).

The only chance the prospective victim has consists either in outwitting its enemy or in taking to flight. This type of contest is a battle of wits rather than a trial of strength. There are constellations in which the individual victim cannot even try to escape or hide; it must resign itself to being devoured, and chances of survival exist only for its species as a whole because of its large numbers.

Rivalry—of food, sex, or prestige—typically occurs among members of the same species. It may lead to violence of varying degrees; the weaker may be eliminated or may withdraw or submit to permanent *domination*.

Within organized human society violence is a more or less marginal phenomenon. Within organized groups violence is restricted or suppressed. Group organization generally has the result that overt compulsion becomes a monopoly of the group's functionaries and may be exercised only under specific conditions. Such compulsion is practiced as a last resort and merely supplements techniques of domination, suggestion, and compromise in settling conflicts of relevance. The pacification of groups, however, is predicated upon a monopoly of means of compulsion; in an area containing several groups where no such monopoly exists, violent conflicts are always possible and occur frequently.

Domination.—A trial of strength may result in the acceptance of domination: a hierarchy is established such that the winner's will regularly takes precedence over that of the loser. Where domination is firmly established, this hierarchy of wills is accepted, so to speak, instinctively. Conflicts of relevance are not experienced as acute conflicts—not, at least, within certain traditionally established limits.

We encounter patterns of domination in certain traditional interpersonal relationships, e.g., in the hierarchical family or between master and servant, etc.; the distribution of privileges among the members of subgroups or classes in a society also reflects a pattern of domination.

In a community where tradition is stable, all members identify themselves with their role, inferiors as well as superiors. The underlying conflict of relevance is no longer consciously realized as such; the pattern of domination determines each subject's conscious attitude toward his own relevance. Thus in the traditional community the servant identifies himself with his role of serving and obeying; it would be naïve to assume that this role is always rejected in a movement of inward protest and that a sense of compulsion is always present. Constant tension of this sort would be more unbearable than acceptance of the inferior role.

It is by no means required, for the acceptance of inferior positions, that the maintenance of a hierarchical order within the group be necessary in the interests of all, as is the case with the crew of a ship or the personnel of an army. Nor is it necessary to postulate otherworldly or afterlife rewards as a compensation, as with lower castes in India. Various psychological factors, such as identification with the strong, repressed fears connected with the idea of transgression, and a yearning for security, may help explain why people in inferior positions identify themselves with their roles. Moreover, we have to bear in mind the nature of adaptation in general. Very exacting and painful roles require a great effort of adaptation; when this effort is accomplished, the subject will be reluctant to seek another role. In societies with little mobility, large numbers of people may become adapted to a remarkable degree to extremely burdensome forms of life. Obviously, this would not be possible without certain subtle devices of compensation and "letting off steam." On the level of the unconscious, the underlying conflicts of relevance may be reopened and the decision reversed.

Traditional hierarchical group structures are, of course, liable to disintegrate. Identification with subordinate roles may, for instance, receive a fatal shock if mobility suddenly increases (e.g., as a result of the discovery of new colonial land). Tradition may also be undermined by technological changes, conflicts within the ruling group, ideological forces, etc. With the weakening of tradition, domination patterns will weaken, too, but they hardly ever disappear totally within a short time. Social elites may be exterminated in revolutions, but some of the old forms of domination will be re-established by a new elite.

Domination in organized society is not, of course, a matter of individual trials of strength (since these are severely regulated or suppressed); power and privilege are distributed among members of groups as such. A certain habitual expectancy of positions in life is reserved for members of each group, either in the form of rigid monopolies or in a more flexible way. There are social structures with more or less vertical mobility, but, apart from this, chances and burdens are unevenly distributed among the various classes.

Where traditional patterns of domination are weak, identification with subordinate roles is low. In such a "democratic" climate, there is constant pressure to make distribution of chances and burdens less unequal. As the role of domination patterns grows less significant, other forms of settling conflicts of relevance—especially compromise, but also compulsion and suggestion—come to the fore.

Suggestion.—The role of suggestion in molding the subject's attitude toward relevance and conflicts of relevance can hardly be overestimated. In a trial of strength, for instance, the beliefs of the parties concerning their chances play a decisive role; these beliefs, however, do not depend on the objective facts alone. They can be influenced by methods of suggestion.

Suggestion is a form of power, derived from playing upon the wishes, fears, foibles, etc., of a person. It is practiced by the use of symbols. Symbols do not control behavior implicitly and automatically, but they always create at least a preoccupation: this is due to the fact that "reading" is automatic (see p. 116, above). It is possible to set up unconscious action tendencies merely by means of repeated symbolic communications. This explains the success of publicity campaigns.

In our present context the most important question is how suggestion influences motivation. We have to note, first of all, that suggestion does not create "new" motives; it merely rearranges, manipulates, and channelizes existing ones. Suggestion influences action tendencies by presenting in a new light the *facts* of the situation having a bearing upon possibilities of satisfaction. The action tendencies of the suggestee are controlled by the suggestor through the introduction of signs which the suggestee cannot help interpreting in such a way that certain emotions will be aroused in him. The involuntary part of the suggestee's response is his interpretation of the situation; the practical decisions he takes will be "voluntary." We must distinguish this from the control of behavior in a relationship of domination. When an order is given by someone to another person who accepts domination by the former, the interpretive responses by the subordinate are autonomous and his practical decisions are heteronomous. To put it in a shorthand and rather inaccurate way, in domination the "will" of a person is controlled while his "mind" remains uncontrolled, while, in suggestion, the "mind" is controlled and the "will" uncontrolled. We may accept, in this sense, Goldhamer and Shils's description of "manipulation" as a process in which behavior is influenced without the desired behavior being made explicit (cf. n. 3, p. 252). Strictly speaking, the criterion given by Goldhamer and Shils does not hold, for very often in suggestion or, as they call it, "manipulation" the desired behavior is made explicit. It is true, however, that it is not the explicit reference to the desired behavior which controls the suggestee's response and that often the success of suggestion depends on the desired behavior *not* being made explicit.

To name an example: when a sign reads, "Buy Vortex blades," the behavior desired by the "manipulator" *is* made explicit; what he wants is precisely that people should buy Vortex blades. Yet the injunction conveyed by the sign is no "order"; there is no question of anybody's accepting domination on the part of the manufacturers of Vortex blades or of obeying their commands. What happens is that people have a need for razor blades; by cluttering up walls with the trade-name of a particular kind of blade so that people *have* to read it, the seller makes them interpret their situation in terms of this possibility of satisfying their need. The imperative, "buy," helps to make the interpretation more emphatic; it is not an "order."

One might object to our analysis that business publicity does create new motives, since it stimulates demand for newly introduced articles for which no need could have existed before. Such cases, however, fit easily into the general framework we have outlined. The publicity campaign for the new gadget also serves to make people reinterpret their situation in terms of the available means of enjoyment—and of the prevailing standards of consumption and "conspicuous waste." Instead of creating a "new" motive, the publicity provides a new outlet for existing motives.

Political propaganda and suggestion also enter into the same general framework, except that the range of motivation affected by it is incomparably wider and more vital. Business propaganda affects just one sector of the individual's behavior—the budgeting of his expenses. Patterns of action involving other people, such as co-operation for pressure, the joining of organizations, or the combating of antagonists, remain unaffected by it. These are the matters with which political propaganda deals.

The political propagandist makes people reinterpret their situations in terms of the possibilities for organized pressure which these situations hold in store. He channels this reinterpretation, depending on the purpose at hand, so as to mobilize emotions of fear or emotions of hope. He uses signs and symbols so as to create the belief that members of *his* group have nothing to fear and that members of rival or enemy groups have nothing to hope for. Here, again, the motives—the fears and wishes—are pre-existent; propaganda merely provides outlets for them. To be sure, propaganda may be seemingly "creative": it may create a vogue for new parties and new programs. What is new in such cases, however, is merely the belief that new instrumentalities are available for the fulfilment of old wishes or that old fears may be substantiated from a new quarter. People who would not think of violence as long as a democratic legal order is intact may decide to join groups advocating violence, once they become convinced that violence can "work." In politics, suggestion supplements compulsion and domination. The latter are "vertical" relationships: they involve a hierarchy of will and position. Suggestion, on the other hand, is a "horizontal" relationship: it presupposes no social hierarchy. The propagandist exercises neither compulsion nor domination; he merely relies on the automatism of the "reading" of signs in order to control the consciousness of his audience. This technique, of course, can be used for political ends: for the creation or consolidation of "vertical" hierarchical systems. The propagandist creates the necessary psychological climate for a "free," "voluntary" decision which leads to the acceptance of domination. One of the prototypes of the political propagandist is the recruiting agent who speaks to "free" people, not his subordinates, trying to persuade them to join. Once they do, of course, they cease to be free; they become the officer's subordinates, and the tone changes. Thereafter, instead of propaganda, it is orders.

Suggestion, domination, and compulsion enter various combinations in political practice. The effectiveness of domination and compulsion can be enhanced by the use of suggestion; on the other hand, the effectiveness of suggestion is increased if there is "real" power behind it. For instance, traditional prestige, which is one of the features of long-established systems of domination, makes for acceptance of suggestion from above.

Much depends on the degree to which single groups are able to control the public avenues of suggestion. If there is widely distributed, plural control, misstatements of fact tend to be corrected; at least, there can be no systematic distortion of the facts which have a bearing on the individual's "free" decisions, e.g., those concerning adhesion to this or that political group. In totalitarian regimes, on the other hand, public avenues of suggestion are monopolized by one ruling group. This leads to a systematic distortion of facts which have a direct or indirect bearing on political attitudes and decisions.[4]

Interest.—A typical source of conflicts of relevance is the scarcity of means of satisfaction. Such conflicts may be settled by a trial of strength or by the establishment of domination, as we have seen; there are certain conditions, however, under which a compromise solution will be worked out. An example of this is barter. If several individuals possess different quantities of scarce goods which have different "marginal utility" for each (i.e., some have too much of what others lack), they may exchange these goods among themselves, so that each will gain. In this way a market community will be founded.

Market transactions can go on only if each of the participants observes the rules of the game and abstains from violence and deceit. In order to insure this, a regulating agency is needed which will intervene if someone departs from the code of pure "interest." This agency must be able to use violence against violence and to detect fraud.

In the ideal case, operations guided by interest can be mutually advantageous to all concerned. This does not mean that, whenever conditions are suitable, everyone will prefer "interest" to "compulsion" or "domination," for a single individual or group with superior means of compulsion will gain more by resorting to violence than by observing the rules of the market. Nevertheless, violence will tend to disappear, once a market is established and is in good working order, because the use of violence then will tend to become precarious. A person may be able to get away with it once, but not always. The advantages derived from market operations can be stable and calculable, whereas violence always involves an element of hazard.

The production of economic goods always tends to be regulated, in part at least, according to patterns of "interest" rather than pure compulsion and domination. Thus, even in slave and serf economies, a compensation proportionate to the work done is often arranged for instead of the arbitrary exaction of the maximum amount of work.

On the other hand, however, economic transactions are seldom exclusively determined by pure patterns of interest. Market transactions are influenced by various techniques of pressure. Economic power, for instance, is used in order to establish monopolies; political power also is being used to influence market conditions. But even where competition is free, the initial chances of the various suppliers of goods

4. See P. Kecskemeti, "Totalitarian Communications as a Means of Control," *Public Opinion Quarterly*, Vol. XIV, No. 2 (summer, 1950).

and services are uneven because of the unequal initial distribution of property. Since it is one of the fundamental rules of the market that transfers of property can be effected only against proper (i.e., voluntarily accepted) compensation, the initial distribution tends to be preserved throughout successive economic transactions, although more or less gradual shifts upsetting the original distribution are by no means excluded. In any case, motivation by interest concerns operations of exchange of goods and services on the basis of an existing initial distribution of resources which is taken for granted. The original distribution may be looked upon as guaranteed by a stable pattern of "domination" or more or less voluntary "consent."

b) APPROPRIATION OF RELEVANCE

"Relevance" is a term which refers to the individual organism and to its enjoyment or well-being. We should bear in mind, however, that the individual organism is not in every respect an end in itself. We find that organisms often accept "sacrifice" for the sake of partners or progeny and, still more generally, that their subjective well-being is influenced by that of other organisms. In such cases organism A will act with regard to an object which affects the well-being of B as if it affected A's own well-being directly. A will then have a motivation to act in such a way as to increase B's primary relevance; in this sense, A may be said to act "egoistically." This, however, is a peculiar sort of "egoism," since it is not self-centered but object-centered. This is what we mean by saying that A has "appropriated" B's relevance.

We find such appropriation of relevance in the animal world, where it may be "instinctive." Among humans, too, it has an "instinctual" basis. Love and hate are "elementary" forces operating in behavior; they cannot be reduced to "reasonable" calculations about usefulness and harmfulness. To be sure, the benefits received or expected from a person play a considerable role in building up love relationships, and so does fear of the loss of these benefits. But there is more to a love relationship than this. There is "appropriation of relevance": what is relevant to the beloved person is *ipso facto* relevant to the lover. The latter is no longer self-centered; he no longer belongs to himself alone. It would be a mistake to believe that there is some sort of hedonistic calculus or economics of pleasure underlying this. The amount of suffering resulting from a love relationship may vastly exceed the amount of pleasure derived from it; yet the lover will be unable to get rid of his love; he is not free; he is possessed by his love.

A salient feature of this state of affairs is that the object of love is seen as a *person* in his own right, somebody whose claims are either unquestioningly recognized or at least acknowledged as demands. It is no longer from the ego alone that demands can emanate. Life has two centers, not one.

It may be suggested with some justification that, by accepting hardships and sacrifice in order to bestow benefits on the object of his love, the lover, consciously or unconsciously, seeks to "impose himself," to conquer and dominate the object. Love is not above being "tyrannical" in this sense. This desire to possess or dominate the object of love, however, is not to be explained by the expectation of benefits to be derived from possession. The explanation is rather that the beloved person is so important, as a person, that the lover cannot help arranging his whole life in relation to him or her: nothing except the closest possible association will do. Everything experienced is judged according to the bearing that it has on this association.

Love is a person-to-person relationship; it should be differentiated from sexual urges directed toward an object. In experiencing love, the loving person becomes transformed. Love somehow depreciates the self; as the feeling of love develops, the lover somehow becomes questionable to himself.[5] This has considerable importance for the evolution of moral sentiments and attitudes. Morality could not develop if the subject did not become questionable to himself in a sense, and love is the first and most natural agency by which this result is achieved. It should be added that, in a love relationship, this questionableness of the self does not remain unrelieved and unresolved. The self which has become questionable will also receive a new justification within the love experience. This also is extremely important for moral life. A morality from which this element is lacking will become cramped and full of repressed aggression. This is why no true morality can exist without love. Capacity for love is essential for a healthy growth of personality, for the attainment of maturity.

The manifestations of love show extraordinary variety; they differ according to age, sex, personality structure, and cultural influences. In all these manifestations, however, one feature—the appropriation of relevance—stands out. That the relevance of another person has been

5. Concerning these points, cf. Theodor Reik, *A Psychologist Looks at Love* (New York and Toronto, 1945).

appropriated means that the subject's own attitude toward his own relevance has changed. This does not mean, however, that satisfaction of primary relevance is absent from the love relationship. The element of "libido" in love represents primary relevance.

The relevance of another person can be appropriated negatively as well as positively. Hate consists of a negative appropriation of relevance: whatever is positively relevant to the object of hate is negatively relevant to the hater, and vice versa. The phenomena of love and hate dwell close together. Love may turn into hate or have an admixture of hate ("ambivalence"). For the hater, too, the object of his hate is important as a person. The former is preoccupied with the latter; he also may suffer from his hate but cannot get rid of it. The hater, like the lover, is "possessed." And hate, like love, cannot be fully explained in terms of loss and gain of pleasure. It is by no means proportional to the actual damage inflicted upon the hater by the object of hate. As we know, many people intensely hate large groups with whose members they have had very little contact. Sometimes actual interests are at stake: members of the hated group are visualized as rivals. This belief, however, is more often a consequence than a cause of the feeling of hate. If the members of the group in question were not hated, they would not be considered rivals.

There is no perfect symmetry or correspondence between love and hate. One of the most important differences is that the lover is conscious of being questionable to himself whereas the hater is "self-righteous," at least consciously. (His aggression toward his own self is repressed and projected upon an outside object.)

It is noteworthy that, while love has a concentric, pinpointing tendency, hate is expansive and tends to englobe entire groups. A beloved person is unique: love is not automatically transferred to those with whom the love-object is associated; to the extent that love seeks exclusive possession of the object, the lover may become jealous of those who are loved by the object of his love. But hate is easily transferred from one individual to those with whom that individual is associated. Hate tends to generalize.

The "appropriation of relevance," whether it is love or hate, is based on a choice or dedication which has a mysterious origin. Once the choice is made, the chooser's whole life is dedicated to the object: it will revolve around that object. In the case of love, such dedication to *another* is typically directed to an individual. When we see a person dedicating his life to love for a group, it is usually his *own* group, or an extension of his own ego; it is a widening rather than a genuine "appropriation" of relevance. In the case of hatred, however, the object of negative, destructive "dedication" is more likely to be a group or category of people than an individual. Passionate love for an in-group or extended ego often manifests itself through passionate hatred of an out-group. In respect to such collective hatred, we must qualify the remark made above that the object of hate is important to the hater "as a person." It should be said, rather, that the object of collective hate is important as *something personified*. The hater in a way creates the object of his hate as a type. The lover both accepts and creates the object of his love as a unique individuality rather than as a personification.

4. GROUP-PERSON RELATIONSHIPS

The interpersonal relationships which we examined in the preceding section are important to our present inquiry because they provide a number of nonegocentric motivations which may either inspire higher-level value judgments or give effect to them in actual behavioral choice. For either judging, or acting upon the basis of, "correctness" or "rightness," identification based upon accepted domination or upon love provides a powerful motive. Another set of such motives originates in a person's orientation toward his group. Quite apart from person-to-person "conflicts of relevance" or "appropriation of relevance," individuals have a need to be accepted within their group. To be accepted and acceptable, they must learn to see their choices from a nonegocentric point of view. I repeat that the motive to be accepted is a motive *of* the person involved and may be called "egoistic" in this sense; but it is nonegocentric in the sense that it can be acted upon only in an other-oriented way.

Social acceptance may be granted to a person in two forms: either in the form of "approval" or in the form of "status." These social rewards are of very different natures. Approval or disapproval as such need not modify a person's rank or the amount of influence he exercises in his group; what it modifies is rather the "warmth" of the atmosphere a person encounters in face-to-face meetings with his fellows. In general, a person whose actions are socially "approved of" will not thereby be propelled into a higher social group. As a rule, he will continue to move in the same circle, and his reward will be the feeling that he is accepted in the circle as someone who "belongs." He may also derive satisfaction from the hope that, when people talk about him, they will use complimentary rather than uncomplimentary terms. Disapproval as such is also more or less limited to a range of sanctions of this kind. In cases of very severe disapproval, a person may be ostracized or become an isolate in his group, and thus also lose status; but mere disapproval by the group seldom has such severe consequences. Expulsion from the group is likely to be a *mark* of low status or a *consequence* of loss of status rather than a result of disapproval of behavior as such.

In addition to informal approval and disapproval, there are also institutionalized rewards and penalties, accompanying conspicuous fulfilment or violation of crucial social norms.

Ranking as to status usually does not follow approval. It depends rather on the assets that a person has and on the means of influence which he commands. A member of a group may have high status because he is rich or talented or attractive or energetic and "dangerous to cross." All this has little to do with the question of whether his behavior is approved or not.

Behavior motivated by the desire for acceptance or recognition may be oriented toward approval maximization or status maximization. In the former case we may speak of conformism; in the latter, of ambition. Both the conformist and the ambitious person may be said to be motivated toward satisfying "social standards"; but the standards are different in the two cases.

We may distinguish in this sense two classes of "social standards": social "norms" and social "goals." A "norm" is a rule, conforming to which brings approval; a "goal" is a set of circumstances, the attainment of which brings prestige and status.

A distinction between social "norms" and social "goals" is made by Merton.[6] According to him, the goals are the things "worth striving for," whereas the norms are that element of the cultural structure which "defines, regulates and controls the acceptable modes of reaching out for these goals." The author says:

No society lacks norms governing social conduct. But societies do differ in the degree to which the folkways, mores and institutional controls are effectively integrated with the goals which stand high in the hierarchy of cultural values. The culture may be such as to lead individuals to center their emotional convictions about the complex of culturally acclaimed ends, with far less support for prescribed methods of reaching out for these ends. . . . The technically most effective procedure, whether culturally legitimate or not, becomes typ-

6. Robert K. Merton, *Social Theory and Social Structure* (Glencoe, Ill.: Free Press, 1949), pp. 126 ff.

ically preferred to institutionally prescribed conduct. As this process continues, the society becomes unstable and there develops what Durkheim called "anomie" or normlessness).[7]

Merton's distinction between "goals" and "norms" is in part analogous to the distinction drawn in this study: the "goals" are common "success goals," while the norms regulate conduct through approval, disapproval, and also institutional coercion and sanction. My definition differs from Merton's, however, in that I do not consider social norms as referring exclusively to prescribed modes of success-seeking behavior. I distinguish between "goals" and "norms" as two different classes or types of socially induced motivation. They *may* enter the combination described by Merton: if *A* seeks a *goal*, that is, a condition which would enhance his position, prestige, and status, he may be restrained by a *norm*, that is, a rule on which his chances of gaining approval or avoiding disapproval (or other social sanctions) depend. But both goal-directed and norm-oriented behavior is thinkable outside this particular configuration. If *A* practices charity, his action may be motivated by the desire to win approval, regardless of whether he will also enhance his social status or rank. In any case, the practicing of charity has nothing to do with the "prescribed methods of reaching out" for social success goals. If, on the other hand, *A* desires to achieve prestige as a sports champion, the methods and rules he has to observe have nothing to do with "social norms." For this reason, I think it is better to keep norms and goals apart as different motivation types, or "social standards," rather than to treat them as two complementary aspects of the same motivation cycle.

My definition, however, does not imply any absolute separation between these two groups of standards. Goals and norms may coincide in certain societies, at least in part; the kind of activity which is particularly approved will also determine status. In our society, money-making is a goal rather than a norm (it gives status without being particularly "approved" of), but, within the family, earning money is a norm. This shows that a line of conduct which is goal-oriented from the point of view of a group may be norm-oriented from the point of view of a subgroup.

The attainment of goals is far less dependent on the individual's own decision and effort than is the fulfilment of norms. Everyone is supposed to be able to live up to the norms set by society for a person in his position; but goals may be unattainable to most members of a

7. *Ibid.*, p. 128.

society, even if nobody is institutionally excluded from seeking to attain them and, what is more, even if everybody is encouraged to seek his life's fulfilment in the attainment of such scarce and elusive goals. Sociologists like Lynd and Merton have strongly emphasized this characteristic of the American culture.

There are many different types of norms and goals. I shall not attempt a complete classification but shall restrict my remarks to a few salient points.

First, as regards goals, highly stratified societies reserve the attainment of the highest goals for closed elites and limit the aspiration level of individuals according to the "caste" to which they belong. In other societies nobody is excluded from *aspiring* toward any goal, but actual chances of attaining goals may still depend on contingencies like one's origin and initial economic position. Since the highest status positions are necessarily "scarce," ambition everywhere is likely to be accompanied by frustration.

In highly developed societies, the goals available for attainment are manifold, and people have a choice among them. Ambition then is a matter of personal preference: an individual may set his heart on prestige or success in a field which attracts him and may disdain all other types of success. Men do not strive for success as such but for success in a particular field; not for status as such but for status in the eyes of a particular group.

As regards norms, they vary enormously as to their origin and content and also as to the way in which they are enforced. Some are purely conventional; others appeal to the individual's autonomous conscience. Some motivate conduct informally; others are publicly enunciated in the form of precise prescriptions, specifying sanctions for noncompliance. I should like to point out, however, that for the "normal" individual the motivating force of the law does not depend on the *specific* penalties it threatens but rather on the mere fact that it is "the law."

Norms may also be classified in a different fashion, that is, from the viewpoint of the social interest which they defend. One large class of norms serves to minimize friction among the individual members of a society and protect legitimate individual interests against encroachment; another aims at insuring the individuals' loyalty to, and solidarity with, a collectivity, the existence and well-being of which depends on the members' readiness to defend it. In the first class belong "moral" precepts, laws regulating conduct that may affect the interests of others, as well as conventions defining "acceptable" behavior regardless of any tangible interest that might be affected by it. The second class contains norms of corporate or national solidarity groups obligating the individual to "stand up" for the group to which he owes allegiance and sacrifice personal interests, or even his existence, to defend it against rivals or enemies. While the first class of norms prescribes or condemns certain types of behavior in "abstract" terms, the second specifies allegiance to an actual, concrete group. Any given individual may belong to different, more or less inclusive, "allegiance groups." There may be conflict among these types of norm—"moral" or "legal" prescriptions may clash with "loyalties," and different loyalties may conflict among themselves.

Usually, a "norm of allegiance" prescribes not only compliance with "abstract" laws and regulations but also obedience to an actual leadership which co-ordinates the collective defensive activities of the group. Such leadership may or may not be removable by the rank-and-file; it may be insecure and exchangeable or intrenched because of bureaucratic "tenure," aristocratic "prerogative," or political "dominance."

As for the degree of permanence and effectiveness of norms, Kardiner outlined a scale which runs from "unconscious" and irrational norm systems to rational norms and ideologies.[8] According to him, the former are the most stable and the latter the least stable. We may also ask which standards are able to impose themselves against greater psychic resistance. It seems that the greatest motivating force is possessed by norms which are fully automatized or norms which are closely associated with goals.

In general, goals have a greater motivating force than norms. In other words, the greatest deliberate sacrifices are made in order to attain status of prestige rather than in order to do what one is "expected" to do. Norms are most effective if they are also goals, i.e., if the fulfilment of the norm also gives status. Thus members of a criminal gang obey the laws of the gang regardless of the risk of punishment at the hand of the authorities; they would lose status if they failed to comply with the gang law (and, of course, they would also incur other sanctions). To mention another example: boys cheerfully submit to onerous discipline in their efforts to attain athletic distinction, on which their status depends.

8. Cf. Abram Kardiner, *The Psychological Frontiers of Society* (New York, 1945), p. 34.

The norm system of every culture is reflected by the slogans, maxims, and precepts current in it. From these verbalizations, we learn what is approved and disapproved of—but not what people actually do or actually force one another to do. In many cases people pay lip service to a maxim but would not follow or enforce it beyond a certain limit. Or the maxim is enforced with regard to members of an "in-group" but not with regard to members of an "out-group." Thus truthfulness is generally praised but actually penalized in many cases; "sharing" is praised and enforced within the family but discouraged when practiced outside the family or in-group.

We have already touched upon conflicts among different goals and norms, as well as upon the discrepancy among goals as such and norms as such.

This topic deserves some more detailed discussion. In social evolution the discrepancy between goals and norms seems to increase; this is one of the manifestations of Kardiner's law, mentioned above. In a more "primitive" society, goals and norms tend to coincide: those who have high status and prestige also are considered "good" (or καλοκάγαθοί, in the Greek phrase); those of low social rank are also "bad." This is generally true of tradition-bound and aristocratic societies. Some philosophers, like Nietzsche, consider the goal-norm discrepancy as a sign of social decay; they attribute it to an illegitimate usurpation of authority by those whose goal-attaining capacity is limited. According to this view, the discrepancy should be healed by striking out all norms that may put a negative valuation upon goal attainment. Other thinkers—the moral idealists—since Socrates have pleaded for the invalidation of all goals attained by counternorm behavior.

In modern Western society, the discrepancy between goals and norms is considerable. Generosity and truthfulness, for instance, are more praised than acquisitiveness and flattery, but the person who achieves wealth and power through the latter has higher status than the person who impoverishes himself through the former. The conflict between the ideals inculcated by the school and the rules of conduct rewarded by success is notorious. Obviously, nobody is happy about this state of affairs; the "realists" deplore the impractical bookishness of school indoctrination, while the "idealists" condemn the iniquity of society. I think the idealists are more nearly right than the realists: education for success would be the greatest calamity that could befall our educational system, except in so far as the youngsters

MEANING, COMMUNICATION, AND VALUE

might rebel against it and thus restore some moral order against their elders. But there is one premise shared by realists and idealists which I reject, namely, that the goal-norm discrepancy in our society should or could be made to disappear altogether.

This ideal could be achieved in two ways: either by going back to an aristocratic ordering of society, in which the "top" people would also be the "good" people; or by going forward to a "perfect" society, in which there would be no differences of status and influence or, alternatively, any such difference would be strictly a reward of useful services and of virtuous actions. Now it seems clear to me (and is, I think, almost generally admitted) that the first solution is unworkable: we cannot go back to an earlier stage in social evoultion. Further, even if we could, this solution would not satisfy our moral sense. This leaves us with the utopian alternative. However, this also seems to be both impracticable and, on closer scrutiny, even morally repellent.

Let us consider first the idea of doing away with the goal-norm discrepancy by abolishing "goals" as motives and regulators of conduct. Everyone, then, would have exactly the same status and influence in society, and all conduct would be regulated solely by "norms." There would be no competitiveness, no ambition; conformism would reign supreme. The society, indeed, would be so perfect that all nonconformism would have to be considered antisocial and immoral. There are grave objections both to the complete egalitarianism and to the rigid conformism implied in this program. Much as we may condemn excessive competitiveness and self-centered ambition, we have to admit that social life cannot be patterned on the basis of a perfectly equal sharing of influence, for most social tasks involving a co-ordinated effort require co-ordinators: it would be just too improbable a supposition to expect that everybody would do, in a completely undirected, spontaneous way, just what the collective task requires. Such complete egalitarianism[9] would be impracticable even if nobody *desired* to exert power and influence. The utopian picture becomes even more absurd if we add to the requirement of complete equality that of exclusive regulation by social norms, that is, complete conformism.

9. The demand for complete egalitarianism is sometimes tempered by stipulating that, while everyone cannot actually have exactly the same position, all at least should have an equal *chance* of attaining higher positions. There is only one way of insuring equality of chances, namely, distribution of positions of influence by drawing lots, a method actually practiced by Greek democracies (see Aristotle *Pol.* 1317[b]). This would certainly not lead to the selection of the "best" government. All other methods, however, must be based on some sort of competition, which the utopian solution now under consideration *excludes*.

To combine these two demands means to assume that, while everybody's word counts for exactly as much as everybody else's, all nevertheless follow exactly the same moral precepts, or at least accept being treated on their basis. Absurdity could not be carried further. We may add that the complete conformism which this version of the utopia implies makes it morally repellent, for it abolishes freedom.

One last alternative remains for doing away with the goal-norm discrepancy: that of retaining some "goals" but making goal attainment strictly dependent on fulfilment of "norms." The socially useful and morally virtuous people would also be the influential ones. This sounds indeed like a perfect society. The trouble with it, however, is that it is impossible to make the recognition of merit and the distribution of influence coincide, for every society needs far more meritorious than influential people. Influential people are needed as co-ordinators of collective activities and conduct; but social usefulness and merit must also exist among those whose activities are co-ordinated. If the influential positions are reserved for those who show the "highest" usefulness and merit, we make competition a dominant feature of life; indeed, it would then be a moral duty for all to compete for the top positions; and the vast majority would necessarily fail. The "many," then, would have to consider themselves *morally* inferior; thus we are back again with the *aristocratic* solution of the problem of goal-norm discrepancy.

In fact, this seemingly perfect society would actually be even more repellent than the most arrogant and iniquitous aristocracy. For the aristocracies of earlier times claimed only that they *possessed* virtue; they did not claim that they achieved their position solely *through* superior virtue. For this, they modestly gave credit to the deity. Their claims of superiority, therefore, were psychologically bearable for the "many." The latter, in fact, were not required to blame only themselves for their "failure": the chance of birth sufficiently explained everybody's position, and nobody was to blame for it. The many could even *identify* with the happy and "virtuous" aristocrats who seemed to possess all good things and good qualities by nature. Those who were excluded could be vicariously happy by identification. This is impossible for people who are, so to speak, defeated candidates for the same positions. For the defeated candidates, only two possibilities remain: either a completely docile avowal of their inferiority in things where they *could* and *should* have done better or some excuse that the competition was rigged and that they should have won. Now I am not denying that competitive success might be recognized by the unsuccessful as completely valid in cases where the successful are obviously the most skilful and best-qualified competitors. Exceptional skill is not too difficult to detect and may be readily admitted even by competitors. The trouble is, however, that most "co-ordinating" jobs do not require exceptional skill and might be filled equally well by a number of people. If these *are* distributed on a basis of pure "merit," to be determined by competition, it is impossible to expect that everybody will bow to the result, at least not unless people are completely docile. Here, too, we encounter the same kind of absurdity we noticed before: an ideal is set up which requires both unlimited competitiveness and unlimited docility.

Moreover, the chances are that, wherever positions of influence are at stake, people will use the social techniques suitable for the securing of influence and power, no matter what the law says. "Merit," therefore, *could* not be the sole basis of the distribution of influence. However, the society would be committed to *claiming* that this was the case; otherwise it would not be the "perfect" society, in which influence is based on merit alone.

I must confess that the thought of a dominant group claiming that it owes its position solely to superior individual merit makes me shudder. These are the people who would be completely smug and self-righteous about their privileges. They would be unbearable even if they actually *did* get their position by honest competition. But this would be too much to expect; no really fair and reliable competition *could* be devised to select just those who are objectively best qualified to fill the influential positions; and even if this were possible in theory, the competition could (and therefore would) be rigged in practice. And in this way the goal-norm discrepancy would once again be with us, except that the basic law of the society would claim its non-existence, so that any hint of a discrepancy would be high treason. Something like this actually exists in the Communist societies, which were founded on progressive utopian principles. That the utopia took the practical aspect it did is no suprise to me. I never expected anything else. And I think utopian progressives who wail that the Bolshevik leaders "betrayed" their shining dream are utterly mistaken. The dream could lead nowhere else.

All this points to the conclusion that discrepancy of goals and norms, however regrettable, should be considered a lesser evil than the evils which would result from attempts to abolish it altogether.

Those who are indoctrinated with utopian progressivism will say, no doubt, that this conclusion betrays a cynical attitude toward human nature and progress. Nothing, however, could be further from the truth. In one respect the cynic's position is far closer to that of the utopian progressive than to mine: in his way, the cynic, too, *abolishes* the norm-goal discrepancy. What he says is that goals alone count for the wise man and that norms should be disregarded as futile and meaningless. My position, however, is that norm-oriented thinking and action are essential, even if we know that they cannot be the sole basis of the ordering of society and that the pattern of goal attainment cannot exactly conform to what the norms would require. According to this position, the goal-norm discrepancy is an evil, and society will be the better ordered, the less such a discrepancy exists in it. The appearance of "cynicism" is created only by the warning that, try as we may, we *cannot* make this discrepancy disappear altogether and that therefore we should not act as if we could.

Such emphasis upon the *limits* of possible improvement always irks the progressive, for he believes that progress can only be inhibited if "necessary" limits are acknowledged beforehand. For the progressive, it is always right to act as if progress could be limitless: in this way, and in this way alone, can we be sure of getting all the progress that is possible; let the limits assert themselves when we reach them. Now it seems to me that such disregard for limits in fact may be a good thing as regards progress in subduing nonhuman "nature": in this field it is true that insuperable limits will simply assert themselves when we reach them and that we cannot gain by trying to guess where the limits are and proposing to stop there. But the situation is different as regards the perfectibility of human society, for what we actually achieve by working for our social ideal depends not merely on "nature" but also on the kind of ideal we adopt. If this ideal fails to take into account certain necessary limits of social perfection, then action based upon it is likely to have grievous effects. Thus, if a group proposing a program based on the *complete* elimination of the norm-goal discrepancy achieves overwhelming influence, it will have to claim either that the social order established and controlled by it is already perfect or that the future attainment of perfection depends on complete compliance with its directives. For progressive utopians, once they are in control, it is impossible to put up with nonconformism. For them, being nonconformist in a society controlled by them must mean the same thing as being antisocial; they cannot avoid drawing this totalitarian conclusion. By refusing to settle for anything less than a perfect society, one is sure to abolish freedom and to achieve totalitarianism.

Let us try to clarify this point a little further. We do not maintain that the norm-goal discrepancy is a good thing in itself. To be sure, in a good society, virtue and service should be rewarded, transgression and waste should be penalized. It would certainly be senseless to aim deliberately at the establishment of a social order in which rewards do not correspond to merit and penalties do not correspond to short-comings. The maintenance of a gap between norm fulfilment and goal achievement cannot be part of our positive ideal. Yet we maintain that, in thinking about the ideal society, one must allow for such a gap and that it is a bad thing to construct a social ideal in which the gap is supposed to be completely filled. How can this seeming contradiction be resolved?

My answer to this question is the following: A good society certainly should provide rewards and penalties based on merit and social utility. But, at the same time, no society could be a good society if it ignored the fact that *all* relative advantages and disadvantages cannot be allocated among the members of society on the basis of merit alone. For this would require, first of all, that all the good and bad things that happen to any individual should be decreed on the basis of a well-reasoned societal decision.[10] To achieve this, one would certainly need an omnipotent state, intervening without limit in everybody's affairs. But this is not all. Even if we accepted the principle of state omnipotence, it would soon become apparent that many things that are in dispute could not be adjudicated to either one or the other party on objective grounds of merit or social utility. It is true of some things in dispute in any society that it is indifferent, from the point of view of morality as well as of group utility, whether A or B has his way about them. Even an all-powerful state, dedicated to the principle that all relative advantages or disadvantages should be based on rationally weighed merit, could not settle such disputes rationally. We must admit, then, that in so far as conflicts of this nature arise, even in the

10. This conclusion would not be inescapable if we could count upon a completely rational market mechanism to distribute rewards strictly in accordance with social utility. Liberalism, in fact, expected the elimination of the goal-norm discrepancy from the working of the market mechanism. But present-day utopians deny that any competitive mechanism could work rationally; on the contrary, they maintain that a market mechanism unchecked by social authority would necessarily destroy the social fabric (cf. Karl Polanyi, *The Great Transformation* [New York: Farrar & Rinehart, 1944]).

best possible society, they can be settled only in a nonrational or irrational fashion. In this respect, then, the goal-norm gap must remain irreducible.

Problems of power distribution belong typically to this class of dispute. There may be a few cases in which the moral good or the interest of society evidently requires that *A* rather than *B* should be in control. And it can certainly never be a good thing to give power to antisocial or completely impractical people. But, when all obviously unsuitable or undeserving aspirants are eliminated, there will still remain, as a rule, a number of contestants for each power position, among whom no rational choice is possible. Such rivalries can be settled only by a trial of strength, which may or may not involve violence. Even the best ordering of society could not eliminate this type of conflict.

This is surely a tragic feature of the human condition, and, as rational beings, we may well deplore the fact that brute power rather than morality and reason will have to decide about so many issues. But it is not enough to deplore this situation; we must also understand its moral implications.

As against those who recognize only *one* valid social ideal, namely, the elimination of the goal-norm discrepancy, I hold that the moral problem of making society better is twofold. First, to be sure, we have to recognize the moral duty of reducing the gap between goal achievement and norm fulfilment as much as possible. Whenever either morality or social utility calls for a societal decision to be made about rewards or penalties, these decisions should be taken. But, second, we must also explicitly recognize the existence of that area where goal attainment cannot coincide with norm fulfilment. And this second duty is also a *moral* duty. It is not merely a matter of giving imperfect reality its due and of renouncing our pursuit of the moral ideal where it is impracticable. Recognition of this irreducible area of the norm-goal discrepancy is an indispensable factor in disciplining our moral conduct. For unless we admit that many disputes to which we are party are morally indifferent, we shall not only combat our enemies or rivals but also disparage them, without having a moral right to do so. There is nothing wrong, of course, in justifying our own cause and condemning that of the adversary when the dispute is *not* a morally indifferent one and we can honestly say that we alone are in the right. But it is surely wrong to refuse to admit that any dispute to which we are party *could* be morally indifferent. There is a peculiar form of immorality which consists in fighting for a pure power interest as if it were a moral goal. To act in this way amounts to disavowing the tragic law under which all human existence stands. By claiming exemption from this inescapable, tragic guilt, we come to deny all human dignity to our adversary, and, by doing so, we deprive our own struggle of the dignity it can have. This is the way of the fanatic. Fanaticism consists in recognizing only one side's right when both, though tragically embroiled in conflict, have rights.

The barbarian also disregards other people's rights whose interests conflict with his. He has no qualms about destroying or enslaving such people. But at least the barbarian does not claim that, in destroying or enslaving his adversary, he is merely fulfilling a moral mission. He does not try to escape the guilt inherent in using force and violence by relegating his adversary to a lower moral plane. For this reason, we conclude that the fanatic is worse than the barbarian. A rudimentary form of moral dignity can still exist under barbaric conditions, since the barbarian inflicts nothing on his enemy that could not happen to him, if fate willed it so. The fanatic, however, claims that he should be exempt from the fate he inflicts upon his adversary, as a matter of right and justice. This claim is incompatible with respect for human dignity.

5. NORMS, CONFORMISM, AND AUTONOMY

A difficulty arises in connection with what we said about a norm-controlled society. We maintained that a society controlled exclusively by means of "norms" would have to be perfectly conformist. It would have to suppress all criticism, all protest. But, on the other hand, the critics, on their part, would also often appeal to "norms"; norm-oriented behavior in such cases would lead to nonconformism. Does this not involve a contradiction?

The apparent contradiction can, I think, be resolved in the following way: Norms, as social standards, may be acted upon both on a heteronomous basis (i.e., on conflict level 2) and on an autonomous basis (i.e., on conflict level 3). Certain norms are pure conventions and allow for no autonomous judgment; others are ambiguous in this respect—they may be satisfied in a heteronomous way (by looking toward authorities and models) as well as in an autonomous way (by criticizing, if need be, even the authorities by whom the norm was inculcated). Thus norm-oriented behavior may be conformist as well as nonconformist; usually, it is a mixture of the two.

Now, assuming that social life is regulated *solely* by norms, it follows that norms can no longer be handled on an autonomous basis if social life is to be orderly and unchallengeably perfect. Approval and disapproval can be the *sole* regulator of conduct if it is not controversial but can always be reliably determined. An "autonomous" norm, however, necessarily leads to controversial judgments. Such a norm is still a "social" norm. For one thing, the existing society explicitly acknowledges the norm in principle. But this is not enough for the co-ordination of conduct in actual fact—for the behavioral implications of the norm in individual cases have to be determined by each person's conscience rather than by authority, suggestion, or coercion. These conscience-inspired judgments still have a "social" content, and in this sense, too, the norms are "social" norms: the judging person has not only himself in mind but most emphatically "all society." Only, in this autonomous case, the society referred to is no longer the existing actual society but an *ideal* society with which the judging person identifies himself. In so far as his conduct is determined (or rather guided) by his conscience, he bids for the approval of an *ideal* society he creates in thought.

The "ideal societies" I am speaking of are not, of course, perfect utopian models; they are idealized constructs in terms of which the "right conduct" here and now is determined. Now these "ideal societies" of the various judging persons are not identical; nor are they meant to be the *actual* voice of existing society. Where judgments are made in autonomous fashion, ideal-society constructs are confronted with one another and with social reality; and there is a very real struggle to modify actual society so as to make it conform more closely to the ideal construct. It is, however, essential to autonomous judgment that it may be acted upon (depending on whether conscience has a strong motivating force), even if the judgment of the *actual* society does not coincide with it.

Society may tolerate, and profit from, such clashing and controversial expressions of moral convictions and appeals to principles without jeopardizing the necessary co-ordination of social action, provided that there are decision mechanisms that provide some common direction while the debate is going on. These mechanisms have to rest on something else than autonomous judgment—perhaps on some formally constituted authority.

In a society which is supposed to be "perfect," there is no room for such variety of views and multiplicity of mechanisms. The definition of this type of society excludes the concept of ideal "constructs" on which the determination of the behavioral implications of a norm can be based. The social content of the norm must be the actual society, than which there can be nothing better. The judging person may use a construct in making his judgment; but he must acknowledge that his construct is identical with his *actual* society, and he must be ready to recant his judgment if he is not upheld by social (i.e., in this case, official) approval. He must be completely conformist.

In a free and "imperfect" society, however, conformism is never an all-or-nothing matter. The normal subject will neither be totally conformist nor totally nonconformist. Since social standards conflict, conformism with regard to one standard may entail nonconformism with regard to another. In general, as Merton has seen, people are more likely to disregard norms than goals, but the opposite is also found. Further, there is not only a discrepancy among norms and goals; some norms, as well as some goals, will conflict with others.

Freedom by no means *excludes* conformism; there is a large part of it in all responsibly free conduct which will be nonconformist only for good reasons and subject to weighing *all* consequences. We must sharply distinguish between "conformism" with regard to a norm, whether autonomous or heteronomous, and "conformism" with regard to the *will* of a dominant group.[11] In general, the greater the amount of autonomy of judgment, the greater the likelihood of partial nonconformism. This will be further discussed in the following chapter, devoted to "autonomous" values.

11. On conformism and nonconformism cf. Floyd H. Allport, "Rule and Custom as Individual Variations of Behavior Distributed upon a Continuum of Conformity," *American Journal of Sociology*, XLIV, No. 6 (May, 1939), 897–921. This paper does not distinguish between conformity toward a norm and conformity toward the will of an established authority or of a ruling group; hence behavior is viewed merely as more or less conforming, but not as both conforming and nonconforming.

CHAPTER X

THE AUTONOMOUS VALUES

1. TYPES OF AUTONOMOUS VALUE

HAVING considered in the preceding chapter the picture of *motivation* on the higher levels of conflict, we now turn to *value judgments* of this level. These we call the "autonomous" values. The standards on which these judgments are based are *value* standards rather than *motivational* standards like "norms" and "goals."

There is more to compliance with autonomous value standards than merely doing what one is "expected" to do; these standards differ in this respect from heteronomous social standards (norms), such as conventions, taboos, and customs. "Autonomy" of judgment means that the judgment is based on insight; "autonomy" in action means that action is free rather than directed by suggestion and coercion. The "autonomous" subject is and feels fully responsible for what he is doing, whereas the subject who fulfils a heteronomous social standard is not responsible for the content of his action; that responsibility rests with the anonymous group, that is, with nobody in particular. But autonomous values can be cultivated only in responsible fashion; we can speak of autonomous values only where an individual feels fully responsible for the intended results of what he is doing, regardless of the actual wishes of the group.

This does not mean that autonomous values *originate* outside every social nexus, for instance, that they are independently discovered by every individual "alone with his conscience" or "with God." "Autonomous" values emerge as social standards; the individual encounters them first as group demands or rather as demands voiced and enforced by the hierarchical head of the family group. Autonomous value-oriented behavior grows out of conformist behavior within the family. But it does not stop there. It is characteristic of such behavior that it implies independent judgment passed over the self as well as over all hierarchical authorities, including those which first implanted the values.

It is sometimes said that conscience is "nothing but" what one heard from one's parents during early childhood. This is entirely misleading. Patterns of behavior imposed during early childhood training remain rigidly unchanged in later life only in fields which are not managed by "conscience," such as cleanliness habits. As for "conscience," it very often becomes emancipated from childhood precepts. A relaxation of conformity to religious precepts during adolescence and adulthood is, for instance, a common occurrence in urban societies; we also encounter the opposite, that is, a "conversion" to stricter religious standards. As against this, it may be suggested, of course, that emancipation is only apparent and that early precepts retain their full motivating force on an unconscious level. Neurotic symptoms, for instance, may be explained as punishments imposed by a conscience of which one is unaware, for infractions against a rule from which the individual thinks he has "emancipated" himself. Such cases certainly occur, but it cannot be assumed that emancipation from childhood precepts always leads to neurosis. Still less can one assume that childhod precepts remain entirely unchanged and unqualified in later life. Even where a person's moral decisions can be said to go back directly to parental injunctions received during childhood, it is not the original injunction as such that motivates behavior exclusively, but the injunction as modified, molded, and qualified by later experience and, possibly, reflection.

That conscience cannot be merely another formula for obedience to parents is apparent from the fact that the formation of conscience is accompanied by a critical attitude toward parents. It is a common occurrence that children discover that their parents or other models or heroes do not live up to the moral standards they preach. When such disillusionment[1] occurs, the typical result is neither that the moral standards are rejected nor that the child will try to behave as the parent or hero actually behaves but that the moral ideal somehow becomes independent of its early human embodiments. A rebellion in the name of value takes place.

Leaving the family circle and entering new groups, the individual is exposed to new group demands, including new values. These also become a matter of conscience and a source of possible nonconformism. Originally implanted by a leader, the value standards become independent of their human representative; the individual begins to

1. Cf. Edith Jacobson, "The Effect of Disappointment on Ego and Super-ego Formation in Normal and Depressive Development," *Psychoanalytic Review*, XXXIII, No. 2 (April, 1946), 129–47.

feel "responsible" for the realization of the value. This feeling of responsibility is, at the same time, a feeling of freedom. The individual seeks to cultivate a value, not to please a group or a leader, but for its own sake, even at the risk of conflict with the leader or the group.

It is clear that no standard can be applied in such a "freely responsible" fashion, unless it involves some "rational" pattern, i.e., one which posits some general, intelligible principle from which concrete conclusions can be drawn as to the line of action to be taken, although the method of inference is not necessarily a strictly logical one.

This means, in other words, that the cultivation of values is eminently "meaning-oriented" behavior. Values could not be cultivated if interpretable "meanings" could not effectively influence behavior "oriented" toward them.

Not all value standards are, however, "rational" in the same degree. In certain types of value-oriented behavior, the value standards are anchored in, or identified with, some concrete, historical individuality —a nation, a class, a religious leader. The value principle is not really universal; conscience is not fully autonomous. Such attitudes are not "pure" value attitudes; they are tinged with other motivational standards, such as love or domination. Still we have to recognize them; in actual life there can be no rigid separation between different types of motivation. Fully autonomous attitudes are in a way extreme, and they are not encountered in every type of society. Yet pure and fully autonomous value attitudes offer a certain interest because they constitute the climax in man's endeavors toward freedom with responsibility.

Pure or rational value standards are truly universal: they are not determined by historical contingencies. We encounter them in historically distant societies; always they ring with the same tone. When we read about a citizen of ancient Egypt complaining about injustice, we know what he means and how he feels. The same applies to "truth" and a number of other moral terms. Whenever they occur, the analogy with our own moral problems is complete; we immediately know what they mean, in spite of differences in social organization and in the "irrational" sector of moral concepts.

We do not assert, however, that universal value standards, as represented by terms like "truth," "justice," etc., are applied *univocally* by every individual in every society. Just the contrary: no question is more moot than "What is true?" "What is just?" "What is beautiful?" and so on. Autonomous values are essentially and irreducibly controversial: they are primarily what men are "fighting about."

What remains unchanged—and, remaining unchanged, renders real controversy possible—are the standards as such. Two people may hold two contradictory sentences to be true, but they assert the same thing about them when they say that they are true. If they did not mean the same thing by "true," they could not disagree. It is important to recognize this constant element underlying disagreements about values.

It is not enough to say, of course, that value *problems* are constant but *solutions* are variable and anarchic. The constancy of problems means that, by invoking a standard, one commits one's self to proceeding in a certain way; not all actual or possible solutions are equally adequate and conform to the standard. As we shall see later in greater detail, there is, even in the case of the most "rational" value standards, a region of uncertainty where a clear-cut and definite decision as to what the "right" solution of the value problem is cannot be attained; but beyond this region of uncertainty it is possible to identify definitely countervalue attitudes. Two people genuinely interested in truth may be unable to settle a theoretical difference; to that extent truth is elusive and uncertain. But this does not mean that deliberate distortion or an attitude inappropriate to the discovery of truth makes no difference. The constant element in value standards is not merely the "problem" they represent but also the basic attitude they require—an attitude which can be defined in terms of detachment toward the individual's "primary" relevance.

We shall now attempt to outline a few basic autonomous value attitudes. We take our examples from different fields, so as to deal with value standards of varying degrees of "rationality." The more "rational" a value standard is, in our sense, the less it is tinged with historical contingencies, "brute facts," and elements of "love" and "domination." Religious and aesthetic values, for instance, are less "rational" than intellectual and moral ones. (This, of course, does not imply that they are somehow inferior.)

a) RELIGIOUS ORTHODOXY

Where the individual members of a religious community are not held responsible for finding the right way of serving God or attaining salvation, the problem of 'orthodoxy" as an autonomous value does not arise. Specific questions involved in value-oriented attitudes do not originate, for instance, in religious groups in which the proper cult is limited to the observance of certain rites and taboos. In such groups religion is a matter of tradition ("domination"): the individual is expected to conform to certain behavior patterns prescribed by recognized "elders" and other authorities. If the individual follows these patterns, he is religiously correct; if not, he incurs punishment for sacrilege. A third possibility does not exist.

Things are different where every individual is held and feels responsible for "doing God's will in the right way." In groups having this outlook, "proper" conduct is not merely one conforming to ritual prescriptions and the like but, above all, one consonant with a set of principles having divine sanction. This means that the individual has to find out for himself, in responsible fashion, what follows from the basic principle of "right" conduct in each concrete case. The religious attitude becomes an autonomous value attitude.

It often happens that a set of basic principles is unanimously held by the members of a religious group, but different conclusions are drawn by members of different subgroups as to the concrete lines of action implied by the principles. This type of controversy concerns the problem of "orthodoxy."

Both parties to any such controversy claim that they are "orthodox," in the sense of being alone right in interpreting God's will; their adversaries are "heretics." In this respect the positions of all contending groups are identical. Their standing in society, however, is not the same: one group usually sides with some established authority; others start out on their own, denouncing the visible authority in the name of an invisible one.

Disagreements concerning the right or "orthodox" belief and conduct often lead to schism and separation. This, however, is not always the case; it may also happen that controversies concerning orthodoxy are settled within one church, where they are submitted to arbitration. This is the practice prevailing in the Catholic church.

Even in this case, however, it remains true that determination to do God's will in the "right" way—to the extent that it is a genuine, autonomous value attitude—may result in nonconformism as well as conformism. A Catholic, for instance, may feel that his duty is to counteract the will of his religious superiors, if his conscience bids him to do so. The resulting controversy may be taken to the supreme arbiter in the church (the pope). At that point, of course, the autonomous value attitude ends.

In view of the high acceptance of authority at all levels of the Catholic church, such nonconformism is, of course, rather exceptional. *Fear* of straying from the path of conformism and *distrust* of "autonomous" value attitudes are more frequent. Such fear and distrust are due partly to the realization that conformism cannot be taken for granted where autonomous value attitudes exist.

There can, of course, be no question of *complete* freedom from authority and unqualified liberty to dissent as long as the supreme goal is orthodoxy of some sort. Orthodoxy always implies the acceptance of some authority—if not that of an established body or dignitary, then that of a system of revelation or of a divine master or prophet. The unquestioning acceptance of this authority sets a limit to the autonomy of the individual's value attitude; there is a point at which the autonomous value attitude as such blends into an attitude oriented toward other standards: love, domination, etc. We may say, in this sense, that religious orthodoxy is a "mixed" value standard.

It seems to me that this "mixed" character of the value standard of orthodoxy partly explains its extremely high motivating strength. There is hardly any behavior goal for the sake of which the individual will run as heavy risks and withstand as heavy pressure as he does for the sake of the "orthodoxy" of his conduct. Complete indifference toward primary relevance may be achieved under the impact of this motive. Apparently, identification with an ideal person, with whom the religious individual is able to reach a high degree of intimacy, without putting himself on the same level, outweighs the loss of primary relevance. Such a result is less likely where the individual has the privilege—and liability—of complete autonomy.

b) TRUTH

When we speak of "truth" (meaning primarily scientific truth) as an autonomous "value," we do not mean "truth" in the sense of a "semantical adjective" applicable to sentences (see above, p. 32). Truth in this sense is not a value; it is not a rule of conduct. The value or rule of conduct that we have in mind has to do, not with sentences as such, but with our behavior dealing with sentences: our asserting or denying them.

As a first approximation, we may try to formulate a "rule of veracity" as follows: "True sentences are to be asserted; false sentences are to be denied." This, however, can hardly be accepted as a rule of conduct oriented toward a value. There is an enormous variety of true sentences, most of them trivial. Is it a value that they should all be asserted at some time? And the same applies to the denial of the whole multitude of trivial false sentences: Should we attempt to knock them all down?

Apparently, if we want to cultivate truth as a value, we have to consider more than factual truth as such or the relationship between sentences and facts. We have to remember that value involves a "level of conflict," i.e., a certain modified attitude toward relevance. Truth as a value concerns the manner in which the recognition of truths affects the individual's (or the group's) relevance.

To cultivate truth as a value means to recognize and proclaim truths regardless of the loss of primary relevance that may ensue. Truth has other aspects—semantical, epistemological, etc.—as well; but this is its value aspect.

One might ask, however, whether truth can be envisaged from this "value" aspect at all. Can the recognition of truth be at variance with primary relevance? In other words, can truth be anything but "useful"? Even to raise such questions must seem utterly strange to those who follow certain pragmatist thinkers in defining a true belief as one which it is *useful* to hold.

Yet I believe that the orientation of behavior toward "truth" can very well be envisaged from the point of view of a possible clash with primary relevance. True beliefs are useful in a very general sense, but in many specific cases truth-seeking or truth-admitting behavior can prevail only in a struggle with powerful urges or interests. This is where the value aspect comes in.

What are these specific cases? We have to remember, first of all, that the discovery of truth is a laborious process. It costs toil, dogged determination, and rigid discipline. Errors can be excluded only at the price of constant vigilance. This means that, in behavior oriented toward the discovery of truth, primary urges toward relaxation must be systematically subdued.

Second, we recall that the recognition of truth is often at variance with self-love or partial interests. Thus the individual tends to refuse to recognize his own defects. It may be argued that it would be more "useful" to him if he recognized his shortcomings; and this is quite true. If the individual stops indulging in self-admiration, the resulting gain of relevance may be a kind of "utility" rather than what we call "autonomous value." But it is possible to face unpleasant truths, even regardless of their "utility." It often happens, for instance, that privileges enjoyed by an individual or a group are bolstered by myths. To the privileged individual or group the myth is "useful," and the truth is "harmful"; yet we demand, in the name of truth as a "value," that the myth be discarded and the truth be recognized by all. Here, also, the pursuit of truth as a value implies the systematic subduing of certain urges.

Thus truth has a double aspect (i.e., it is a "mixed" standard like that of religious orthodoxy, although in a different way). In one respect, truth is useful for survival, and, as such, as a value it belongs to conflict level 1. In another respect, however, it is an "autonomous" value, since it involves detachment from such utility, as well as from "conventional" standards.

Truth-seeking and truth-admitting behavior as an autonomous value attitude exhibits the specific characteristics of all such attitudes: responsibility and freedom. To assume the scientific attitude means that one feels responsible for bringing the truth to light, whatever it may be. Such a responsible attitude is not possible without freedom. Where there are limits to the acknowledgment of truth, nobody can live up to the responsibility for truth, at least not without conflict.

Truth-oriented behavior, as a value attitude, may result in conformism as well as in nonconformism. Truthfulness as a standard is recognized in every group, since social life would be impossible if the members of the group could not rely on the dependability of at least some types of communication. Groups, however, usually differentiate between situations and types of communication in this respect. Dependability is held indispensable in some; it is subordinated to other standards or held undesirable in still others. Thus the man intrusted with a military intelligence task "must" tell the truth to his superiors; in social intercourse, truth must often be suppressed in order to avoid conflicts; the enemy "must" be deceived. Truth-oriented behavior cuts across these distinctions and thus may result in nonconformism.

Within the scientific community the pattern of conformism and nonconformism also stands out. Activities in the community are governed by the rational principle of fact-finding as a pursuit that should not be affected by extraneous considerations of relevance. Basic techniques and standards of fact-finding must be learned from "masters"; they are social norms transmitted by authority. Yet, after the pupil has learned to master these norms and techniques, he is able to look critically at the authority which implanted them. Disciples may part company with masters, if necessary.

Attitudes oriented toward scientific truth and fact-finding are wholly "rational" and autonomous. In the pursuit of truth, no standards extraneous to fact-finding as such need be recognized; there is no question of accepting arbitration by authority or by contingent, historically determined principles. This practically pure rationality, of course, can be maintained only as long as the truth to be established concerns empirical facts, subject to "detached" observation and experimentation.

This narrow definition of truth, however, is not the only possible one. We may also speak of "truth" outside the realm of empirical science proper. Thus one often discusses religious, aesthetic, or moral "truth." This manner of speaking is misleading, if one wants to suggest by it that one's religious or aesthetic or moral attitude is wholly "rational" and "autonomous"; but it has a certain justification if it serves merely to indicate that those extra-theoretical attitudes are *relatively* autonomous or rational.

c) JUSTICE

The proper field of the application of the value standard of "justice" is that of "conflicts of relevance" (see pp. 65; 251 ff., above), especially in so far as they affect "legitimate" interests.

A "legitimate interest" is a claim to satisfaction which is justified under a set of principles which are or ought to be accepted by society as a whole. This concept is a by-product of the cultural regimentation of the satisfaction of primary urges (see above, p. 263).

Norms of justice concern the behavior of the individual or of society as a whole or of its representatives in protecting "legitimate" interests. The most important cases that may arise in connection are (1) that a legitimate interest is violated one-sidedly, without any legitimate reason, and (2) that a balance has to be struck between various legitimate interests, since none can be fully satisfied without curtailing satisfaction of the others. To these cases correspond the "protective" and "distributive" aspects of justice, respectively.

There is a great variety of legitimate interests in various societies, and these may be affected in manifold ways. In all such cases, however, the general principle is valid that a "just" settlement of conflicts involving legitimate interests must be invariant toward considerations of relevance. If a decision is materially influenced by the question of *who* is to profit and *who* is to be penalized, it is not a just one. In order to arrive at a just decision, it is necessary to consider all the persons involved in the case as interchangeable. This is the general or formal principle of justice: the "principle of impartiality." It implies that justice is an autonomous value, since it prescribes conduct based on a rational principle, invariant toward relevance, utility, or convention.

Justice requires that one should adopt the viewpoint of an ideally detached or ideally neutral onlooker, either one who is not personally interested in the conflict under arbitration or one who is able to overlook completely his own stake in the conflict. The question of whether such an ideally neutral or detached attitude can actually exist is beside the point; what we are concerned with is only a standard that is presupposed when one is discussing questions of justice. What we mean is simply that we cannot consider any conduct or decision just unless we can accept it as detached or neutral in this sense.

It is possible to make an honest, deliberate effort at blotting out considerations of relevance, as well as others of lower "conflict levels," and approximating the attitude of the ideally detached observer. Those who do may be said to feel and act "justly." They are, however, relatively few in any society.

At the same time, however, no battle cry is more often heard in society than that of "justice." It is used by those who want to enlist the aid of the "neutral" members of society in a conflict, by pointing out that their legitimate interests have been wronged. They should get redress, not in their own interests, but in the interests of "justice" or of the "whole." Such a procedure is effective, because one is more likely to find supporters if one claims to have been wronged than if one merely states that one desires some satisfaction. Nevertheless, the desire most often is more real than the alleged interest in "justice."

The simplest criterion of the genuineness of a person's interest in justice consists in finding out whether he himself is to benefit by the settlement which he proposes as "just." There is, of course, nothing wrong with demanding justice if one has been wronged, but something very decidedly is wrong with a society in which practically every demand for justice is made by those who are likely to gain by its being granted. I, for one, find it impossible to have a high estimate of the sense of justice of persons or groups who speak of justice only when their own interests are at stake.

Such practices are a sure sign that the principle of justice has degenerated into a cloak or camouflage of private interests. This degeneracy, however, is nothing uncommon. The term 'justice,' as well as many other terms of moral commendation or disapproval, has the paradoxical property that its average, normal use is a deceptive one. "Intensionally," such terms mean something right or wrong *in se;* but "extensionally," in actual designation, they are used in referring to things which are advantageous or disadvantageous to the speaker. If it were true (as Carnap asserts in his discussion of "pragmatics") that the "meaning" of a term should be ascertained on the basis of its use in designating things, terms such as 'just' or 'right' would turn out to have a meaning very close to 'desirable' or 'expedient for the speaker.' It is, however, plain that, if one claims that a certain state of things is 'just' or 'right,' one means more than that it appears desirable to him.

The point is that terms like 'just' and 'right' are normally used in a deceptive fashion; they are effective because of this deceptiveness. But they could not be used deceptively unless the *meaning* of 'justice,' etc., were clear to all concerned as a value concept, implying detachment from relevance. References to 'justice' and similar values are understood in terms of these "deictic rules," even if their application is defective.

An example of the deceptive use of the term 'justice' is found in Thucydides iii. 52 ff. (Arnold ed.), where it is related that the Spartans, who were besieging Plataea, urged the Plataeans to surrender. If they did, the Spartans said, only "lawbreakers" would be punished, but "nobody will be harmed unjustly." After the surrender, however, the Spartans specified that, in order to be granted the immunity which had been promised, each Plataean citizen was to prove that he had "rendered services to Sparta or her allies in the present war." Since Plataea had fought on the Athenian side, no Plataean was able to offer such proof; their argument that the promise of "just" treatment had nothing to do with services rendered to the adverse party was unavailing, and all male citizens of the town were put to death, while the women and children were sold as slaves.

Pareto, who cites this passage of Thucydides, makes the following remark concerning it: "On peut ajouter cet exemple à une infinité d'autres qui montrent qu'en s'engageant à agir selon la 'justice,' on ne s'engage vraiment à rien, car la 'justice' est comme le caoutchouc: on l'étire comme on veut."[2] This is a classic example of the misunderstanding which consists in confusing the meaning of a word with some actual response or actual usage. It is obvious that one does not

2. V. Pareto, *Traité de sociologie générale* (Paris, 1932), § 2350, n. 1.

"commit one's self" to anything in promising to act justly, in the sense that one may or may not live up to the promise. But it is absurd to conclude from this that the promise itself has no precise meaning. If *A* promises *B* to pay him a thousand dollars on a certain day, he may or may not pay as promised; but, supposing he had learned that somebody had promised to pay a thousand dollars and actually paid only two hundred, would Pareto have concluded that the term 'thousand dollars' had no precise meaning and "could be drawn out like rubber"?

It seems to me that the Plataeans were far more accurate than Pareto in appraising the semantics of the case. According to Thucydides, they replied to the Spartans: "If you make it a criterion of justice whether the enemy has rendered services to you and your allies, you do not seem to be correctly judging what is right but rather to be interested in mere expediency" (τοῦ μὲν ὀρθοῦ φανεῖσθε οὐκ ἀληθεῖς κριταὶ ὄντες, τὸ δὲ ξυμφέρον μᾶλλον θεραπεύοντες). In other words, the Spartans had used certain value terms in a way incompatible with their deictic rules, especially in so far as the "interchangeability" of the persons involved and "detachment" from relevance were concerned.

The standard violated in this case was one of "protective" justice: legitimate interests were violated in a one-sided manner. In other cases the question is how certain means of satisfaction should be distributed in a "just" fashion; this question concerns the "basic distribution" of property rather than the mechanism of exchange under the laws of the market. Where all claimants are exactly alike in their circumstances, the equal distribution is the just one; then the problem of justice can be reduced to a question of "order," admitting of a clear-cut solution. This case, however, hardly ever occurs in large groups made up of people of divers conditions and functions. Hence, the "just" distribution cannot be determined on a formal, quantitative basis alone; it is affected by qualitative factors. These, however, cannot be appraised in a completely objective fashion. The question "What is just?"—as regards either "protective" or "distributive" justice—cannot be solved on a perfectly "objective," reliably "factual," basis.

The standard of justice is "rational" in so far as the formal character of the value attitude toward justice is concerned, namely, in so far as it implies detachment from individual relevance and utility. Viewed from this angle, "justice" involves the same task for all men at all times. But the actual content of decisions oriented toward justice will inevitably be influenced by certain contingent, historical perspectives. This is a limit to the rationality of the value standard of justice.

Like other values, justice may inspire conformistic or nonconformistic behavior. Many revolts have been due to a passion for justice; peace or conformism are often preserved at the price of tolerating injustice.

d) BEAUTY

It may appear doubtful at first glance whether beauty and other aesthetic properties can be considered "autonomous values" in our sense. Beauty is, after all, something to be enjoyed, not judged—and 'enjoyment' is a term of relevance, not of value. Aesthetic enjoyment is something spontaneous: an immediate factor of well-being rather than something due to an elaboration of primary impulses.

I do not deny that the experience of beauty has a component of basic relevance. Unlike "justice" and other values, it cannot be envisaged as a task that must be solved correctly under a rational standard. It emerges spontaneously, as we contemplate certain objects. Yet enjoyment in contemplation does not exhaust the meaning of beauty.

We may enjoy the contemplation of this or that object for various reasons: they may evoke pleasant reminiscences or raise hopeful expectations and the like. On a primitive level all such experiences may be lumped together under the term 'beautiful.' As experience grows more refined, however, we come to discern a specific "aesthetic" element which sets itself off against the rest. There is a characteristic attitude which corresponds to this "aesthetic" element: that in which appearing forms are envisaged purely as such, divorced from practical and private associations.

We can indicate the meaning of the terms 'beauty' and 'beautiful' by relating it to this attitude. In other words, once again we do not seek to define our value term on the basis of its actual use, that is, by finding out what objects people actually designate as "beautiful." No doubt, this question has considerable psychological interest, but it is a different question from the one we are interested in now: what the terms 'beauty' and 'beautiful' mean. If two people disagree as to whether a certain object is beautiful, they may still agree as to what is meant by 'beautiful.'

We have said that, in adopting the aesthetic attitude, we envisage appearing forms "purely as such," apart from practical associations. We enjoy the form; but we enjoy it purely as such, not because we interpret it as a sign indicating the imminence of a good meal or of some material success. What the form does to us it does purely as "verbal," visible, or audible form. Its significance is encompassed within its "verbal," visible, or audible appearance.

This does not mean that aesthetic beauty is necessarily purely abstract and devoid of all "worldly" associations. The associations that are excluded from the aesthetic experience are "private or practical" associations, that is, those pointing to the spectator's own primary relevance or to other matters of relevance or to utility or, on the level of "autonomous" valuation, to convention. If we look at an object as something that will make an excellent dinner, we do not see its "beauty." But the significance of the form of the aesthetic object may very well have representational and other associative factors. It is essential to the beauty of a landscape painting that it represent trees; but we do not perceive that beauty unless we go beyond the abstract, general idea that trees are represented and observe how beauty is achieved by the unique form of the trees in the picture. It is in this sense that we say that the significance of aesthetic form is encompassed within a visible or audible or "verbal" appearance. This consideration is also valid for any social or other "message" that a work of art may convey. Such a message may be essential to the aesthetic value of a work; but what matters from the point of view of aesthetic experience is how the message is shaped by just this unique form.

The meaning of the aesthetic experience is that enjoyment in contemplation is focused upon a unique formed object as such. This means that we have to do with an experience of conflict level 3, inasmuch as, in the aesthetic experience, all considerations of relevance or value not related to the unique form as such are somehow blotted out. This meaning of the aesthetic attitude is constant throughout all vicissitudes of aesthetic life. Any intelligent or worth-while discussion of art or beauty presupposes this attitude.

If people disagree about the beauty of a certain object, it makes a very great difference whether their attitude corresponds to the above pattern or not. Not every opinion has equal weight. If the approach taken by a person shows that he is not sensitive to forms as such, his testimony should be thrown out of court. As for the others, they may disagree; but they will at least speak about the same subject.

There is nothing arbitrary about this delimitation of the subject matter of aesthetic discourse. It is not a law we lay down but merely the analysis of the conditions under which discourse of a certain general character can alone be meaningful. It is not certain that people "always and everywhere" feel and discuss "beauty" in the sense specified by us, but it is certain that no discussion of beauty can make sense unless the participants approximate the attitude we have described.

If, however, it cannot be rightly charged that our criterion of the meaningfulness of discourse about "beauty" is arbitrary, there would be more point to the criticism that it says too little. As we said, an appearing form may be "significant" as form in an infinity of ways and for innumerable reasons. How do we come to recognize whether a form is significant and how significant it is? It is clearly not enough to say that we have to focus our attention upon the significance of form as such; we also have to indicate how that significance can be detected.

To this question, we have to answer, first of all, that aesthetic significance cannot be defined in a shorthand formula, since it does not correspond to a "rational" operation. The aesthetic attitude does not involve a principle from which pointers for decisions can be derived by rational deduction.

In order to perceive aesthetic significance, beauty, and other aesthetic properties, one must have, first of all, aesthetic sensibility. This is differentially developed in different individuals. Besides people who are able to perceive at once all the intricacies of polyphonic musical patter, there are others to whom all they hear is just noise. A form, of course, cannot be appreciated unless it is perceived. Thus the first prerequisite of aesthetic judgment is the ability to perceive the forms in question.

But this natural ability is not all. It must be developed; aesthetic judgment is also a matter of education. And this education cannot be based on rational, timeless principles. The appreciation of forms can be developed only in contact with existing objects, works of art, which constitute a historic continuum. Significant forms are those which are created by artists; the spectator cannot do anything but follow the leadership of the creator. Hence aesthetic significance is not timeless; it bears the mark of the historic occasion, the climate of its creation. Its appeal, however, is not limited to that historical occasion. In spite of differences of style, the substantial greatness of a work of art can be perceived by spectators of a different age. Works bearing the signature of their time have timeless appeal.

The various historic styles are no mere conventions, embodied in standard works and assimilated by contemplation and imitation of forms. Besides this conventional element, they also involve a relatively rational body of doctrine: a principle defining what the artist seeks to achieve. Works of art may be judged in the light of this principle; they may be analyzed according to a conceptual pattern. Such criticism, of course, can be only an "immanent" one, i.e., each work of art can be judged only in terms of the body of doctrine underlying the style to which it belongs. There can be no complete understanding of art without it; but it is not sufficient all by itself. Spontaneous sensibility and receptivity are as necessary for aesthetic understanding as conceptual analysis is; the two somehow must strengthen each other. In our present context, it is important to stress the relatively "rational" element, since the status of beauty as an autonomous value is primarily based on it rather than on either the spontaneous or the merely conventional components of the aesthetic experience.

A pattern of conformism-nonconformism, characteristic of every field of value, is closely connected with the relatively rational factor in the creation and appreciation of art. Basic practices, techniques, conventions, and principles of the various arts must be learned from masters; but in this field, too, pupils may emancipate themselves. They are primarily helped in this by some articulate doctrine. Innovators in art are often theorists.

2. UTILITARIANISM

Since autonomous value standards are, as we have seen, "inherently controversial," they do not offer a reliable way to reach universal agreement on the issues judged. These standards have, indeed, a "universal" reference: the point in applying them is to determine not what is good, advantageous, and pleasing "to me," nor yet what is actually approved "by my group," but what is right "in itself," from the point of view of an ideally "impartial" group, taken to embrace all "men of good will." This universality in intention, however, is not matched by universality in actual application. What is the reason for this lack of universality?

It stems, apparently, from two factors: one is the height of the conflict level on which autonomous valuations are made and the other is the admixture of "irrationality" or "contingency" in these standards. In other words, autonomous judgments cannot command universal agreement, first, because "too much is at stake" and, second, because everyone making them necessarily has his own socially, historically, and biographically determined "perspective." The first reason means that, try as one may, one cannot be absolutely neutral toward one's own interests; the second, that presuppositions other than such neutrality or impartiality always enter into the definition of the standards.

Now it is obvious that communicative standards which do not permit universal agreement but always leave a residue of irreducible controversy are defective. The problem arises as to whether this defect could somehow be remedied. Can we construct a value-language which will give us reliably and universally decidable judgments?

We might attempt to solve this task in two ways: first, by reducing the height of the conflict level; second, by eliminating the contingent, perspective component of value judgments. The first method involves a translation of the third-level value problems into problems of a lower level, such as level 2 (convention) or level 1 (utility); the second points to elimination of all "irrationalities" from value discourse. The two procedures may be combined—we can try to achieve both results at the same time; but we can also choose one method to the exclusion of the other. If, for instance, we try to achieve universal decidability by adopting a second-level, conventionalist standard, maximization of rationality in judgment will be irrelevant: rational or not, our standard will be reliable. If we reduce the "level" of value discourse to that of utility, we may also hope to obtain a better, less controversial communication pattern, again without necessarily increasing the "rationality" of our discourse. If, finally, we try to reduce, say, ethics to a rational formalism based on a "categorical imperative," we emphatically maintain our value-language on conflict level 3 and hope that its universality will be insured by its sheer rationality.

Another approach consists, as indicated, in combining a reduction in "level" with an increase in "rationality." This may again be done in two ways. One consists in translating all "autonomous" (and other) value judgments into statements of fact *about* what each person prefers, without indicating whom we consider right from any point of view. Since it may well be postulated that all fact statements are reliably decidable, this would radically improve communication; but a defect of this approach is that it will leave all controversies untouched: after agreeing about all the "facts" concerning individual preferences, we shall be no nearer to achieving agreement among discordant individual preferences. We have, in fact, maximized "rationality" and reduced the "level of conflict," but it appears that, in doing the latter, we have overshot the mark. For, in our effort to lower the conflict level, we maneuvered ourselves out of the field of "relevance" altogether and limited our discourse to a pure standard of "order." If we are not content with this but still want to improve decidability by combining greater "rationality" with a reduction in the "level of conflict," we can revise our program. This revised program will consist in reformulating our judgments in terms of "utility" and trying to make our "utility" judgments as scientific and factual as possible. In this way we shall eliminate the irreducible controversialness of "third-level" value discourse but will still retain a standard by which divergent preferences can be judged. I shall use the label "utilitarianism" to designate this position.

Now I do not believe that this procedure is fully adequate—that is, that it will enable us to achieve all that third-level value thinking can achieve, while doing away with the undecidability from which third-level discourse necessarily suffers. But it seems to me that it is worth considering, for it promises something that would be extremely valuable, namely, a value-language that would be genuine and, at the same time, both highly rational and maximally decidable. None of the other solutions of the problem of decidability promises to satisfy all these requirements; hence I shall confine my discussion of the proposal to achieve decidability by reducing the conflict level and by maximizing rationality to the utilitarian position. I shall consider two versions of the utilitarian thesis—one "classical" and the other "modern."

a) CLASSICAL UTILITARIANISM

Utilitarianism consists essentially in a complete and unqualified rejection of the very concept of autonomous value, as we have set it forth in the preceding chapter. According to the utilitarian, discourse and thinking on "conflict level 3" is not only undecidable and hence inconclusive but also positively harmful. Instead of promoting what it purports to promote, namely, "autonomy," "fairness," and "impartiality," such thinking actually hinders it. The use of "ethical" value categories and right-wrong terms is not only "unscientific" but also antisocial.

Not that the utilitarian rejects the *material content* of traditional ethics and the principles of "autonomy" and "impartiality" that underlie it. In this respect he is firmly on the side of the angels. His point is, however, that the realization of these ideals depends on discarding specific ethical categories like "right" and "wrong" and recognizing that exactly the kind of actual behavior that is *meant* by these categories will result if we base our conduct on different standards.

The utilitarian argues as follows: "I accept the 'postulates' that conflicts of interests should be settled as impartially as possible, and that choices affecting such matters be as 'autonomous' (i.e., as free from compulsion and suggestion) as possible. But both objectives can be realized if all members of a society make intelligent choices serving solely to maximize their *own* self-interest. An 'intelligent' choice, by definition, is free; and it can be shown that 'intelligent' choices made to further the chooser's interest as much as possible will lead to an impartial settlement of all conflicts."

The thesis deserves careful consideration. Its central concept is the ideal of the "enlightened egoist": the person who bases all his decisions on complete and rational knowledge regarding all consequences. Such decisions, the utilitarian maintains, will result in "impartial" settlements, even if "impartiality" as such is not among the enlightened egoist's consciously entertained motives.

Can we assume that things in any actual society would work out in this way? It would appear that this cannot be expected if power is being employed to any significant extent in that society. For, if anybody uses power, the enlightened egoist must, too; otherwise he would be eliminated. But, in relying on power, the only question which the enlightened egoist will consider is to what extent the use of power will promote his own ends. He will refrain from using power (including violence) if his intelligence tells him that a possible victory would be short-lived: for instance, counterviolence might be mobilized against him later. It is easily seen that when decisions are arrived at on this basis, the ensuing settlements are either not impartial or not "autonomous": either the egoist will get away with more than his due, or he will act under some anticipated or real compulsion. In other words, the utilitarian position does not allow for any voluntary and autonomous limitation of power, as the "ethical" position does. But this argument in itself by no means clinches the case against the utilitarian and for the "ethical" position.

The utilitarian, in fact, may oppose this argument with two very weighty counterarguments. The first is that reliance on power in itself shows lack of "enlightenment." In a society composed entirely of enlightened egoists, nobody *would* use power; whatever conflicts of interest might arise among them, enlightened egoists will never fight, for they can always discover some arrangement more advantageous to both of them. Mutually beneficial arrangements are, by definition, "impartial" as well as "autonomous"; and enlightened egoists would never settle any difference on any other basis. If, on the other hand, some people are not enlightened enough to follow such a course, then, to be sure, power will decide, and it will not be "limited" by ethical considerations. But—and this is the second counter-argument—is such self-limitation to be expected in any case? It is an illusion to believe that justice or "impartiality" can be achieved to any extent by the "self-limitation" of power.[3] Mutually beneficial voluntary agreements alone offer any hope for a social order that is just as well as free. If for any reason people prefer other arrangements, the two postulates of a "good" society cannot be satisfied.

Moreover, the utilitarian might add, a society of "enlightened egoists" would not even use mutually beneficial bargains as the sole basis of decisions. An "enlightened egoist" may also act out of sympathy; there is no contradiction involved here. "Maximization of self-interest" does not mean that one would never spontaneously benefit another person, simply for the pleasure of doing it. It is a classic utilitarian argument that "human nature" is basically sympathetic and outgoing; let everybody follow his bent, and there will be, on the whole, more good deeds than bad actions. "Neutrality" toward one's own and everybody else's interest position is not necessary to achieve a good society; since it will inhibit spontaneous kindness as much as it would inhibit unrighteous selfishness, its net effect may even be harmful.

All this sounds convincing as far as it goes, and there are some points in this utilitarian and liberal argument which I shall grant without further discussion. I admit that, in any acute conflict of interests between two parties, the possibility of a compromise based on mutual interests offers *more* hope than that of spontaneous, ethical self-limitation of power. The point about spontaneous kindness is also well taken: an ethical position that would rule out such "egoistically" kind actions would be extremely ill-advised, and, in general, the assumption of a rigid separation between "altruism" and "egoism" is as wrong from a psychological as from an ethical point of view. The main issue, however, is not decided by these considerations.

3. Cf. the proposition that "the amount of power tends to increase till limited by other power holders," in Harold D. Lasswell and Abraham Kaplan, *Power and Society* (New Haven: Yale University Press, 1950), p. 94.

The real dispute is about the question of what kind of discipline we should impose upon our motivations. That some such discipline is necessary is conceded by the utilitarian: he certainly would check his motives to avoid taking foolish decisions that would lead to more suffering later than they prevent now. And he would also educate his children always to use such checks. All that he rules out is a certain *kind* of check, that based upon impartial right-wrong considerations; these, he says, are at best superfluous, for either the situation is such that a mutually satisfactory agreement can be had (and then we need not ask what is right and wrong), or there can be no voluntary agreement, and then power will have the last word; it would be illusory to expect that habits of "checking" impulses in terms of right-wrong would lead the more powerful adversary to restrain himself.

Now I submit that this analysis is valid only for two-person power conflicts without "outsiders." In large groups, however, there are usually "neutral" onlookers in every conflict situation—outsiders who are not interested in the outcome of the conflict one way or another but *are* interested in ending the conflict somehow. On the utilitarian principle, however, such an outsider could come in and try to settle the conflict only in either of two ways. He could form a coalition with the party who makes the highest bid for his help; or he could toss a coin to determine what settlement he would impose. The first method would make him an interested party in the power struggle; the second would leave him neutral as to the outcome of the conflict and interested only in restoring peace. I think that exclusive reliance on these two alternatives would be an extremely poor way of settling conflicts in a society. It would certainly run counter to our two "postulates"; for it would actually rule out "impartial" settlements other than those based on the impartiality of chance.

If there are *any* power conflicts in a society, the disinterested outsider has a great opportunity and obligation to seek a really impartial settlement. To do this, however, he needs the kind of "check" or discipline" that the utilitarian rules out: acting toward the *consciously entertained goal* of achieving a just and impartial settlement. It is true that his own interests are not at stake, and hence he need not use checks to insure that he will be neutral with regard to his *own* demands. But this is true only before he begins to arbitrate; once he has assumed a role of arbiter, the possibility of forming a coalition will arise, and he can resist the temptation of accepting a bribe only if his impartiality extends also to himself.

Here, then, are my conclusions:

a) In a society of "perfectly enlightened" egoists, we would not need "ethical" checks and disciplines of motivation, provided that in each case of conflict of interest a mutually satisfactory compromise could be reached without resort to the use of power. This, however, would require not only a universally high level of intelligence but also the absence of any critical scarcity or dissatisfaction in the society; for, no matter how intelligent we are, there *may* be situations in which one party can be satisfied only at the expense of another. The utilitarian assumption that intelligent egoists would never use power must therefore be rejected.

b) If, then, we accept the fact that some conflicts will be settled on the basis of power, the problem will arise of how to make these settlements conform as much as possible to our two postulates. One possibility is to call in disinterested arbiters; their function, however, presupposes that impartiality (as well as incorruptibility) is a consciously entertained goal. This form of an "autonomous self-limitation of power," based on considerations of impartiality, is not illusory, even if we could expect no such voluntary self-limitation from the participants themselves.

c) If an entire community is squarely divided into two camps, with no disinterested outsiders, no solution will work, but, in actual fact, the utilitarian method of a compromise based on intelligent calculation would offer relatively *more* hope than reliance on ethical checks. The reason for this is not that intelligence is more widespread than morality (perhaps it is not) but that, in actual conflict, moral self-restraint may be suicidal. In general, where conflicts are very extensive, so that large groups are arrayed against one another, ethical solutions become difficult, for hardly any other large group will be able to remain a neutral outsider.

d) The "neutral arbiter" must himself have power to enforce his decision. This would seem at first sight to destroy the whole argument; for we did not want to achieve impartiality only, but also freedom—that is, societal decisions not based on compulsion. It is not problematic that an all-powerful social arbiter can enforce just, as well as unjust, decisions. But the question is how "just" decisions can be arrived at in a "free" society. If we need an arbiter to do it, why not admit with the utilitarian that free and just solutions are possible only on the basis of mutually satisfactory compromises?

The answer to this is that the power of an impartial arbiter rests to a great extent on everybody's willingness to co-operate with him, as they share with him the goal of being "impartial." The arbiter can exercise his function of judge only if he is both impartial and incorruptible; he can enforce his judgment only if he is voluntarily helped by everybody, including, perhaps, the conflicting parties themselves. To do this, however, it is necessary that the "ethical" ("right-wrong") checks upon motivations be consciously entertained and exercised by all concerned. If everybody were interested merely in maximizing his own advantage, in no matter how intelligent a fashion, this voluntary enrolment behind an impartial power would not be possible.

e) An example of this "arbitration" function is, of course, the legal order. No legal order is entirely just and impartial; moreover, every legal order protects "vested interests," unequally distributed. To say, therefore, that a legal order existing in a society makes that society a "just" one would be an exaggeration. Nevertheless, both "impartiality" and "incorruptibility" are essential to the conception and administration of the law; and no legal order could function if the individual members of the society did not as a rule observe the law voluntarily (i.e., if they *did* use every chance to evade the law). I think this state of things can prevail only where people think in "right-wrong" concepts and where the prescriptions of the law correspond to people's "sense of justice." Where there is a substantial divergence between legal norms and the people's moral sense, the law tends to become virtually unenforcible, except by terroristic measures. Thus a functioning legal order presupposes moralistic (right-wrong) thinking.

The utilitarian might deny this and say that the individual participants in a legal order could also uphold it without any "moralizing," purely as a means of maximizing their self-interest; after all, a legal order is also "useful" and could not remain in existence unless it served the interests of the majority. I do not think, however, that insight into the usefulness of a legal order would be a sufficient basis for the voluntary co-operation on which the legal order depends. First of all, we must be clear about the "maximization" concept that we want to use here. Agreement among the majority of people that the maintenance of the legal order would maximize the *aggregate* of their satisfactions might be sufficient, but this "maximization" concept is incompatible with the utilitarian thesis as defined here. The classics of utilitarianism (Bentham, Mill) indeed used the concept of the "greatest happiness of the greatest number" as a criterion of the good society; but it is impossible for a utilitarian to suggest this ideal as a goal *consciously entertained by the various individuals,* without destroying the whole system. For the principle of the "greatest happiness of the greatest number" brings in ethics through the back door; if I adopt it as a conscious check upon my motivations, I take an *ethical* position, implying that the interests of others are as important to me as my own. Within the utilitarian system the "greatest happiness of the greatest number" can be considered only as an *end-result* of innumerable decisions *not* consciously directed toward it. What the utilitarian has to show, in the context now under consideration, is, therefore, that it is sufficient for voluntary co-operation in a legal order if the various individuals consider the question of whether they should co-operate merely from the point of view of the maximization of their *own* personal interests. This thesis, however, cannot be upheld. For any individual may believe, indeed, that it would serve his interests best if *all others* voluntarily observed the law; but, since his observance or nonobservance does not influence the decisions of others, his own evading the law, if profitable, would not detract from the benefits he would derive from the law and would, in addition, provide a surplus gain. The consideration "I have myself to act in a way I expect other people to act in my own interests" is an *ethical* consideration and presupposes a "right-wrong" check upon motivations.

In order to obtain voluntary co-operation with the legal system, we need, then, a "check upon motivations" not based on maximization of self-interest. The overriding motive needed here may be described as that of maintaining self-esteem—an image of the integrity of the self—which depends on doing the "right thing" regardless of the consequences.

f) All this does not mean that "ethical checks" upon motivations are either sufficient or without danger. It is not enough to think in terms of "right-wrong" impartially, and, moreover, "moralizing" thinking of this kind occasionally does great harm. Moralistic affect may lead to grave injustice in individual cases. Too great preoccupation with questions of right and wrong may also interfere with a healthy and spontaneous emotional life. This aspect of the question is stressed by a contemporary version of "utilitarian" thinking to which I am now turning.

b) MODERN UTILITARIANISM

This contemporary version of utilitarianism may be summarized as follows:

The basic mistake involved in the "ethical" position is that it considers thinking in terms of "right" and "wrong" and of behavior checks based on it as instances of "autonomous" conduct. In actual fact, none of these things can be classified under types of "autonomous" behavior. All "right-wrong" thinking is produced by *suggestion;* the moment we adopt this approach, we have already sacrificed freedom. In fact, *all* autonomous conduct is purely ego-oriented and based on the maximization of ego satisfaction. A "free" and "impartial" resolution of conflicts can be founded only on ego-oriented conduct. The reason for this is not merely, as older utilitarians assumed, that a purely rational, "intelligent" analysis of the situation will always suggest profitable compromises, though this is acceptable as an ideal model for conflict situations. But, in addition to this, we have to stress that "ego-oriented" conduct is, at the same time, "socialized" and "outgoing," sympathetic toward others. "Ethical" conduct, on the other hand, tends to be antisocial and barren of love and sympathy. In order to realize the ideal of a "good" society, we must, first of all, get rid of moralizing "right and wrong" thinking. All "ethical" categories are the myths and figments of a noxious superego and must be eliminated. Conduct centered on the ego will give us not only "mutually beneficial bargains" but more: a general atmosphere of sympathy and love and the untrammeled functioning of man's intelligence and creative impulses.

The first point to be considered here is that concerning the role of "suggestion" in the development of ethical thinking. It is true that ideas of right and wrong originate on the basis of parental suggestion. But this is true of all "motivation checks," those serving to avoid "foolish" decisions as well as those which serve to prevent "wicked" ones. We need education—and that means, in part, suggestion—to initiate *any* type of regulated conduct, quite emphatically including "intelligent" behavior. An ideal "free" society cannot include children at the initial stages of social training. The question is not *whether* motivation checks originate in suggestion—they cannot originate in any other way—but whether, once implanted, they can become the basis of autonomous conduct. I think that ethical checks of the "right-wrong" type accomplish precisely this in a way no other behavior checks can. For "moralizing" in the adolescent is the principal instrument of his *liberation from* parental authority.

In the typical biography of modern Western culture, a phase occurs in which the child discovers that the parents do not do the things they preach—that they have "feet of clay." Such judgments come about on the basis of the indoctrination provided by the parents themselves. At a still later stage, there is often also a reconciliation—the young man discovers, so to speak, his own "feet of clay" and, no longer being under actual parental control, acquires enough serenity to judge more leniently. In this way, one learns to live with and by ethical precepts, using them to challenge every authority but also realizing the necessity for toning them down.

It seems that this typical biographical sequence corresponds to intense needs of growing children in our culture, needs that must be satisfied if grave disturbances are to be avoided. Children of about ten take to moralizing like ducks to water. They "understand" the meaning of the ethical terms perfectly and develop an unerring sense in detecting unfairness and partiality. This is, as I said, one of the ways in which they develop their autonomy and independence vis-à-vis adult authority. The categories of right and wrong, understood in the sense of right and wrong "in itself" rather than in the sense of conformity with adult orders, serve as a guide in determining choices autonomously.

The modern utilitarian thesis is that this autonomy is not the right kind and that *another* system of making autonomous choices—that based on ego-centered "intelligence"—could and should be cultivated exclusively. Some modern utilitarians believe that this second system can develop without any parental suggestion at all. They postulate an instinct for acquiring "knowledge" about everything; if this instinct is not interfered with, they hold, the child will discover all he needs to know to avoid "foolish" decisions. At the same time, he will socialize his conduct (for antisocial behavior will be discovered to be "foolish") and will develop marvelous sympathetic attachments, happy "object choices," and a creative mental life. There is a tendency among psychoanalysts to cherish such expectations, and this is not hard to understand. Psychoanalysis has shed a sharp light upon the tremendous, nearly destructive stresses imposed upon the infant by the necessary process of the "socialization" of conduct; the early interest of psychoanalysts was focused upon the problem of smoothing out this "socialization" process and eliminating from it those elements which make it unduly painful and leave neurotic developments as their residue. Harsh and strict parental intervention appeared as the main source of later difficulties; and the late-nineteenth-century scientific atmosphere in which psychoanalysis was first developed by Freud was particularly favorable to the tendency to hold traditional moral and other authorities responsible for all the ills of life and to look to purely "objective," nondirective, nonmoralizing, scientific analysis and counsel as the means to rid mankind of those evils. This led to firmly held beliefs that the socialization process should be handled in a new way, by substituting for parental "authority" and all it entails a new scientific technique of letting the "ego," untrammeled by the authority of the "superego," discover by experience the way in which satisfaction can be maximized and harm can be avoided. Roughly speaking, the superego (and, with it, all concepts of "right-wrong") came to be regarded as "bad," together with the unregulated, antisocial "id," while the "ego" was looked upon as the proper authority to curb antisocial impulses.

This outlook, which originally characterized psychoanalysis, has been tempered somewhat in the meantime, and many psychoanalysts now recognize the legitimate role of a relatively autonomous and rational superego. But, by and large, the superego is still suspect, and the rational ego, defined along utilitarian lines, is considered to be the chief agency for normal regulation of conduct. Psychoanalytically inspired education still avoids indoctrination in right-wrong terms as much as possible, on the grounds that interference with normal and healthy aggression would merely direct aggression to other targets, including the self, and foster the formation of an unhealthy and irrational superego.

It is difficult to formulate any reasonable hypothesis on the likely effects of the adoption of such educational principles upon personality formation in our culture. Experiences with "permissive" education have been partly good and partly bad; and it is difficult to say how the point that interests us here—the retention or abandonment of moral indoctrination in "right-wrong" terms—has influenced the observed results. I think such moralistic concepts have seldom, if ever, been completely eliminated from education, even of the most "advanced" kind; hence we cannot have any evidence as to the probable consequences of their *complete* elimination, which is the only issue interesting us at the moment. That less emphasis on moralizing, more tolerance with the spontaneous impulses of the child, and, above all, a reasonable, noncapricious handling of right-wrong concepts and principles of conduct would have beneficial effects is hardly in doubt. But I do not think that a radical *ban* on superego formation could do any good.

In the absence of any systematically controlled evidence, I shall give a few admittedly speculative reasons for my skepticism. My main objection to a purely "ego-oriented" personality formation is that the emotional burden it would put upon the child would be infinitely *greater* than that imposed by even a fairly demanding "superego" schedule. The emotional conflicts likely to result from the task of differentiating between "safe" and "harmful" impulses seem to me far greater and more destructive than those resulting from the application of ethical, right-and-wrong criteria. This point—which I shall develop a little more fully—is generally overlooked by utilitarians; this shows how the specifically "adult" and abstract perspective of theoreticians can lead to radical misconceptions where emotions are concerned. (Experienced psychonanalysts are less likely to be doctrinaire on this point, since they know too much about emotional needs to ignore them.)

The typical utilitarian reasoning is this: If I have to renounce some drive satisfaction in *my own interest*, in order to save my chances for greater enjoyment in the future, no great emotional conflict can arise, since it is done "for my own sake" and is also profitable. What is bad about the frustration of some keenly felt desire and what makes it emotionally hard to bear are, first, its finality and, second, its being imposed "from without," against my wish. Hence, if some satisfaction *has* to be renounced, it is best to make the "ego" the judge; once the ego has learned to forego "foolish" decisions, this will be done without great emotional difficulties.

While this view certainly contains an element of truth, I think it is, on the whole, erroneous. To be sure, a renunciation without *any* compensation and imposed by compulsion alone is emotionally hard to accept and, if exacted in a systematic way, ruinous. But it does not follow that the *only* compensation through which the emotional stress can be alleviated is some future benefit. And it is wrong to believe that no emotional conflict can arise if the ego itself is required to reject some "foolish" choice in the name of self-interest. The emotional difficulty involved in having to renounce some tempting enjoyment may be much less if some other regulative mechanism than pure self-interest is mobilized. Both the desire to please some emotionally accepted authority and the determination to achieve self-esteem by renouncing satisfaction "for honor's sake" may work more smoothly than the totally nonauthoritarian and ego-oriented "gain-maximization" mechanism.

It is true that, whatever regulatory mechanism we mobilize, the ultimate decision will reflect "maximum satisfaction"—no choice can be made on any other basis than that of adopting the one alternative that is preferred to all other available ones. But this is a purely analytical truth which will remain unchanged, whatever actual choice is made. The question is not whether the choosing subject will choose the most satisfactory alternative; it cannot do anything else. What matters is the standard on the basis of which the "most satisfactory course" will be determined. These standards may be ego-oriented and based on the calculation of maximum egocentric enjoyment over time, or they may involve nonego-oriented (second- or third-level) decisions, such as "earning the approval of" an authority or "earning one's own self-esteem by satisfying honor," regardless of the quantity of primary enjoyment. My point is that the last-named standards may permit an emotionally smoother and easier handling of impulses that have to be checked than the first-named one.

There are situations in which the child can indeed work out the solution of goal conflicts on an experiental basis in terms of primary enjoyments without any great emotional stress. But this is not generally the case. It is often extremely difficult to resist a "foolish" impulse in order to avoid its unpleasant later consequences if there is neither an accepted authority nor some "ethical" standard that demands such a course. For we must not forget that one way of dealing with unpleasant future possibilities is to *ignore* them. If there is an emotional pull in this direction, then the subject must resist not only the immediate urge to enjoy something that is "dangerous" but also the tendency to forget the danger. This emotional problem may be agonizingly difficult to cope with, whereas either the precepts of the accepted authority or the internalized principles of an ethical code may provide an emotionally easy way of resolving the conflict. In both these latter cases there is an immediately felt compensation, based either on identification with an authority or on self-esteem. These compensations may be emotionally more "real" than the realization that some pain will not be felt in the future. In fact, such a realization may provide no emotional gain at all, since the future pain can also be made nonexistent by simply ignoring it. The avoidance of a possible painful experience is made psychologically real, on the whole, only by a previously experienced trauma. If the impulse that is to be resisted is associated with an earlier traumatic experience, then, in fact, it *will* be resisted without the counsels of either an accepted authority or moral conscience. But it would seem to me an extremely harsh method of the "socialization" and "rationalization" of conduct to base it on a series of traumatic experiences. Rousseau, the first modern apostle of completely nondirective education, saw clearly that trauma is needed in the absence of identification and, in fact, based his educational system on the administration of judiciously selected traumatic experiences made to appear as emanating from "nature" alone. My objection to his advice is that it is too hard on the children. As we see, the traditional roles of the spokesmen of "conservatism" and "progressivism" in education are easily reversed. I am pleading for an attitude sympathetic to the emotional needs of children and for the avoidance of traumata. Rousseau sternly condemns this "coddling" in the name of his lofty moral principles, which reject any meddling with the self-contained sovereignty of the child.

I am far from rejecting the "permissive" trend in modern education as a whole. It is bad if the spontaneous impulses of children are checked in an arbitrary manner or systematically suppressed as a matter of discipline. But I am dealing here with the necessity for checking *some* impulses in order to make conduct "socialized" and nonself-destructive. To base such checks exclusively on sober calculations of the child's self-interest is out of tune with the emotional needs and capacities of children. And so we see "progressively" educated children often disoriented, torn by emotional crises, because they are obliged to work out their goal conflicts by rational calculation, without any compensatory short cut to help them over the emotional impasse. It is pathetic to observe "progressive" parents desperately and endlessly "yak-yakking" about the simplest matters, trying to make the children agree that to do or not to do a certain thing would really be good for *them*—and the children just as desperately and silently despising their parents for not having enough courage to end the torment by making a decision or a clear judgment about right and wrong.

This has nothing to do with permissiveness, rightly understood, or with respecting the spontaneity of children. We are speaking about goal conflicts for which no power on earth can provide a "spontaneous" solution. Spontaneity should not be confused with being left alone. Nor does respect for the spontaneity of the child mean that it should neither be relieved of responsibility nor given the means for coping with it. Compulsive nondirectiveness always creates more problems than it can solve. It can go to absurd lengths, but an end will be reached sooner or later, and the parent will have to reverse himself and use authority when the situation becomes impossible. Thus what happens in practice is not that the child will never experience parental authority, but that it will never know when to expect it and will be forced to experiment to find the limit beyond which it cannot go. Those who are indoctrinated with the gospel of fluidity and experimentation may think that this is just wonderful. But in actual experience within the family it is more likely to be infernal. It is absolutely impossible to reconcile this constant "politicking," this jockeying for position, with the emotional warmth, confidence, and understanding that the child needs.

I have said that in the "typical biography" characteristic of Western culture, there is a phase of "ethical revolt" against parental authority. This revolt may assume various forms, some perverted and self-destructive. Often it is a decisive step toward maturity. In this case the ethical principles first inculcated by authority remain intact; their authoritarian origin is forgotten, and they are considered as the expression of the rebel's very own innermost aspirations and ideals. In this way revolt and self-emancipation can coexist with continuity; and during the later stages of the "typical biography," the rebel may mitigate his ethical rigorism after having discovered, so to speak, his own "feet of clay" and learned to see his parents from a distance.

How would things look in the "typical biography" determined by a purely utilitarian education? I think that in this case, too, there is likely to be a revolt. For it is not true that men revolt only against tyranny; they can also revolt against weakness. Furthermore, it seems to me that the revolt against the nondirective parent runs the risk of being more bitter and poignant than the revolt against the authoritarian one. In the latter case there may be a feeling of superiority and triumph, of getting even, of coming into one's own. But the feeling characterizing the revolt against the nondirective parent is more likely to be one of pure, irretrievable loss—of eternal regret at not having received from the parents what would have really mattered—a capacity for identification, confidence, respect, and judging by principle. The rebel against nonauthority cannot "get even" for wrongs inflicted; he does not even know what a "wrong" is. He has to fight against shapeless shadows.

Of course, there are substitutes for everything. In the absence of identification and an autonomous ethical conscience, the child may learn "socialized" habits by becoming sensitive to being approved in the peer group.[4] A compulsively nondirective education often leaves no other resource. What we get in this way is neither "spontaneity" nor "independence" but utter dependence on others. Of course, there is nothing wrong with "good social adjustment" and "popularity" as such. But if this is the *only* moral support a child may hope to obtain, the results will be pathetic. For the real prize of "popularity" in the peer group will always be won by those who do not need it desperately. The prize will go to those who either possess gratuitous gifts of beauty or social distinction or attain some excellence by sheer competitive doggedness and sometimes to those who have received strength of character and a well-rounded personality from a happily integrated home life. The others can "belong" only by conforming and following the leader. The peer group is never nondirective. In it the children may find outlets for their need to feel respect and to perform clear-cut duties—a need which their parents refuse to satisfy. This will help them mature in a way; but the peer group cannot give everything. In it the child is not accepted unconditionally for its own sake. This is possible only in the family. "Peer-group children," those who have no real home but the gang, are "Saturday's children"; they truly work hard for their living.

Some utilitarian parents by their compulsive nondirectiveness force their children into the peer group, where the need for direction can be satisfied. Others try to transform the family into a simulated "peer group" by becoming "pals" to their children. This solution is as bad as compulsive nondirectiveness, and possibly worse; it is certainly more dishonest. For the genuine peer group is a freely chosen group in which authority is spontaneously accorded the leader; the parent, by pretending to be a pal, fraudulently seeks to obtain such recognition which the child cannot refuse (since it could hardly claim to play the role of gang leader) and cannot honestly grant either. The illusion of palship can be maintained only by endless lies—the parent must pretend that his interests are exactly the same as the child's, since otherwise he would cease to be a "pal."

My conclusion about modern utilitarianism is, then, that, while it has great practical as well as theoretical merits, its ultimate position—

4. Cf. D. Riesman and Associates, *The Lonely Crowd: A Study of the Changing American Society* (New Haven: Yale University Press, 1950), pp. 65 ff.

that is, its complete ban on "moralizing" concepts in education—is unsound. This movement has greatly benefited both children and parents by stressing the evils resulting from harshness, rigidity, and suppression of spontaneity. It has also performed a great service by elucidating the origin of many neuroses and maladjustments. But its theoretical assumption that right-wrong concepts should or could be eliminated completely would, if acted upon, result in stresses and crises as bad as, if not worse than, those created by the other extreme. And this is the only point which interests us here; our question is whether utilitarianism in all its forms is right in its contention that the use of properly ethical categories can lead *only* to antisocial results, whereas guidance of conduct by "enlightened self-interest" *alone* will insure as good an ordering of society as is attainable.

Our preceding analysis seems to suggest that the debate between the "utilitarian" and the "ethical" position cannot be decided on an all-or-nothing basis. The analysis does not countenance the position that application of ethical categories is all we need to guarantee a good social order; nor does it support the view that the use of such categories contributes nothing of value to the social process. We may now try to assess the respective merits of the utilitarian and the "ethical" (or "right-wrong") approach.

It seems that society needs, and can profit by, orientation of its members toward autonomous values to the extent that it is a fluid society, one in which groupings are to a great extent unstable and indeterminate and where the over-all situation depends significantly on many individual choices. For the kind of social situation which the autonomous value judgment has in mind is one in which a group has to *constitute itself*. The autonomous judge of value *creates* an ideal society in his mind and adjusts his conduct to the requirements of *this* society. This idealizing procedure will not, and cannot, correspond to social reality; nor can it serve as the *sole* regulator of social processes. Actual social co-ordination requires something more tangible than such idealizing constructs. But these are indispensable wherever the orientation of society is in flux, where groupings have to be evolved in keeping with the meaning of a social situation. What I mean can be illustrated by the example of subgroups in which co-ordination and consensus are, by definition, left undetermined and must be created afresh every day on the basis of autonomous judgment. The scientific community is such a group, and so is the community of the letters and the arts. It is unthinkable that these communities could exist without constant orientation of their members toward "third-level," autonomous values. In the various religious communities the element of fluidity is less and that of predetermination, suggestion, and compulsion greater; but they, too, are aware of the need to re-create themselves anew by fresh acts of faith. They also depend, or should ideally depend, on continuous creation.

Our problem, however, concerns society as a whole rather than subsocieties clearly founded on the service of more or less "rational," autonomous values; and our question is how and when this inclusive society can use ethical orientations among its members. The answer is: It can use such orientations in the process of regrouping itself in such a way that some, or many, of its members pass from a neutral position into a nonneutral one or pass, for conscience' sake, from one camp into the other. If these shifts were dictated solely by the self-interest of the various individuals or homogeneous subgroups, the "postulates" shared by the utilitarian and ethical positions would quickly fall by the wayside. Rigid fronts would soon emerge, with all decisions dictated by indivisible group interests.

When such a state *is* reached, however, utilitarianism, with its stress upon "enlightened self-interest," offers the only real hope. When the lines are drawn and no neutrals are left, nobody can shift his position; fluidity has disappeared, as far as the autonomous decisions of the participants are concerned. In such a case some "reasonableness," some fluidity, can be provided only by factual analysis of the most advantageous action to take. As far as people can still be reasonably egoistic enough to see that their interests would not be served by fighting, they can yet remain at peace by compromising their differences. Insistence on "rights" and "wrongs" *might*, in such circumstances, make things worse rather than better. With a rigid delimitation of fronts and with very radical differences between the conflicting parties, the voice of self-interest, too, may be silenced; that, indeed, is a desparate situation and one that offers little real hope. For no matter how moral and how enlightened one side is, it cannot save the situation if the other side is unenlightened and immoral. In such a situation, fighting may be unavoidable, and ethical considerations will again be socially useful: the consciousness of being "in the right" is a greater source of strength than the idea that one is fighting to maximize his self-interest. But an exculsive emphasis upon morality tends also to have harmful results in war. Both in the conduct of the war and in the making of peace, indignation against the enemy should be tempered with considerations of cool self-interest. We should remember that true morality is an impartial affair; if ethical thinking is not directed against the self as much as against the other, it becomes falsified. This is why it cannot achieve much in the terribly immoral situation in which fighting for one's existence is the only recourse. A society can be ethical only when its business is to create, not when its business is to destroy.

It is possible that all present-day societies are losing their fluidity. This is quite apparent in the international community and also within the totalitarian societies, where the process has already reached its ultimate culmination. But within the democratic societies, too, fluidity seems to be on the wane. Maybe the utilitarian counsel of enlightened self-interest is the last word that human reason can speak. This, at least, is still in a sense an autonomous voice because, while it disregards "ethical" value autonomy, it still upholds the autonomy of the "order" standard of pure fact-finding. I admit, in this sense, that in the last resort "science" alone may save us; this would be true, in fact, if we were to destroy the social basis of ethical value autonomy. Whether science can long retain its vitality when the other forms of autonomous value thinking have withered away is, of course, open to doubt. It may, in any case, be the last to go.

In a happier time Hegel, too, expected science to speak the "last word," and he also interpreted this as meaning that the cultural cycle was reaching its end, that the times of creativity were over. It is dusk, he said, when Minerva's owl takes wing. If science can "save us," it is only because we have reached the stage of rigidity, so that the "data," the "facts on record," are sufficient for guidance.

I must confess, however, that all my instincts and convictions call for the "fluid" society in which thinking and action oriented toward autonomous values have a place. This ideal may already be antiquated. If so, that would mean, for me, that all that is best in life is gone from our world.

I affirm in this sense my faith in the "open society." By this I do not mean a society controlled by the "social engineer" or one which has no firm beliefs in anything except the dogma of the unlimited reversibility of all convictions. "Vertical social mobility" is also something different from the "openness" I have in mind. Such mobility is, I think, a very desirable feature in the competitive framework of free society, but it is not this possibility of "getting ahead" which is needed to make autonomous value thinking possible and socially meaningful.

The rigidity which the "open society" in my sense excludes is that of "fronts," of combative alignments within the society; the fluidity it requires is the possibility for the free man to take sides with those who are wronged and against those who do wrong, reserving the right to shift his demands when the victims of wrongdoing, gaining ascendancy, in their turn risk becoming oppressors. An example of this is again the legal order, which protects society and individual victims against the lawbreaker but is also ready to protect the rights of the lawbreaker when *they* are threatened. Such changes of alignment and practical orientation have nothing to do with a change of principles; on the contrary, firm principles of justice alone can motivate them. The moment "principled" behavior is taken to imply the assumption that one group alone can do or suffer wrong, it ceases to be ethical behavior; and those who act on such maxims betray the principle of the open society, no matter how righteous and progressive they consider themselves to be.

All this is not meant to imply that firm alignments and loyalties are always "unethical." Group solidarity is socially indispensable, and—to repeat—ethics does not *condemn* the pursuit of self-interest as such, whether individual or collective. All it requires is merely readiness to limit and check the pursuit of self-interest when it runs counter to the conditions for *creating* a grouping based on the autonomous principle of impartiality. Such ethical thinking cannot make over all society in its image; but it can make society better. It can, however, have such effects only to the extent that fluid regroupings are possible. Such regroupings can be meaningful only if they are guided by unalterable principles. We cannot have both complete mobility in alignment and complete variability in orientation. We must choose between unchangeable social alignments and unalterable principles of right and wrong. The "open society" chooses the latter.

This does not mean that its concepts of right and wrong will be rigidly frozen. To have "unalterable" principles of right and wrong does not mean that one will never revise his judgment about what in particular is to be considered right and wrong; what is unalterable is only the principle of impartiality itself. The scientist's attitude offers a parallel: he is always ready to revise findings and theories, but he can do this only on condition that his over-all principle—that of "admitting the evidence" and "thinking logically"—remain unalterable. It is a complete misunderstanding to believe that the scientific attitude excludes all "absolutes." On the contrary, it is based on an "absolute."

Once this is understood, it will be easier to see that the morbid fear of admitting "absolute" positions, so widespread in the intellectual community, is utterly unwarranted. It cannot be based on the scientific ethos, since, on the contrary, it negates it; and it cannot be the magic means whereby tyranny can be eliminated. The widespread notion that those who affirm absolute beliefs by the same token countenance absolute rule is an absurdity. Absolute rule can be combated only on the basis of absolute principles. The moment we try to do completely without the latter, society will provide for the necessary stabilizer in other ways, for instance, by freezing its "fronts" without the possibility of change. Those who are happy in a stable combative alignment may prefer the latter; but their society will emphatically not be an "open" society.

CHAPTER XI

THE VALIDATION OF JUDGMENTS
OF VALUE

1. VALUE STANDARDS AS POSTULATES

OUR analysis of "utilitarianism" has suggested the conclusion that the "open" society—which is not, and does not pretend to be, a "perfect" society but which corresponds to our idea of a "good" society—requires that the behavior of its members be oriented in part toward autonomous values. But this conclusion leaves us in a difficult position; for we have admitted that communication in terms of "autonomous" values is defective: there exists no reliable "decision method" for them. To be sure, each individual who uses such concepts has some internalized standard, some decision method, that he applies for himself. But if two individuals judging about the same value problem happen to disagree, there is no objective, logical, or cognitive test by which their disagreement could be safely resolved. This seems to imply that all discussions about values are futile, or at least that neither opponent can force the other to come around to his position by using a rational method of persuasion. In case of any controversy, then, we could hope to generate agreement only by using irrational methods of persuasion—for instance, suggestion; barring this, we would have to fight or agree to disagree. To accept this, however, means to abandon "autonomy" in the field of conflicts about values, a conclusion which is fatal to our entire concept of "autonomous" value thinking. I now propose to consider the question of whether the conclusion just formulated is really inescapable.

In doing this, I shall examine, first of all, the logical structure of any argument about autonomous values. Such arguments are neither about facts nor about the logical consequences flowing from axioms or assumptions. Yet they are not unstructured, wholly unmanageable controversies, just pitting one ultimate position against another. For in all value judgments—and, indeed, in all judgments—it is possible to distinguish several components, some of which are postulational and others factual. When we spell out the full meaning of any judgment

314

of value, we obtain an expression corresponding to the schema: "Given the standard S, which is, from the logical point of view, a postulate, and the facts F_1, F_2, . . . , and so on, the object we judge, A, has the value V." A controversy may center either around the "postulational" strand of the judgments made or around the "factual" strand. If the latter, the controversy may be resolved by sifting the evidence. In this case we obviously do have a method of "forcing agreement" by rational means. But if our disagreement concerns the postulational strand, neither logical analysis nor factual evidence will give us a rational method of resolving the controversy. In such cases rational discussion is possible only if we have a technique for analyzing postulates which is rational and autonomous (that is, not based on coercion or suggestion), although it can be reduced neither to logic nor to scientific fact-finding. My position is that such a technique of analyzing postulates exists, so that value controversies are not entirely hopeless even if they center around the postulational strands of the judgments involved; but I think the technique—which I shall outline in a moment—falls far short of the finality and reliability of logic and empirical science. It will not enable us to force agreement reliably in every case; but it will help us lay bare a rationale which is binding upon autonomous participants in a type of common undertaking. This result, I think, is important enough to warrant debates bearing on the postulational rather than merely on the factual strand of controversial value judgments.

An analysis of value judgments based on separating their "factual" from their "postulational" components has been carried out by Stevenson.[1] He takes the "postulational" part of the judgment to be a demand or imperative, whereas the "factual" part refers to the causal conditions on which the realization of the demand depends. On his theory, controversies about values can be fruitful only to the extent that one of the disputants can convince the other, by adducing factual evidence, that the latter could realize his *own* desires by acceding to his opponent's demand. This means that agreement is possible only if the two disputants discover a postulational ground common to them, in the sense of their sharing a demand, thus reducing their controversy to one about facts.

Now I agree with the idea of breaking down the value judgment into a postulational and a factual part, and I also agree that agreement

1. C. L. Stevenson, *Ehics and Language* (New Haven: Yale Universiy Press, 1944), pp. 26 ff.

is possible only if a common postulational ground exists. But it seems to me that the postulational component involved cannot be simply equated with "demands," "imperatives," or "desires." In my view the "postulates" on which the disputants may agree or disagree are not simply desires but standards of a conflict level higher than 1, that is, the level on which "desires" may conflict with "facts." If A and B disagree, say, about the "rightness" of some past or projected action, the problem for A is not to convince B that, all things considered, B would be well-advised, in his own interest, to come around to A's appreciation of the matter. What he has to show is, rather, that B must come to the same value judgment, provided that he accepts some "higher conflict-level" standard, regardless of what his demands and interests are. On this analysis, too, the discussion must be broken off if no common postulational ground can be discovered. But it does not follow that such ultimate postulational differences boil down to a question of "taste" or of arbitrary demands of preferences. For third-level standards, though mere "postulates" from a logical point of view, define the "meaning" of a type of social situation; and their rejection, though it cannot be shown to involve either a logical contradiction or a factual error, nevertheless has a *stringent* consequence, namely, that those who reject them can no longer participate in the type of social situation which the standard defines.

To make this clear, let us consider, instead of ethical standards, that of scientific fact-finding. As a "value standard," it defines the meaning of a social situation—that of people engaged in collecting and evaluating evidence for the purpose of constructing a comprehensive and economical theory. Now controversies about what is "scientifically true" can certainly be fruitful only as long as all participants have a common *postulational ground*, that is, agree on certain basic principles prescribing respect for "facts" as well as "logic." Everyone is free, in a sense, to reject these basic principles; he may choose, if he wishes, to disregard facts and to prefer inconsistency to consistency. But, if he does, he can no longer maintain that he is taking part in the type of co-operative situation defined by the meaning of the term "scientific fact-finding." A choice like this is neither "factually false" nor "illogical," for the simple reason that choices cannot be either. We cannot "force" our opponent by either factual or logical arguments to accept our postulates. Yet we cannot help feeling that our postulates themselves are eminently "rational." Why? Because, it seems to me, the social situation they define is one in which every participant behaves in autonomous fashion—we postulate a type of behavior not based on either suggestion or coercion.

This much will probably be granted by all those who consider scientific activity rational; but one may accept this and yet deny the possibility of rational discussion about basic value standards and postulates other than those of science. According to this view, the two basic postulates we mentioned in the preceding paragraph—respect for logic and respect for facts—are the *only* rational postulates that one may formulate. They alone can be used for purposes of "rational" persuasion. As soon as we adopt postulates or standards which go beyond respect for facts and logic—for instance, standards of "right" and "wrong" behavior—we must either renounce all attempts at persuasion or frankly use irrational techniques of persuasion.

This is the position I want to refute, and, in order to do this, I shall consider the "meaning" of the social situation of two (or more) participants in a dispute about what is the "right thing" to do. The meaning of this situation, in my view, is not simply that the opponents have conflicting demands or desires. Their desires do, indeed, conflict, in that each would prefer to see the course followed which he deems right; but the judgment "This is right" means more than the statement "I wish people would act this way." The judgment presupposes that there is a standard on the basis of which one may distinguish right from wrong, regardless of all momentary demands or interests. Agreement is possible only if all disputants have such a standard in common.

Ethical standards or postulates used in distinguishing "right" from "wrong" actions may be autonomous or heteronomous, that is, they may or may not exclude coercion and suggestion. A discussion about "right" and "wrong" can be rational only if it is conducted in terms of an autonomous standard. The view which I reject asserts that no ethical standards are or can be autonomous. If this view is correct, then it follows that ethical persuasion can only be irrational and that we must renounce all persuasion if we want to avoid irrational discourse. But if some ethical standards are autonomous, then ethical discussion may in some cases parallel the one about scientific fact-finding that we have mentioned: it may appeal to a "rational" standard rather than to an irrational one.

In ethics, I think, we do have an autonomous standard, and that is the "principle of impartiality" as such. This defines the "meaning" of a social situation, namely, that in which the participants agree that the correct decision concerning the matter under dispute must be invariant with regard to their personal interests or demands. What the principle says is that the decision must be wrong if it can be shown that it would come out different if the situation were "rotated," that is, if the participants changed places in terms of the advantages or disadvantages allocated on the basis of the decision.

I am not asserting that all actual norms about "right" and "wrong" behavior by which societies regulate the conduct of their members boil down to this principle of impartiality or that all are autonomous in the sense defined. Actual working norms may be, to a large extent, heteronomous: their acceptance or internalization may depend on suggestion or coercion. What I assert is merely that ethical persuasion can be rational to the extent that the social decision under dispute may be influenced by considerations of impartiality.

A judgment about the rightness or wrongness of some action is not necessarily a judgment about the "impartiality" or "fairness" of that action; it may be based on taboos, conventions, or submission to authority. But every properly "ethical" judgment, even if its material content is extra-rational or irrational, has at least a rational dimension, a dimension of impartiality; for it would cease to be an ethical judgment altogether if it were understood that the action judged would have a different value if the agent were a different person. And this dimension of the judgment is autonomous: it presupposes a standard free from coercion or suggestion.

The principle of impartiality is, logically speaking, a postulate. It is not an analytically true formula, nor is it a statement of fact; hence, in a sense, everybody is free to accept or to reject it. And yet we cannot say that it is "irrational"; it is "rational" in the same way and for the same reason that the basic postulates of scientific activity are. For these postulates, as value standards, are not "rational" because they are logically or empirically demonstrable; in fact, they are neither. Their rationality consists merely in their capacity to generate consensus, in a social situation, without recourse to suggestion and coercion. The same, however, is true of the principle of impartiality, although to a lesser degree. For to the extent that the disputants can "see the point" of a free, impartial ordering of society and can come to judge their own demands and those of others in this light, they also work toward a consensus which is not based on either coercion or suggestion. The difference is merely that, in the case of our ethical principle, the shaping of actual decisions according to the standard is very much a matter of approximating an ideal in a more or less imperfect way, subject to many limitations. The ethical standard of impartiality does not lead to reliably ordered conduct which comes near to fulfilling the ideal in every instance. Nor does it permit exact measurement of the extent to which actual behavior approximates, or deviates from, the standard. If we define "rationality" in terms of the facility with which consensus can actually be generated in each case, then our principle of impartiality is not rational in the same sense in which the basic postulates of science are; for ethical judgments are always inherently controversial. But it seems to me wrong to define rationality in such a way, for then we deprive ourselves of *any* possibility of improving social decisions and of making them as rational as they can be. It is all very well to insist upon maximum standards of rationality in discourse, and definitions are free; but the price we pay for discarding all discourse that falls short of the scientific standard of rationality would be too high.

When it comes to regulating our own ethical conduct and influencing that of others, a procedure rational both in the sense of being "autonomous" and in the sense of being completely reliable is strictly impossible. For the task of regulating conduct in an autonomous fashion involves detachment from our needs and demands; this can be achieved in near-perfect fashion in the context of fact-finding, for here we can simply ignore conflicting needs and demands. In the ethical context, however, detachment has to be achieved while we are *focusing upon* conflicting demands. This can be achieved imperfectly at best. To the extent that we rely on this being done autonomously, without coercion and suggestion, we must expect great imperfection in practice. If we insist on perfectly reliable regulation of conduct and judgment, we must adopt an authoritarian, nonautonomous solution. If, on the other hand, we renounce complete reliability in order to preserve freedom, we cannot say that with the abandonment of perfect reliability we have also rejected all rationality. Such a judgment would be both scientifically and ethically wrong. For, in spite of the scientist's contention that the ethical subject's conduct lacks a rational basis, the latter will apply rational standards as well as he can, and the actual process of social life cannot be adequately interpreted without taking this into account. If the ethical subjects were to take the scientific verdict of the irrationality of all ethical decisions literally and ceased to educate themselves and others in terms of impartiality, then freedom would degenerate into anarchy; and, since society cannot tolerate anarchy, an authoritarian solution would again emerge.

It seems, then, that we cannot take the postulational strand of value judgments simply for granted, as something that admits of no analysis in terms of rationality, and limit such analysis to the factual strand alone. In the following section, I shall try to carry out such an analysis for a few types of value judgment, making a distinction between "fundamental" (or "maximally rational") and "secondary" (less rational) standards. The idea from which I start is that, while all value judgments imply postulates, not all postulates are equally indispensable for the maintenance of the social activity which the value defines.

2. The Hierarchy of Postulates

It is entirely normal, and necessary for intellectual and moral progress, that *some* postulates be rejected from time to time and replaced by "better" ones. New intellectual worlds, such as non-Euclidean geometry and the theory of relativity, may be opened up in this fashion. But such revision and replacement of postulates cannot proceed in an arbitrary and haphazard fashion if the behavioral system organized around the postulates is not to be disrupted. If we revise or replace one postulate, we have to justify this with reference to other, more "fundamental," ones which are not supposed to change. Thus we come to the concept of the "fundamental" postulates of a field; these are the postulates which cannot be abandoned without making further operations in that field impossible.

There is, however, a certain relativity about some of these "fundamental" postulates. In this or that science, we may need today a "fundamental" postulate in order to go on with our research; tomorrow the postulate may become superfluous: we may discover a way to organize scientific thinking and activity without it. Even such extremely general and basic theoretical postulates as the principle of causality have been challenged and abandoned in a certain formulation, although it is doubtful whether science can do without some sort of belief in a type of causality. Certain other "fundamental" postulates, which are behavioral rather than theoretical, on the other hand, seem to be "fundamental" in an absolute sense. These are the basic postulates of scientific activity we mentioned in the foregoing section: those prescribing probity in reporting observations and logical soundness in making inferences from them. These postulates are "absolutely" fundamental to science—no scientific activity could go on if they were disregarded.

In science there is a general tendency not to admit any general postulate unless it is either relatively or absolutely fundamental; the scientific position is that we *must* either postulate certain things to have a coherent theory at all or produce some factual evidence or logical proof for our assertions. (This principle is known as "Occam's razor.")

We shall not go into a detailed discussion of the postulates of either formal (mathematical) or empirical sciences. Suffice it to say that in the sciences all fundamental postulates serve to insure the orderly continuity of fact-gathering and theory-building activities and that some of these postulates (like the postulate of the "orderly" nature of natural processes, however defined) are theoretical, while others (like that of "respect for facts and logic") are behavioral. Although it is often said that the scientific temper recognizes no "absolutes" but is ready to revise any position in the light of conflicting evidence, it seems that the fundamental postulates of science are organic to any scientific activity and "absolute" in this sense. Hypotheses and factual assumptions may be revised, and axioms may be changed or dropped, but all such activities stand under the rationale of scientific conduct which justifies and requires them; it would surely be absurd to say that the principles of scientific conduct itself are subject to change in the light of further evidence. After all, we need these principles to evaluate any evidence whatever.

The fundamental postulates of scientific activity define a task: that of formulating those general hypotheses which account best for the known observational facts. The task itself is the same, no matter what the content of the observations made. We thus have in this field an invariant task calling for varying solutions. The rationale of scientific activity is itself unchanging; but the content of the activity changes, and methodologies change, for procedures and methods which at one time seem adequate to solve the task may turn out to be inadequate when new facts are discovered or new questions are asked. The "rational" postulates of scientific activity can tell us only in a very general outline what the scientists of a future time will actually do. Most of the details of future scientific activities cannot be anticipated from knowing only the rationale of those activities. In other words, the rationale as such is formal and nearly empty. What will actually happen is determined, to a large extent, by whatever future observation will bring to light; what we can predict is only that future theories will be inspired by the task of accounting for future observations as well as for past ones.

But even this is not sufficient to characterize the extra-rational component of scientific activity. The "task" of accounting for observations cannot, in general, be solved by proceeding in a "rational" fashion, in the sense of applying learned routines to the new material. The elaboration of new hypotheses requires intuition and imagination; in general, we could not predict the content of new theories even if we anticipated correctly the new observations that will be made. The postulates of science do not predetermine actual procedures and methods; what they do predetermine is merely a general attitude, the "meaning" of a social situation. What specific judgments and choices this "meaning" of the situation will call for depends to a large extent on extra-rational factors ("brute facts"). These judgments and choices, however, must fulfil one basic requirement: they must be "reliably decidable" in each instance. No matter how large a part intuition and imagination may have played in the conception of a hypothesis, its confirmation is not a matter of intuition and imagination but of methodical observation and calculation that anybody familiar with the required techniques may perform.

In science nothing can be deduced from the basic postulates alone; and even the basic postulates and the observational facts together do not enable us, in general, to "deduce" a new hypothesis. For that, imagination is necessary. But we can specify, after imagination has done its work, whether its product is or is not consistent with the basic postulates; the latter are sufficiently firm and clear-cut to guide the critical work of checking on new hypotheses.

We cannot *prove* that acting on the rationale of scientific activity, as we know it, must and always will make consensus possible in each instance. It is conceivable that the communication system of science will one day break down. All we can say is that the scientific community is constantly endeavoring to prevent this from happening; for, if it should happen, the community as such would cease to exist. The scientific community is one that is continually in the process of creating itself, and to this end it maintains a constant watch over its communication system, so as to forestall the intrusion of symbols which would not make consensus reliably attainable. This activity is a selective one: both observations and questions on which reliable consensus does not appear to be feasible are weeded out. Thus far this selective activity has been successful, and it will presumably continue to be so;

but we must recognize that the scientific community has been able to preserve its existence because of such a selective practice, that is, because scientific activity has not been turned loose on all facts that may be observed and on all questions that may be asked. It chooses its own universe of facts and ignores those which are impervious to its methods.

In the case of science, then, the "hierarchy of postulates" seems to have the following character: No postulate, whether methodological or theoretical, is adopted unless it seems to be required by the rational "task" of science; in this sense, all postulates are rational. Specific formulations may, however, prove untenable and call for revision. Thus some theoretical principles, such as that of the conservation of mass, are subject to change; the only "absolute" principle is that of "rational" scientific activity itself. In the day-to-day work of the scientists, moreover, we may observe "hierarchical" features not concerned with postulates as such but with the "ranking" of hypotheses, constructs, and observational materials. Both well-controlled observations and logical principles "rank" higher than theoretical constructs and hypotheses. It is easier for the scientist to give up such constructs as the ether or "absolute" Newtonian space and time than to ignore, say, the Michelson-Morley experiment or to discard the results of calculation.

Things are in part similar but in the most important respects very different as regards the postulational system of "rational" ethics. The "rational" ideal or fundamental postulate of ethics is in a way similar to the fundamental postulates of scientific activity: if the principle of impartiality is rejected, autonomous ethical judgment and activity themselves become impossible. We then cannot even try to create an ethical society in which consensus about the "right" thing to do may be based on ethical insight rather than on suggestion and coercion. We have to remember, however, that this ethical "task" cannot be accomplished, as the scientific "task" can, by organizing a community apart from the "big" society. There can be no specialized community of ethics, as there is a specialized community of science. All ethical appeals are addressed to all men, whether they have committed themselves to observe a basic "rational" postulate or not. This means that we cannot, in ethics, expect with a high degree of confidence actual consensus to come about on a basis on which rational consensus would be possible in principle—an expectation which is actually fulfilled with great reliability in the specialized community of science. When we think about "possible" consensus, we may concentrate upon our rational principle of impartiality as such; but we cannot act and think as if actual consensus were to materialize in each case on this basis, uninfluenced by "irrational" pressures, goals, and influences. The ethical person, then, might feel tempted to withdraw into his ivory tower and let society pursue its irrational course until it dooms itself. Such withdrawal, however, would in itself be unethical; for the essence of the ethical "task" itself is misconstrued if it is reduced to preoccupation with the fundamental postulate alone. The task does not consist merely in working out solutions which would be just and fair, whether people accept them or not; it also has another dimension, namely, that of maximizing rationality of conduct and judgment in the actual society in which many working norms and goals are in part extra-rational or irrational. This means that the ethical person must come to grips with a mixed postulational system which is actually in force in his society; he must distinguish between postulates and norms of greater or less rationality and try to find a way to defend and maximize autonomy and rationality.

The fundamental postulate of impartiality refers to the task of "creating" a society. But actual society cannot be created anew every day (as the "scientific community" in a sense can). Actual consensus and co-operation, "as things are," requires compliance with norms not rational in themselves; and an actual working order in which social decisions are reached without resort to violence, coercion, and overt suggestion is not, in itself, a matter of indifference to ethical value thinking, even if it fails to reflect pure impartiality and embodies many irrational features of power and suggestion. Social laws and norms which are able to elicit consensus *in fact* may not be absolutely fundamental to autonomous ethical thinking, in that we might conceive an autonomous ethical society, and even a better one, without them. They may be only "relatively" fundamental, in the sense that autonomous co-operation would be impossible or at least severely reduced if they were radically challenged by many members of the society. Such "relatively" fundamental norms change, of course, as the culture changes. This happens not as a result of conscious elaboration or excogitation but as a result of the interplay of social stresses, of the impact of new techniques, and of moral and intellectual initiatives on the part of individuals. They may also break down: a society may find itself in a situation in which no system of norms and regulative principles will elicit even the necessary minimum of consensus.

Society cannot forestall such crises in the way that the scientific community can, that is, by singling out those problems on which consensus can be reliably generated and ignoring all others. For social decisions must be made whenever a conflict arises; we cannot achieve harmony by eliminating conflict-generating symbols from the communication system.

Ethical symbols and demands may play a powerful role in such crises; often they supply a dynamism by which the crisis is aggravated. Although autonomous ethical principles always purport to specify social decisions on which free consensus is possible "in principle," there is no guaranty that social decisions inspired by ethical principles will always make free consensus attainable *in fact*. A social decision that can be enforced with a minimum of actual coercion is not necessarily one which is maximally rational, that is, one which would be adopted if all members and subgroups of the society were maximally committed to impartiality. If, however, we try to enforce such a "maximally rational" decision by using force, our action will be self-defeating; for we diminish rather than increase the scope for autonomous thinking and action in our society if we actually rely on coercion, no matter whether the regulation we impose by force "would" appeal to the members of a perfectly ethical community. Without freedom, there is no scope for ethical action and thinking in any society.

In the social situation defined by the rationale of scientific activity, actual consensus corresponding to the requirements of the fundamental postulate may be taken for granted. In the social situation defined by the rationale of ethical judgment and action, however, such consensus can never be taken for granted; the ethical subject must always confront the "ideal" group, oriented toward his fundamental postulate (or standard), with the "real" group, whose motivations are mixed. His role, therefore, will be a dual one; for not only will he criticize and challenge the actual group to persuade it to be more similar to the ideal one, but he will also determine actual social decisions, for which he may be responsible, in the light of what the actual group may accept without coercion. We may say in this sense that ethical action in a society cannot be undemocratic, although the question of what is ethically "right" cannot be answered by determining what actual group demands (whether those of majorities or of minorities) are.

In our analysis of the scientific "task" we have seen that its meaning, or fundamental standard, required "rational" procedures to be applied to extra-rational materials and, further, that extra-rational abilities and operations (imagination) were also involved in the performance of the task. It appears that, in performing the ethical "task," we have to reckon with an even more extensive intrusion of extra-rational and irrational elements. In science we merely have to acknowledge and account for "brute facts," which in themselves are impervious to reason. In ethics we must find a way to square our "rational" principles with egocentric demands—our own and those of others; this is a less manageable task than that of "accounting for" the facts.

Nor is this the only way in which ethical behavior necessarily depends on extra-rational factors. Thus far we have considered only one principle of ethical behavior, that of impartiality; and we have discussed extra-rational and irrational factors only in so far as they must be "compromised" with. But this is not the whole story; impartiality and justice do not constitute our whole moral life. Considerations of right and wrong, in fact, tend to interfere with the spontaneity of our actions, and ethics, rightly understood, has to protect this spontaneity. It is essential for our autonomy to know how to think about right and wrong and how to judge impartially; but it is also essential to be able to give and take spontaneously, regardless of considerations of right and wrong. Scrupulousness about right and wrong should not go so far as to inhibit and falsify action from appetite and action from love. From a "hierarchical" point of view, love is "higher" than fulfilment of the "law." The reason why our discussion has centered upon the "law" rather than upon "love" is that we are concerned with an analysis of "values," and love is not, properly speaking, a "value" category. A value is a property to be judged in terms of a standard of high conflict level. Such judgments indeed require a great deal of self-consciousness and analysis. Love, however, is spontaneous and unanalyzable. Our value analysis must take it for granted; we may say that all genuine moral life is suffused with love, but we cannot characterize love in terms of "principle" and "method." The place of love in our analysis of ethical value is somewhat analogous to the place we have assigned to "imagination" and "intuition" in our analysis of the scientific task. These "extra-rational" capacities, as we have seen, are also essential to the performance of a "rationally" defined task. But love is more sovereign in ethics than imagination is in science. For, after imagination has done its work, pedestrian reason and method can catch up with it; but the rationale of the ethical task, impartiality, cannot "catch up" with love. Even when we censure actions stemming from love which are counter to justice and impartiality (as we may have to), we must acknowledge the unique dignity and creative nature of love.

So much about the "hierarchy of postulates" in ethics. The "fundamental," maximally rational postulate is that of impartiality: it is "absolute" in the sense in which the fundamental postulates of science are, meaning that all autonomous judgment becomes impossible if the postulate is rejected. But, in ethics as in science, actual judgments cannot be deduced from the fundamental postulates alone. To be sure, the principle of impartiality is less "empty" than the fundamental postulates of science are; in a sense it determines the content of our judgments rather than merely the "attitude" we have to take in judging. But it cannot by itself determine the entire content of our judgments. In judging about right and wrong, many things besides impartiality have to be taken into account, notably the "gap" between the ideal and the actual group and between free consensus "possible in principle" and "attainable in reality."

So far, in our analysis of fundamental value postulates, "autonomy" tended to coincide with "rationality": we have satisfied ourselves of the "rational" nature of our fundamental postulates by pointing out that they were "autonomous," i.e., that they did not depend on suggestion and coercion but merely on insight. Upon closer inspection, however, it will be seen that rationality, although it implies autonomy, is not synonymous with it. Rationality has an element of method and regularity: a standard is wholly rational only if it can be reduced to teachable rules. To the extent that value activities are not entirely reducible to the application of such rules, they involve "extra-rational" elements. In science, for instance, such extra-rational elements, as we have seen, play an incidental but vital role. In another "autonomous" field of value to which we now turn, that of aesthetics, the role of the "extra-rational" is even more essential.

In the field of aesthetics the contention that judgments of value are a matter of "taste" has some merit: "taste" is, in fact, an aesthetic category, and in many aesthetic disputes there is no appeal beyond it. Yet in this field, too, we can specify a hierarchy of postulates. While nobody can or should be persuaded to prize what he does not like or to reject what he does like, it would be wrong to consider the aesthetic life of a community as consisting merely of a multitude of individual likes and dislikes. Art also is a co-operative activity; we may even say that, as such, it is more highly organized than the co-operative field of ethics, for we can distinguish an artistic community (the artists and their public) set apart from society at large, although less specialized than that of science, since it gives a larger place to the mere "amateur." In art, then, we also have to do with a "social situation" which has a "meaning," and we may try to spell out this meaning in terms of "postulates."

In this field, too, it is possible to distinguish between "relatively" and "absolutely" fundamental postulates. In classic periods every art is a craft to be learned from masters: the presupposition underlying the aesthetic activities of the community is that, unless the craft is mastered, the activities cannot go on. The requirements of the "craft" may change or be relaxed, although the "craft" aspect of art cannot evaporate completely, even in anarchic periods like ours. But, in addition to this, there is also an "absolutely" fundamental postulate of aesthetic activity, namely, that, to those engaged in the production and enjoyment of art as such, the organization of visible and audible materials as such must be a matter of interest. Those who can see in a work of art nothing but a stimulant of daydreams or an adjunct to propaganda are not concerned with art at all. Artistic activity can be a matter of "autonomous value" only where this postulate is not wilfully neglected. Any individual or group may reject the postulate, but then they must accept the consequences: they cannot have a conscious aesthetic life.

I do not assert that art has always been cultivated in this spirit as a field of "autonomous" valuation. In earlier, and particularly in primitive, times the creation and enjoyment of works of art seem to have been devoid of self-consciousness; art was not experienced as a "value" category involving a high "level of conflict." Nor can we say that the "value" aspect of art even today reflects the full essential content of aesthetic activity. Creation and appreciation of art are largely unconscious processes. We may speak of an aeshetic "task"— and the self-conscious artist will always be aware of it—but we cannot specify its rules and methods. That is something for creative or re-creative imagination, drawing upon unconscious resources. Nevertheless, in our society the cultivation of art as a "value" seems essential. For, though in earlier, more primitive, societies aesthetic creation and enjoyment pervaded all society, we are now dependent on "creating" an artistic community. This requires thinking in terms of value standards. While many working standards are contingent and changeable, so that art (and even better art) would be thinkable without them, the fundamental standard of aesthetic valuation as such is "absolute" in the sense that the aesthetic community could not be continuously "created" without its being accepted.

3. The Structure of Value Discussions

So far, the outcome of our analysis is the following: Discussions about values cannot be fruitful unless there is a common postulational ground for all disputants. This, however, does not mean that they must "happen to" agree about demands; it means, rather, that they must recognize a rationale as defining the meaning of their social situation. All are free to reject any rationale that may be proposed, but then they must accept the consequences: they then will not be able to create a co-operative group of a certain type.

We shall now consider the logical structure of the disputes that may arise when a common postulational ground of this type exists. Then one of the disputants may hope to "force" his opponent to accept his position, if he is able to show that the opponent's judgments lead to consequences which are incompatible with the commonly accepted postulate.

But what kind of "consequences" is meant, and how can we demonstrate that they *do* follow from the position we reject? One might argue that, once the "postulates" are not in dispute, all disagreement can be reduced to questions of fact or of logical consistency. Scientific discussions, in fact, are structured in this way. But it seems to me that this analysis cannot do justice to ethical discussions; for what seems to be at issue is neither some actual "state of things" that will emerge, depending on which position is accepted, nor mere logical consistency, but rather something in between: states of things which are "ideally" implied in the positions adopted by the antagonists and not "actual" consequences. What is in dispute is not so much the future state of the world as the "ideal" state, the "integrity" of the community that is to be continuously created by the participants; and this "integrity" is something different from mere consistency in the communications exchanged by the members of the community.

This is not to say that consideration of facts is irrelevant to dispute about matters of value. All our judgments of "right" and "wrong," as well as of other types of value, presuppose that the facts of the case are such and such. But, even so, the relevant facts are not always, and not primarily, those concerning "future states of the world." For instance, if the question we are debating is whether X had a "right" to act as he did, or *would* have the right to act in a certain manner, some *past* events seem to be more crucial than the expected consequences. Did X, in fact, "promise" to do a certain thing? Did he assume an "obligation" to act in a certain way? If so, he would be "wrong" to act differently, whatever the consequences. This, at least, must be our first answer to the question; and the answer will not be changed if it is merely shown that, if X acts in conformity with his promise, the resulting state of the world will not correspond to his desires. And the reason why we hold X to his promise is not that we foresee some actual bad consequences if we are lenient with him. It is often said that, if a person does not keep his promise or is allowed to break it, social reality will be changed, since other people will then go back on their promises also; and I do not deny that any norm may be "hollowed out" if it is sytematically and conspicuously violated, and particularly if this happens with the connivance of authorities. But in our case this point seems to be irrelevant; for the moral behavior of "most" people does not depend on the actual fulfilment of norms and obligations by everyone. The wrongness of a wrong action is entirely independent of its effect on the law-abiding behavior of others. Wrongdoing is not inherently contagious, and, even to the extent that it may be, its wrongness does not consist in its being contagious. Very few people will feel impelled to commit murder because someone else did, and the wrongness of the crime has nothing to do with its consequences in this direction.

All this does not mean that actual future consequences are entirely negligible in ethical debates. In connection with X's promise, we may discover some probable consequences, not foreseen at the time the promise was made, that would work great hardship on X if he were to fulfil his promise. Then the right thing would seem to be to release him from his obligation. But even in this case foresight of the future case merely serves to reinterpret the past. We do not act on the general principle that the "right" action is one which leads to the most desirable state of the world, but on an entirely different principle, namely, that an obligation is no longer valid if the factual premises assumed to hold at the time when it was contracted turn out to be false.

Not all ethical disputes, however, are of this form. In the case of X's promise, the crucial thing was what happened in the past. But when we discuss the merits of a general rule or prescription, our criteria have more to do with future consequences than with past events. This is true, of course, also of the general rule that promises must be kept. If one were to deny the rule, while accepting the general postulate of impartiality, all we can do is to show that, if we were to discard the rule, the actions to be expected would be inconsistent with our postulate. My point is only that such an argument, while it does refer to the future "state of the world," does not commit us to a complete specification of the actual course of events that is to be expected. In this case it is sufficient to spell out the "ideal" consequences.

An examination of the actual consequences to be expected if a rule is adopted or discarded seems to be relevant only if we are not ready to uphold the rule on ethical grounds, that is, if the rule itself does not seem to follow from our fundamental ethical postulates. Rules about sexual behavior are a case in point. One may argue that insistence on these taboos causes much unnecessary suffering or that it leads to neuroses and other undesirable social consequences. These arguments will be convincing to those whose fundamental postulates do not include the norms and taboos in question; and it is clear that the principle of impartiality as such does not imply these norms. The critic of sexual morality argues on the basis of an ethical principle, namely, that it is wrong to cause unnecessary suffering. To this argument foresight of actual suffering or illness is relevant: one may, indeed, argue against extra-rational norms in this fashion. But the argument will not be convincing to those whose system of postulates includes the traditional norms of sexual behavior. They may admit the suffering but will deny that it is unnecessary; they will counter the argument by asserting that, if the norms are relaxed, the reduced suffering of the victims of the taboos will be matched by increased suffering of the victims of laxity. We may say, in general, that facts can subvert a postulate only if one is ready to abandon them anyway. Those who hold a postulate to be fundamental, for whatever reason, are, by the same token, ready to accept undesirable factual consequences for its sake.

It seems, then, that, in deciding ethical issues, consideration of factual consequences is not our main criterion. Our judgments are based rather on a kind of introspective datum concerning the integrity and consistency of principled action to which our "ideal" group is somehow committed. In ethical judgments, whether about individual acts or proposed rules, we have to use an "introspective discipline," enabling us to ascertain whether an act or a rule is consonant with a general principle of conduct. Such a discipline may be called "phenomenological" in Husserl's sense of the term. "Phenomenological" discipline consists essentially in carrying out thought experiments to find out what would or would not be consonant with the rationale of a certain system of conduct.

I hold that, when disputes arise among people who accept basic value postulates but disagree on what judgments are consonant with them, the phenomenological method is indispensable in clarifying and, if possible, settling the issue; and the same applies to resolving one's own doubts as to what the right action or judgment would be in a situation. Man has far better methods than this for resolving problems: both logic and scientific induction are better in the sense of "forcing assent" more reliably. But these methods cannot be applied, or at least not exclusively, in the ethical field, where we have to use, to a large extent, idealizing models of a group activity for which we are responsible. This field is one of constant potential conflict with powerful drives and interests; on these, techniques which can "force assent" only in matters of logical consistency and recognition of facts have no hold.

The "introspective discipline" of phenomenology smacks of the a priori, and for this reason many will consider it unsound in principle. It is often said that no finding based on introspection, even on "disciplined" introspection, can have any validity. Whether this complete rejection of introspection is consistent with empiricism may be doubted; after all, introspective experience is experience, and hence empiricists should treat it with sympathy. Nevertheless, distrust of introspective findings, particularly if socially relevant decisions are to be based on it, has a point. The feeling is justified that nothing should be accorded public recognition if it is founded merely on the fleeting and self-centered "inner experience" of one man; the collectivity can be asked to give credence only to findings arrived at in a public and co-operative fashion.

But is it true that phenomenological findings, such as moral judgments based on "conscience," have only private significance and are devoid of any justifiable claim to public recognition? This view seems to me unwarranted. Obviously, a moral conviction and judgment which are backed up by an individual's conscience are something very different from a well-controlled scientific finding and should not be treated in the same fashion. But this does not mean that it should be treated like the individual's private affair which can embody no moral "truth" to be recognized by others. It is possible to argue that individual consciences are the products of early "conditioning" by environmental influences, and I shall not deny the element of truth contained in this argument. But I would suggest that, in addition to "conditioning," the genesis of moral conscience also embodies cumulative and co-operative experience in group creation and in the development and maintenance of harmonious social relationships. The "phenomenological" method of which I spoke consists in attending to this accumulated moral experience; and for this reason we may say that it has a cognitive status which we are obliged to recognize. Autonomous ethical behavior, no less than autonomous scientific behavior, is a product of a long series of successive generations gradually discovering ways of realizing human potentialities.

Judgments based on conscience are not one man's private affair, and whether we agree with them or not is not our own private affair. Every judgment based on conscience represents an appeal and a challenge to the group and concerns every member of it; and the question of whether to concur or dissent is one which the isolated individual as such can neither meaningfully ask nor resolve. Hence recognition that the instruments at the command of the scientific community are unable to deal with this material should not be taken to imply that no community can deal with them rationally. The only justified conclusion is that, in ethical matters, either everything is irrational, or there is a moral community with a specific rationale underlying its co-operative task. It is the latter view that I adopt.

All this does not mean that any individual's or group's judgment in moral matters is infallible. Judgments based on conscience may conflict among themselves, and the "moral community" has no way to establish a firm truth to be accepted by all its members. To say that moral questioning has a rationale is not to maintain that there is a reliable decision method to settle any difference of opinion that may arise. What it means is only that we have a fundamental postulate that tells us how an autonomous group can be created in principle and a phenomenological discipline that helps us determine the practical implications of the principle; these two conditions are not sufficient to insure consensus in each case but merely enable us to make some progress toward a better approximation of the ideal of the autonomous community.

Of course, even the decision method available to the empirical scientist is not absolutely infallible. Nothing is more fundamental to the methodology and philosophy of science than the recognition of the tentative character of all scientific findings. What distinguishes the scientific "decision method" from all others and gives it a unique reliability is that in science, if we do not know how to achieve perfect truth, we at least know how to minimize error. Everything is so contrived that error will be detected sooner or later, so that we may at least be assured of not getting farther away from an unattainable truth. In matters of value, where in essentials we have only principles and phenomenological discipline to guide us, we do not even have this guaranty. We can never be sure of making the "best possible" choice under the circumstances. Moreover, the best things we may achieve are those we achieve without a conscious effort, by love or by the grace of God. Nevertheless, the moral "effort" to achieve the autonomous society is not wasted, for our human dignity depends on it.

The conceptual tools of the ethical community—its rational fundamental postulate and its phenomenological discipline—cannot achieve the certainty of attaining truth; it cannot even achieve the certainty of minimizing error. Nevertheless, these concepts alone provide us with a basis on which we can confront one another as free men and yet enter into essential communication. If we renounce the attempt to create our groups on this basis, we must sacrifice either freedom or communciation; we can then only choose between isolation and slavery.

4. Values Absolute and Relative

We shall conclude this analysis with a few brief remarks about a question which may have occurred to the reader, namely, whether, on the view adopted here, autonomous values should be considered "absolute" or "relative." In order to clarify our position about "relativity," we shall first attempt to formulate the question in a meaningful way.

What do we mean by saying that a value is "absolute" or, respectively, merely "relative"? Such assertions seem to refer to the nature of the standard on which value judgments may be based. One may try to define an "absolute" standard as one which is recognized at all times by every society or as one derived from insight into ultimate, incontrovertible "truth" or "reality." Standards not satisfying these conditions, then, would be called "relative."

Now such a definition of "absoluteness" and "relativity" does not seem to me to be fruitful. The fact of universal recognition does not seem to correspond to our intuitive feeling of "absolute" validity, for the point in claiming such validity for any standard or for any judgment based on a standard is that it is somehow independent of actual recognition by any group or individual. This would leave us with the second formulation presented above: that defining "absoluteness" metaphysically, as derived from contact with ultimate truth or reality. But this formulation is also unsatisfactory, for actual contact with, or possession of, ultimate truth and reality is not something that can be rationally demonstrated or even debated. If "absoluteness" is defined in either of these two "extravagant" ways, the conclusion that all standards are "relative" will be inescapable. For even if the criterion of "universal recognition" were internally consistent—which it is not—it clearly specifies a condition that is not actually fulfilled by any standard. And the "metaphysical" criterion also is empty, if we insist upon rational demonstration. I am not asserting that metaphysical terms such as "ultimate reality" or "ultimate truth" are necessarily empty or meaningless; what I am saying is that the object to which they refer is, in any case, so transcendent and remote that it cannot serve as a criterion for our applying standards and making judgments.

If, however, we stop our analysis here, we shall make no progress toward understanding the real problem involved in the concept of "relativity." No insight into the status of value standards can be gained if we merely note that they could not possibly be "absolute" in an extravagant sense. We cannot even meaningfully say, then, that these standards are "relative," for we do not know to what they are supposed to be relative. It seems advisable, then, to make a fresh start and to attempt to clarify our problem by assigning some clear meaning to the expression that a standard is "relative."

Usually the problem of "relativity" or "absoluteness" is posed in an all-or-nothing fashion; that is, one asserts either that all value standards are "absolute" or that all are "relative." The former assertion may be taken to mean that any value judgment is demonstrably either true or false; the latter, that no value judgment can be either. It is not customary to start by assuming that one might distinguish absolute from relative standards and work with both in different contexts. This, however, is the position that I shall try to defend.

Let us consider the "relativist" thesis that no value judgment can be either true or false. The thesis means that no value judgment is a meaningful communication; all such judgments represent, rather, merely a "conditioned response" and are "relative" in this sense: they are "dependent on" the conditions which give rise to them.

To assert this amounts to saying that standards of value cannot be explicated in terms of a "task" which one may perform well or badly. Such a view, however, is incompatible with the conclusions that our analysis has led us to accept. Thus we shall reject the "relativist" thesis, according to which value judgments are merely conditioned responses, and standards nothing but conditioning factors. We shall say, instead, that judgments of value are meaningful communications, implying by this that each standard that may give rise to such judgments defines a meaningful "task."

We may, however, distinguish two types of "tasks," corresponding to "absolute" and "relative" standards, respectively. All meaningful tasks may be performed in different ways; but we may judge the performance, either in terms of a set of specific rules which vary as the task is performed in one or another way, or in terms of a "meaning" which is invariant with regard to the various possible solutions. If we do the former, we employ a "relative" standard; if the latter, we employ an "absolute" one. To mention a simple example: the "task" in question may be that of describing an object. If we judge the performance from the point of view of "correctness" according to the rules of one language, our standard is a relative one; if we judge it in terms of "truth," whatever the language employed, our standard is an "absolute" one. In this case we attend to the "meaning" of the description, which is invariant, whatever language is used. Clearly, this "absolute" standard of truth is not "absolute" in the metaphysical sense, namely, in that of reflecting "absolute" reality; it is still "relative" to a definable task. But it is "absolute" in the sense that it presupposes a task with an invariant meaning, a rationale.

My contention is that some value standards are "absolute" in this sense while others can be defined only in "relative" terms. A conventional standard of "correctness"—e.g., "correctness" in performing a ritual—is a "relative" standard, in the sense that we have to specify a body of rules in order to apply it; we cannot formulate the task in terms of a rationale invariant with regard to a set of different bodies of rules. Our autonomous standards, on the other hand, are "absolute" in the sense that they refer to a task defined only in terms of meaning.

It is possible to maintain that man has only "relative" value standards. This assertion means that our concept of "autonomy" is empty, that is, that no judgment of value implies an invariant task with a specifiable "meaning." If this view is correct, all value terms have to be explicated as referring to norms and prescriptions promulgated by a certain group. Then we have to say that any such formula as "the action X is right" is incomplete and, in this sense, meaningless; to spell out its full meaning, we have to amplify and say that "the action X is deemed right by the group Y." On my view, however, this explication is demanded only by conventional standards and not by autonomous ones. The latter imply a task which is not regulated by actual groups but confronts possible groups to be created; and, if we want to create our group in an autonomous fashion, we must attend to the "meaning" of the task.

This concept of an "absolute" standard has nothing to do with a metaphysical absolute or with the claim that a judgment based on it embodies ultimate, incontrovertible truth. On the contrary, relative standards are more "certain," more reliably applicable than absolute ones. For using an "absolute" rather than a "relative" standard means that we have an understanding of a task as such without necessarily knowing what operations are needed to solve the task. With relative standards, we cannot know the meaning of our task without knowing the operational rules for solving it. We may say, in this sense, that an absolute standard defines a task only incompletely; it is the user of the standard who has to complete the definition by "doing." Absolute standards are "open-ended": to be guided by them means to embark upon an adventure, a creative undertaking. This excludes complete certainty that the task will be performed in perfect fashion. It also excludes the stereotypization of any operational solution; when we are guided by absolute standards, each situation is a new one—one that cannot be met by the mechanical adoption of old solutions. An absolute standard represents an ideal to be approached rather than a definite command to be obeyed.

In a sense, absolute standards are immutable; for we cannot embark upon the creative, autonomous venture of solving tasks defined "in terms of their meaning only" unless that meaning, the ideal rationale of our activity, remains unchanged. Some philosophers consider intolerable the acknowledgment of such unchanging task meanings; for do they not deny man's freedom to set his "goals" as he sees fit? The answer to this is that "freedom" in the sense of an arbitrary choice of meaningless goals is a very degenerate ideal and that all zeal in defending it is completely misplaced. Real freedom, freedom worth defending, consists in being able to do what the meaning of the situation demands. We can act freely only to the extent that we understand what we are doing. Understanding, however, presupposes a pre-existent standard and is not a matter of choice. We can seek understanding, but whether we attain it or not depends on our mental organization and learning rather than on a decision. Our capacities, potentialities, and experiences determine what situation meanings we can understand and in terms of what standards; and we have to cultivate our potentialities and capacities and accumulate experience, in order to be able to understand and act in free and autonomous fashion. When we reach that point, we can grasp absolute standards as such. Far from pressing our behavior into a rigid mold, this achievement alone enables us to be really free, creative, and flexible in our behavior.

Absolute standards represent timeless tasks; but this does not mean that man has always recognized them and grasped them in conscious fashion. This is possible only where autonomy is achieved, and the attainment of autonomy is a late cultural product: it depends on many psychological and sociological conditions. It may be admitted that all behavior is "relative" in this sense: the extent to which social intercourse and activity are consciously guided by absolute and relative standards, respectively, and by which ones, depends on cultural and sociological conditions. But these conditions determine only whether absolute standards are grasped as such; they do not determine the standards themselves. Nor does the absence of conscious recognition of an absolute standard mean that the task defined by it does not actually underlie and influence part of the culturally prevalent behavior. In a nonautonomous society all consciously applied standards and norms are relative and are operationally defined; but the outsider can still relate the actually observed patterns of behavior to the meaning of a task as such. That meaning itself, which is an absolute standard, can be made explicit only in relation to a process in which community is created continuously, on the basis of a rationale. We cannot define such absolute standards arbitrarily. Neither philosophers nor leaders nor the common man can create situation meanings and goals out of nothing. Our basic cultural ideas, such as truth-finding and impartiality, point to the ways in which, in view of our human potentialities, we can act in autonomous fashion; and, as far as we can look back, the same absolute standards, whether narrowed down to a "relative," operationally fixed, code or recognized in their true generality and indefiniteness, have always to some extent influenced cultural behavior.

One might ask whether social evolution does not actually produce ever new autonomous standards leading to new foundations of group-creating behavior. Such a possibility cannot be ruled out; we cannot predict in what ways mankind may change in the future. All we can say is only that thus far, in all the welter of changing norms and institutional forms, just one cluster of absolute standards has emerged; and we cannot define, even speculatively, a new one that would not be related to those we know. The emergence of new absolute standards would signify the beginning of a new cultural cycle, a radical change in man's potentialities. We could not interpret such a new culture; for the symbols at our command are defined within the framework of our absolute standards. The possibility of communication always presupposes some common absolute standard, whether consciously recognized or not.

To mention an example: if the task of "describing an observed event" involved no absolute standard but only relative linguistic conventions, such a description could not be translated from one language into another, and the possibility of communication would be restricted to members of one language community. The reason why the circle of symbolic communication is all-inclusive is that mere difference in relative standards does not hinder communication. The latter becomes impossible if and only if absolute standards are different. Radical cultural pluralists and relativists may maintain that multiplicity and mutual exclusion of absolute standards is the prevailing condition among human cultures, whether viewed in their simultaneity or in historic succession; but to me it seems more natural to recognize as absolute only those standards which make universal communication possible in principle. For, where this condition is not fulfilled, the meaning of "absoluteness" gets lost: we cannot maintain that our behavior is guided only by the "meaning of the task as such" if, at the same time, we restrict the understanding of this meaning to some empirical group.

Our absolute standards set the outer limits of our possibilities of communication. Whatever language we use, we can talk only within one universe of absolute standards. Within this universe, however, we cannot define our absolute standards operationally. Our meaning-oriented behavior can be said to follow an absolute standard (whether consciously recognized or not) only in so far as it cannot be reduced to a ready-made formula. To dogmatize the absolute is, then, to falsify it; but refusal to recognize the absolute because it cannot be "operationally" dogmatized is merely the other side of the same fallacy.

INDEX

INDEX

Absolute and relative values, 334 f.
Absolute standards, 336 ff.
Absolutes: in ethics, 327; in the scientific attitude, 312 f., 320 ff.
Abstract words, 144 f.
Abstractness, degrees of, 178
Acceptance within the group, 262
Actor and knower, 50
Actual behavior, 223
Actual situation, not extensionless, 152
Adaptation, 37 f., 223
Aesthetic significance, 291
Aesthetics, 208 f., 289 ff., 327 ff.
Ajdukiewicz, K., 71 n.
Allegiance, norms of, 266
Allport, F. H., 276 n.
Ambition, 265
Analytic and nonanalytic discourse, 68 f.
Analytical communications, interpretation of, 28, 30
Anarchy, 319 f.
Animals, live in nonsaturated environment, 34
Anticipation, 195
Application of scientific theories, 221 f.
Appropriation of relevance, 251, 259 ff.
Approval-disapproval, language of, 198 ff.; differs from preference, 202; does not refer to maximization of welfare, 205
Approval, social, 262 f.
A priori, 69, 332
Apriorism, 96 f.
Arbitration, 298 f.
Arguments about values, 314 ff.; logical structure of, 329 ff.; phenomenological method used in, 332 f.
Aristocracy, 267 ff.
Aristotle, 45, 268 n.
Arrow, K., 223 n.
Art, as co-operative activity, 328
Automata, 113 f.
Automatic and nonautomatic behavior, 113 ff., 214
Automatic response to symbols, 116, 255, 257
Autonomous ethical judgment, 208, 249, 317
Autonomous norms, 274
Autonomous values, 277 ff.
Axioms, 181, 321; for logical operations on occasional sentences, 162 ff.
Ayer, A. J., 82 n., 150, 151

Bally, G., 4 n.
Barbarism, 274
Beauty, 289 f.
Behavior and conditioned response, 112 f.
Behavior sciences and interpretive variables, 219, 224; deal with meaningful data, 6, 10, 20, 214; and intuitive language, 77; and quantitative data, 215; and value, 245
Behavior theory and contextual behavior, 56 f.
Behavioral randomness and its reduction, 34, 114
Bentham, J., 233, 299
Bergmann, G., 72 n., 73 n.
Biology, 11, 20
Braithwaite, R. B., 165
Brand names, 139
Bridgman, F. W., 83 n.
Britton, K., 103 n.
Brugmann, K., 154
Brute fact, 9 f., 322, 326
Buehler, K., 154, 155

Calculation, 179, 322
Capitalism, 229 f.
Carnap, R., 9, 57, 68 n., 72, 73, 74, 76, 80 n., 82 n., 180 n., 182, 183, 186, 287
Caste, 265
Catholicism, 281
Charismatic authority, 228
Choice: absent in reflex responses, 37; in contextual behavior, 119; and information, 49 f.
Coalition, 297
Collectivities, 145
Commands, 105 f., 256
Communicative meaning, 26 ff.; distinguished from situational meaning, 32; invariant of a range of actual responses, 102
Communism, 270
Community: of art, 328; of science, 309 ff.
Compromise, 252, 298
Compulsion (coercion), 84, 86, 310, 317 f., 324
Conditional responses, 111 ff., 336
Confidence, 87, 307
Conflict: of goals, in judgments of utility, 195, in judgments of value, 240 ff., 283 ff.; levels of, 246 ff.; social, 221 f., 295 ff., 325; of standards, 224

343